PIMLICO

303

I'LL STAND BY Y

SYLVIA TOWNSEND WARNER (1893–1978) was born in Harrow, Middlesex. The daughter of a housemaster at Harrow School, she received no formal education. During the First World War she worked in a munitions factory. In the 1920s she was on the editorial board of *Tudor Church Music*, and published a first book of verse, *The Espalier* (1925), and her first novel, *Lolly Willowes* (1926). She went on to become one of the finest short-story writers of the age and a distinguished poet and novelist: her best known novels include *Mr Fortune's Maggot* (1927), *Summer Will Show* (1936) and *After the Death of Don Juan* (1938). She was also the translator of Proust's *Contre Sainte-Beuve* (1958), and biographer of T. H. White (1967). A fellow of the Royal Society of Literature, she received the Prix Menton in 1969.

VALENTINE ACKLAND (1906–1969) was educated at Queen's College, London and in Paris. She published a collection of poems, *Whether a Dove or a Seagull*, with Sylvia Townsend Warner in 1934. A collection of her poems was selected by Sylvia after her death and published: *The Nature of the Moment*, 1973. *Further Poems of Valentine Ackland* was similarly published in 1978 by Julius Lipton of Welmont Publishing, a friend from Communist Party days. Her autobiographical essay, *For Sylvia: an Honest Account*, was published in 1985.

I'LL STAND BY YOU

Selected Letters of
Sylvia Townsend Warner and
Valentine Ackland
with Narrative by
Sylvia Townsend Warner

———

EDITED BY

SUSANNA PINNEY

PIMLICO

Published by Pimlico 1998

2 4 6 8 10 9 7 5 3 1

Copyright © Susanna Pinney and William Maxwell 1998

Susanna Pinney has asserted her right under the Copyright, Designs
and Patents Act 1988 to be identified as the editor of this work

First published by
Pimlico in 1998

Pimlico
Random House, 20 Vauxhall Bridge Road,
London SW1V 2SA

Random House Australia (Pty) Limited
20 Alfred Street, Milsons Point, Sydney,
New South Wales 2061, Australia

Random House New Zealand Limited
18 Poland Road, Glenfield,
Auckland 10, New Zealand

Random House South Africa (Pty) Limited
Endulini, 5A Jubilee Road, Parktown 2193, South Africa

Random House UK Limited Reg. No. 954009

A CIP catalogue record for this book
is available from the British Library

ISBN 0712673717

Papers used by Random House UK Limited are natural, recyclable products
made from wood grown in sustainable forests. The manufacturing processes
conform to the environmental regulations of the country of origin.

Typeset by SX Composing DTP, Rayleigh, Essex
Printed and bound in Great Britain by
Mackays of Chatham PLC

Contents

Editor's Note

I started to work for Sylvia in 1970. This collection of letters was the second piece of typing she gave me. I was touched that she should place such trust in me, because the letters revealed an intimate account of her relationship with Valentine, and Valentine was so newly dead. This perhaps, was naïve, for Sylvia was proud of their relationship and wanted it known, though not while she was alive; she would have found it too painful, she told me. She also did not want others hurt. Therefore she sent the top copy to the Berg Collection in New York with instructions that the letters should not be published until certain named people were dead.

The originals she sent to two American friends and writers, Joy and Marchette Chute. (They are now in the archive at the Dorset County Museum.) The second copy she kept with her in the house at Frome Vauchurch.

In the month before Sylvia died, she asked me to remove the letters and keep them with me until they could be published. It was only then that I discovered she had written a connecting narrative and annotated the letters as well.

When they were separated they often wrote more than one letter a day, and the collection was too large to be published in its entirety as Sylvia had planned: roughly 400,000 words. It had to be severely cut by almost two-thirds. (The elipses in the text, however, appear in the original copy and should not be mistaken for cuts.)

The notes Sylvia placed in clusters at intervals throughout the text. For ease of reading I have changed their original position to footnotes on the relevant pages. I have kept additional notes to a minimum, and where identification was accessible and unambiguous. My additions are shown in square brackets.

The narrative, however, is all her own.

I would like to thank William Maxwell for his unfailing trust and guidance; Jenny Uglow for her encouragement; Roger Peers, Janet

Pollock and Claire Harman for their help and support; and George D. Painter, Denis Enright, John Charlton and John Powys.

Susanna Pinney

THE LETTERS

1930—1934

The course of our future life was determined by an unamiable farmer.

As Theodore Powys would not stir out of the landscape of his novels, his London admirers had to go to the remote village of Chaldon in Dorset if they wished to meet him. I was such an early admirer that I counted as a friend and from the mid-twenties onward I used from time to time to stay with him and his wife, Violet, at Beth Car – a small red brick house on a grassy hillside. It was from Violet that I first heard of Valentine. Valentine rented a cottage in the village. She lived by herself. She had married before she was twenty but the marriage had been annulled. She went for long solitary walks, wearing trousers (at that date, a novelty). She did not eat enough to keep a mouse alive. She and Theodore lent each other books. She was believed to write poetry but never spoke of it. Her mother, a widow, lived in London and was well-off. The village approved of her; she was polite to everybody and very open-handed. When Mr Goult let her drive the village bus, she drove it much faster than he did. Violet omitted to tell me that this rustic solitary had been finished in Paris.

This is the world exactly as Adam had it –
Spring now, and willows flowering, and I alone
In an ash-wood, with the birds around me
Clamouring and flying, the small birds like leaves' shadows
Threading through the hedge.

As Adam may have done, I sit
On a felled bough in sunlight,
Admiring how my hair glitters –
The bright gold blown lock over my brow –
As Adam must have sat, the whole world his.

All around me slender branches, felled for sticks, not flowering –
Ashboughs, grey and smooth, and withy wands
Silk-berried still, and the lambs' tails falling

Tasselled from the hazel sticks – straight sticks and brittle –
I snap them in my hands, making a summer noise.

Between this wood and the field tall ash-plants stand
And bend beneath the wind, their smooth stems making
Noise like footsteps – as if someone went
In nailed boots over the stony plough of the field;
But no one is near.

No one is near. The sunlight on branches,
On black ash-buds, on my glittering hair –
The sunlight and the trees conspire,
Banish time, outwit time –
There is no one to come here.

The wood comes up to spring, thirsty,
As a horse comes to clear water –
Drinks long and lazily,
I, with the world gone, with earth my own,
Sit solitary and glad, watching my Kingdom thrive.

When the solitary came in, halfway through Violet's tea-party, I was not prepared for someone so romantically young and elegant – tall, slender as a willow-wand, sweet scented as a spray of Cape Jessamine, almost as silent, too. Our meeting was not a success. She had come to meet the writer of my poetry, found her talking among talkers, thought her aggressively witty and overbearing. I was disconcerted by feeling myself so gravely and dispassionately observed by someone I was making a poor impression on. She was young, poised and beautiful, and I was none of these things. I recouped my self-esteem by deciding we could have nothing in common and that I need think no more about her; and in my pique I allowed this decision to be slightingly obvious.

I thought no more about her. Once or twice on later visits to Beth Car, I saw her sliding out of the house by the back door as I entered it. Once or twice when I was walking alone over the downs I caught sight of her, turning off in an opposite direction. Forgetting that the company of my black chow-dog made me immediately identifiable, I assumed it was a fortunate coincidence. Sometimes Violet spoke of her: she had pleurisy, alone and unfed in her cottage; so-and-so was in love with her but she would not have him; she had been riding Katie's[1] mare; she was in Italy.

1 Katie [Powys], a sister.

6

I suppose it was a year or so after our first encounter that I got a letter asking me if I would like to borrow her cottage during the summer. There was a walnut tree. She would be away between such and such dates. I replied, truthfully as it happened, that I was unable to leave London, that she was very kind, that I was fond of walnut trees. This generosity from someone I had slighted, and the warrant of the dates that no involvement hung on it, abashed me.

I was to be more abashed. In a village, everything becomes known. The unamiable farmer heard that Valentine had offered me her cottage; assuming that she would be sub-letting it at a vast profit, he swelled with resentment and turned her out at a week's notice.

This, and that Valentine was now lodging elsewhere in the village, I heard from Violet when I next visited Beth Car. My conscience pricked me. As a result of meaning to do me a kindness, Valentine had lost her cottage, and with it her independence, her privacy, the way of life she had chosen. All this had come about through me; I was not responsible but I was the cause. I could do nothing to amend it; but when next we met I would try to mend my manners.

As our meetings hitherto had been merely accidental collisions this intention might have proved difficult to carry out if it had not been that we were both very fond of Theodore.

I thought he was looking unwell and Violet uneasy. This afforded a decent pretext for going to call on her. I asked if anything was wrong at Beth Car. She told me that everything had been going wrong since Theodore's younger son had given up his job on medical advice and come to live at home. Savage with boredom, he was avenging himself on society by tormenting Theodore, frightening Violet and making mischief between them. I would soon see for myself, she said. I did, and was as much concerned as she. There was nothing we could do; but as onlookers we drew together, and before I left I asked her to let me know how things went on. When she came to London that winter we met to share letters from Violet, to find no comfort in them, to think of no way to better the situation – and to explore happier interests we had in common. One of these was poetry. I was curious about hers, but whenever there was an opportunity to ask about it, she whisked the opportunity away. So we went on walking round each other till a letter from Violet reported that Francis (the younger son) had written enough of his poems to fill a book, and wanted to find a publisher. I groaned, knowing what would be expected of me. Had I seen them, she asked. I replied that I had seen as many as I cared to – and went on: 'The poems

I want to see are yours.' She did not protest or disclaim. 'I expect they are bad,' she said. 'I know they are weak. But how is one to tell for oneself? What I need is criticism – savage criticism.' She took a folder of poems out of a drawer, hesitated, discarded, exclaimed, 'All this fuss about nothing!' and gave me a handful to take away. As I read them that evening, I felt as though I had carried away a lapful of pebbles from a sea-shore – they were so weighted with intention, these brief poems. Like pebbles, they gave no impression of accomplishment, or skill – though some were remarkable skilful – or knack. Like pebbles, I thought, like those fragments of broken glass worn smooth and sea-coloured; like knives and arrowheads shaped out of flints. Some were bad. None were sham. Of the comparisons which occurred to me, I went back to pebbles, poems sleeked and shaped by the working of a restless mind. I could see they were immature; but it was as written poems they were immature: there was no immaturity in the intention.

Some poets have facility – which is a kind of innocence – in their stars. Others – and here was one of them – are born with the destiny of difficulty. Hard task-masters to themselves, they mistrust their natural flow, and at the same time savagely reject what is not authentically their own. The difficulty extends: I had undertaken to be critical. But what the devil was I to say?

Praise, encouragement, technical niceties, would be risky offerings to this well-mannered young creature whose reserve masked such a lonely and sardonic mind. More than ever I regretted that lost cottage.

> As it cries out from under the cover
> Of mind, he rises up, leaves his lover,
> Leaves his house, wealth, food behind
> And goes out.
>
> As it cries to him, he answers, but obeys
> Nothing he knows. Intermittently throughout his days
> He follows, alone; scared when it shows,
> Terrified when it dies to him.
>
> And so on. He trembles when it calls him,
> But must follow. Suspicious of all that then befalls him,
> He loses peace, love, zest, and finally life –
> And nothing done.
>
> And nothing done. For at the end all he masters

Is the route of the way of numberless disasters,
No more – and where all others have found their way to grief
He comes, too, to grief – alone.

At the Easter week-end of 1930, I went to Chaldon for Violet's birthday, which was also her silver wedding day (she had got up at daybreak to admire the splendid iced cake garlanded with silver doves which Valentine had given her). It was a late spring; no one had seen a swallow; but on Easter Monday it suddenly became warm and benign, celandines opened on every bank, rooks were building. Valentine appeared in a summer shirt. During tea Theodore spoke of taking a walk up the Drove – a lane leading northward out of the village and over the ridge called The Five Marys because of the five tumuli along its summit – and after tea we set out. We were partway up the Drove when Violet asked me why I did not buy Miss Green's cottage? Which cottage was that, said I, and who was Miss Green? Before she could answer Theodore said he was sure I would be happy there: Miss Green had died in it. We turned back to look at it. It was a small slate-roofed cottage with nothing to be said in its favour except that it was totally unpicturesque and stood by itself. Planted in front of it was a notice-board with a placard: FOR SALE. FREEHOLD. We fetched a very large key from the Inn. We unlocked the door. It opened into a fair-sized living-room, smelling of rust and cold soot dominated by a rusty kitchen-stove. Behind it under a salt-box roof was a back-kitchen with a copper. A narrow corkscrewing stair, shut off by a door, led to two communicating bedrooms above. Everything was peculiarly dingy. But it was for sale: Freehold: an unevictable tenure. I looked at Valentine. Her face told me nothing. *Freehold.* 'If it could be put into order, would you live' – I stopped myself in time – 'would you move here, and keep it warm for me, be my steward?' Even with this last moment emendation, abolishing the constraint implicit in a gift, I did not expect her to say yes. 'I should like to very much.'

So that was settled. We returned the key and walked on up the Drove, agreeing that a back door to escape by was an essential amenity and must be added. She had noticed more than I: that the living-room was floored with Portland stone flags, that the bedroom windows looked out on a view of the hill called High Chaldon, that there was a row of young ash-trees on the high turf bank between the garden and the field beyond.

As for the unamiable farmer who had brought all this about, after acknowledging the word, Freehold, I never gave him another thought. And next morning, I was gone. I had never bought a house – I was not in that walk of life. But after writing to the house-agent, I somehow remembered that people who buy houses get a surveyor's report before they make an offer. Headed: *The late Miss Green's Cottage* the report stated: 'This is a small undesirable property situated in an out of the way place and with no attractions whatsoever.' Then came a grudging admission that it was structurally sound. I made my offer, wrote to Valentine, and bought a dusky wall-mirror with gilded plasterwork scrollings, a pair of bellows and a wastepaper basket. She undertook to provide a satinwood *bonheur du jour*, two papier mâché chairs and a folio bible. Other essentials would gather in time.

While the house-agent and I bickered about the price and Violet's letters became full of rumours about other possible buyers who would pay enormous sums, and a nephew who wanted to live there himself, I made some more purchases and a great many lists. Though I was too busy to be systematic (I had arranged to be very busy and animated that summer, to distract my thoughts from a personal unhappiness), I was practical by fits and starts. Kindnesses and windfalls came in. My mother promised kitchen equipment. Valentine, suppressing comment on my theory that things like hammers could be got from Woolworth, bought garden tools, an axe, a chopping-block, and a vintage spade, smooth as silver. In July my stepfather, an architect, met me at Chaldon where we spent a day conferring with the local builder about the back door and the brick hearth which was to replace the rusty kitchen-stove. The garden was full of pink shoe-rose poppies – too fleeting to be sent to Valentine, who was at her mother's flat after a wisdom-tooth extraction which had brought on a haemorrhage, lying flat and pale with Browne's *Pseudodoxia*, *The Historie of the World*, a Siamese cat and two by-blow kittens on the bed. I had been to visit her the day before, meeting her mother for the first time.

I was still contracted to that emended invitation about keeping the cottage warm for me. I had thought this would be easier to assent to, and when Valentine assented I felt I had done the right thing. Now I was not so sure. My first honest intention was accumulating a good many false pretences, including my own, as when I had to assure her mother that there was no call for anyone to be grateful, unless it were I. I wanted no gratitudes, no assumptions that Valentine might be under an obligation to me. She would not think it so; she had none of the shabbiness of mind which suspects patronage in a kindness; but she might well resent being tricked. I would have done better to offer her the cottage straight out, for as things were now she might come to dislike it, yet stay on out of politeness. (Here I misjudged her; if she had not wanted to stay, nothing would have kept her.)

But I did not think very long or intently about all this. I had a great many other things to think of: Miss Green's Cottage was an airy habitation still, in spite of all the hardware I was amassing. As it came nearer, I believed less and less in it. If in the end it all came to nothing, it would be a pity: but more was lost at Mohacs – a proverb often on my lips at that date. This did not prevent me, when Valentine had gone back to Chaldon and was at work on the neglected garden, from writing to her with a variety of enquiries, recommendations and demands for measurements.

On September 23rd she drove me down to Chaldon with a final assortment of incompatible objects creaking and rattling in the back of the car. Watching her hand on the wheel, abandoning myself to a suavity of driving which was like the bowing of a master-violinist, I felt that everything was bound to go right. And there, at the end of the journey, was the Late Miss Green: her windows open, her walls milk-white, the coral-pink paint on her woodwork and Mr Miller the carpenter at that moment putting up shelves. There was the garden, cleaned and dug and raked smooth, and looking twice as large for it. There was old Mrs Moxon with a bunch of flowers, waiting to tell me how well Valentine had dug and what a great heap of bindweed and couch-grass roots had been burned to wholesome ashes. And there was Valentine, to whom all this, so astonishing to me, was a familiar sight – and already, I thought, looking ownerly. Later, when we were by ourselves, it would not be difficult to tell her of her ownership, and the reason for it. But the disclosure had to be postponed because she had promised to take the Beth Car party to Portland Fair.

Even with a move when the contents of a house are put in a van and decanted into another house, things go wrong. I had made a generous allowance for things going wrong over this move, which involved loads of furniture coming from three different places. What I had not allowed for was that a providential little dog should bite me in the wrist the day after our arrival. It was not a bad bite: Valentine's bandaging was far beyond its deserts; but it put the move under new management. I sat with my arm in a sling while she did everything from lighting my cigarettes to getting a chest of drawers upstairs when nobody else could, and all without the least parade of efficiency. From time to time she would say how well I had organised it all, till I began to think so myself. For a siesta (her management included siestas) we would dawdle up the Drove and sit on a Mary, listening to the wind in the grasses and admiring our small undesirable property from above. Covertly, I also admired her, her long limbs and small nut-brown, nut-smooth head with its golden forelock – *chiome d'oro*, like Morgana's – which the lifting wind blew forward to dangle over one eye. Then we would dawdle back to do some more unpacking and prepare for the influx of afternoon visitors, coming to see how we were getting on. A raree-show was their due, and Theodore and Violet were much the livelier for our bran-tub entertainment. But our dearest visitor was Grannie Moxon, that loving, giving and doing character, who lit the first fire on our new hearth and watched it take hold with passionate intensity, as if Valentine's fate depended on it. 'There, my sweetheart! He's going up nicely. You'll be all right.' I can see her now, with her burning, dark-rimmed eyes and her battered hat, and hear her laugh, sudden and screeching like the cry of a jay. That evening we walked to the cottage half expecting to find it burned down. There was a smell of woodsmoke from the warmed chimney, the embers were still drowsily alight. We stood looking in through the window as though there had never been a fire in an empty room before.

And still I had not told her about the ownership of the cottage. Haltingly, I explained that I had bought it, hoping that it would be good to write poetry in; but got no further. I had chosen a bad moment. She was barren of poetry, she said; for a long while she had written nothing and despaired of ever writing again. Too quick despairer . . . Only a little while before she had written in her notebook: 'Last afternoon I made a poem from a beginning which I had had in London. I am fairly well-pleased with the finished work. It is what I mean, anyhow!' But I didn't know of this; and even if I had, I already knew better than to encourage unasked.

> Space is invisible waves. In leaves of trees
> Space-water rustles, and the sway of these
> Is only movement of sea-weed under tide
> In restless sway and swing from side to side
> While in the invisible air and in the sky
> Spirits like deep-sea fishes are sweeping by
> And I on a hill-top in summer, where grass is brown,
> Lying beneath the sky, and likely to drown
> In the vast ocean of space passing to and fro –
> Here, on the floor of the sea, starved thistles blow.
> And the wind is no wind but a fast-flowing current of tide,
> And the spirits are blown and are driven and cannot abide.

By the end of the month the last of the last-moment difficulties had been overcome, and she went back to London. On the fourth of October I moved in. I made up the two beds, proud of my linen sheets, pleased with the eiderdowns in their scarlet madapolan covers, like the eiderdown in the nursery. I hung the curtains, put out soap and candles, put away my clothes and went from one room to another (she had chosen the inner room) debating which of their identical views of High Chaldon was the better. I arranged the store-cupboard and washed the china and polished the glasses and whisked the dust off the scrollings of the oval mirror and fixed candles in its two sconces. I felt pleased with the house for being well-found and for looking carefree – which was due to its contents being so fortuitous, as though Autolycus had furnished it. I hoped it would look as engaging that evening when Valentine would arrive, bringing herself, her mother and her mother's chauffeur: by which arrangement, she had explained, her mother would be repossessed of the car and immediately driven away for dinner at her hotel. (I had refrained from saying, 'And if you change your mind on the doorstep –'.)

I had miscalculated how long it would take to roast a duck in a brand-new oven on an oil-cooker; everything was behind-hand when the car stopped outside. I hurried to the door. She stood in the porch, slightly a stranger in her London clothes. In a flurry of belatedness and apology, I kissed her. There was a momentary stiffening and I realised I had never done so before and would do better not to do it again. The car was greeted and farewelled and drove away. She had brought some wine and a bottle of brandy and after dinner we sat for a long while drinking coffee and conversing. Conversing, not talking. The formality of 'conversing' matched the tall candlesticks, her Regency coffee-spoons, my egg-shell porcelain coffee-cups, white outside, lined with sugar-almond pink. With these and the mirror we declared against the grated carrot, folk-pottery way of life. Outside the quiet room the wind from the sea blew in gusts. We sat in our cocoon of warmth and subdued light and it seemed odd that we had not been living there for years.

We continued to be formal. Living at such close quarters and dependent on each other's consideration for freedom of mind, a degree of formality was essential. So was the framework of routine. From the first morning when Valentine in silk dressing-gown and green slippers laid and lit the fire, our parts were established, and we never contested them. Our relationship was a sort of unintimate intimacy; a relationship between two people who like each other's company and leave it at that, fortunate castaways on a desert island. We read. We listened to music – she had brought her Gramophone. Stone embellishes strings, and her record of Beethoven opus 132 (one in an assortment ranging from Handel to Noël Coward) sounded very well on our Portland flags.

We learned more about our likings and our opinions, but not much more about ourselves. She did not talk herself, I did not ask questions; it was the code of good middle-class manners we had been brought up to practise, and the fashion of the day reinforced it. Confidences were out. 'Let us be very strange and well-bred; let us be as strange as though we had been married a great while; and as well-bred as if we were not married at all.' We followed Millamant's prescription. Besides, why go deeper? In another ten days the conversation would close. I would go back to London for the Winter. Valentine would be left in possession of Miss Green. I would miss her company; miss the composed low voice and the sardonic turn of mind and the velvet good manners; miss, even, the impersonal surveying regard which had irked me when I was making a bad impression at Violet's tea party.

'Walking one day in the country,' she began
'Alone, and beside a wall, I saw a stoat which ran
Level with me, but on the other side of the wall. Jerkily it ran,
And often too,' she said
'Getting a little ahead
It stopped, front paws on the wall, and reared its head.'
For the story, that was all. But more truth grew
Out from it to my mind than ever before I knew,
So clearly I pictured myself there. Beyond all questions I knew
That so am I, beside you on your way,
And curious, intent, and not in play –
Sheltered from you, and watching, and never in play.

If a village is sufficiently small and remote (and Chaldon was both) it always finds something to be excited about. After the incongruities of Miss Green's Cottage, plain white wash on the walls and pink paint sent from London, the grandeur of its saucepans and not a single upholstered chair, there was Harvest Festival and the rivalry of decorators. Then everything was swept aside by the girl who tried to run away from the Old Vicarage. Vicarage no longer, for Chaldon had been merged in the neighbouring parish of Winfrith, this gaunt dwelling was tenanted by a lady who received mental deficients for training as domestic servants. I suppose we were too gentry to be told about the escape and recapture (gentry are assumed to side with authority). We knew nothing till some days later, when we were at Beth Car and heard from Violet that the girl had made two more attempts to escape, that the policeman had found her hiding in a ditch, that the village was in an uproar of indignation and that really something ought to be done about it by somebody.

Valentine got up. Even if we could not help the girl, we could tackle the lady. But how to begin? It was her little dog who had bitten me, but this scarcely amounted to an introduction. Theodore said it would be best to make a pretext of neighbourly concern for her and then dwell on the savage nature of simple villagers, and how skilled they were at stone-throwing and fire-raising.

Uncertain what to do but agreed that we must do it, we walked to the Vicarage and rang the bell. An old woman opened the door wide enough to tell us the lady was not in. We said we would call again. When we called again, no one answered. We went back to the cottage, snatched a meal of undercooked chicken, still pink at the joints, collected a little public opinion (Violet had not exaggerated) and set out for a third try. This time it was the lady who let us in. We explained our errand; but her repartees about these hopeless creatures, you know, and how P.C. Wintle had actually addressed the girl as 'Miss' made it impossible to keep up a show of neighbourly concern. So we told her, plainly, that the village was suspicious and angry; that the girl's repeated attempts to get away appeared to justify such a reaction; that if the village temper went from words to deeds, no one would raise a hand to help her. She resorted to toadying, felt sure we would understand her difficulties, assured me I could have no idea how strong the hopeless creatures were – it was impossible to tire them out. Valentine sat by, silent and implacable. I left it to her silence to conclude the interview. As we were walking away, speechless, she thrashed the air with her walking-stick. It was one of our formalities that we did not talk after the door between our bedrooms was closed. I had blown out my candle and was half-asleep when I heard a screech-owl hunting up the valley, and Valentine saying she hoped it would put the woman at the Vicarage in remembrance of a shroud – though it was more likely to do that to her captive. Somehow – I was still half-asleep – we got on to the subject of human relationships. I said I found it easier to love people than to like them. There was a pause. A voice of convinced desolation said, 'Sometimes I think I am utterly unloved.' I jumped out of bed, in a flash. I was through the door and on my knees at her bedside, crying out that it was not true, not true, that she must not say such a thing. She gathered me up in an embrace to lie beside her.

Love amazes, but it does not surprise. I woke to daylight and saw her standing by the bed, looking down at me. 'Well?' she asked, rather sternly. I could not conceive why there should be any question, or why her voice should be stern. I was at home in an unsurmised love, an irrefutable happiness. It was early morning, autumnally silent. Realising how mistaken we had been about each other and how in my precipitate ignorance I had thrown out all her experienced calculations, we laughed as people do who have escaped, by a miracle, from some deadly peril and find themselves safe and secure.

1930

Chaldon, 13 October 1930

I meant to give you this today – anyhow it is obviously yours because your hands are so beautiful. But a mourning ring is not suitable to our state. However, the design is delicate and charming, and the curve and texture of the setting is lovely enough to remind me of you, but nothing is adequate. There is not anything which could speak to you for me.

This is not a letter. I am awaiting your word. I shall tell you nothing, except that I have not yet started to tell you how I love you.

This rose came from the front garden. A month[1] seems an intolerably long time, but I shall spend it in devising pleasures for you. And you will come to taste them? The sun is coming in through the sitting-room window and trying to put out the fire – but that legend is not true. I am not put out. And there is a blinding sun shining upon me. You will enjoy it, and be happy, my dear – and not forget me?

Valentine

London, 14 October 1930

My dear love

The ring is on my finger. I look at it, and remember seeing it on yours. And the rose is beside me, sitting a little self-consciously in a liqueur glass. It must have been the warmth of our love flowing out of the window that

---

1 I had to go back to London to comply with various engagements and obligations which I proposed to despatch by early November.

bloomed it, for I saw the bud a week ago, a small cross thing, and thought: you will never open before the winter.

You spoke with such determination, and I believe all your words so implicitly that I did not expect anything, not even 'This is not a letter' this morning. So though I woke early I shut my eyes again, and imagined, rather successfully, that you had come in and were looking at me. Afterwards, I found the parcel, with your falcon[1] sealing it, and you inside. My hands are not beautiful, my dear. They were once, but now they are spoiled, like most of the rest of me. I say most; for by some strange mercy my sensitiveness has remained unbattered. I can give you that without self-reproach or sighing. But I am not good enough for you, Valentine, and there are moments when I wonder if it would not be better that I should go away, like Mr Fortune,[2] leaving you with love. But I can't. Even though the wonder were certainty, I don't think I could. I have so little strength left, except to love you. Instead, I have been walking about in Kensington Gardens, visiting the trees that have been kind to my old distress and bewilderment. I said nothing to them, just showed myself . . . the abandoned avenue, and the plane-tree whose banana-coloured serpent branches were so stripped and voluptuous and defiant, swinging in last winter's gales (Cry down the winter skies) and the thorn-tree that always comes out so much too soon, and the frost has it with frozen thawings, and the other thorn-trees where the rushes grow among the grass. And William[3] followed, keeping an eye on me, and saying: She's often mooned about like this. But today it seems rather different.

Last night I walked into the cottage, and saw you, sitting alone by the fire, and thinking about me. It will not be long before I come again, not all of a month. And it would take you much longer than a month, my darling, to finish devising pleasures for me. I know you, and how there is no end to your generosity and patient skill to please. I want no pleasure but to be with you, but I will take all you can give me and be grateful.

You can have no idea how many people there are in London. Yet so far I don't seem to have seen anyone. They are there, and I talk to them, and answer their questions about my cottage (the poor ignoramuses still suppose it to be mine, for I hide most jealously the so much richer possession that it is yours) and they seem to hear my answers. But it is hard to believe in them. They are like the bleached shadows one opens one's eyes to after looking at the sun with one's eyes shut. My eyes have

1 A peregrine falcon, sitting on a gloved hand: motto *Inébranlable*, her family crest.
2 Of my novel, *Mr Fortune's Maggot*.
3 My black chow-dog.

been a good deal shut lately, my sun, as you know. No wonder my vision is affected. However, the bores and nuisances have a certain lifelikeness.

I thought of a ring, too. But you will not put it on till tomorrow, for there was a little pearl to be replaced. Meanwhile, here is an ivory armoury[1] for you to play with. I am sorry that it has no cross-hilt daggers;[2] but it is pleasant to find the wise Chinese first discovering the croquet mallet, and instantly recognising it as a weapon of offence.

I will send you my hindward poems tomorrow. And when some claret comes from Harveys, you are to drink it everyday. It is an anonymous Margaux, a pleasant drink with no airs and pretentions. You might drink it for breakfast and no harm would come to you. My dearest, these words chill me. Take care of yourself, I love you so desperately.

Sylvia

3: VA

Chaldon, 15 October 1930

My most dear love,

How well you know me already. The armoury has occupied me for over an hour. I came downstairs in my pyjamas and my dressing-gown, duly lighted the fire, and sat at the table, selecting first one and then the next delight. The effect of that array was so entrancing, even by daylight, that tonight, I can tell, it will be completely bewitching. They are so slender, and so formidable. I have already selected the finest and sharpest as deadly weapons; to be used on your guests, with your consent, if they really outstay our tender patience. They will have the ineffable consolation of a delicious death. Your gloomy foresight is justified in me. I have had to spend many anxious and cross minutes in searching for the hiding holes which conceal various cereals and spices. I find that, during all your careful tour of the storeroom, I was noting down as carefully each movement and form and shape of you. I can walk from larder to cupboard and shelf to shelf with you, even now remembering accurately the shape of your hands and the feel of your lovely shoulder.

But find the pepper I cannot. Although now, by a stern effort of

1 A set of Chinese spillikins.
2 Valentine had added her 17th cent. cross-hilt dagger and a contemporary pistol to the furnishings of Miss Green.

concentration, I can run most of the sardines to earth. I wonder, and I am afraid. What will happen when you realise how unlearned I am – and how I know nothing of wit and wisdom. How undeveloped my mind is and how slow. And when you are forced by proof to believe all this – lack of ability, cowardice, and all the rest. When you see, at this moment, how I shy away from a full list of my weakness and vice. While you, your fine, sharp handwriting, the sure rightness of your words, your wit and understanding, wisdom and courage and steadfastness. All this is an endless delight to me, and for the beauty of your body, which I worship, and the achievement and mastery for which I adore you – Dear love. I love you. Let us not speak of unworthiness.

I have nothing to give you which is worthy of you, except that my love is great. You must *desire* the pleasures I am devising for you. I think you will. You would not receive love so beautifully unless you enjoyed and desired it. There can be no end to the delight of making love to you. It hurts me when I read your words. It scared me, too. If you leave me now I may well misunderstand – and compel you to return. Because I would hope you were being Mr Fortune, while you would probably be simply tired of me. But really it went deeper than that and I can hardly bear to think of it now. My dear love – why did you say that to me? I call your hands beautiful because it is the most adequate word I have – they are really far lovelier than that. I tell you that you are lovely, that I love you, that I am still dazed and dreaming, and only half comprehending that you love me. I have always thought myself fastidious. It is my one means of grace and hope of glory. You deny it to me. You tell me that I am loving something which is spoilt. Such a cruel word that I am nearly weeping.

You must promise me, my darling, that you will never think such thoughts again. You must promise me that you will not talk of leaving me. If you will consider carefully the sin against the Holy Ghost you will realise how nearly you have committed it by those words and moods of yours. But, my sweet, you could not escape from my love now, unless you ceased to love me. Until then, my hands, even my finger-tips, could bring you back. And would – would now if only they might, because my hands are idle without you, and quite as useless as you first thought of them.

Betty[1] terrified me by saying you looked ill. I became panic-stricken last night. It was only by a really stern strength that I prevented myself from flying to you. And I never thought to bully a promise from you, about that. Now that you are out of reach must I descend to meanness

1 Betty [Muntz], an artist, living in the village.

from majesty? I hate to make pathos a weapon, and I will not. I did not see you clearly, as you went away. But these women know, I suppose, how you should look. My dearest love – how can I make you promise to tell me? You must know how much worse it is to be anxious and disturbed all day than to know if anything is wrong – when it is. Besides, we owe such a gift to each other. The weight of care and responsibility is a very precious one, in these circumstances.

I have to be angry with you again. I have to tell you not to do something. And by that I shall risk your hatred, I know – but anyway – My Dear, you are not to buy me wine. You are not to buy me anything like that. You are not to spend upon me anything more than three-halfpence a day,[1] and a certain amount of time. As much of *that* as you will; when it is not being put to its right use, which is the writing of poetry.

But about this I am really serious. I am so deeply earnest about it that I feel like a stony rock. I know the dreadful accusations which can be flung at me – ingratitude – lack of sensibility – lack of imagination – but spray never yet hurt a great rock.

My most loved one. I long for you so much that the weight on my heart is intolerable. Everything which gives me happiness here (and in this house each thing does delight me) and everything I see: small things to please me when I am walking, or shapely things, or rude and angry and strong things. Clouds especially, and trees. They all bring you to me – literally, as if you were led by the hand and my heart cries out because each time you go away unkissed.

When we meet. What *will* happen – probably no more than a kiss. But let it be soon.

Valentine

The Brahms sonata[2] is another reason for your return. We shall often feel like that.

4: STW

London, 16 October 1930

My lovely, my dearest, my long lass, tomorrow is the next best day to

1 Letter postage at that date.
2 A record of the violin sonata in A.

today. I went to Whiteleys – if I am one of those unfortunate quick (and another specimen of early theology: for I took the quick to be those who dodged round the corner) on the last day I shall probably be seen hurrying to that beastly shop for a pair of reach-me-down gloves – to look up your trains. There are two earliest trains, Mrs Hall's[1] 11. something, and an earlier than early, which reaches London about 10.40. I shall expect you by both. There will be elevenses for you by the earliest, lunch by the second. And Friday is a heavenly blank brought me by the Dove, who has fluttered me away from any engagement except a very short tea with Oliver's[2] aunt Elinor – a nice old lady who can do my joy no harm. I cannot believe that I shall see you so soon, that you will lighten upon me. My darling, is it possible that we can be happier than ever? I have two clean breasts to make. Yesterday I went out to dinner and ate, I hang my head to confess it, boiled cod followed by roast mutton. I also – O Valentine, this is worse and worse – drank an African wine. And I sinned against your shade which said to me, Ask for bread and water. But I had not the courage, ate the accursed things, politely agreeing how serious it was about the Empire. And I was paid out, as I deserved to be. For it was not till three hours later, when Oliver had driven me round Hyde Park, smelling of rusty grass, that I recovered the airy joy I had worn all day. How can you love a woman who has eaten boiled cod?

The other breast is that I had already ordered the offending Margaux when I wrote about it. I would of course have counter-ordered it, but this morning the note that it had been sent off arrived by the same post as your letter. I can't do anything now, can I? Except I make amends – it is very cheap Margaux, being a farmhouse vineyard and not château – by working it out in penny halfpennies, and saving them by being with you instead of writing letters to you? Would that do? I could not answer your yesterday letter properly owing to the world being so much with me (the tea-party was a great success, all the cakes eaten but two) and so I had not time to enquire into why you were abashed by Francis's[3] remarks about the publication of worse poetry than his or yours. Why were you abashed? For his bad manners, I hope, not for your good poems. Do you really think that I don't know good from bad? Of course, one might believe anything of a woman who had rioted in Empire wine, but am I to be punished for this by the loss of all your confidence? I shall not be perfectly easy till I see you

1 Mrs Hall, taxi driver.
2 Oliver [Warner], my very remote cousin. I shared 113 Inverness Terrace, W.2, with him and his wife.
3 [Powys]

knowing the respective positions of yourself and that little whipper-snapping Snodgrass, and keeping yourself in your proper place. Your poetry, I say it again, is true and good, and beautifully and cleanly made. It has really got your quality, it is proud and violent and controlled. I was haunted by it long before I had opened my dull ungrateful senses to you, and I feel exactly about it now as I did then. I read it through again the other day, to see if love made any difference. It made none. And I cannot conceive a sharper test than that. With every achieved line I love *you* better, but the poems still kept me at my distance; and it is the prerogative of good art to do that to the reader – to be haughty and arbitrary. How did you make those snail-shells' smell of you so unmistakeably and excitingly? If you had sent me two of your shirts they could not have plagued me into trembling more. They lie on the table, and I eye them, every now and then, their defiant smooth colours, their polished slopes; and I shy away, and hear my heart hurry, and know that presently they will have their way with me, and I must pick them up and smell them again. And then what will the Bettys say of my complexion? 'These women know, I suppose, how you should look.' Oh, what scorn, fury, jealousy, in those words! You suppose, do you, my tyrant? And haven't you some rather definite views as to how I should look, too? No, my lover, I must put those shells away presently. They are more ruthless than you, for I can do nothing to them in return. And if I feel like this now, how shall I live out the muffle of time still between us? Oh, strip off these hours, one by one, till I feel your flesh against mine again . . . Hemlock, Henbane, Agnus Castus, waterlily . . . which of these am I to feed on for the next twenty-four hours? And I don't really trust waterlily, it is much too like you to be a reliable counter-aphrodisiac. 'It helpeth much to procure rest, and so settle the brain of frantic persons.' Credo. No, I cannot write any more. I have a great deal to say about globe artichokes, but I cannot say it now. I can only express a vindictive wish that when we meet I may get a little of my own back for this rape and outrage. I looked at your window today. I could just see the top of your door which will let me in. Then I walked on and had an entirely new view of Inverness Terrace – A Valentine's-eye view.

Tomorrow.

My love, my tremblings, my hurrying heart's blood.

Sylvia

How comparatively calmly I began this letter.

---

1 Two delicate little yellow snail-shells which she had steeped in Fougère Royale.

Narrative 2

It was a five minutes' walk from my door to hers. When she came to London I reversed the sun. My day began when I went to spend the night with her, lying in a narrow bed under a lofty ceiling. Into the four days between my departure from Chaldon and her arrival in London we had packed a month's impatience and curiosity. We had liked, now we loved; we had to learn each other all over again.

'O my America! my new-found-land.' My America was a continent of many climates: reckless, serious, fastidious, melancholy, sophisticated, compassionate, self-willed, self-tormenting, shy, sly, proud, suspicious: a continent of all climates of love, from vehemence to delighted amusement, from possession to cajolery. I had not believed it possible to give such pleasure, to satisfy such a variety of moods, to feel so demanded and so secure, to be loved by anyone so beautiful and to see that beauty enhanced by loving me. The nights were so ample that there was even time to fall briefly asleep in them, to waken and eat chicken sandwiches ('tonight I thought we would be vulgar and have champagne'), to admire her by candlelight, to stroll across to the large bare window and look at the northern sky, to be swept into more love-making, to fall asleep in her arms, to wake and admire her by light of day as she lay asleep. Waking or sleeping, it was the stillest face I have ever known, her lips betrayed nothing unless amusement slightly sharpened them into a fox's smile; to learn what she felt, I watched the pupils of her eyes.

And for the remainder of the twenty-four hours I went about my obligations with an affable pretence of being aware of them.

Towards the end of the month I was taken to Winterton in Norfolk, where The Hill House, the holiday house her father had bought when she was a small child, was still kept up, though not often lived in. This day, too, began after sundown. We dined late. When we set out, it was raining. After we were away from London the curtaining rain and the speed seemed to make our road, calling it up and dismissing it. We went by Six Mile Bottom, where Byron stayed with Augusta, through Newmarket and on to Barton Mills. There we stopped for petrol. I sat in the car with the window down, listening to the splash of weir-water and the tap of her decisive high-heeled shoes. The sky was clearing. As we drove on I lost the sense of being pursued which the rain and speed had given me. Nothing, I thought, could be more assuring than to be driven through unknown country to an unknown destination. Thetford, with the tall memorial column starting up from the heath; Wymondham, where everybody had long been asleep; Norwich; Acle, with the car going faster; a pale tower suddenly looming over us and Valentine saying that Winterton Church tower was boasted to overtop Yarmouth's St Nicholas by the length of a herring; then a steep narrow drive and a low house on a plateau.

The sky was clear, there was a light on-shore wind; I heard the noise of the sea. Speed was over and done with, there was time to walk from room to room, and through the run of narrow greenhouses smelling of heliotrope, with a naked Eros sitting marble-cold and solitary in the last of them, grieving over his broken arrow.

It was the severe presence of the sea which made the rather ugly house romantic. Below the plateau the dunes stretched far as the eye could travel, harshly mossed to the landward (it was impossible to think of them as land), prickled with marram grass as they rose into sandhills and subsided into the beach: a grey pebble beach till the tide went out and left a belt of sand streaked with watery light where the sea lay caught in pits and furrows.

It was the severe presence of the sea which provoked us to be childish, to run, leap, snatch mouthfuls of foam, write our initials on the sand with a heart round them and an arrow through the heart. The sand showed me the secret of her lovely gait: the footprints were exactly aligned in a narrow track, regular as machine-stitching – the gait of a superlative riding-horse. All that morning on the beach we saw no one till a small boy appeared and hung about at a distance, waiting to catch her eye. This was Roger, a village boy, she had taught him to box. He addressed her as 'Miss Maaalie', dragging out her discarded *Molly* as if the vowel were rattled from a capstan.

He told us the herring-fleet was in. That afternoon she took me to Yarmouth to see the boats packed cheek by jowl along the quay, the nets hanging in the drying-ground, looped like vines from port to port to gut the catch for the packers. Standing at stone troughs they slit and gutted, flick-flick, the herring running like a silver chain through their red hands. They wore black sea-boots and black oilskin aprons with bibs, uniform as a flock of sea-birds except for their bright-coloured mufflers.

There was a visit to Caterina[1] – her broad face and pug nose transfigured as she showed me photographs of Valentine as a young lady

1 Caterina, also Trina, married and living in Norfolk: 'My maid, when I was young. She was a darling and my greatest and best friend. She had such respect for the poets I read aloud to her that she used to ask me "Please may we have a poem by Mr Blake" or "Could you read that lovely one by Mr Wordsworth?"' – so Valentine, recalling her in a letter of long after.

of fashion, as a bride; visits to several windmills; to the chapel at Somerton, roofless, sunk in a wood, with a sycamore grown tall where the priest had stood before the altar; to inns, churches, other beaches. On the third day, after a turn-off to see Hickling Broad where a ghost skates across the water, we went back to London.

*

5: VA

London, Sunday 2 November 1930

My Darling,

This day has passed so slowly and I have been waiting so long. But there was a sharp thunderstorm, which pleased me, and reminded me of you.

Just now I was made very angry indeed because I was called 'soutenu' by you. This is a grave charge. It has, a little, shattered me. Now you know me as your lover you will not suspect me of cowardice when you see I write to you and do not wait to speak it. Here there is no question of fear, but I am more able to write than to speak.

Please will you bend your thoughts to this French word, and will you, when we meet tomorrow, have prepared for me an explanation, but not an excuse?

At present my two minds are at war, and I know nothing certain from either front. My handwriting is bad – worse than usual because I write this on my knee. I had not allowed for that word and that rudery, and so I was surprised. Please, my dear love, do not feel chivvied by annoyances when you read this. Please forgive me for telling you, selfishly, as it seems, but this is a very solid shadow, and, unless you wish it, I would rather nothing of its kind should be between us.

I love you with all my strength. I love you so utterly that I am unshaken, even by this sort of word. I love you passionately and very truly. For as long as you will you can rest on my love, and find shelter there – and find strength, too. Sometimes I am afraid in case all my store of love will give you what you most desire. If that is so, you must leave me. I will not allow your desire to be lessened to fit my power. But while I can hold you, I shall.

It is just possible that this vile word will sicken you, and that you will think it makes clear something you had not seen before. If things happen so you must let me know and I will not see you tomorrow. But whatever happens to or between us, now or in the future, we must have perfect good faith and truth always.

I shall be in at about four-thirty tomorrow, and I will telephone you then.

Valentine

N.B. This early morning the silence broke and I made a complete, and not too bad poem. But this may be only a god's wink, and not to be taken too seriously.

The part of me which writes poems is considerably slowed down. It is a separate engine and set to a more deliberate speed. This refers back, as far as I know, to the evening I walked up and down the room, and finally stood behind your back, and from there questioned you. So it is not valid now. But for all that, it uncorks me, I hope.

> You with your despair
> Have plaited my desire
> Entwining dark and fair
> With art I bitterly admire.
>
> You have made my pain
> Meet your different woe
> And burnished it again
> Until the strands too fiercely glow.
>
> You have dared to use
> My single talent thus
> Making by this abuse
> A shroud foredoomed to cover us.

If it is as bad as I now think it, I am indeed doomed. Especially as I have altered the other one.

6: STW

London, 3 November 1930[1]

My love, my liking

It is a really good poem, to the last verse. There it wants tightening. A short bitter lyric like this must turn back its tail and sting itself in the head, like the scorpion in the ring of fire. *Shroud* won't do – too peaceful a way out of the implied tangle; and the statement of the first two verses, ought, I think, to sharpen to a threat. 'Since you dare to use' you should threaten – you shall damn well be caught in this net as well as me.

And, my fierce one, that ending will be a very much closer rendering of the mood you were in when you stood behind me, threatening me with joy and trousers.

But the wording, and above all the fingering, of the first two verses delights me. You can do it, and I thank God.

This letter is wild as me in a bramble-bush. I am not only writing on my knee, I am talking to Mrs Keates[2] about her husband and my stockings. And I shall forget half I want to say, I might almost forget to say that I have asked Master Francis[3] to tea – so as to be sure he won't drop in for dinner, am I not a politician – and that I ask you to dinner and to my most, most loving breast.

I bend my thoughts to that French word; but the one response my mind can give to anything so unmeaning is to think you should spell it with a final e, shouldn't you?

I am not even annoyed that it should be said. It is too insignificant, I hope, to have worried you. We are both of us tethered to savage senses of honour, no arrangement to which we could have consented would have cast on either a slight.

Till tonight.

Sylvia

1 Was slid under her door, to be there before the 4.30 of her return.
2 Mrs Keates, my charwoman.
3 Master Francis [Powys], again in London.

7: VA

Chaldon, 5 November 1930

My dearest love,

There has been no letter from you this morning, but as I am not permitted to be possessive I pretended not to be angry, and as I love you I did not reproach you in that telegram. This last forbearance used a good deal of fortitude. No doubt, what with one threat and another with which you have assailed my ears, I shall need a vast amount of Edith Cavell's virtue. I will do my best.

An excited Violet[1] visited me last night. She chattered and jumped about like a child. This plan of going to London has caused her to forget that Francis is her son who is about to be sacrificed. Theo, too, is happy and well, so they say. You have done a good thing here, by your skill and diplomacy. I tremble in case you do not come early on Friday. How hard, if you do not, when everything is so shining and spotless and warm and excited.

I have to take the two of them to Dorchester now, and Ruth.[2] I bought a lanthorn.

There has been little time, but I have changed the last verse of that poem. It is not to my liking yet, but it is only eluding me, as you do, with a kind promise of capture.

Please, will you bring those poems down when you come? I would be very much helped if you would pull out the dead ones for me. I need to learn, if you will teach me – although, my dear love, it is a sorry prospect for you, though not a thankless one.

Your telegram put health into me, I charge you to be firm, sweetheart, and not beguiled by Violet to remain even for one train. I dread that some misfortune has touched you. The lack of evidence that you are well is worrying me. If no letter comes this afternoon I shall be distraught. But do not be moved by this, and do not be put out. Do not think of me as a nuisance, yet – at any rate. My darling. This letter is full of instructions and requests. Reading it, one would almost forget that I love you. But I do – most passionately. The gale which is gathering outside makes me

1 Violet was coming to London to farewell Francis. My machinations had worked and he was about to travel to France to be secretary to W.D. This was an American lady, who had written to me from the South of France, suggesting I should live with her as secretary-companion. Seeing this as a chance to get Francis away from Beth Car, I hoped he might be accepted as an alternative.
2 Ruth, her mother.

want you desperately. The might of my love is more fierce and powerful, but you can shelter from it in my arms.

Remember your promise, freely given, and therefore binding, that you would tell me immediately if you were ill or unhappy or anxious or alarmed. In thee have I trusted, let me never be confounded. – You did promise constancy too.

Valentine

8: STW

London, 5 November 1930, 11.30 p.m.

Darling,

For a moment I have the house to myself, and have read your letter. I needed a little comfort. At 7.5. Francis rang up from your studio, asking could he bring Violet round. I said, come both to dinner, but come soon as I have other people dining, and a dinner that will spoil. At 8.5 I rang you again, and at 8.30 we sat down to cold hard-baked eggs and a stew like the marrow of Sodom and Gomorrah. During dinner Francis sat like a fossil while every one else tried to carry plates. I thrust a bottle of claret at him, with a curt word, and he bested me by driving in the cork and spilling half of it. Now, thank God, they are pulling me to pieces at 2, whither they went to retrieve luggage. How I dislike the thought of Francis there. Dearest, why did you let him? 'Tis profanation, Nay, 'tis sin.

He leaves (D.V.) tomorrow by the 8.20 p.m. This lands him at the Nord at 5 a.m. with six hours to wait. If only a taxi would get him. I am feeling a little more real. Your letter and a book which we shall read together have just come. The book is by Bill Empson – *Seven Types of Ambiguity in English Verse*. It looks entertaining. That smell which gave me to you is the apples in the cupboard. Going bad, my dearest! Schiller liked them, but I don't think Schiller would have liked me. But to know that the real me is safe in your arms appeases the savage ghost who sits here. I did not think I was capable of such frantic impatience – Damn, they are back again!

2 a.m. Now I am consuming cake and sherry, and trying to sleepify myself. But how can I sleep, apart from the rigours of the occasional bed,

to which I condemn Master Francis so blithely? The wind rises, it tosses the dead leaves against the door, and Violet has given me your letter, and I think of that other gale . . . and am shelterless. Well (I must write small, this is all my paper down here) I have heard from Violet, calling you Sylvia and me Valentine – which pleased me. And I have put her to bed, and kissed her goodnight. I knocked, there was no answer so I looked in, and there she was in a long white nightgown, starting guiltily up from her knees, like a pigeon rising from a forbidden cornfield. I have washed up the dinner, and prepared my bed in the dining-room. And if you were here you could certainly tell me I am tired – I am – and send me to bed. But I defy you, I will write as small as I can and write to the end of the paper. Then, with all this practice – for I am improving – I will engrave the Lord's Prayer on invisibility. How cross I was with Francis three hours ago! The gunpowder has all run out of the heels of my boots now, I am sorry I was cross. Still, you had better know it. You had better see that I, who can with tolerable equanimity, endure outrages upon the spirit, fly into the devil's wrath if my flesh-pots are kept too long in the oven and spoilt.

And you got no letter this morning, and you worried about me. Darling, I am penitent. I should have been rounder with those persons from Porlock; but yesterday I had not a kick in me. But I am perfectly well, do not imagine me otherwise. But till I see you I am a vain show. How lovely to have a lanthorn! I shall see your long legs by it and your slender hand. I have ordered Mrs Hall to meet the 1.43 and I have bought my ticket. You do not really doubt my coming, or my constancy. There is triumph in your insistence that you do. This night is whittled so about, for I must rise early, that I can almost say, Only one more night. And you in your now can say it without a proviso. My love.

Sylvia

Thursday
The Gill photographs[1] came this morning, and I have been arranging secret assignations with them ever since. But they are not as beautiful as you, my dear.

I had Violet and Francis to breakfast, every one in the highest spirits, and Violet at Woolworths revelling in artificial red-hot pokers, and cut-glass bowls because they were like hedgehogs. I bought some practical

1 Photographs of two nude studies of her by Eric Gill.

night-lights, and a bread platter, and a memorandum book. I was in the most tearing gaiety all the morning until I saw a little dog run over. It was a baby Pekinese, it rushed into the traffic like a dead leaf blown by the wind. I went to the vets with its mother, but it died on the way there. I had to tell her. She held it in her arms but dared not look at it, and the slow blood dripped from its nose on the sleeve of her slaughtered fur coat. If I had not vowed truth to you, I would not tell you such things.

I began to tremble, and to think that joy was as rash and as easily made away with. But I have been extremely sensible. I have had lunch and reasoned with myself. I was thinking of you at the very moment I saw it happen before my eyes. That was partly what made it so terrible. It was as though it were you. By this time tomorrow we shall be together. My dear, dear love, I love you.

Sylvia

1931

London, 1 January 1931

My dearest,

We can go to Lavenham as soon as we like.[1] I have just had a letter from Kenneth Rivington[2] to say so. He was in London all Christmas time – it was evil chance that whenever I rang up the house was empty and my letter had to be sent on from Lavenham, which is why it seemed so interminable to get an answer.

So now, what shall we do? Go there soon, don't you think? We could meet in opposite directions, me by train, you by car – or I could come up to you at Winterton first, or whatever you like.

I do long to show you that place. I did not tell you, and it doesn't show in the print but the church is on the side of a hill, a grass slope leading up to it, very crumbly-crusty underfoot on a winter's night, and at the foot of the slope a pond where in July men cut the water-lilies, standing in a boat and scything under the water.

By the pond is the church path: It abuts on to a garden, and the owners did wickedly move it three feet to the left. So now whenever I approach by that path, duty obliges me to climb over a fence, tread down some seedling conifers, and climb back again a few yards further on, in order to preserve a national right of way. You will be of great assistance in this, the fence is high and tottering.

There is also, but rather in tatters, the house where Jane and Anne Taylor lived when they were small. And in The Barn, besides the

---

1 She had gone to Winterton in order to be alone after a fortnight in London. It was a wretched fortnight. She had several migraines. Her heart was troubled by the reproachful conclusion of a long-standing friendship. Haru, her Siamese cat, sickened and had to go to the vet for nursing; on Christmas day we heard she was dead.

2 Kenneth Rivington lent his house in Lavenham, Suffolk, to fortunate friends. I was one of these.

unparalleled collection of Sax Rohmers, there is a photograph album of celebrated beauties in the 90s. Cowlike countesses, and a tart, in bed, in her night gown, but with stays on underneath. Also a lovely picture of Queen Alexandra with a young George in one hand and an umbrella in the other, not very well rolled, saying: these are my jewels.

Have you got the dominoes? If not I will collect them from 2[1]: it is the perfect place for dominoes, there is a slightly snuffy comfort about it, due to the faint popping sound which comes from the gas, and the chairs deeply upholstered in carpets.

We will be very happy there, my lovely, and very warm, indoors at any rate. And if we have the car there are dozens of places to visit, especially Little Gidding if we feel brave enough to go so far. It is a tiny church, with an Inigo Jones-ish west front entirely taken up with a large and formal clock. It is in a field, one approaches it through a farm barton, and the mossy flagged church path emerges from muddy grass. But car or no, doesn't much matter. We can be happy without architecture, and if we want a diversion we can go to church and hear a nice plain C. of E. Tell me when you would like to go there, and I will write to Mrs Parker to make ready for us, I leave the dates and plans to you. It has grown colder and colder since you left, or else it is that I feel more and more forsaken. In a few hours time I may even be looking forward to that whiskey!

This is not a proper letter, because people may come to tea at any – here they are – moment, so I cannot let myself go.

Bell.

Darling, I love you.

Sylvia

Wasn't them, after all. Was boy with fish, very clammy, in newspaper, for upstairs. Did abstractedly shake fish, mistaking for hand of guest. Was rather livid sensation.

10: VA

Winterton, 2 January 1931, 8.30 a.m.

My dear love,

I will make calculations in my new diary and write to you about Lavenham. Only I cannot do that yet, as I have not the diary. It will be

1 [Valentine's flat]

bought in Yarmouth this morning, when I have been to the Quay for my trousers and for your ship's boy's jersey.

A dreadful journey. Intensely cold, and belly-pain snarling and biting at me for almost all the way. I sat delightfully wearing your coat, and smelling you – so lifelike it was that I was beguiled into a state of keen desire for you. But this was not much good, and I expect you paid no heed to my anger as you sat coldly playing on your typewriter.

My chief comfort last night was in discovering what you had written in 'Lavengro'.[1] My darling – when I read those words in the book I referred them to you. Remarked them in a protective voice. So we are each steadfast to the other, you see, and I expect we shall need to be. It is not likely that such love as ours will be smooth and easy, and it would be a waste of good power if it were.

Today is fine and white – very blue sky and the air is frozen stiff and still, and the sea is making a great clatter on the beach. My sweet love – I want you to come here again. The place is asking about you so eagerly and continually that I think we should be here alone together, sans Ruth, because I want you to be delighted – which is how you are when you are with me, my heart.

I am longing to go to Lavenham. We will be very happy, of course, and how lovely to be together where you were alone. Will you regret your lost estate, and wish to be solitary again? Perhaps I shall pick up scent of that outworn Sylvia, and track her out from her sleep, and learn what she was like. But I believe that her sleep will slide into death, and that haunted and despairing creature I saw[2] in the street will never come back. Nor do I wish to fetch her back unless her ghost ever troubles you. If it does, I will lay it at Lavenham. You are so lovely and so complete and fulfilled when you are happy, my darling, and your melancholy grows well in this soil. Sometimes I feel a fear that you will become impatient with pleasure and joy, but I think that is foolish of me. Love does not lack sorrow or rage. But anyhow – you have done it and I do not think you can slip out of this net, however slim and agile you are. Besides, will you want to escape away from such tenderness and such deep love.

Later. What about Friday 9th? I will motor to London on that day, and

1 *Lavengro* [by George Borrow]: 'Never heed,' said the girl, 'I'll stand by you.' I thought she resembled Isobel Berners in more than stature, and I had written this in a copy of *Lavengro* I gave her.
2 It was catching sight of me thus as she was driving down Inverness Terrace which impelled her to offer me her cottage.

fetch you, and then either bring you here to stay until Monday, or straight to Lavenham. Let us be together this day week anyhow – and I will do as you please about where we go.

My darling, I hope you are feeling rather gloomy without me. Not so desolate as I am, because I am so much in love with you.

Valentine

11: STW

London, 2 January 1931

My dearest,

At the last glimpse of your smooth pale hunted face yesterday, being swallowed up like the moon in that welter of luggage and dirty linen and what not I remembered.

> Constrained by their Lord to embark
> And venture without him to sea,
> The season tempestuous and dark,
> How griev'd the disciples must be.[1]

But though I remained on the shore, darling, did pray; and your wire from Newmarket with glad tidings of J.M. being beLorded was an answer to prayer.[2]

All your vows and ordinances are being carefully observed (I shall save up my remarks on the whiskey for a later paragraph). Victor[3] came to dinner, or rather came for a drink and stopped on, and told me that the Indian Conference is at sixes and sevens, chiefly because Ramsay tried to hector the Moslims and put their backs up instead; and in return I told him the last instalment from Beth Car. He said that Powyses were like Proust or Les Thibauds; if you have a volume once a year nothing could be more entertaining, but God forbid he should have them all the time. Should it be Les Thibauts? Did learn once, but can't remember. He liked Mrs Moxon. He also said he had never seen me look so well, so there is

---

1 *Olney Hymns.*
2 A rumour that James Maxton, a Labour MP, was in the New Year's Honours List.
3 Victor [Butler].

confirmation, if you want more.

After he had gone, I turned out a drawer and found all manner of entertainments. Several early poems of mine, one with illustrations, and also this, which is so beautiful that it was ungrateful of me not to wear it embroidered into my memory.

Lines Inscribed on a Drinking Fountain
attached to the Workhouse wall
in Marloes Road

Lord, from thy blessed throne,
The griefs of earth look upon –
God bless the poor!
Teach them true liberty;
Make them from strong drink free;
Let their hours happy be –
God bless the poor.

I hear that the proofs of Opus 7[1] are coming through, so with luck it should be out in March. I wish that I had not this snobbish feeling that it is rather trifling to come out at 2/- and I do still yearn after my blue frog-spawn. But a dolphin is a nice damp animal, too, it might be worse.

Now it is almost time to begin mentioning that whiskey.[2] I looked at the label, wondering if there was room to inscribe that line Dante saw written up over the gates of Hell: Wisdom and power and primal love ordained me; but there wasn't; then I wondered a little if I should crack the bottom and draw my measure up to your pencil mark instead of down to it; then I shuddered and decided to put it away till bed-time. By then, though I shouldn't have guessed it, the worst was over. For when I came to drink it, I was in such a knot over re-writing the last verse of 'Night's Worst' that I swallowed it almost automatically, as I might have swallowed water or prussic acid. It immediately made me extraordinarily drunk. I felt drunkenness rushing up me in dark warm waves. Then I got into bed; and while I was falling asleep I composed several epigrams with childlike fluency. Some I remembered, here are three, all about still lives.

---

1 My narrative poem, about to be published at 2 shillings in the Dolphin Series.
2 I did not like whiskey but a bottle had been left with injunctions to drink it as a prophylactic.

Faithful to an old design
Chardin painted bread and wine
But with private fancy blent
A knife into the sacrament.

Closed is the book, and on it lies,
Blind, the accomplice of closed eyes.

Unrotted by the fall of man
This apple painted by Cézanne
Smirks on a dish and looks as nice
As ever it did in Paradise.

I dreamed of you all night. In one dream I embellished you with two aunts. They were extremely like you, only their eyes were a shallow dusky blue, and they were at least a foot taller. They sat on either side of a table turning over photograph albums while you and Ruth had a painful altercation. Ruth kept turning round and saying things about you to me in French; in the end I rescued you with a very ingenious strategy, which was to say to Ruth and each aunt in turn, in a very confidential whisper: 'Excuse me, but your sister wants to see you in the next room'. This got rid of them beautifully.

Tonight, with luck, I may get a letter from you. I shall not really begin to miss you till then, for I still can't believe you are away, it seems only a longer and chaster interregnum.

It is nearly six. I must rush out with this into a very sharp evening, bristling with stars. At least, it feels as if it would be that, for the fire crackles and when William last came in his coat was icy cold.

Do look after yourself, my dear, and make a prudent owl of yourself, and keep out of mischief, and eat that good Winterton food. I am glad for yet another reason, now, that you took me there, for I can see you indoors and out, very clearly in that easterly light.

My love, my love.

Sylvia

I am extremely well, not a sniff or snuffle.

12: VA

Winterton, 2 January 1931

My love,

Opening this box I discovered your poem (Death is more sure than I) which I had been thinking of as I undressed. Believing that I had left it in London and being angry at the thought of that. Now I read it again, and put it among the others, and see it there, and see how all these latest ones have a new unity and folded completeness – each one like a Russian toy or like an impossibly well-ordered life, sense and spirit or body and soul and mind, all weighted and perfect. I am most glad of all that I loved you first because of your poems. You should be glad of that. It means that now, however proudly I prance in my possession of you, I am still in love with you as carefully and humbly as I was when that was all I had. It would be unforgiveable to love you without worship – but I doubt whether you have been so loved and worshipped before – or anyhow, so thoroughly.

But apart from all this (and I did succeed in getting apart from it for one short and cold moment) I am entranced by the poem. I finger its skill with more joy than I have from my dagger, and with exactly the same excitement as I felt from touching the lovely hinges of your body. Just the same compact and well-mastered working.

Perhaps you don't like your poem touched just so. But it is *not* impertinently fingered. It is watched and admired and observed as if I were standing above you as you lay in bed. And you are so proudly naked that you must rejoice – and you do not shrink from my stare, and you do not glare reproachfully – so obviously you are glad of your beauty.

I am now in bed. Trying not to think of the boy who will be hanged to-morrow and yet in my mind scorning my own terror. It is bad, and weak, to fear any fact of this sort, and yet I shrink from it, and fly from it, dragging my imagination after me as if I were trying to avoid a dog-fight.

My poem about Raveney[1] is wrong and quite false – which is a pity. I realise now that, on the last night one would not have any connected thoughts at all. So the third section, which I meant to be the thought in the front of his mind is really both foolish and untrue.

Sunday
I was nearly destroyed by carelessness last night. The radiator of the car

---

1 Raveney, also a boy who was hanged.

boiled, and blew off its cap, and a jet of boiling water sprang at my face – but I ducked and only got my brow a little scalded. How horrible for you if I had been altogether mutilated. But I should never have seen you again.

Yesterday I found a book on Bisexuality. After reading it carefully I discover that you and I are admirably suited to each other. Which is a comfortable thought, my darling, and should support you all day long, but it is little consolation at night. The only frightening thing is that the author of this book recommends one to become a Member of the Order of Woodcraft Chivalry. But I think we may escape that, with care. Please do not have any truck with that Order while I am away.

I had a letter from you, after my panic-telegram had gone. I am sorry that I panicked so quickly, dear love – but glad too. Your words came to me on the telephone first – in a deep Norfolk accent. Now no more can you twite me with 'Woffor?'

Whiskey's claims are vindicated by your childlike epigrams. If this were not Sunday I would send a bottle of White Horse – and I only fail to do it because no shops are open and no parcels taken. No other reasons could stay my hand.

Today has been mixed weather. It snowed, rather feebly, this morning, but quickly that turned to rain. The sky has been grey: not really grey, either, but that heavy pink which shows that snow is about. After lunch the sun shone, and I walked to the last high dune at the edge of the shore. The sea has been very kind to these fishermen: they are rich and can be as drunk as they please.

Caterina told me of an old woman of 72, called Jane Rogers, who has had a very great many children, each by a different man, and who has brought them up most tidily. She wears a grand silk dress, of black, and goes to church. She has many grandchildren, a lovely figure, and speaks no evil of any one.

Valentine

13: STW

London, 5 January 1931

I am writing this at the hairdresser's, with my head in an Egyptian bag. For this is one of those days when everything has to be fitted in, and I have dropped you into this interval as though I were shutting up one of your shells in a box.

Oh, how lovely that it is to be Thursday. I have been prancing ever since, have ordered a special brand of tea, and some drinks. The drinks, let me state, have been ordered for my behalf. My constitution has always needed alcohol in Suffolk – but I will let you share.

Thank God your telegram came and wiped out the picture of you having your face scalded. I felt sick and trembling after I read that. Are you sure that your forehead is all right. You shouldn't wear a hat that might rub it. Do be careful that it has every chance to heal properly, for no part of one scars more easily than one's brow. My heart, my darling, do let this be a lesson to you. I believed you when you said once that you were always careful with cars – now my faith is rather rocked. I should love you exactly as much (but how regretting your beauty) if you were scarred all over – but I should rage and despair, for all that love, when I thought it might have been averted.

This morning I had such a long and closely-written screed from Ruth that glancing at it I thought: This can only be an expostulation. However, it wasn't, as far as I could decipher – merely a very protracted explanation of how nice she had made Winterton for you. Do you know that she intends travelling back on the return half of her motor coach on Thursday. Should this be dealt with? I also gather that Willie[1] has a boil on his buttock. This is hard on Ruth who, I am sure, would like to deal with it directly.

Young Mrs Keates has been loosed at 2. I have encouraged her to give it a good clean-up, as I think it needs paint washing and so forth. I went there last night and put away letters, poems and odd papers. The poems are in the escritoire, the rest in the top of Dorothy.[2] I also laid away some clothes, including an odd glove. I enjoyed trotting round among belongings like a good wife (that word is GOOD).

How nice that we are bi-sexual. I seem to remember Remy de Gourmont making that point, but the order of Woodcraft Chivalry is new to me. I think I would really prefer to be an Ancient Buffalo. I suppose buffalos might be as bi-sexual as we.

Do we do it in alternate spasms, do you think, like synchronised oysters ('Tithonus, or the Future of the Oyster'[3]) or is one both at once?

1 Willie [Goffin], chauffeur.
2 A massive bureau, given by a lady of that name. She had burning red hair and a temper to match; during a pre-Christmas visit to Valentine she had suddenly knocked her down and tried to strangle her.
3 A series of sociological essays had titles on these lines.

And can we have a child by those means? Which reminds me, the winkle season has begun. I ate some on Saturday and, darling, you know I *do* believe they're boiled, because inside one winkle was a very small crab; *and that crab was scarlet.* At this interesting point I am taken out of my bag and must go away. Goodbye, my dearest Love, be very careful, remember you are mine. And bless you for saying Thursday.

Sylvia

14: VA

Winterton, 5 January 1931

My dear love,

I went for a walk on the beach early this morning. The dunes were frozen stiff, and I walked on the crest of the grasses. The beach had patches of white frost beneath every stone and in every dent and hollow – even the ripples which the tide has marked on it had frost in them like shadows on a film negative.

I walked for about three miles along the shore, and then turned back, and drove my shadow home in front of me, over the frozen sand, following the course of my yesterday's foot prints, which were today hard and encrusted. There had been a high storm tide and the beach is littered with rubbish rolled into parcels and tied with sea-weed. I found three boots – one with a wooden sole – a great many bottomless tins, an enormous and intact mackintosh sheet, plenty of straw, some half-peeled carrots, a turnip, a child's shoe, some green boughs of tree, two dead gulls and a piece of wood painted seagull-grey. Upon this I inscribed our names very carefully and the date of this year and of last (which looked very grand and extravagant) and then I cast it far into the sea.

After this, I ran a great deal, with Bunny.[1] Who was so intensely happy that he yelled whenever he had enough breath. I tried to make him jump over a fairly wide lagoon which we found. But he would not. I did – and after a great many leaps I trod on some quicksand and got soaked.

My blue trousers had an overwhelming desire for seawater. They led me directly into the waves, and did not flinch when those jaws yawned at

1 Bunny, a Pekinese domiciled in Norfolk, whom she had bought out of a pet shop because he looked disconsolate.

me. But I ran them away. They are in league with my belt for it came off and nearly got us all drowned, because I had to rescue it.

I sat on the sand in the sun, and got very warm. Then I said aloud the last Sonnet, with such passion that I was impressed and did it all over again. Then I walked across the beach and, to my mild astonishment, a large fisherboy who had been approaching me but was still too far off for me to know him, came rapidly across the beach, mistaking me for a friend. Theo-like,[1] I fled. These perils! But they have made me take much violent exercise, which has done me much good, and, though you need not fear my returning to you red-faced and yokel-like, you should be ready for great strength and a very much increased power of endurance. Psychologically bi-sexual. Not physiologically, which would be dreadful. Anyhow, you are neither. Darling – do you want to have children? If you really do, I must ask the O.W.C. what to do. But think it over seriously. Perhaps you had better read all about extroverts, which is me, and introverts, which is you, before you develop any new desires.

My dearest Love. You have been grubbing in that cold room and although I am grateful I have to reproach you for it. You must not and shall not tend me so. I will talk to you when we lie in darkness together, and I can prove that my words are wise and kind and not harsh, as they would look in this letter.

Take care of yourself, extra care during these days. If I arrived at ten on Thursday, would you be awake – and, if so, would you be out?

I find that some damned fool has given Ruth *Mrs Dalloway*. If I had selected my own powers I should be able to write as Virginia Woolf can. I love opaque honesty and transparent cunning. And skill. The sunshine is so warm and bright, I believe it *could* put the fire out if it shone directly on the flame. The fire would die of jealousy of your powers. Dearest heart – please, if you do the catering and not Mrs Parker, do not think that I have been living on true Winterton fare here. I have cut everything down to the minimum; toast and tea for breakfast, it's true, but cheese for lunch, no tea at all and one dish (usually soup or egg) for supper. No drink at all, except once as a medicine. All of which has suited me even though the air here is hunger-making usually.

I await developments from Ruth. She is becoming quite maddening once again. It is my fault. Being happy myself I have found it difficult to be sour to her; and the moment I relapse from my ill-temper she encroaches and makes life impossible. I should have been warned when

---

1 Theodore took evasive action at sight.

she proposed living in a larger flat again, after selling this place, so that I, when I was in town, would live there with her. Now Caterina is full of prophecy – and I must take care. I'm afraid you have married into a bad family, but it shall not affect you, my love.

Valentine

Later

A ghastly telephone conversation with Ruth. Who wants, slyly, to come here to-morrow and motor up with me on Thursday. Which would mean the hell of a fuss about an early start, endless reproaches from my most dreadful family, because of Ruth having to arise so early – *and* the loss of my looked-forward-to down-drive. Intolerable.

Ruth breathed down the machine, from Sussex to Norfolk, so powerfully that I felt like the mouse¹ when we bellowed it. How that innocent beast has avenged itself. Its ghost smirked at my rage.

'But, surely, darling – I might have *one* day with you. And I so *love* motoring. It couldn't hurt you – could it?' (exaggerated). If the jersey is not nice, return it AT ONCE and I shall be able to change it at the shop and bring you an ordinary one, not pulled in at the waist and not double-knitted. Do this, because, who knows, the weather may be dire at Chaldon, and it is only in wet and icy weather that you realise how warm and wise fishermen are. I walked in heavy rain yesterday, and my trousers were waterproof, although they cost under 15/- and claimed no virtue but of being hardwearing.

I will be so happy to return to the cottage, dear love; I feel us to be grateful and none too kind if we leave it long alone. None too wise, either. It has blessed us more than anywhere. Me with you, and you with fine poems and a most true lover. In Mother Goose I found this account of our coming meeting: 'their discourse was not well connected, they did weep more than talk, little Eloquence and a great Deal of Love . . . They had but very little sleep, the Princess had no Occasion . . .' I am also told that very often Hymen's blisses sweet, Altho' some tedious obstacles they meet, Which makes us for them a long while to stay, Are not less happy for approaching slow; And that we nothing lose by such delay.

But that I am less inclined to believe.

How nearly have you finished your story?

Darling – I am so impatient for you.

---

1 We had tried to eject it from behind a cupboard by puffing the bellows at it.

15: STW

London, 6 January 1931

Blast the weather, devil take the fish-harvest! I know that my letters are cold and flat – that I cannot write love-letters, that here is still a recess you have not thawed . . . but that is no reason why you, who write so well of our love, should threaten me with fish-harvests. But darling, the inadequacy of my letters is another good reason to your hand why we should stay together; though except for a collector's point of view there is no reason for you to want good reasons. Still, you may have them, like your daggers.

I am fixed and hung and aimed on Thursday. But this morning, walking in the cold I began to wonder if it is needful for you to come all the way to fetch me. I could so easily manage it by train, and you would have less than half the journey, and none of that crawling in and out of London. Though God knows why I should say crawling, when the word I mean is snaking.

My heart, are you sure it wouldn't be wiser to go straight to Lavenham? You have never said a word how you are; how are megrims,[1] do you still have headaches, are you really and truly, apart from me and the Stoicks, fit for such a long and cold day's driving? If I were someone else, if I were Nuttlesnip's[2] nieces, would you be well enough to fetch me?

Please think. I implore you by all the times I have hauled the bedclothes over you, think twice!

I like all three new poems, and especially the chimney stars. It is so baize-bottomed, the lines slide in and out so easily, and fit so close. I have read it over and over, trying to see how you manage that impermeable quality where all is so thronged, and yet nothing falls out, no loose ends or joins, no declamation of being intricate. Your body has the same quality, and your love-making, when however strongly and ruthlessly you hold me, I am never jolted.

I have been thinking a good deal about last verses. I feel more and more that when one writes in stanzas, as I do, something must be done about a finish. If the poem is short and can turn round and bite itself, well and good. But one doesn't always want to do that, so what to do then? There ought to be some sign, some formal sign of ending, like the formal clinch

1 Migraines.
2 Miss Ursula Nettleship, Augustus John's sister-in-law, who lived in the flat above Valentine's.

of the last two lines of a Shakespeare sonnet, or the Alexandrine after-couplet, or Dryden's bracketed triplet. But these are all implicit in the form, stanza codas will be hard to manage. I did one in that poem in Time Importuned about the nurses in Kensington Gardens, when I turned them all into mermaids. That stroke I added long after, on the proof, I believe, and on an impulse I didn't then examine. But I am sure that impulse was a sound one. Another advantage of the twiddle at the end would be that it might stop one from that damnable straining for a chic last line. So I shall experiment. I have indeed been experimenting; for the story sticks and will get gluey if I work on it in this state, so I have been taking old dissatisfied stanza poems and trying experimental codas on them. It is damn hard, because the coda has to refer back to the form of the poem. I thought of course what could G. M. Hopkins do. And was immediately quelled by remembering the 'Deutschland', stanza after stanza marching on. But 'Binsey Poplars' has a sort of coda, a final flourish, almost, if you come to think of it, a fol-de-riddle, toorahoora scene. I don't think we talk about poetry enough, not shoppily enough. Being poets we are always dug into the agony of doing the thing. But there should be time for the kind of talk that does artists so much good: where to buy the best alizarines, and what is the best way to deal with cerulean. Which reminds me. Have you any idea what he meant in 'Deutschland' by *thy unchancelling* poising palms? It pleases my blind mind, just as I liked Empson's *unvalenced air of heaven* vaguely referring it to bed-frills; but I was so ashamed of that liking when I discovered what he meant that I should love you to know unchancelling, or at any rate to have views on it. I suppose it is something akin to chancellor, and I imagine chancellors dispense something, like exchequers. But what's the etymology? Shall we invoke Harper? You know, darling, I think it would be highly good for me if you saw to it that I read a page of a dictionary daily. Not more than a page, and attentively. But then I forget again. I have just remembered looking up piacular because of Sweeney's *piacular pence*, and I distinctly recollect that it was a revelation to me, but I have forgotten what piacular does mean. It would do me a great deal of good if you would really take my mind in hand, coil and comb the same. Think what four month's attention has done for my behaviour; more, apparently, than you believe, walking out and embroiling me with dinner-parties, while I have sat at home, cooing peevishly like a turtle, every evening since you left.

But only two nights more, two more objectless unlighted evenings, except that at nine o'clock a letter comes. Then – I shut my eyes and leave off writing. O my heart, this nearness is such danger! Do take care of yourself, do make Willie go over that car thoroughly, and see the wheels are on and all that. Do put on warm clothes and take hot drinks, and those ammonia things, and for God's sake don't start unless you feel perfectly well. Wire, and I will come at once to you instead. And above all, please, please don't tackle that drive to London.

Your Sylvia

When I read this over I suddenly understood that I shall be in an anguish of fuss about you on Thursday, lest you have another megrim while you are driving alone. I know you will rage at me for saying so, but could you bring Ruth too, if she is coming to Winterton the day before? It would be a little abrupt for her, I suppose, straightaway to be borne back; but then she did get you out of Whiteleys very promptly that day.

I am sorry, my love, it is loathsome for you to be intruded on by my fears and my fusses. Later on I swear I will be more rational . . . But my fear is still so raw, I must wince and cry out. You asked me seriously on New Year's Night if this illness had weakened you to me. But it is I who am weakened by it; or have been forced by it to acknowledge my weakness.

But you must decide.

Narrative 3

On January 11th, we broke our stay at Lavenham to go to London for a Schnabel concert at the Queen's Hall. He played three concertos: the Schumann, a Mozart and the Emperor – the opening, she said, was like Dr Johnson saying *Sir*. In the taxi going back to 113 we spoke of acquaintances we had recognised, and I said that looking round on all those known and unknown listeners I knew that I wanted none of them and only wanted her. The spell of Schnabel's playing and the spell-bound concurrence of his hearers, perhaps, or perhaps my remark, for I made it as a simple statement of fact, annulled her lurking mistrust that I might not be wholly hers, that I might not stay. (This mistrust was partly owing to me: in my anxiety not to tie her down I had declaimed against any transactions in love, any tenure beyond the moment's; and to the slip of parchment on which I had written in a scrivener's hand, *Item: One Fidelity Freehold*, I had given a libertine air by including it among the frivolities of a Christmas stocking.) That night, our love-making had a new depth and serenity. When we woke she said it had been a marriage night. She said this so gravely and with such conviction that I took her word for it. For my part, why not? I loved; I increasingly honoured, and if being bewitched into compliance is obedience, I obeyed. As for fidelity, it seemed as natural as the circulation of my blood, and no more meritorious. While we lay talking I asked her how she knew. Her body told her, she said: the body is older and wiser than the soul, being first created; and like a good horse, given its way would go home by the best path and at the right pace. I took her word for that, too. She knew about horses, I didn't.

Her field of knowledge far exceeded mine. Back at Lavenham that evening, stretched on the sofa at her six foot length, trousered and smoking a small pipe, she broke an essential silence with, 'I once had a long controversy with the head of The Mothers' Union.'

*

16: STW

London, 22 January 1931

My dearest love,

You are but half an hour gone. I suppose you have passed that friendly sign saying To the North. I hope . . . W.¹ Her voice is like a melancholy little dog at the end of a string. I am so glad for her sake that you had your good idea and that we turned back that evening. And I believe she will be a comfort to you, at any rate a solace and pass-time.

How long it is before I can even begin to think of you arrived, and in the warm, and eating and drinking, and eyeing your bed. How one length lengthens another – for if that is so long, how much longer till you get this letter, till I get yours. And on Sunday there is no post. Damn. This absence had need to be shorter than the last, for it will be much worse. All that has happened since then makes me a sad shadow out of your light, a

---

1 Whatever I hoped is lost in a crease of the letter. Francis had exhausted W.D.'s patience. She had come to England and wrote to me from a hotel near London. We went to see her. Though it was clear her kindness had been abused, we surmised that she might have been difficult to live with. After we had left, Valentine, who was due to spend the week-end at Winterton with Ruth, turned back and invited her to come too – much as she had bought Bunny the Pekinese because he looked disconsolate.

busy ghost, the poor soul of an engagement book.

Your falcon[1] sits on my smallest finger, waiting to shake off her jesses and spread wing when you come back. Your snowdrops look at me with their whiteness and small firm shapes. One of them has in miniature the curve of your smooth shoulder. The fire babbles, the air darkens and clears with dusk, the wind hoots and laments and fingers the windows. And as I sit here the ghosts of all the other winter afternoons when I have sat here come thronging round me, and say: This was your solitude, your peace, your contentment. You could dwell like this once and be glad that you felt no revolt. What has happened to you now, that you are so changed? What have you heard in the wind since then, what gales have wakened you, what firesides have you sat by in the dusk? O my dearest, when I remember what I was like, how covered in my decent black, how cowled with my abnegation, how disgraced and smutted with resignation, how complacent to think that a growing dusk and a teapot best fitted me, then I understand indeed how you have loved me, and do love, that you should have had the power to smite this away from me with a kiss, and hold me from it in your arms. Hold me still, never slacken that hold. But not from fear, now, that I should slip back. I have, I truly have cast away the works of darkness. But it is your courage only that saved me; and all the time when I was scornful of you and thoughtless of you, you were whetting and tempering the only sword that could have cut me free. My darling, how I am yours.

Sylvia

17: VA

Winterton, 22 January 1931

My dearest love,

At last in bed — feeling very tired and fairly sleepy. I am very much alone without you. The coat smells of you and makes me deeply angry that I am not holding you now. What fools we are to ever be parted.

I hold your heart.[2] It is very pretty and trimmed with ermine, as, probably, your real heart is trimmed with mischief or even as I would

1 Her signet ring.
2 An enamel locket I wore as a child, an exchange hostage for the falcon.

prefer to think with constancy.

W. has been exemplary. She is not an Aborigine – but I do not like her as much as I intended to. There is something to be wary of which looks out of her for a second sometimes. Although really she is very nice and unspecial.

I am not yet quite sure that she does not hate me. I rather fancy she does. I lent her *Lady Chatterley*, but I shall not be at *all* astonished if she leaves tomorrow because of it. I believe she is a Romantic and Universal Lover, and in that case she will hate the word 'fucking' and be angered to remember that that is exactly what happened to her. She shows a distinct disposition to confide.

I am very tired, my Sweetheart, and so deeply in love with you that I don't want to think of anyone else. I love you and hold you in my arms, and I ask you to remember all that has happened between us. Once you have summoned that into your mind you will know how closely I hold you, and with what power. Because you are so small and slender, and lovely and because you are my Love.

Valentine

18: STW

London, 24 January 1931

My dearest love,

I have just walked in, hung all over with parcels like Diana of the Ephesians, and found your telegram. Such a pretty one! Darling, among the other good uses of our love, we shall teach poetry to the Post-Office. And think how my cold voice must heighten the moral tone of the telephone exchanges.

It is a most ravishing morning, so gay and crisp that it almost beguiled me out of my widowhood. And as I walked I called up pictures of you from my mind. It is curious how surprise etches in an image; for almost the clearest of them is you as I met you early one morning on your way to Harper's – a summer morning – and you looked the embodiment of it, fresh and composed. And then I said to myself, but now I must see her in trousers; and instantly you were sitting on the sofa at Lavenham, smoking a pipe and making your celebrated statement about the Mothers Union.

Did you see in the Lit. Sup. that old Bridges, like you, had found out

Darley, and written an essay on him? And that the reviewer speaks of Bridges in the present tense? This of course is as it should be, but it was a queer and pleasant shock to find it so: I don't think I have ever before noticed immortality being put on under my nose.

When we go down to Miss Green I shall start planting shrubs and flowering trees. We must have lilacs, guelder roses, the common scrambling fuchsia, syringa, and a cherry, don't you think, a bird-cherry, and a laburnam.

And what do you think about a may-tree? It is a pity that there are no blue trees. I can't think of a single example. And let's have a quantity of laurustinus. But it *is* a pity that there are no blue trees. Now that I have allowed my mind to dwell on it, the need is almost as pressing as a winkle. Sky will mate with water, but scarcely with earth. When we are old ladies, I think we will have a small green-house. Even when Mrs Moxon's prophecies have caught me and I am too stiff to kneel on the damp earth, I suppose I shall still be able to potter and snip. I shall never forget how, early one August morning at Little Zeal when I could not sleep and didn't want to, I went out into the cool damp and dusky garden and from there into Nora's[1] small green-house. It was like an unspeakably melodious brass band, all that pounce and riot and strong cloistered colour and warmth. It almost fulfilled my child-dream of being able to get inside a stained glass window. That was partly, though, because I wanted to re-arrange the Cardinal Virtues' cloaks and sashes. There was a row of them that I used to stare at for hours on end, thinking that when I was grown up, I too would dress after that manner, have a claret-coloured dress like Charity, not only touching the ground but wallowing on it – or a green cloak like Mercy or Fortitude's wood-brown skirts and silver breast plate.

At other times my taste was less chastened, as when I said to Nora: When I am a lady I will have an orange ball-dress with violets on each lung.

I must leave off this letter in a minute, for the world is beginning to shuffle on the doorstep. There is the matter of that cold tap to be dealt with, and several invitations to be refused on the lovely grounds of not being in London then, thank you, and H.[2] with his confidences to tea and as soon as I have seen his heels I must go down to Amersham[3] to be a dove. But it is a good plan, really, that I have all these things to do, they

1 Nora [Eiloart, my mother].
2 [Harold Raymond.]
3 [The home of] Arthur and Purefoy Machen; Purefoy was my aunt.

will pass off the rest of the day well enough till the moment I get home late, find your letter – please God a bulgy one – and read it in bed so that it may remind me of you as immediately as possible.

I love you so much, my love, so lovingly, so loving to love you. Look after yourself well, do not catch cold in churches or allow the radiator to boil.

Sylvia

19: STW

Little Zeal, 24 March 1931

My dearest Love,

The Austin did very well, and got me here about 11.30.[1] The last part of the journey where the landscape was all familiar and real was painful, and I was glad to have it over. I found Nora up, and very glad for a minute or two to collapse on me. Then she became, and still is, rather over-braced, very full of arrangements and certainties. Determined to stay here with the dogs, and so forth. So I say nothing, and wait till she is more herself.

Poor darling, she had a cruel time of it. Yesterday morning Ronald complained of a dull pain under his collar-bone, but did not think enough of it or feel ill enough to stay indoors. He spent the afternoon working on the unfinished garden-house he was putting up as a studio for Nora. She, going into the kitchen to get tea, looked out of the window and saw his feet sticking out round the corner. She ran out and found him dead. The unhappy creature was alone in the house, with the nearest telephone two hundred yards or so away. She rang up the local doctor, then got help from the farm near by. People were very kind to her – neighbours flocked in, wrote letters for her, stayed all night and so forth.

It was, apparently, angina. He must have died instantly, if he had cried out she would have heard him. There is to be an inquest, perhaps a post-mortem, but I hope that may be avoided. He is to be buried here, on

1 The evening before, I got a telegram from my mother, saying 'Ronald dead.' (He was my step-father and I was much attached to him.) Early next morning I set out for Little Zeal, my mother's house in Devonshire. I left with my heart in my boots. Though I esteemed my mother's good qualities, no tenderness was possible between us. She despised me, and during my youth I was afraid of her.

Thursday or Friday.

She is being extremely brave and sensible, and carried on by an extraordinary excitement. The shock being so great, has, in a way, left scarcely any impression, a deep, imperceptible cut, rather than a wound. 'I want you to stay here with me till I have got things settled,' she said. 'For a week or perhaps a fortnight.' Not to be frightened, my dear. A week without you, not longer. If I can't get her to Chaldon after then, you must come here. It is a weight off my mind to find that she has no thought that I should stay here indefinitely.

I miss you quite unspeakably, my love. It is like some crowded dismal dream, with that mixture of crowdedness and *longueurs* that dreams have . . . an unmoving jostle of things happening. The parson, telegrams. 'Ferdinand will be with you at 6.55.' Ferdinand is Ronald's elder brother, and we did not ask that he should be with us, and he will by commandeering the little spare room obliterate my last hope of avoiding what I knew must be done – that is, sleeping with Nora. She had taken it for granted, as she did when my father died. It is a misery, but can't be helped. If, after two or three nights I find I can't bear it, I shall say so. Don't worry about her influenza. If she has had it, it has quite gone – and the draughts in her bedroom would disinfect a pest-house. But it will mean that I can't, as I had hoped, write you a long letter every evening, for she goes to bed early. I shall lie and remember you, my star. With that to hold on to the nights will not be as long and exasperating as those other nights.

It is two o'clock. Lunch over and Nora lying down. I write in the living-room, which is warm. The clock ticks, outside the little river brawls down under the leafless oakwoods. Spring is not so advanced here as with us. It is cold, only a few birds sing, hungry finches are feeding on a raw bone outside, winter's colours hang on haw and hillside. I am glad. I could not endure to be shown Spring while I am here, absent from you.

Ronald's body lies in the room upstairs. Nora, with a curious touching pride, showed it to me. He looks extremely beautiful, with that queer *secret* look that my father's face had also. 'Behold, I will show you a mystery,' those unmoving lips seem to say. I mourn him deeply. Yesterday it seemed only Nora's loss – today it is mine, too.

The parson did his best under difficult circumstances – administered nothing he was not asked for; which was arrangements about the funeral and the grave. Nora, rambling a little, on seeing he wouldn't bite or pray, was moved to remark: 'Well, then, he must be buried beside Colonel Rogers. Poor Ronald: He always found him a terrible bore, it seems a pity they should have to lie side by side.' An expression as much as to say – 'Poor woman! Grief, no doubt' – passed over those clean-shaven features (the man has absolutely *no* back to his head, but we must remember those 39 articles), then he said hastily, 'Yes, yes, very sad, very true,' and asked if we would like a hymn.

My love, I can't thank you for all you did for me. As I unpacked, your love met me all over my suitcase. Your love shelters me, even here. Your care, your grave care, wards me. Think, remember, how I too run after you with love and exhortations. Take the greatest care of yourself, know yourself loved for ever by me. Do not be too worked upon by my poor William. He will be at his worst, I expect, for the first two days. Ah, how real you are to me as I write. We cannot be far apart, with this love gathering us into one. My true one, my heart's love, do not pine too much, or worry over me. I will take the greatest care of this myself which is yours. Do you so too, for your part. I love you.

Sylvia

20: VA

Chaldon, 24 March 1931

My love,

I have taken this time to write that letter to Bo,[1] telling her definitely of how I love you – so that, if it may be, I release her from any hope of me. This time when you are away – when my trust in you and my love make me unafraid. It is a good time to write to poor Bo, whose love, under circumstances broadly the same, failed and refused to flower. I shall copy here a sentence or two, so that you may know more or less what I have said.

But in this I have been given everything, without any possible reservation – and even in this test I believe Sylvia will remain mine . . . I do believe that she will return to me, and I seemed to have flowered into trust and responsibility now. There must not be any talk of her as my 'mistress' now. The thin relationship which just wantonness gives is no longer ours . . . Now our duty to each other seems quite clear . . . I do not want to hurt

---

1 Bo [Foster].

you. Our love was far too dear to me. But the last yielding was not there. You had a separate life. Our love did not ever *compel* us to live together. There was no duty either of us could claim from the other.

I am afraid, my sweetheart, that you may feel resentment at my speaking of our love to Bo. But think and remember that I had from her love and care for many years – and although she will not generously accept this – or would not – she does seem still to expect my penitent return. I am sure that it is right to clear away this poor dead hope – which must by now be foul anyway, and I prefer our own brave truth to any niggling falsehoods or evasions. I love you and I have looked at you and known you my wife – I cannot any longer let you be my mistress – even in Bo's eyes. And after this I expect we shall hear no more. In which case we need not think any more either. And anyhow – only *our* life lives.

The copper cries with that burlesque of your voice. Your little, amorous cries which I love so. And how I love the cause of them. Your loveliness is with me, and whatever I see of new life in this spring reminds me of your beautiful renewal.

William watches me in my comings and goings rather as you do, when my poor love, you think me angry with you – or remote. And yet I have never been angry, never been remote. But William's eyes are troubled and wise as yours have been. I comfort him, but not as effectually as I can comfort you. His grief is very dignified. I do not fuss over him. We go on as we went when you were here and all was well. Only it lacks any interest or vitality. We eat, and talk occasionally – and William lies, looking very good and quiet, and very sorrowful. I don't know what will happen tonight. Neither does William. We watch the day pass over us and dread the night, which seems strange – to me, anyhow. Although it should be a more familiar state than any happiness.

It is a very bright day; rather cold and boisterous, but very sure of itself. All those birds are singing, but I feel as if their sounds were unheard sounds. My ears reject them.

This lovely and happy house is as warm and confiding as a hole in hay would be. It folds itself and presses itself around me and promises your return, and the return of our joys.

I am sorry to write such a sober letter. It is useless and rattling to write you a cheer-up letter. Far better to stretch out, as William has just done, and sigh and lie still – eyes open and watching and paws quite slack and resigned. But joy like ours is *not* fleeting. Our joy no man taketh from us. And you, my sweet one, are so deeply hidden in my heart that I can safely carry you wherever I go. No one can see you and no one can wish you harm. You are my dear and I love you. You are my life and all my joy. This pain of being parted is not a lost pain. We are one and we cannot be divided – unless you consent to it. For I will not.

I shall have Fred Payne to clear the garden, and I shall dig a little in the cleaned patch. I am having your dear bed made up, so that if you can persuade Nora to come here soon, it will be ready, or if William seems unhappy in my room I will sleep there.

If my letters are gloomy, sweetheart, you must not be too distressed. You would not have me love you less – ? I would not have you deceive me about your unhappiness. I would not have even such a shadowy and insubstantial lie between us. So I will not make any pretence of happiness. You are the whole light of my joy – without you even the casual delights of this weather, of this place, are dark and formless, and I resent them.

Mrs Way[1] has cleaned and polished. The beans and flowers I will plant. The haddock shall be eaten. I will take all care and all comfort. You are so present in this cottage that every beauty is like you – is of you.

But William droops on his mat, and I droop on your chair. Our hearts are with you, and you must not keep them apart from our poor bodies for too long, my beloved.

I hope it is not too horrible for you. I dare not think too much of your anxiety and busy-ness and trouble, or I should be flying to help you, and get in your way, probably – but if you need anything, practical help or care and comfort, you must send for me. You have no longer any right to suffer or to endure alone. Remember that and give thought to it.

I love you and my thoughts are with you all the day.

Valentine

21: STW

Little Zeal, 25 March 1931

My dearest Love,

I can hardly bear to look at the two locks of hair, so neat and meek in their screens of paper. Your letter I read over and over again – carry it about, and dive into it whenever I have a moment. How well I see you by

1 Mrs Way: our charwoman.

the fire (have you ordered coal from Edward's?) sad and pensive with your resigned paws.

I slept with the little silver snuff-box in my hand all night. It is so smooth and finely curved I might almost believe it to be your hand I hold. Slept, I say. But at 5 a.m. poor Nora woke, made herself a brew of strong tea and began to converse. I feel like the crumbs at the bottom of a biscuit tin as a result. However, and for all this, I do not regret that Ferdinand is with us. He came about seven last night, and Nora immediately cheered up and obviously felt a deep relief to have a man in the house. She now leans on him entirely. I suppose that when he leaves after the funeral there will be a secondary wrench. But as he is tiding her over these days I don't worry about that. He is a long thin melancholy creature, not in the least like Ronald, except in being sensible. I pity him acutely, I cannot imagine a more painful situation, as Nora long ago quarrelled with his wife, and indeed more or less with all the family. He moves sadly about the house, banging his head on the beams and doorways, and makes reasonable remarks in a sad diffident voice.

One cloud has been lifted: for we got a message last night that the Coroner has waived the inquest. So the funeral will be tomorrow afternoon, and I will pick up the daffodils from the post-office on my way here. Our poor garden, robbed of its legendary pride: But Ronald was so kind to Miss Green that I should like something from there to put on his grave, rather than a London wreath.

The moment one is dead one is a great loss. But it is really true of Ronald, and his are the best mourners, the poor and lowly. Even the tradespeople of the village, a glum lot as a rule, are doing Nora every kindness they can for his sake. And poor fat Mr Cranch, the local carpenter who is also the local undertaker, when he came last night with the coffin was almost speechless, and bemused with grief. A hard task for him to coffin his friend.

As for me – I feel not only a personal loss, but I now realise how much of my own good relations with Nora depended on him, and are gone with him. I feel myself sinking back into that helpless bruise of being unavailing and a nuisance that I felt after my father's death. She clings to me automatically, but I can do her no real good. I have said nothing about ourselves to her. She would not understand, nothing is real to her and while she is in that state it would do more harm than good. She did once realise your existence, when I broke one of your sausages[1] under her nose,

1 Ampoules of strong smelling salts.

and said you had sent them. But in a moment you were dismissed again. But do not think that for this, my dear, my heart wavers a moment in its duty. If explaining, at any rate, abiding by our love and living together is to be difficult or painful, that only strengthens and enforces the need to explain and abide by. And if I am not to be yours on easy terms, I am the more yours; and the better wife in my own eyes, to be thought a bad daughter. But equally, do not think I am worried about this. I have a real belief in letting the morrow look after itself. At present there is nothing to be done except daily things about the house and what cosseting I can prevail on her to accept from me. And I am quite content to go on so for the present, knowing that there is an end, and that end in your arms.

My love, I am very glad that you have written to Bo and as you did. I feel no resentment, I deeply approve of your truth. How should I resent that you know and acknowledge my entire love?

You are being perfect with William, respecting his solemn sorrow. But do not give him *all* your food, my dear. Kiss his nose from me and tell him I will come back soon, and that he is to look after you and guard away all evil-doers.

I say *soon*. But this is only the second day, and already I feel as though I had waded through an age of being without you. Nora is now lying down, and I, with Edward Thomas, shall go and do likewise. You must not think that I am not taking care of myself.

My love, my dearest one.

Sylvia

22: VA

Chaldon, 26 March 1931

My darling,

I think about you today, which is, I suppose the day of the inquest. I am fevered with desire to be with you for I fear that such a proceeding is very trying and macabre. And you, my sweetest Love, should never have to endure such horrors. Of all people, not you – whose courage needs no testing and whose heart is so kind. But I am worse than useless. I feel sometimes as if I were paralysed, and doomed to watch you working and never be able to help you, whom I love so deeply and so passionately.

But physically I am *not* paralysed; I have planted the bulbs, had the garden cleaned, the manure carted and the roses fed and blanketed in it. I shall go out soon to use some for the shrubs.

Last night Theo and Violet and Doris[1] came. I gave them coffee and biscuits and almonds. Theo spoke endlessly and rhythmically about your woe. He reverted to it all through games of dominoes and whist, until Doris began to look haunted and afraid, and I protested, for decencies' sake, and then he was moodily silent.

I have maintained a silence about drives in the car, in case you send for me – or better still, let me fetch you both away. I shall detain the car, by main force if need be, until our dreadful week is up. See how I trust your word; but do not fear to contradict that trust, if you really have to; nothing will ever shake it.

Bo's letter, enclosed, is a noble one, I think, and justifies my desperate patience – final though it seems to be. And certainly, if you left me, I should not ever see you again – but for a different reason. Unless perhaps mine is only different because I admit it: my desire and physical love for you would make it impossible to see you. But I cannot bear to think of this, nor is it right to, when you are so sweet and true.

Fred Payne, the nice yokel, patiently trailed his barrow over and over our new garden, being warned off the shrubs and mysterious plants. I hope our flowers pleased you. They looked so many and so beautiful when I had picked them. My sweetheart. Do not be burdened by my love for you or your sweet love for me. I have heaped it rather heavily upon your pretty shoulders. I repent, but cannot promise, or even *purpose*, amendment. I love you.

Ruth sent some steak. William and I ate it. He is still all right – very fond and very grave. He pines a little, although he eats well and walks gaily enough – but he *does* pine and small wonder. You are so enmeshed in both our hearts, my lovely one, that in nothing can we escape. William, even when he rushes after rabbits, seems to be pulled back and jerked by you. It is well.

Florrie[2] can put me up, if your mother will come. Your bed is made up, and kept aired. I have kind Mrs Way everyday – for company, chiefly, and so that I can talk of you.

Later.
I have just come in from a walk on the hill with dog William. I did not go

1 Doris: Violet's niece, then living at Beth Car.
2 Florrie [Legg].

to the Marys, but only on the road, and then sat by the old harrow in Jacob's field. It is an ideal day for love-making. A light opaque mist between the hill and the village, and sky as blue and as tender as speedwell. That moon is up there, like a tuft of cottonwool, very soft and untidy. I sat there, being warmed and coaxed by the sun, until everything grew too insistent. Then William and I came away. He bounding and I lagging down the lane. Now I shall go and work with manure, which is more suitable than this seductive and lustful world which is outside our gate.

I love you, deeply and tenderly, and for ever.

Later.
My hand is shaking from digging. I hope you can read this. My beloved. Your letter has just come. It is melancholy and dazed. Not that I mean as a reproach to call you so – but I stretch out to comfort you, and yet perhaps it is best not to breathe life into you yet.

My dear one, please – from compassion – tell me in each letter that you will not delay. Tell me that we are not parted, even *now*, for more than a week? I love you so much – even importunity is excused by this. You are wise not to have me with you, I realise that – but I tremble before it. It seems to lengthen time, and these days are already like stretched elastic. I cannot bear it to be tried further.

Please will you still persist patiently in your care-taking? Eat more than you need. Sleep as much and whenever you can, drink well and incessantly, do not over-smoke. Let your heart lean on me, as it should, because my love can never fail you.

Valentine

I carry the hair from your sweet beloved head. I kiss you. Daisy from the Marys road – let us walk there soon.

23: STW

Little Zeal, 27 March 1931

My dearest Love,
Never say again that you are no help to me. Where should I be now, and in what strait pit of despair, if it were not for you? After I had posted

my letter to you I sat on the low bridge over the little brawling river, and read among your sonnets[1] – your hand pointing my way through them. It was almost as if you were beside me, and I could hear the wood-pigeons crooning in the oakwood without stuffing my ears with stoicism.

It was a whining cantankerous hateful letter, and the moment it fell into the box with its sullen thud I knew it. It can do two things. Make you more distressed about me, and make you think me a contemptible sniveller, like Mr Potts. So I thought; and then pulling out the little way-worn book, I began to read.

> Till whatever star that guides my moving
> Points on me graciously with fair aspect,
> And puts apparel on my tatter'd loving.

Darling, my love was very tattered just then, wailing like a peevish child, and I should not have written as I did. But you have re-apparelled it and now though I am as sad as ever to be without you, I am not in such frantic despair at being here. Also, having read and meditated and water-stared myself into a better frame of mind, I came back to the house determined to put a better shoulder to the wheel and by dint of a god-sent flow of enthralling conversation, and Nora's own abetting efforts, have got through the remains of the poor beautiful day quite well. Such a lovely day, and I have been almost ready to curse its innocent face.

Thomas was exactly the right poet to send here with me. I read every morning in bed and find deep beauty in those melancholy uncouth dignified lines.

And tell my William,[2] won't you, that his sonnets are always tucked somewhere about me.

When the dogs are slightly more accustomed to the newly installed telephone, I will telegraph you an assignation for a trunk call. At present they stand round baying it – and with all the Chaldon P.O. at your end, and all this bow-wowing at mine, conversation would be more of a mockery than a comfort. But I could hear your voice, and have that *immediate* sense of you which letters can't carry. For with every letter after I have read it the thought comes, that is how she was *then*. But now?

The squashed daisy and the yellow primrose were very real-making. I

---

1 A purse copy of the Shakespeare *Sonnets* which she had lent me for the time of my adversity.
2 She said William was a reincarnation of William Shakespeare, having such small wise eyes and a knowledge of human weakness.

should have known the daisy for a drove daisy anywhere – so impudent, staring back at the churchyard, and all the goings-on that go by.

I return Bo's letter. I agree with you about it in all things save one. I don't read it as final. It is a very dignified renunciation of what is past, but I don't think it implies no future. I suspect she will go to her Italy and Hungary and come back adapted and reconciled to friendship or some such. But I think she will come back. Anyway, it is a fine letter, and a befitting answer to yours.

Do not work too hard in the garden. I did not intend you to deal with manure. Somehow I always shuffle out of all the unpleasant and hard work there, and return to beam and walk about praising.

Ah, my dear, but won't I? We shall have all the summer flowers coming out, the poppies and the phloxes and the Pretty Fannies in the light of my beams, and the strawberries ripening at my heat of delight. The thorns will fall off the gooseberries.

You can never desire me too fiercely; never avoid my bed for that. Love as you will my consent shall match you. And though I outcry the copper and say, No, Oh No, I shall never say, please stop. Love stinted, Love in leading-strings, is the only unnatural love.

The owls are crying round the house, and presently I shall go to bed, with Thomas, and the snuff-box and the box with Sarah's hair[1] and your poems beside me, and your rings on my wedded hand. You are quite right to say my hand looks married. It does. And I look at it constantly, and am comforted to see it looking as married as ever, though it droops for lack of you to touch and caress.

How pass the days till we are together again? So much harder for you, my poor darling, my fierce tear-stained one whom I love so for those tears, though they do infringe my prerogative. Would it be a good plan to go up to London with Ruth and see Huddie?[2] I daresay a dentist might be diverting. And dog William would be happy with you, for he loves you indeed, that outsized hairy sparrow. Are the mice a comfort to him at all, do you think? – a distraction as the dentist might be to you? And how are the young adders? My love, do be careful and fondle them with caution. I believe adders are detiparous or whatever the right word is. So was Genghis Khan, and Richard Crouchback.

My Love, my beauty, my bird with soft breast and ah, bright wings, do

---

1 An ivory toothpick-box she gave me with a plait of ash-blonde hair framed in the lid. We decided on no evidence that Sarah Ponsonby gave it to Eleanor Butler.

2 Huddie: her dentist; she had toothache.

not be too much grieved while you wait. My love, my true love has never strayed from your side, and now when I go to bed I shall lie down with my head on your shoulder, my body in your arms.

Sylvia

24: VA

Chaldon, 28 March 1931

My sweetheart,

Your letter to Ruth caused me great trouble and disappointment; I flew down to open the door directly I heard Mrs Lucas,[1] I tore open the envelope – saw 'Dearest Ruth', faltered a little, decided that a thin page was hers and the rest mine. Then, struck down by your own hand, saw the clear address on the blood-envelope.

Well:
The mice have bred. Four hearty pink sweets. Mrs Way drowned two for me – in the most nonchalant manner possible. I winced squeamishly, and buried them.

I have bought you, at Warminster, a *lovely* little light fork to dig with – so that you can play to your heart's content, and mine – and take no hurt. Too, I bought you a lesser fork, like your long-handled trowel, to weed with, and a pretty hatchet so that, if I am called away from you, you can cut fire-wood without injuring yourself by the heavy axes or endangering your precious limbs by that vile hook!

Then, at Weymouth – but these are Easter, or at any rate celebration presents and God knows when I shall be able to *celebrate* and *rejoice* again. (This habit of underlining, used cautiously, is pretty.)

I took kind Ruth to Beth Car. Gertrude[2] and the egregious Betty were there. The latter very prim and fixed. I was intolerably rude to her, spurned her advances, mocked her gently, flattered Gertrude and received the honour of a slight sparring-match with Theo – neither of us receiving more than the most loving scratches, and I a sly and most penitent and beguiling kiss, in the dark tunnel of that hall.

1 Mrs Lucas: the post woman.
2 Gertrude Powys: Theodore's sister.

Your chair is quite enchanting. Return to it soon, dear heart. How pretty you will look in its lap – how it longs for you, and sits spread-kneed to receive you. And shall not, I swear, receive any less lovely and beloved body upon it.

Ruth has been kind. She sat with me for a long time, and comforts me for your absence as best she can, listening patiently to my constant talk of you, and accepting my desolate lack of life with complete understanding and sympathy. I took William with me to meet Ruth yesterday. Gave him a picnic in a very beautiful larch-wood, where every tree sprouted clouds of grey pigeons, like smoke, while William forged about beneath them. There was a strong smell of fox.

It is warm, and grey, I have a vile headache. It may be that thunder is about.

I have had a slight (very slight) return of influenza. But now it seems to be better, even gone – I expect. And maybe it was chiefly mope. Which is absurd (as I learned to say, bitterly, towards the end of a geometrical problem). That I cannot live without you is humiliating – is ridiculous, and should be untrue. But it is not, it is not.

I have started three separate poems, and all of them seem to be all right, but none will finish. And you cannot wonder at it. *Sorrow*, or rage, or indignation are all good fertilisers. Pining is not.

I dug in a good deal of manure last evening, and Ruth, by my commands, went weeding.

My darling. You have all my heart.

Valentine

Your poor letter just come. Do not fear, my beloved. I can wait for you, and will, most willingly, as long as my waiting relieves your burden.

Do not pity me, so as to cause yourself pain. I have my heart in your keeping. So long as you nurse it tenderly I am whole. My desires are always for you, but they must learn to wait; and *shall* learn.

Do not fear, my sweetheart – and do not come to me until you are easy about your duty.

Do as you will, and know that it is with my blessing. You have all my love.

Valentine

25: STW

Little Zeal, 29 March 1931

My dearest Love,

It was not like a dream¹ – your coming here. It was like some sudden short waking. You did have to take me by the shoulder and shout in my ears, didn't you?

Nora's comments were few, and of a rather discreet (or stunned: I don't know which) nature. She said of Ruth, 'She seems a very kind woman; but rather fatiguing.' I feel that the latter clause may well have been used by Ruth about Nora. I hope she, Ruth, is none the worse for her noble behaviour as a stalking-horse, or a Troy-horse, or whatever. And that you did not have too unbearably cold a journey back. Why hadn't you a coat? And with that disgraceful cold, too.

I have said nothing about Friday. I shall say nothing yet. Tonight poor Nora said: 'Don't tell me when you are going. I don't want to know too soon before.' It is things like these that are so hard to stand up against. The honey must have unmanned Samson much more than the lion.

Do not worry about me. I am sorry that I looked ill today – if I did. I daresay I did. When we have been married longer you will know that I can look iller on less provocation than any woman breathing. A day will make a hag of me, two days a walking corpse. Here, just to convince you, is a picture of what I looked like before I left New York. You see, then I had even begun to go bald. It came today, most providentially, with some cuttings, and you carried it here, little knowing what you carried.

Anyhow, you were Satan rebuking sin. *I* have no cold in my head. I cannot quite believe I am writing to you, you are still so much here; though the state of my bed should convince me you are not; alas! So quiet and cold. It must be the kiss still tingling on my pillow. My poor fierce darling, I don't think you can have enjoyed this afternoon much, though you *did* bite and bully me. O lovely, to be confronted with your fierce will again, your savage tenderness. I feel now as though I were almost home again – as a tune might feel after grinding through one extreme modulation to another, when it gets into the sub-dominant and begins to smell its stable, and curl itself towards the cadence.

Yes, you rushed me – with that threat of fetching me on Friday. But

---

1 Ruth, on a pretext of condolence, had been brought for an afternoon call. The ensuing hospitality was so charged with my mother's enmity towards Valentine that my shaking hand dropped a pat of butter into my teacup.

while you stood in the drive, threatening over my enchanted willing ears – Oh, who suborned my ears, so that now they listen to no one but you? – my mind was blackly meditating upon the Passion. If only it were not Good Friday it would be so simple either way. I could ask you to wait one day longer, or the meat would come. As it is, my mind is screwed and wrenched with Good Friday. Because, my heart, this day so dreadful to you is a day of rejoicing, apparently, among butchers – all this is queerly Doone-ish and conceited – who shut their shops. Now ordinarily the dogs' meat comes, a vast bloody package, on Friday; and it was always dealt with by Ronald for Nora, the unpacking, hacking and cleansing of. But on Good Friday it comes on Saturday.

I cannot avoid the thought that if I stayed till Saturday I could deal with this for her – and I can't quite bring myself to stomach with any peace of mind the picture of Nora, already rather raw at my leaving her, standing among all this butchery with the feeling that this is what falls to the widowed who are serpent-chilled. Whereas an unmatrimonial devil at my elbow whispers that if I stay on to deal with the meat on Saturday morning – all over by one, it comes up from the station by twelve – I leave with the decent finish of performing a last good action and grace. And Nora would be spared an exasperation of her sense of being deserted and helpless, and might even feel that a compliment had been paid her.

But then this Good Friday is your dread, your black pit. And to spare my own feelings I propose to leave you in it. I can't work it out. I must go on with this in the morning, and wait to hear what you say.

The truth is, I am still too towzled and revived by you to be capable of any thought at all. My darling, it was such rapture to see you, and such reality, that I am now quite stupefied and dumb, and could only express myself by turning into your arms with a whimper and some grunts. I love you, I love you. I desire you and am yours. Take care of yourself, my heart's love, my melancholy mope-alone.

Sylvia

26: VA

Chaldon, 29 March 1931

My Most Beloved,
   I write this after mature thought, and a conversation with Ruth, on the

way home. I wish you to keep this as a confidence! It seems that your mother, immediately we had gone out, asked Ruth her opinion of our 'sudden and intense friendship'. (Save the mark) Ruth sensed, she says, that the question was hostile, and parried by observing that it was 'so nice for us'. Then it went on. You have perhaps heard how. Ruth is anxious that you should know that she uttered no word against us or our relationship, played Nelson manfully, and nailed her blind eye to the telescope throughout. But resentfully found how hated I am.

None of this really dangerously affects us – or I choose to believe that it doesn't, for I trust you. But, my sweetheart, *why* did you not tell me that you had had 'words' on this subject, me under discussion, and our life together made a stumbling-block?

Do not think from this that I am angry with you, or that my rage today was directed against you. Neither would be true. But I wonder what your reason was, and whether I approve of it. I believe I do not, for it might so well have landed us in a false position.

Now, I don't want to hurry you, and I especially do not want to add to your complications any more than I have done: I shall not belabour you about Friday, although I repeat – I intend to fetch you, or to send for you, on that day four days from now. My reasons are worthier, if possible, than just my passionate desire for you. I think you have spent all the *good* you can do for your mother, and I think every day henceforth you and she will scratch upon each other's nerves, and by staying with her you will render her far worse service than by leaving. You are *not* in a fit state yourself to give any repose – and that quality is what she is desperately looking for. She would not, my sweetheart, *rest* in you, or you in her – and what else could give her healing from her misery and shock? I realise that the practical difficulties are very great; that she cannot be left alone, that she dislikes the idea of a domestic to sleep there and that, when you mention going, she immediately clings to you. But the first she will have to overcome in time, and better to suffer any lesser discomfort which a greater pain is applying, than when it has subsided and one is left, tender and very tired. The second will salve the first, and that she will see if she has to. The third *has to be tackled*, and I do verily believe that, once you are gone, she will be glad of it; even begin to make headway then, against her grief.

I do not want you to think that this is all a device to get you here to me. I should hate to use such weapons, even to get *you* back. Besides, I am not a child – I *can* wait for two weeks and not one, if the need be. But I have confidence in my own judgement, and also confidence in Ruth's (more especially as she rejoices to see Mother Love – Daughter Love – triumphant over Perversion). And she has been repeating all this all the way home. She too is confident that part of your mother's trouble now is her peculiar relationship to you. Ruth also agrees with my worried anxiety and says that you look really ill, and should – and *should* come away.

My dear love, my own one, my true, my wife – I felt a brute and a bully most of the time I was with you. And yet here I am doing the same thing again, and feeling as determined as if I'd had no attack of conscience. If I seemed unloving, or harsh, or unsympathetic, my darling, you must remember that, though I arrived full of pity and real sympathy, I also carried love in my heart. And when I saw you, *my* Love, looking so pale and wan and thin and so deeply unhappy – saw you looking *frightened* once or twice – it is natural, and right, that my heart became angry and resolute, and that the resolution still stands firm.

Do not worry over this. Do not dread. Take my early-childhood's dear text 'Be strong and of good courage: dread not nor be dismayed'. Be patient and forbearing as long as you can, but if you want to lose your temper, lose it *well*. And above all, rest on me, and in me. I will do nothing to cause you the least terror or pain. I will cherish, comfort and caress you, be faithful to you, and forever desire you. But my love is strengthening, is growing lusty and strong, and it is protesting and it is demanding – and you must listen. It is your duty which you vowed. And I *love* you.

Valentine

Ruth has written a Collins to your mother – she insists – blandly remarking how nice it is that we are as we seem to be. I refuse responsibility for this.

P.S. This has precipitated a discussion with Ruth, who, however, is very wise and most tolerant – utters no word of criticism, and merely reiterates how she likes you.

27: STW

Little Zeal, 30 March 1931

Monday night in bed.

'In Mrs. Inge's bedroom much has been done by the untiring efforts and the devoted labour of the Clerk of the Works to the Cathedral.'

This is not quite what one would hope for the poor lady, being from an account of restorations in that grave house you admire so much.[1] But it is a pretty beginning. You, my darling, embellish my bedroom in other and better ways.

I can write this freely because this letter, I deduce, will be delivered to you all uncontaminated in the sacred vessel of the Royal Mail.[2]

I am in bed, I am very sleepy, I am quite perceptibly sprightly. Ever since I saw you yesterday my spirits have been going up. Perhaps it was the champagne too. We had half the first bottle for lunch, and finished it for dinner. Do you shake your stick at me? It was Nora's idea, not mine. Nora drinks like a mouse, and has gone to bed under the impression that this has been a day of signal debauchery and elegance. She is much the better for that idea, and for the champagne. Tomorrow, under pressure of a threat that my uncle will come to dinner and rob her of her share of the second half, I may persuade her to finish the other bottle for lunch.

Moved by the champagne, and also by my statement that the Machens will want more than tea (however strong) and crème de menthe, she allowed me to look into the wine-cellar. Not an easy task, it being blocked with a table, a sewing-machine, and a vacuum cleaner. However, I exploded these and had an interesting rout round. And there, among lamp-glasses, candlesticks in baize bags, lamp-shades stoved in, and, O Iacchos! a milk-tumbler, I found a remaining bottle of the 1815 Madeira. God knows what it is like by now, but I am bringing it with me, and we will try. At any rate, it will be an interesting experience.

Poor Ruzzie,[3] he would have grinned, albeit wryly, over that milk-tumbler. He stocked this little cellar seriously, and I have a good memory of him and it. Some people were coming to lunch, and came too soon, while he was still buttling. Furious at being interrupted, he remained like an ostrich with his head in the cellar and his incognito behind unbendingly present to them as they walked past. They hovered round it, trying to howd'yedo; but there was no response.

I believe we shall be the only people living in the country who do not arrive before they are expected. Damn and blast this candle, it is going

1 The Deanery of St Paul's.
2 Which delivered our afternoon post at the door. The morning post was delivered through the post-office. This delivery was erratic, which seemed to bear out the village rumour that the postmistress was not above steaming letters open.
3 Ruzzie: my father [George Townsend Warner].

out. But do not let us arrive too often — you are not likely to let us, are you?

Darling, if I am to address that envelope, I must leave off. I love you — and seeing you has made me so much happier I should hardly know myself except for that same loving and desiring.

Sylvia

Kiss my dear William. I never thanked you properly for his good and well-cared-for and comforted estate.

28: VA

Chaldon, 31 March 1931

My Angel,

Your friend Betty has just been here . . . telling me about 'a wee lamb, just born ten minutes or so, which I found in a field. I saw its mother give it its first kiss — it was rather wonderful. Then the shepherd sent all the other sheep up the field driven by the dog. What an entry into the world! All the old sheep around you hurrying away, the dog barking and men shouting —'

She is, my love, a *very* stupid woman. But I gave her some potato wine.

Your telegram came. I sent off mine at once. May it be balm to your soul, my sweetheart.

I love you with all my heart and strength. Come back before that heart and that strength become too formidable . . . This is a threat.

Later.
Katie to tea. Ruth out at Burton Bradstock. I finished a poem just as Katie came. Here it is. I believe it may be very bathetical (this is a coined word and may be false) but if it is not, then it may be good. I am now roasting a pair of plump, pale pigeons against Ruth's hungry return. I feel as desperate as Herr Jaeger when he flies out and forages for that greedy wife of his and their palpitating twins. Meanwhile, if this poem, as I shrewdly suspect, bites its own tail clean off, then that only shows how unwise it is to give advice . . . not that I'd have you stop. In this I certainly and very thankfully bow my head before you (and beg from you).

The pigeons are snapping vigorously. Ought I to baste (?) them?

Later.

I did. I wonder why it does not burn cloth? It burned my thumb.

Saturday is *too far off*. I pant for it. This very day, a day, I suppose of good news – since at least *definite* news came – has dragged along until I could rage at it. But that would do no good.

Flu' I have kept at bay by one, chaste, half-bottle of Margaux consumed at supper – but tonight hot whiskey and milk will be pressed into service.

Those damned pigeons are raging again. I don't see why they should not wait. They were pale as ever, last time, only shiny.

Oh my Love – I am speechless with desire for you.

Valentine

31 March 1931
(only *2* in this month, darling!)

> As he grows old he leans closer to the earth
> Cossetting the ground, preparing it.
> And testing it with prods and stamps and so forth,
> Before, being still living, he'll lower his bulk and sit.
>
> Rest there alone he will, for hours together.
> One square of short grass on that dried-up hillside
> Will be his indifferent home, in any weather
> He'll climb there slowly, poke it, and sit and abide.
>
> For he is watching the earth, learning to sieve
> From others its truths. He knows now that these concern him –
> Yet not so nearly as it comforts him to believe –
> For when his end comes you may be sure they'll burn him.

(This last 'they' seems to apply to one set of truths or another – The only escape that I can see is to use that damned Americanism, and say something soothing about his 'folks' –)

(At first I had the second line of the last verse reading thus:

> 'Its truths from others –')

I have kept this.

29: STW

Little Zeal, 1 April 1931

My dearest Love,

It is still raining. It has now rained for three days; but from the moment I got your telegram[1] I have had the impression that it isn't real rain.

And all this is because of my admirable uncle, who has worked like a charm. Did you ever get so far as the passage in the Carlyle translation of *Wilhelm Meister* – but you can't have, for it comes right at the end, and I don't believe any one but me with my gift for enjoying being bored in print could get so far – where one of those mysterious characters says of another 'I joyed in him as in an uncle.'

Now I have further cause to joy in him. For would you believe it, my dear, I might have owned a hereditary three sixteenths of the Black Dog Inn at Broadmayne? It was the property of my great-great-grandfather, Samways Oke, who left it in shares between his three daughters, Susan, Mary, and Anne. Susan married my great-grandfather and imported, so it is said, a culpable flightiness into the family. It was she who after duly mourning for a husband who didn't approve of artificial flowers as tending to the worship of idols broke out in a bonnet entirely smothered in forget-me-nots.

Anne never married, stayed in Dorset, and spent her life in hunting up family tombstones. Mary was the old lady whose apparition in a crinoline I saw when I was a girl.

I am glad to have this strand of Dorset blood. We must go and drink a pious drink at the Black Dog one day.

A perfectly florid garland of conversation is going on as I write, so forgive me if this all sounds flimflam and distracted. But it is too cold to do anything in my bedroom but drink secret draughts of brandy. I held off the bottle more or less till today. Now I am drinking, not because there is anything the matter with me, but I must celebrate somehow.

Perhaps when I saw Mary she had come to point me to Dorset. It might well be, one can trace back any event to any cause. The same night I went to my first dance, and except when I was dancing with Ruzzie, didn't like it. This naturally would turn me towards country life and perversion. Yes, I shall certainly believe that smooth-band-haired lady appeared with a

---

1 My mother had consented to the dogs' meat being fetched on Thursday. My uncle was staying over the week-end. I could leave with a clear conscience.

purpose.

I shall expect the car at 2, about, and have no views as to finding you in it. If it is a day like this, cold and wet, *you are not to come*. As to coming here, my darling, as you please. South Brent is a dingy place to wait, I think, though I once heard comfortable words about an inn called the Royal Oak. I think, though, it would be needlessly unpleasant for you to come here and risk affront. But as for caution, that I despise. But I repeat, if it is a bad day, you are not to come.

The blackthorn is out. I can't believe it, I feel as though there can have been no spring anywhere – till today, perhaps. Today anything might come out, the mice have another family, the Winterton wallflowers and rosemary put forth, and yellow stars shine out on the Persian Briar. O my darling, I can scarcely believe it. Only one day more of this bondage, and then I am in your arms and your head pouncing to my breast.

But I can't write as my heart would speak, being a net to these brisk volleys of conversation. I shall march out into this unreal pain, and post this.

Always.

Sylvia

30: VA

London, 14 August 1931, 5.30 p.m.

My sweet Love,

The boy at the garage, I was informed by a rather impudent and gentlemanly foreigner, goes off at 5.15. I put the car[1] in at 5. The boy was there – and the foreigner, and a very superior chauffeur. They watched giggling. God fought on my side – hard. I drove in in *one*. They ceased from giggling. I strolled back to the studio, and a fierce thunderstorm (still going on) broke over me – but I heard the noise of the car! I sallied forth, and saw the nose of it in the yard again. I went in, told the boy the car must on no account be driven, EVER, by any one but only by me. He nearly wept with anguish. I said I knew the noise of the engine, and that it must remain pure and unsoiled. He agreed – but had not a key. I arranged that one should be made tomorrow – and the car oiled and

---

1 A second-hand Triumph two-seater I had given her in July.

greased for us (I shall watch that, on Monday). So that is all right, as far as it goes. The thunder goes much further, and rages over us.

I sent a wire – R.P. – to Janet,[1] asking her if I might fetch her for lunch to-morrow – intending to take her to a show of some sort (*not* to give her a driving lesson unless you are there, in case of trouble – for, although I pretend the car is my own, I look on it as a case for exercise, at least, of stewardship) and, if not, to early supper (so as to take in a cinema) on Sunday – fetching her and conveying her back. All carefully stated (When the telegram girl heard me dictate 'Fetch you about twelve, return you about seven' she commented 'Sounds like a parcel' – and was mildly astonished when I said seriously, 'It is').

There is a present for you in the car. I have not had any real poem yet. I am trying desperately to keep to my arrangement about not grieving[2] – until this late evening. It is bloody difficult. All *sounds* are leagued against me: taxis, just on the note of our taxi, draw up at the door in the wall; a man calls 'Echo – Echo –'; a boy whistles, for hours on end, some foolish tune which I have teased you with; and in Whiteleys – of all places – someone behind me cried out 'Darling!' and I whipped round, and saw a handsome but quite unfamiliar young woman greeting another. So I came out.

I am awaiting your telegram. All this is like a dream, and a pretty nasty one; if there is that quality of mechanical horror about this letter, you will know why. And, dear heart, forgive me – I meant not to let out my sorrow till yours was spent – so that, at least, you could feel the grander griever! but mine will not be stuffed away – I love you so desperately, and you have become so cunningly a part of my life, then the half of it, and then, very swiftly, the whole – and now, when you withdraw for even eleven days, I am in a desert while I am without you – and there is precious little hope of anything with which I can save myself from dying of weariness and thirst.

If you were going to be here tonight, I would, by now, have assembled our midnight supper, our vulgar sparkling Burgundy – and our bed. I would slyly make our bed, and rejoice over when laid – but supper meek upon a tray; and I would set two glasses, and a little baby chicken for William, and a truffle for us, and – Here a wire from Janet (saying Sunday suits best) – so we must starve on a truffle and wine, and feed full on our

1 Janet Machen: my cousin in her early teens.
2 She had just seen me off on a visit to my mother. Synchronising our filial offerings, she was accompanying Ruth to Paris.

74

rich love.

About 8.15 p.m.
After a dinner of peas and olives (bottled peas, I confess, because I could
not dare face the silence and loneliness of shelling true peas – but the
bottled ones were very good. They were grey and fat and rather sweet –
like Ruth's eldest sister). There is a cloud of tiny moths all over my
bedroom, and I have had a gentle but most enduring attack of hiccups.

My sweetest Love – were the handkerchiefs a pleasure – and has the
Koran come? I did not inscribe it, for the pen was bad; and the young
man, although he was sympathetic, was not all that encouraging (He put
it in paper for me). I cannot write poems – I wish I were to spend a quiet
and happy holiday – being alone and melancholy. For I should have you
back sooner, or see you anyhow – because I would journey to you, in
desperation. As it is, I can do nothing, unless I force you to return, and I
must not do that.

How empty and sorrowful my arms will be tonight. How blessedly
long since I lay alone. I bless you for that, my dear, my pretty dove; I bless
you for your softness, and your generous yielding, and your passionate
truth. My love for you is far stronger and sterner than you know. It is like
a tree which you notice suddenly, like a strong and violent jet of water
from the ground; springing straight to its height and refusing to be
assaulted by anything, admitting nothing stronger than itself, being itself
the most passionate of all creatures. That is how my love looks, in my
heart, alive and shining with a million trimmings of leaves . . .

Later.
The telephone rings. Of course I thought it was you. It was really Ruth,
Tickets for Havre – 7 hours of boat. Cabin, though – she is cross about
me not going to Winterton, uppish about the fact that I had a cold when I
answered the telephone (a choke!) '*Not* a cold, surely? Just when
Bleadon's bill has come in, and it *was* a blow –' 'My God', I said. 'Oh
well,' said Ruth – gaily – 'I suppose we have been a good deal ill.' (That's
my 'flu.)

Bunny comes up to-morrow and goes home on Monday, when we
leave. I shall be glad of him. I am more desolate than I meant to be, even
more than I expected. And Ruth was beastly. 'Has Sylvia gone?' No reply
from me. Eagerly 'Did Sylvia leave to-day?' No answer, only an evasion
– then 'Are you alone? Did Sylvia go?' Me 'Oh, yes, yes.'

Naturally, perhaps, furious about my passport. 'You will never get one

in time – never. You must look for yours. Please do look for a long time.'
So I grew angry, knowing by her patient voice that Alec[1] was hearing. 'I
am tired,' I said. 'I shall soon go to bed – Is Alec there?' 'Here, beside me,'
she said. So there, you see. I cannot be anything but vile when Ruth is
being so especially forbearing.

My Paris address is: Hotel de Blois, Rue Vavin, Boulevard Raspail,
Paris.

I stare at the photographs of you, and curse myself for not taking many
more, far better ones. Of you in bed, of us, of you closer-to, of you, side,
and front, and back, and again sideways – But above all, I kick myself for
not having let you miss the train . . .

No poems come, nothing is done, I haven't even been out to buy, as I
meant, an evening paper. It is still, now, between-storms, and I must hunt
for that bloody passport, which is to remove me further from you, and
bring me no happiness until it brings me back. I would give all my
treasures, even those I love and protect, to have you back, and in my
arms, and in my bed and loving me again – my sweetheart.

Reading over a poem I made (which I think you also have: 'All today,
Melancholy') I was moved to break the form, and add a last line to the last
verse, rhyming 'to-night'. It came like the ending of a rather obvious and
easy tune. Shall I?

The Charles Jewel[2] is such an intense delight to me, my Love.

I am wearing the garnet ring, having discarded the signet, during the
time you are away and I am out of trousers.

Oh Sylvia, Sylvia – how deeply and passionately I love you and desire
you. How desperately I long for you, wait for you and conjure you into
my arms. How I stretch out my arms to you, and urge you to give yourself
to me – and then find that 'you' are only what I made in my half-sleep –
in my pain.

A hundred poems go from my head to you, but none can be born, none
can be born, I am far too deeply stirred. These bubbles of air will not reach
the surface for a year or more, and God knows if I will live till then.
Meanwhile I lie in bed – trying not to compel you to me, and yet
desperately trying to pierce our future time. As I try to pierce back, in the
wireless, turning and turning, and never getting the past, and now, never
wholly believing the future. But all the time, all the time, desperately

---

1 Alec [Robertson]: her cousin.
2 A 17th cent. paste and enamel locket sold as a memorial portrait of Charles 1st, King and Martyr
– but a surpliced martyr, so not Charles.

needing you. Perhaps, you know, my body has reason to be peevish: these visitors, our tiredness, our ensuing chastity, our rare and our wildly lovely nights – all these things have gone together now to overset me. I love you, I desire you, my sweet, my beloved, my wife. I must imagine you.

Valentine

31: STW

14 August 1931, 4.40

My Dearest Love,

I am in that damned Devonshire now – at Newton Abbot. Thus far the miles are measured. Opposite me sits an old lady, deaf and dignified with whom I have exchanged a few courteous nods, and grimaces about raising and lowering of the window. William lies at my feet, wide-awake but with his eyes shut – incessantly trampled on and caressed by a family who got in at Reading – and well they might. They have pebble eyes and shiny noses. Thanks to your kind untruths, I lunched in great peace and quiet – and drank Guinness and shared roast beef with William.

I am acutely conscious of being miserable and disgruntled – and yet I can't yet realise why, and that I have truly left you behind in that shadowy den of noise and smell, to make your way back to a lonely 2. After I started I had a sudden vision of William's bowl of milk undrunk on the floor – and you, melancholy, my dearest Love, stooping with a sigh to pick it up.

Does it still rain with you? Here the sun shines, but that is no better. Take care of yourself, my lovely. Take special care, care for your mind, too. Be easy with your sad self, practise the kindness you have for Sylvia on Valentine. If your tenderness were not so dear to me, I would grieve to remember how last night and this morning you did everything, fed me and cosseted me, and carried my luggage and my griefs, when I should have been looking after you.

I have no sense of time. I only know that you are not with me. It is too soon for revolt, even, far too soon for resignation – and tonight the day I cross off is still the day begun with you, and in your arms; your arms so strong to hold me, so quick to gentle me, so honourable to let me go on this accursed pilgrimage of piety. I love you, I love you. Every way and always I am yours. Oh my dearest one, my only love, take care of self.

Sylvia

32: VA

London, 17 August 1931, about 10 a.m.

My Sweet Love

You are a blessed and a kind one to return the drafts. One I have messed up, but it's not worth exchanging a birthright for. I have not touched the other you like. My mood is not propitious – very far from that.

I love you, still today!, so violently that the whole, busy, flouncing day will be utterly out of my interest. I have been either pacing the room, in my dressing-room, or else writing at this rickety table, since about half-past eight, Bunny snoring in the big grey chair. I did start packing, and thus discovered the little, mild pearl ring you first gave me – which I have pressed down upon the wedding-ring (and a pretty pair they are – just like us. You fine and deceitfully meek and most rare, and I corrugated!). If you were here, I expect, in fact I am quite certain, that by now we should have forfeited our tickets abroad, we should be in bed, we should be most happily (if a little dizzily) launched on our own familiar sea, in our dear boat – with my heart its sleeping captain and you, not yet afraid, being more and more driven by our storm. I *know* that I should make love to you, today, better, more cunningly and more fiercely than ever before, and gentle you more tenderly, and hold you more strongly between my thighs. I would not let you go. I will not let you go. When you are here again we will not delay a moment. We will go to the kind bed, which will instantly receive us. We will lie upon it and make such love that you will lean your sweet head upon me and, being tired, pretend to be afraid. Not really so. You will be mine again, as you should be, in my arms.

Let the time go quickly, my sweetheart,

Valentine

Please keep the Charles ring for me and wear it sometimes. I am wearing the garnet.

33: STW

Little Zeal, 17 August 1931

My Dearest Love,

Your long fierce melancholy letter came this morning, and tore my heart. O my poor wild Cat, moping and yowling, with blackened eyes, and nothing but air to claw. God knows, *I* was unhappy enough yesterday – frozen with fears, a stone with a heart banging in it. And the sloth of time . . .

I know what a solace the Charles Jewel must be. Do I not take out, handle, hold to the light, try on, all the various pretties that you have given to me, and remember when they were given, and how? And the emerald steadfastly eyes me, and has me in charge. Today I am wearing Francis Butcher[1] and my grey dress, and your nosegay, miraculously preserved, sits on the writing-table. A frond of asparagus fern, clinging unbeknownst to my sponge, was encountered by poor Nora in her bath this morning – and she was extremely puzzled by its appearance, supposing it to have come down from the moor *via* the cold tap. It upset her botany.

Tilleys have sent the certificate of the car insurance, and the Policy will come in a few days. Lovely to think of you garaging it in one, and lovelier still to think of it sliding so nimbly into the Royal Parks. But it is your car, you know, however you may please to play at stewardship. Poor lamb, it will bite its paws in idleness now, but not feel forsaken, wearing the bracelet of our names.

This damned wind still blows, and I think unhappily of your seven hours on the Channel. How fatuous to take seven hours to cross that fretful ditch. I do not know what time I am in which end of this letter – whether you are now reading it in Paris, or still harried with packing and passports; nor which sympathy to feel.

Now what to tell you? I am well, I am taking care of myself. I eat and drink and sleep – though not too well, since I am continually woken up by being alone – every time I turn over in my sleep and find you not there I wake to make miserably and savagely sure of it. I work – poetry evades me, but I am doing a potboiler. I have plenty of time to myself, since Nora is busy painting, and while she paints is glad to have me out of the way. The brandy is delicious, and stood me in good stead in yesterday's cold.

1 Mourning ring.

And I cook an occasional dish, which is a blessed sedative. And so, I suppose, I shall go on. But there is no sureness anywhere, or peace, in this prospect of regular days and nights. A quiet life can prey on one as surely as catastrophe. And when I say quiet, all it means is that I force it to be quiet, and hem it down, this waste of time, neatly stitch by stitch. No timepiece, not even Grinnie,[1] comes to my aid. It is always an hour earlier than I think it . . . I know the faces of every clock in this house, and the pattern of their discrepancies.

And sometimes I look back at other visits here, when I thought myself pitiable, a slave to slow time, and deprived of love. And it is like looking back on an eiderdown quilt from a bed of coals. O my love, you need not ask me, as you do, if I ever loved more or more deeply than I do now.

Sylvia

34: VA

On the boat, 11.20 p.m. but still at S'hampton

My beloved one,

I am desperately pining for you, I am feeling my heart torn from my side, as I get further in distance from you, but how much closer in desire every moment of time. I think of you. I hold your sweet, most precious body to me. I clip you again, I tease you, I kiss you and ravish you, I am yours and you are mine. Truly and indeed we are one flesh, one spirit. This – for all its pain – is my joy, the proof of my pride and happiness – that we are in truth married. 'Our married steps.' My Love, my darling. Do not fear – we will not stumble. I love you, my Pretty – you are beautiful – you are my own one, my wife, my beloved, my cherished one, my loving and my most loved. And now the boat is off. We are passing a large and lighted steamer. Goodnight, sweetheart. I fold you in my love and hold you closely, warmly – and gentle you and rejoice over you. How many most blessed nights I have spent in gentling you. More soon, my Pretty, my pride, my Love.

Paris. Tuesday about 2.30 p.m.

1 Her grandmother's watch, the only timepiece she trusted to get me punctually into the train I was coming back by.

Sweetheart,

We got here about 10.30. Tired, but not sick. A baddish crossing, and interminable. Fierce storms, as you will have read in the papers. So I telegraphed you in case you were at all fussed.

I am in my old room – just below the roof. I had brains meunière for lunch, with tomatoes cooked with chopped garlic and parsley, and then wild strawberries and cream. The whole lot and Margaux ½ (1925) costing about 3/- including coffee and bread and an iced hock, to begin with.

I set out at once to look for a little pistol for you, but only got a ridiculous but fierce miniature one, which Ruth is bringing you, as a present. I have seen already about six dresses for you, and about 50 hats, and countless pretties of various kinds which would delight you. But being silk, cannot be brought.

I pine bitterly for you. I, like Mole, sniff at my past fun and yet weep. You have so much of my heart that I resent that any part of it was ever not wholly yours. That comes of your refusal to be jealous – I do it for you, and most thoroughly.

My sweetest Love, my heart, – How I curse the river of time which is still broad between us.

Normandy was looking exquisite. Rouen shone in dark sunlight and a storm swept it away from my eyes and churned up the broad river with waves which pounced up like cats as our train drew out of the arches of the bridge.

I have seen some pretty and even two beautiful girls here – but to my horror, and wry joy, I look dispassionately and then my gaze travels to you – and rests – and is pleased. Sweetheart, I love you.

Valentine

35: STW

Little Zeal, 17 August 1931, 6 p.m.

My dearest Love,

In future you must think more kindly of Totnes; it has just done me a great deal of good. And I have bought you two presents there, and so I feel much happier. One of them – for I can't leave you poised on two curiosities – is a celestial globe – a smallish one, not larger than two footballs. I don't quite know where it will go in Miss Green – perhaps it might stand on one of the new bookcases, or balance the Family Bible. It is a yellowish firmament; and there is a small hole in one of the constellations, with a little dribble of plaster. But it can be stopped up. It is faint and stained and defaced – which is why I got it remarkably cheap – but if one looks closely one sees dim bears and giants and oddities. And we will ask Llewelyn and Alyse[1] to explain its workings to us, and see if they know how. I shan't be quite unconsoled if they can't. The other present[2] is not in the least like this.

I also did some other shopping, with a view to Christmas. Buying so early, one always has time to change one's mind and keep things. But I shan't keep – since I have a so much lovelier one – a small papier-maché desk with mother-of-pearl whiskers radiating from a bunch of flowers. Nor, I think, a copper lustre jug, even though it has on one side a vignette of an 1830 couple drinking wine at a small al-fresco table, and on the other a clock-face showing 8.20 . . . so that was how they breakfasted, and now we know what sort of couple they were; but another couple I am undecided about. I found the female one first, a small wooden idol, Javanese, I daresay, or East Indian, carved with a tail of hair down her back and afterwards improved with a plait of real black horsehair, wired on, and earrings, nose-ring, necklace and stomacher of glass beads. Also anklets. The girl in the shop, a bouncing county school Miss, then hunted out my lady's husband; a wasp-waisted elegant with an unmistakable penis. Quite, quite solemnly she said – 'This is the male one, I suppose. It hasn't a pigtail.'

But the present I am not telling you about is, to my mind, much the most exciting and exquisite. It is exactly what I wanted for you, only I had not thought of it in this medium. It is intensely elaborate and as smooth as a fish – but it is not a snake.

It was a melancholy blow to walk out, feeling secret and excited and not to find you waiting suspiciously on the pavement, with an expression of ruthless savagery and a rival (and lovelier) parcel under your arm. Do you remember how I suddenly viewed you through a topaz in the Westbourne Grove?

18.8.1931
Your letters, Charles' ring and Galen this morning. And it is a shiny sweet-aired day, and I am wearing my grey dress with the two

1 Llewelyn and Alyse Powys. They lived near Chaldon, and tended to be omniscient.
2 A Regency straw-work cabinet.

handkerchiefs fastened corner to corner and pinned with the Christmas brooch – extremely pretty, O that you were here to think so! – and the little amethyst mourning ring.

At four a.m. William woke me by a sudden whine. I was terrified, and in an instant wrecked you . . . then, to my gradual trembling relief he began steadfastly to scratch. I don't *think* wraiths would have that effect. He was restless, so I took him into the garden; a marvellous stillness and starriness. But too late to do you any good, I'm afraid. I do hope the crossing wasn't too hideous.

My darling, what a bore about your thyroid, and what a dreary dietary to go to Paris on. Boiled fish, my God! absolutely without nourishment, for look how starved people come out of nursing homes, where they live on it. And it oppresses me to think how I have been feeding you on all the forbidden things, peas, beans and pork. And sardines.

Dear Bunny, I am so glad you had him for the week-end. Bunny's small ghost sits whimpering in a corner of my conscience. I could deprive, though I didn't set out to, Bo with calm philosophy; but I am very compuncted about Bunny always. He must have been a comfort, I am sure of that. Fur is; even a fur coat can be kinder than people, and fur warmed with a heart just the mixture of sympathy and ignorance one needs. I hope he spent Saturday and Sunday nights in your bed, and soothed you with affectionate snuffles, and was squudged lovingly by you.

I like the tree exercise. It is small, compact and wry as a crab-apple. I should certainly keep frivolity instead of puerility. I think it is a pity that puerility should have acquired this deep taint of something scornable, because in its meaning it is a good word, and being led astray one has to fall back on childishness, which carries now a shade of Anglo-Cat sentiment (that old rogue Coventry Patmore,[1] I suppose, being sorry); whereas it would be a blessing to have one unjudicial word that one could drive in like a plain nail.

I don't see how you could have written with all that rumpus without and stir within. As one gets deeper into poetry, I believe, one needs quite different mental conditions to strike root in. The poem struck out in a moment of violence is almost always an early poem – like those amazing sunflowers that grow in the first year of a garden – you can see them in any new council house settlement; but less the next year, and then not again until the soil has been converted into garden earth. But the recollection of how one wrote one's first poems persists; and

---

1 Coventry Patmore, 'sorry for their childishness'.

hampers one with the suspicion that one is less quick or less genuine than one was. But really it is that one is less fortuitous, less at the mercy of circumstances. I should imagine that with your sort of poetry, so much less objective than mine, this change towards recollected in tranquillity would be even more definite. Your poems will more and more proceed from the texture of your mind, not from assaults on it; and I shall not be surprised to find you, before long, working best in such a manner as Theo's — every day after breakfast with the Bible beside you.

I looked out of the window and saw, then, two wood-pigeons, preening, coquetting and quarrelling on a bough. They think it is a good morning to make love; and so it is. If you were here, we would climb into a tree and outdo the wood-pigeons. Now they are telling each other affably how much they liked it.

My love, my bird, only eight days more. Time *does* go, however heavily. We are down among the single figures now. Never doubt me, and don't worry about me, I am well, and I love you.

Sylvia

. . .

36: VA

Paris, Friday, about 11 a.m.

My Sweetheart,

Your letters brought relief and pleasure to me last night, except for anxiety about poor head of; but today your telegram gave me inexpressible joy, and I bless you for its promptness. What is the secret present? The globe is exactly my idea of a really exciting treasure. I long to see it. Where is it now? Will it accompany you? I shall need it, of course, on the boat.

I have not got you a pistol. They do not now make decorated ones, except one which I saw, but did not approve. It was not at all well-built. I would not let your fingers play with such a jerry-built thing. Your pretty, nimble fingers must never have to handle anything so stiffly-hinged or so tin-like. The small black revolvers are not safe. I should not know a moment's peace, in case it blew up in your hand. So I have got a pretty and delicate present[1] for you. After two days spent in making R's life a misery by roaming from grove to grove, hesitating between three or four objects of clothing (all to be brought to you – all to be smuggled) and a hat or else this – which I have bought. It is a thing which, perhaps on principle or perhaps just through habit of non-use, you dislike. But it is pretty and well-made. At least, I hope so, and the young woman who sold it to me spoke the most impure American I have ever heard, from the most charming mouth I have ever watched. And swore to me that this toy will last, anyhow for three years, guaranteed, and of course one may hope it will last for ever.

Here is the weekly menu of a restaurant I found – it is extremely good. I had cassoulet (goose in it) and Vin Rosé de la Loire, in carafe, at 6 Frcs. Then Aubergines (iced Pilsner with the first, and Rosé with the second) and the coffee. It is the most superb cooking. Rather swaggering, but that is what it should be, I think, for such dishes.

You *will* come?

Last night I had plain roast veal, with mushrooms, fried. Then tomatoes grilled with garlic and parsley, coffee and very nice (probably well-matured) vodka.

Now, my prettiest love, I must go out. Poor R. is crackling her Continental *Daily Mail*.

I love you most deeply, my darling. Take heed to yourself, begin to trim, for our night is nearing and our days and the lovely crescendo of happiness which is our time together.

Later about 6.30 p.m.

Sweetheart,

A fearful storm – the worst, except that it was brief, that I have ever known. And the most fierce rain I have ever watched, really worse than that rainstorm on that miserable day in London – which seems now so many ages ago.

I had a belated idea. Parisot and Lucile[2] are most desperately poor. They are nice – at least, he is – and sensibly complimentary because, when he asked if I was happy, I replied Yes. You were right.[3] He gently presented to me a young woman called Jeanne. She is charming. Very

---

1 A wristwatch.
2 Parisot and Lucile: friends from earlier sojourns in Paris.
3 I had forecast complimentary pimping.

quiet and serious, a face shaped a little like D.W., aged about 25, I believe. I arranged to have Parisot and Lucile and her to supper at about ten-thirty. I have said nothing to Ruth. She is in a queer mood since our argument. But it is still thundering. I shall remain quietly here if it goes on. Anyway – dear Parisot is kind, and thoughtful – but I am puritanical (truly) about it, and as I find no desire in my heart I cannot have any truck with it. But I can, and will, be very nice and also properly grateful.

My own most beloved most sweet one. But what violent storms of desire I suffer for you. I did not know I could stomach such a prolonged thwarting from anyone. But you, my sweetheart, by being reluctant to thwart me (you are, I think) make it more bitter still.

> Shall I, wasting in despair,
> Die because a woman's fair?

Wasting has begun. I pine. I stare with cross approval at every pair of lovers, and curse and bless them, all at once.

I love you intolerably. God help you when I do get you – but God help me till then. I wish I were a Catholic! I'd burn all the candles in France to witch us together again, and light them from my flame.

Valentine

Perhaps it is because you are such an accomplished cook, that you fry me so well.

37: STW

Little Zeal, 21 August 1931

My dearest Love,

Today – for a day – has been quite adventurous. As you know, I went down to bring back the meat, and finished my letter to you in the Post Office. I then bought one of the new 5/- stamp books, so much recommended to me by the Post Master that I feel sure they have been issued with instructions to press their sale – so that people may lose them, as they do the 3/- kind, and so redeem the Excquerer. I mean exchequer, but really excquerer is as good. Then he told me I was his first purchaser. So I overlooked his blotting-paper and we wished each other many happy returns. Then I cashed a cheque at the grocer's. Then I went to the station and looked up trains. My usual 11-ish train has been put later, and doesn't reach Paddington till 4.30. So I propose to catch an 8.5 and be at Paddington at 1.15. So I shall see you more than two hours earlier than I expected – and I do truthfully say O rapture, Oh bless the 8.5!! And when you remember what I feel about early starts – but you don't doubt my love, do you?

Then, as if this were not adventure enough, I walked out William in the afternoon, and met a waggon loaded with fern and two very supple sheep-dogs. *And* a farmer I didn't know on a white horse. I was relieved to see him. One of the creepy things about this place is that the ground carries sound to a most unnatural distance. And in a clear and visible landscape I had heard these thuds and stampings; and was beginning to see another rider on a pale horse when, far off, I saw the real one.

I have been reading the Koran every night in bed – about six surahs and then my elbow gives out. I like Mahomet's original sentiments extremely, but I grew rather weary of the day of judgement, and arrived at it each time more like the wicked appearing with downcast eyes and unwilling steps.

This evening I beguiled Nora into a long account of her Lesbians, H. and E., and how E. carpenters and looks after the garden ('just like a man') and was in a fearful twitter when she had to have some teeth out (which Nora also thought just like a man, though if that is true I must be a great deal more manly than you suspect); and how romantic and delightful it all is. Their meeting *is* rather romantic. H. went to Stoke Fleming and took a house there, and furnished it, and then went to church. In church she saw E. The moment church was over she walked up to her, began to talk and invited her to tea. E. came, sniffed around, asked a few questions, and then said: 'I have been living with an uncle and aunt, but they are leaving to go to London and I don't want to go with them. I think it would be a good plan if I came to live with you. I can bring my uncle's gardener.' And since then they have lived together in great content, only disagreeing about the Creation and the Ark, since E. takes both these stories verbatim.

She looks like that. I only saw her broad, locally-tailored back at Ronald's funeral, but it had faith in every line of it: faith in tailors, too.

I hope one day some one will be writing in a letter about us, only they will never be able to say that you have a faithful back, believing back, I mean. For your lovely straight back and proud shoulders speak your truth and integrity. I would love you if you were covered with prickles and sackcloth; but how glad I am that your lovely outside bespeaks your nature – so clean and proud and fine.

I am a hypocrite ingrain, my darling. I was just going to put my head on one side and say, O what a pity that not one of the slenders or the slys or the willings caught your fancy. And only just in the nick of time did I find myself out – my deep female pride and content that they didn't. And as soon as I'd written *that* I found myself cautiously going on to say that if by any chance one of them had done so, since your letter, I was, of course, delighted.

Now I shall go to my large, empty mockery of a bed – wearing a nightgown, pooh! and probably a small coat, too, since it is cold. But we will be warm on 2's narrow kind bed. My love.

Sylvia

How nice to have a fierce pistol – how charming and inappropriate from Ruth. May I fire it with feux de joie all the way to Winterton? I am going to give the little writing case to Ruth. I have oiled and polished it, and it has come up like those Kingdom Collars.[1]

I mean to put in a loving border of postscripts. Darling, I love you. Take the utmost care of yourself. Eat!

I dreamed last night that Timothy[2] sat on a cane chair and ate Penny. I smacked him and he sprang on to my neck. I was terrified – but you appeared, plucked him off, and threw him out of the window.

I have done a lot more patchwork. And drunk a lot more brandy. But no poems. I can't sing unmated.

38: STW

Little Zeal, 22 August 1931

My Dearest Love,

After I had finished my letter to you last night I got into bed and felt, as I curled up, my warm shoulder – and thought, This is Valentine's wife.

You have no idea what you have escaped. I found in a book of sayings about weathers and signs and times of year a set of sooth-sayings about

---

1 A current poster of a smiling laundress saying 'These Kingdom collars come up fine.'
2 Timothy: a cat at Winterton; Penny was one of the 'family' of mice.

the character of wives according to the month they are married in. If you had waited a month later you would have married 'a chattermag' – in August, a spendthrift. But a January bride, it says, will make a prudent housewife and has a sweet temper.

This morning, when I least expected such a windfall, a cheque from New York came. £45. So I have a balance again. What is even nicer is that Opus 7 has sold over 1000 copies in U.S.A. which, for a poem, in such a bad year, is flattering.

It remains to be seen if I bring the celestial globe with me. The other affair has gone to London by rail, and should be at 113 – where if we can spare the time, we must go and unpack it. But the little car certainly won't be able to take them both – and I don't know if Ruth and Alec, coming in the Austin, would want to toss a celestial globe with legs from one to the other. So perhaps it had better stay here, till I can drive over for the day and fetch it.

How lovely to be making such practical plans – almost packing for 26th.

The clocks in this house, having got slower and slower, have now stopped. However, they will be wound up tomorrow, I suppose. And there shall be no mistake about catching the 8.5.

I shall start looking for the alarm clock – I think I saw it last in the W.C. – so suitable – tomorrow, and telephone for the exact time on Tuesday night.

You with your wireless – perhaps before I see you, you will have voyaged into some other time.

Before I see you – not long now, I say to myself. But it *is* long. You are not the only one to ache and pine, my poor darling. This morning brought me your letter of Wednesday – and I think it was not till the next day you telegraphed; and then I did not get the wire telephoned till nearly eight. I can only hope telegrams in Paris go on later than they do in London. I tear myself, all so belatedly too, thinking that this happened, and am at a loss to see how. For I have written every day, and posted myself. O my love, it breaks my heart to think of you so unhappy and distracted, and all because of me. Even Ruth, in her Wednesday letter, said you looked tired and ill – and explained it by the thunderstorm.

23. 11 a.m.

Then the largest Daddy Long Legs I have ever seen began to climb up the candlestick. So I went hurriedly to bed, and listening to the river almost made it into the regular sound of a calm sea – and thought of you on the channel. But then I fell asleep, and had horrible dreams about falling off the Aquitania in that gale, and knowing, as I clawed at the last hope of a railing that if I were drowned, then I should never know Valentine.

This is an exquisite morning. The air says you are back and a very light wind has blown my dreams away.

This morning I feel myself so nearly home with you that I can babble. Only two days more – for the day one is in never really counts – and I shan't have a word to say for myself – partly because I shall be too happy for anything but sighs, and partly because you will be kissing me. And I will heal you of this miserable absence, my dearest. In our first night it will all be forgotten.

Sylvia

39: VA

2, London, 23 August 1931, Sunday about 4.45 p.m.

My love, You must be patient with me if I indulge myself by writing to you a long letter in each of these interminable days which spread between us.[1] I will only post once a day (unless something acute happens) but it eases me a little to write to you, although it may be hard on you. I will try to make my letters legible anyhow.

I have been scrambling out my fairings from the box. I got a small, a very pretty, bag for Janet. She seemed so pleased to have anything elegant and not too childish given her that surely this can do no harm? I did not want to offend her parents' tastes, but more still I wanted to avoid shaping hers. Still, it is an anonymous little thing, and yet feminine and slightly luxurious. I hope you will not think this choice indiscreet. I spent three separate hours of three separate days in choosing this, and enjoyed myself.

If I can find a suitable box in which to pack it, I shall post to you your small present[2] (it is the size of my thumbnail, I should say – or, at most, of the butt-end of a cigar and much the colour of the latter). It is a strangely ironic and moving piece of work – made by an old man whose pastime is the making of bone skulls (this is not one) most carefully fashioned, each

---

1 But I cut short my stay in Devonshire, and was back the next day.
2 A bone carving, ½ inch high, head of the man of sorrows; reverse a death's head.

differently shaped and each perfect in all detail. The first time I met him over there (some years ago) he smiled at my admiration, and, tapping my bony finger said dryly: 'I could make one out of that. I make them of bones.' His profession is that of stationer, and he sells vile post-cards and deckle-edged, expensive writing-paper.

His shop is called: 'A Jeanne d'Arc' and he Weibel. However, everything depends on my chance of finding a suitable little box.

I am quite desert-dry as regards poetry. Perhaps you are right (you always are) and it is not astonishing or necessarily bad. It always takes *me* in. But I think I must try to have an *idea*. About anything, really, so long as I have it, and do not be just a baby-farmer. But today, though I am most restive, and angry, at my impotence and sterility, it is possibly true, for once, that I am tired. We left Paris at 7 last evening, and reached Waterloo at the ghastly hour of nine-thirty: on a Sunday! Now I am trying not to have my relief and hope dimmed by the melancholy noises of this place – thin whistling from the street, little breathing-noise of the gas, trees rattling like rain, and the extraordinary quietness (after Paris almost like the country) and pattering footsteps which cannot, today, quicken my heart and draw me swiftly to the window, to see you and William turn in at the door in the wall, come pattering along the flagstones and running up the stairs.

The train made a gentle sound last night, conveying me to Havre. I loved it. I sat, seraphically contemplating you, listening to the quiet and comforting noise that French train made, reassuring me, saying: 'Nearer, nearer – all right, all right' until I almost wept. Then I lay flat on my bunk, on board, to all appearance most resigned, but really chivvying you up and down this room I am now in, hurrying you here and there, and seeing that there was N O time wasted between our entering this door and getting into bed. 'Hurry! My darling. Oh damn William. I'll give him some water. That'll do for him' (and he got an enormous bowl of milk and a tin of fine and juicy salmon). 'Blast your skirt – damn your belt. *Pull* it off. Well, tear it then.' But you know quite well, by now, how things go. But do you? Are you quite sure that you know what I am like when you have wilfully deprived me of eleven tedious days and endless nights? Ah, my Sweetheart. You had better take that early train. An earlier, if possible. We will need all that remains of that day, and there's no *chance* of my being willing (and would I be able?) to wait until the night. I am making enquiries about trains. There may be an earlier one yet. I have a shrewd, uneasy suspicion that you have grown *cold*. That you have suppressed your desires so thoroughly that now they will not flame? Tell me if this is so, please.

Well, my beloved one. Take heed of these threats and instructions. Love me. Charge yourself, over and over again, every minute of the day, with carefulness. Remember, you are taking care of my most precious, my unutterably dear prize. Above all things, sweetheart, guard against all misfortune and be *wise*. Take no risks with my only riches. Without you, my life would be gone. If any harm, however slight, came to you I should hardly be able to support it, if anything hurt or flawed you, my light would die. None of this is exaggerated. It is all dearly truth. My love for you is a terrible thing - as I warned you when I first told you I loved you. It is the earth and the sweet seasons, and the smell of hay and honeysuckle and the shadow of trees and the lovely shapes of winter trees or of Chaldon hills – but it is also the fire in the belly of earth. Do not ever forget that. We are lost if we forget that.

I love you, my Love – for ever,

Valentine

Narrative 4

While we lived in the houseboat on the river Thurne, hearing the slap of water and the windmill's creaking refrain leap its minor seventh and fall back, we agreed that we must postpone our return to Miss Green and spend the winter in Norfolk. Ruth was proposing to give up her flat at St James's Court and settle economically at The Hill House. She would repine less, Valentine said, if we were in the garage flat. By mid-October we were there, laying up a stock of wood against the winter. The landscape, stripped for winter, the skies tall as the horizons were wide, was as compelling as a chaconne: one never knew what variation of light would come next.

We were still engaged in learning more about each other, and she had Norfolk to teach me. I had never known a winter sea. I had never encountered the East Coast climate, nor a wind so strong that it blew me off my feet. All that rigging of fishermen's jerseys had prepared me for a stern climate but not for such a fickle one. After an easterly gale which raged for three days and wrecked a ship by driving it up the beach, we woke to a morning so calm, so blue, so mild, that we strolled out in dressing-gowns to walk on the plateau. A south-bound vessel was travelling smoothly through a halcyon sea. I said it was a boat by Shelley. Valentine, whose mind was more positive, fetched her binoculars. The

Shelleyan vessel was lettered: *Huntley and Palmer*.

While we were still settling in a succession of women from the village arrived with presents of jam and pickles. I remarked on their kindness. 'We don't want all this jam,' she exclaimed. 'Come on! I'll take you down to the Three Mariners and display you.'

I remembered that Ruth, condoled with on my emergence as yet another of Valentine's loves, was reported to have said, 'Well, at any rate, she's a gentlewoman.' 'Miss Maaalie's latest,' I commented. 'Will you feel embarrassed?'

'Why?'

We sat in the snug. More and more people came in.

Winterton was like no village I had ever seen. It was a small closed community, violent and feuding, where everyone was related, and known by a nickname, like characters in the Icelandic Sagas. It had two public-houses, a church, a chapel, and a sacred stone which only the old men might sit on. During the summer half of the year old men and boys were the only males in the village; the men were away in the herring-fleet. In autumn they put in at Yarmouth, got their money, came home, saw the children born while they were away, begot more, bellowed sentimental hymns at the Fishermen's Thanks-giving Services, put fresh coats of tar on their seaward flint walls. The women, a six-month matriarchy, were as outspoken and upstanding as the men. 'Popularity' is a servile word. At Chaldon, Valentine was conditionally popular. At Winterton, she was unconditionally accepted.

She was accepted; she had position too. An undefinable swagger acknowledged this. One morning, I watched her pause on her way from the flat to the house for a word with John[1], the gardener. Willie looked out of the garage. 'What did his Lordship say?'

Against all reason it was believed that she would inherit the place, rule there, and restore a former state of things. Against all reason, she half-envisaged doing so. There was still so much worth saving – a traditional amplitude, a Victorian solidity and compactness. But in the ten years since her father's death The Hill House had been left to go downhill. Everything had the blurred look of having known better days. In her childhood, it had known those days. In her childhood, she had been passionately attached to the place. Later, she outgrew the attachment, largely because it had been exploited by Ruth as a means of tethering her. Now, with me to show it off to, she felt ownership – ownerly fury at the

1 [John Powles]

way it had been allowed to fall into neglect, ownerly despair because, even if she should inherit, there would not be enough money to ransom it. What I saw as a stanza in the interminable English poem of 'The Triumph of Time', she saw with practical censoriousness; while at the same time the intimacy of childhood rainbowed what was disused, out of repair, not what it used to be: the rusted enormous roller which used to be pulled over the lawn by a pony wearing boots (we found one of the boots in the potting shed); the tattering reed-fence which had been so tight against the wind, the well under the lilac bushes, the ash tree where she sat writing poems and hid them in the crevices. 'No chance of a poem now,' she said. In fact, there were several, though it took the detachment of influenza to release this one.

> The winter woods against this yellow sky
> Stand like embroidered trees
> Worked in memorial hair;
> So still against the clouds the branches lie,
> Drooping as if to please
> The grief that placed them there.
> The stable cistern, like a funeral urn,
> Outlined in strong relief
> Stands up beneath the boughs;
> As if with evening nature would return
> To mourn some ancient grief
> No younger heart allows.

The belief that she would inherit The Hill House, rule there and restore the old order derived its conviction from her resemblance to her father. 'Mr Ackland to the life,' said the village. 'Same way of walking. Same way of giving you a look.' He was consistently remembered. Only Ruth seemed to have forgotten him, taking a widow's licence to cut him down to her own size, ignore a formidable perfectionism, and implacable streak of melancholy. But she habitually falsified: it was her expedient of possessiveness. For the first week or so of our stay at Winterton Valentine's presence was pleasure and support to her. But possessiveness cannot accept; it cannot even strike a fair bargain; it has to confer. We lived on the end of a string, incessantly tweaked across to the house for small celebrations – shrimps for tea, a pheasant, some relative's birthday or death-day – or sunk in return hospitalities. The intention of being there so that Ruth should repine less was lost under demonstrations that Ruth was doing all in her power to keep us from repining.

We did not repine. We were together, Norfolk was wide, we were often blazingly happy; but we could not call our happiness our own. Valentine took time more seriously than I did. My casual consent to its wastage exasperated her; she would suddenly lose control and let fly at me. No comfort came of this. Her mechanism was too intricate to receive anything but damage by explosions.

At intervals as if it were something of great importance I hadn't been attending to, I would remember the sea.

'Let's go down to the beach.'

This time – we were nearing the end of our stay, and we both had colds in the head – it was a grey afternoon, stone cold and windless. The sea was so calm that the waves did not break. They travelled to the shore and died on it. During that first visit to Winterton, which now seemed a visit to some quite different place, I had told her she had mermaid blood. I had meant it lightly, a comment on her beauty and beguilingness. But there was more than that to mermaid blood, I thought, looking at the stern quiescence of the winter sea. She picked up a small, pure white, pebble, showed it to me, tossed it high in the air, caught it again.

'Sometimes I love you like that,' she said.

1932

In the train,[1] 19 March 1932

My Dearest Love,

I have just looked at the little clock, and it is 11.45, and I am in Berkshire. The sky is dappled blue and white, but mostly white.

You are still at 2 packing, my poor one. You walked away such a stiff proud cat; I still see and admire your lovely straight back, your long haughty legs. Darling, you were so sweet to me, I cannot thank you even now and certainly could not then. And I am as gloomy and as limp and as helpless as any animal that has to be put into a guard's van and foresees it.

But this is a nice quiet van, I have nothing to say against this carriage, unless I cavil at the exceeding ugliness of the woman opposite. I have lent her *Vogue*, and she is embedded in it, turning each page with yearning, and reading how at Master Cecil Beaton's country house the cushions are of silver lamé, covered with fringed dishcloths.

. . . . I have had lunch; the rabbity little attendant was most sweet and kind and offered me second-helps, joining in this halloo of the Poor Invalid. If anything could make travelling alone tolerable, your foreseeings would – excepted, of course, the 8 a.m. for Paddington. On that train I require no cossetting.

Several smuts have settled on my nose and been blotted out by beaver puff. Everything I use is of you and your love. Your goodness and mercy follow me everywhere. And even now I have not come to the dear little poetry book, and the shell which I pulled out and snuffed the moment the train started. You do these things, these givings and graces, so perfectly, my Dear. I am such a dull dump compared to you. But only in love am I,

---

1 Having been seen off on a journey to Little Zeal after a great deal of invocation and tipping of the head of the restaurant-car service. (She went back to Winterton that afternoon.)

much more than you will admit, your equal. I love you with all my heart, my dearest. I love you with a wedded love.

I am in Somerset now, I have seen the first field of red earth and made a face at it. I have seen lambs, too, with their large ears looking so pert; and all alone in one large field, a married goose and gander, extremely solemn, almost with umbrellas tucked under their wings. They were gravely arguing about a dandelion. I look with pleasure on all sober respectable married couples now . . . though I never see our variety of sobriety and respectability matched. But then they are not so much nor so happily in love as we.

My darling, I love you always and everywhere.

Sylvia

41: VA

Winterton, 20 March 1932

My Sweetheart,

Dear little John is sitting blandly in the garage – longing to be off – but awfully pleased to know how soon we'll see you again. That little car is a great delight to me. You do *know*, don't you? He has been a comfort to me before, when we were away from each other. For longer, last time I wonder how we stood that separation? But the strength of time between us seems *always* interminable. Even when you are out, or I am out, for half-an-hour. My heart grows colder and colder, like a dowsed coal. Dirty and shabby and dull and damp. And my temper *most evil*.

The freesias know it. They are pouring their sweetness like oil upon my storm, but, poor lambs, to little purpose, except that they do sweeten my rage to melancholy.

The sun is out. The heavy grey cloud which blanketed the sky has been pushed aside, and is lying low over the sea – rolled back from the other side too – so that there is a slit of horizon against which little tiny clear ships go along. Small and neat, little models drawn across a stage. One brown smack is becalmed opposite the look-out.

My love for you is bewildering me – making me feel lost and as if I were in a strange land. My love for you is true – true and steadfast and unshakable. Look at the falcon on your little clock. I love you like that.

Monday 20 March 1932

Dear Heart,

I've been reading the expurgated *Lady Chatterley's Lover*. Lawrence was right to say 'the book bleeds'. It's bled itself white. There is nothing left but limp flesh now, and rather revolting flesh, too.

I smile to remember Lady Mary Wortley Montagu's poem (from memory, as I probably misquote), 'And when the long hours of our parting are past and we meet with champagne and a chicken at last –'

That, sweetheart, was a practical and amiable woman! I hope she was very happy and pleased. Willing and greedy and complaisante she certainly was – and so are you – and what could be higher praise, from a lover? This bed creaks at the memory of our strife upon it! But its sound is doleful now – until we are both back.

I told my ash-tree all about you, yesterday. All its branches quivered. You must go and talk to it yourself. The skin of its newest branch was as smooth and as warm as yours, and the wildest and most passionate vibrations made the branches quiver beneath my hand – just as you have done, as you *will do*. The wind stirred the tree and the sun teased it and the earth itself was throbbing yesterday, like a waking womb. The sun has been most amorous – my Sweet, my Love – my Love – as I would be to you – as I would be.

Valentine

42: STW

Little Zeal, 21 March 1932

My dearest Love,

Dear Cole, and Charlotte[1] came this morning – a comforting pair, and to look inside Cole and see your hand was almost as though you had suddenly spoken over my shoulder.

No letter this morning. But it is Monday, and that comforts me; and such a lovely thing happened last night that I am still the better for it.

I was just going to bed, about eleven, very moped and dead-hearted,

---

1 W. Cole, *Bletchley Diary*; Charlotte Charke (she was Colley Cibber's daughter), *Account of My Life*.

when *I heard a blackbird sing* . . . his whole strain, his whole chime. It was a very still moonlight night, a grey moonlight not a blue – so much the colour of dawn that as I leaned out of the window I was almost persuaded that the bird must be right, not I.

Presently, I heard a chirp or two, and then, another burst of song. He sang like this, with a flourish, and then a pause, and then another flourish, for almost half an hour; and then as though he had at last kindled it, his song was immediately taken up by a second blackbird, very close to my window, unbelievably sweet and exciting.

And then, as though having kindled the response, he was satisfied, he didn't sing any more.

I longed for you then, with your eyes black with excitement, your listening look, the joy you would have had at this.

Il pleut, Bergère. I wish you could gather in your sheep. But it is a gentle rain, and pleases the trees and the birds and the weary winter grass, so I bear it no malice.

Nora is being affable. She can't resist prodding a bit, but there isn't much animus behind the prods, it is habit of mind and curiosity more than any specific passion. This morning her eye fell on the brandy flask. 'What's that? Brandy?' 'Brandy.' 'Do you always take a flask like that with you?' 'Yes, always. Years ago you said one shouldn't travel without it, and I still follow your advice.' A short pause, during which she contemplated the size of the bottle. 'What do you take it for, may I ask?' Sitting up in bed I described with animation my powers of diarrhoea, telling the story of the Winkle, but with embellishments, and introducing other incidents, striking impromptus, to prove how easily I could be upset inside. Nora listened with more awe than conviction, and extricated herself with credit by saying, 'you must have inherited it from me.'

But I expect I have now supplanted Dorothie[1] as the family dipsomaniac. Nora's mind has become extremely rural. She sits meditating like Marvell's nightingale, and builds up the queerest convictions about her relations. 'I should like to think that Evelyn[2] isn't a liar', or 'I hope he doesn't really embezzle' – and so forth. All about the most blameless bourgeoisie, too. It is horribly tempting not to feed the flame with little puffs here and there. The queer thing is that having worked herself into these beliefs she is sincerely concerned at having to believe them.

The little clock is a reservoir of kisses. I read in your books, fondle

---

1 [Dorothie Purefoy Machen.]
2 [Evelyn Huddleston, Nora's and Purefoy's sister-in-law.]

your presents, eat and drink to you, and think of your poems. O my far love and unkissed. This morning I saw you as I had seen you when I looked up from the Davidson poems to you standing by the dresser, staring at me, already alone and desolate. And again I threw my arms round you, and felt your head bow down to my shoulder, and shake there, mournfully, steadfastly denying comfort. But be comforted, my darling. It is not long, I will soon come. I will be in your hold, and be yours and be happy.

I take the greatest care of myself. Sometimes I wish you were not where there is so much to remind you of me, to catch your thought and say – Here she was. She left this behind. This, too, is hers. Then I think how the bleakness of this place, that scarcely acknowledges that you have been here, is worse. But there is nothing but a wilderness of worsts, when we are separated.

My dearest one, my bird, not long to mope, I love you and love you, and shelter in the thought of your love, and light myself with the thought of your beauty. Everything that I see clear, strong, unswerving, swift, sleek, living, is you to me. Take care of yourself, my dearest love.

Sylvia

43: VA

2, London, 22 March 1932

My sweetheart,

Your lovely thought of me is scenting all the room – yellow daisies, polyanthus(?) freesias. I bless you for them.

Keates is here. She is well, and kind, and sends you her devoted love. She will write tomorrow.

I am abed – chiefly laziness, partly being unwell. Nothing to fuss about, and by the time you get this I shall be up again and misliking it more than being here.

I shall write to you a good and long letter after lunch. This brings you my love – my true and devoted love – for ever, my dear, my pretty. I think of you ceaselessly. Thank God – Tuesday is half over and only one more desert – but two nights – ah, my desire, my Love, take care of self.

Valentine

Do not worry; all is quite well with me. I long for you and long for you, and bid you remember your duty, and *catch the early train*!

That blackbird was my heart – a night-singing bird, and proud and wild and dark – and all yours.

44: STW

Little Zeal, 17 September 1932

My Dearest Love,

I was happy to get your telegram, and to know that the Pembroke Arms had opened so kindly, and that you were well. I immediately spun the top, and it fell to 'passionately'. You must have trained it before sending it out. It is the prettiest top – and how did you contrive to buy toys in the Burlington Arcade while I could have sworn that I had tight hold of you all the time?

My arrival was much enhanced, as I thought it would be, by Apollo.[1] And from tea to dinner I heard all about Phoebe. She sounds a most objectionable woman who spends all her time complaining of her husband and running away in the middle of the night to sympathetic neighbours. Meanwhile, she being comforted and kept for the night, her Basil is left alone with the gin-bottle and drinks himself worse. She tried to get him certified as insane. I am glad to say the doctor refused to hear of it. Another night, when he had been drinking, she sent for two superior policemen, and concealed them in the house. In the morning a restored and sober Basil walked downstairs and found these two fellows sitting in the hall. He asked them what they thought they were doing there. They replied, sheepishly, that they had happened to come in for a little while (like dead leaves, you know). So taking out his watch he gave them ten minutes in which to decamp and they decamped. After this he left for Bristol, to see his lawyer, and is still there. I hope he may stay there, since he is, apparently, a dangerous driver, and liable to have fits while driving. But he may come back at any moment; so, darling, I should be easier in my mind if you didn't peruse through these damned lanes too often, in case you come on him having a fit at 50 m.p.h. I am being taken to see the celebrated Phoebe tomorrow (I'm sure I shall hate her); and I will try to find out what make of car he drives, so that you may know what to look out for.

1 Apollo: our canary.

I have written to Mrs Goult[1] about the measles. And I have begun the centre star of my patchwork quilt, using the new prints you gave me. I had to stitch rather hard, since I found Nora assuming I was going to stay for a fortnight. And of course, me being new, she was upset to hear I leave on Friday – voice a little veiled, magnanimous scarcity of reproaches, all rather distressing. It is my own silly fault. I did say a week in an earlier letter; but I should have rubbed it in more, instead of being pusillanimous and vague. But I think she went to bed tolerably consoled, conversation having flowed into more pleasing channels of her new shoes (she had a burst, and went and bought four pairs of evening slippers, *all* coloured) and her new discoveries at the China shop.

It is really unfair that I should be feeling a slight laceration of the conscience. For earlier in my arrival I was filled with righteous fury at her failure to enquire after your health. She had to in the end. Since she caught the telephone delivering your telegram. But even then it was so grudging that I turned the conversation.

This place is much tidier than usual. The gardener has been cutting its hair. I am glad. I hate overgrown bowers when I am not with you to hide in them. Not, for that matter, that we trouble much about taking cover. I read in dear Remy de Gourmont that the root of sexual modesty was the proper fear of being caught at a disadvantage. Wrong, I daresay. But pleasing to me.

The American *Nation* and the *Saturday Review of Lit.* have both returned the poems I sent them. So now I really expect with confidence that I shall write some more. After this, I hope you might begin to lean your mind to the thought that the *Sat. Review of Lit.* may have taken yours because they liked it, not because they smelled me round the corner.

Sunday
I have found out about the establishment kept by two old ladies. It sounds so suitable that I'm sure you won't hear of it. It is a converted country house with rough shooting, smooth, too, at this time of year, a great many acres and riding-horses. The food is looked after by a retired hospital matron. Of course, if you had brought a pair of trousers and felt drawn to the riding-horses you might overlook the matron.

I am well, William is well, Apollo is very well. He talked incessantly throughout breakfast. I think a night spent in the warm kitchen has agreed with him. It is hot and pouring with the usual rain. I am wearing my grey

---

1 Mrs Goult of Chaldon, asking about an outbreak of measles there.

snake's dress, and the white coat, and grey kittens round my neck and earrings, and a grey handkerchief and the first mourning ring. And my face is most carefully painted, to keep up my morale.

I need it. When I think of you arriving today[1] into this climate, my heart goes into the heels of my green slippers. When I say to William, poured out in an attitude of patience, 'Poor Valentine!' he moans. My bed is so double and so comfortable that I could slash it to bits; and the house is so crammed with whim-whams that I want for you that my bowels shrivel with frustration. In fact I am in a sullen temper, and well-set to pine. In the mirror opposite I see myself looking positively handsome with contained rage. My only comfort is to look at the little watch, and take it off to refresh the kiss on its back. No, that's not true. *You* are my comfort, my darling, and the remembrance of your promise to take care of yourself.

I long for you all the time, I think of you incessantly. Your looks of beauty and truth are steadfastly before me, I walk about clinging to your hand, as I did yesterday. I love you, my dearest. You were never so beautiful as you were yesterday standing outside my cattle-truck. So beautiful that looking at you I forgot to cry. Take every, every care, my true love. I kiss you a hundred times, my senses fly towards you like a flock of birds. Remember that I only wait your word to come to you. I love you.

As for this letter, so talkative and reasonable, I could tear it up. But what to do, my darling? One cannot write down a cry.

Sylvia

45: VA

Hexworthy, 19 September 1932

Monday 9 a.m.

Good morning to you, Valentine's.

I've had breakfast and taken Kaolen and incautiously asked Ruth if she had ever read *Women in Love* — and been unendurably irritated by her reply (in the most artificial voice you can imagine) 'No — is it *Wonderful?*'

---

1 At Hexworthy, on Dartmoor.

'NO' I snapped. However, I grinned over Hermione's blow[1] with the paper-weight. Like aunt, like niece, I said.

I had 2 sedebrol last night, and slept until 6 sans waking and woke sans backache. That was a pleasant change. I woke with the first line of a blasphemous hymn on my lips 'Praise the Dad for his posterity.'

There is a little cat crying outside, it fetched me out of bed directly I woke, but I can't see it from my window. I can't see anything but a sloping stretch of kitchen garden. It's raining, of course.

Ah, when I get you back again, sweet love.

If we can't go to Chaldon immediately, shall we go for a short tour in the car? I'd like very much to stay two nights at Wilton again – it is so very beautiful and yet frail now – like your old little gold ring – so thin that one day it will wear through and cease to be itself. There aren't many places in England like Wilton now, I think. And I'd like to be with you in this odd feeling of freedom you get by journeying rather aimlessly, and staying to stare, admire and poke and pry and then getting back to the large, impersonal bedroom in the hotel – and lying together, very close and tender all night.

I shall get a little tin box today and tomorrow, Tuesday, unless I hear from you saying No, I will bury it in the hedge – a present for you and for William and for Apollo. I shall come at about 3 o'clock – up the lane, beyond your house, towards the cottage and on that side. I hope a tramp won't get the present!

Beloved – in this damned damp moist weather remember to change your feet. I've got your new mushroom slippers here . . . Won't that fetch you? There are no pretty young women in this hotel. No one in the least particle alive or dangerous. All grim or else affable – curse and blast them. Some a little too apt to talk. I've got Wrooth on a b.b. and a short lead, except in the evening, when I let her off to run by her self, and go myself to bed.

I like the row of raindrops on the garden railings opposite my bedroom window. I feel like them (for I feel better) light and smooth and round, reflecting the light. There are two little bushy trees beyond the garden, up the hill; but they are rather messy and not solid enough.

There is only one pleasing person here – that's the Outside Man who looks after the cars. He is very fierce and smiling and a lovely shape. He likes to terrify people about the hills and dangerous roads. I saw Ruth move hastily when he was speaking, as if he burnt her. Of course, the cat

---

1 The model for Lawrence's Hermione was aunt to the redoubtable Dorothy (see p. 41 n. 2).

may be nice too, but I fear it will be a fat and fluffy creature – like the Devonshire voice. My dearest pretty Love – my Doll – write to me. It is desolate without a letter. Why *can't* I telephone you? The boy in dungarees is gardening, his buttocks are almost as pointed as yours. Sweetheart, how *halved* I am, without you. How I hate the feeling. You'd much better come home. What time on Friday will I fetch you? Wire me about measles. I love you – and time will *not* hurry.

Anyway, I'll have to fetch you early Friday – about 11 – or else you won't see Ruth to say good-bye. She has to be in London at mid-day on Saturday for certain. I'll post this in Princetown. Look out for the box in the hedge tomorrow afternoon.

Bless you, sweet Love. Keep yourself most carefully. Take care of every atom of yourself. My dearest heart, know that I love you.

P.S.
I've found a divine Spiritualist book – here is an extract. 'There are lovely lyrics composed out here and impressed on the receptive minds of earthy poets. A poet told me it was easier to do with a short lyric than with an epic or a drama, where a long-continued effort was necessary.' Which explains, much to my satisfaction and relief, many of my Holy Hymns and laboured lyrics. To continue: 'Whenever you go to a concert where beautiful music is being played, there is probably all round you a crowd of music-loving spirits, drinking in the harmonies . . . But no sensitive spirit likes to go near a place where bad strumming is going on. Of all earthy things, sound reaches most directly into this plane of life. Tell that to the musicians.'

Well, well, well. But it does explain a great deal which is otherwise *very mysterious*.

Now I am going, D.V., to Chagford and Grimspound. And I want to see a Beehive Hut. And I've written to Wilton to engage our room (thank God, not rooms!) and we'll go to Stonehenge. Friday and Saturday, anyway, we'll spend there, my darling.

I love you as I love life and as I love rivers. And *trees*, for I adore them. Sweetheart, my sweet Love. Wait impatiently for our day – and our night. I love you.

Valentine

46: STW

Little Zeal, 19 September 1932

My dearest Love,

Your erring and straying Tibby[1] smiled for the first time when she read that you had a pisky on your door. Actually, Ruth ought to be careful what she says; for pisky is the term used in Edinburgh to describe members of the Episcopalian church; and when my father was young he used to hear the street urchins singing outside the Episcopalian building on Sundays.

> Pisky, Pisky A A A - M E N !
> Down on your hunkers and up again . . .

a criticism of ritual that I'm sure Ruth would not wholly agree with.

Meanwhile, wonders do not cease. This evening, while Nora and I were straying round the china cabinet she suddenly handed me a small object, and remarked – By the way, I found this and thought that you and Miss Ackland might like it.

I looked. It was a China pomade pot, circa about 1870, in an early Goss manner. It was dark fig-green, and had on the lid a transfer picture of two ladies out walking. One was tall and one was short, and both alike wore black riding-boots, black cloaks, and black top-hats. They were walking past a Gothic cell, and a greyhound precedes them; and underneath (have you guessed?) it says: The Ladies of Llangollen.

I thanked like a bird, and was as pleased as Apollo at groundsel. For indeed, it is a nice addition to our china, and isn't it pleasing to think that the Ladies had so lasting a renown as to get on to memorial pomade pots? And what do you make of my mamma? Personally I am much pleased with her for this spirited and affable little dig in our ribs. She's pleased, too. She's gone about beaming all the evening.

I visited Totnes, and bought a not very practical tea-set, but it is so pretty that I hope you will like it enough to view it as a 4th October[2] present. It is six coffee-cups and four tea-cups and ten deep saucers and a plate of Derby wheat-ear pattern: grey, black and gold on a dull white ground. It is very fragile, and most of the cups have cracks about them;

---

1 Tib and Tibby were names for the domestic side of my character.
2 The day we set up house together at Miss Green.

but I think it is tea-tight; and it is as beautiful as a winter landscape of snow at dusk.

I also bought, bearing in mind that junket may have to take place in your diet-dinners, a font-shaped junket bowl, with a mixed-up flower pattern transfer. I know from experience that one reason why junket seems such a dreary food is that it is always served in a flat glass dish. It is *really* nicer in a proper personal shaped bowl. With flowers.

I also bought you a small curiosity as a surprise and meeting present.[1] I will only mention that it is flat, contains a thunderstorm, a rainbow and an old gentleman in a yellow dressing-gown, reminds me forcibly of Theo's writings, and marries Thomson's *Seasons* to the Bible.

I knew that Wilton would be nice with its prancing Lombardic church. Alas! I had hoped that you would stay there a little longer. But you are in this deplorable county. I could wish you, with all my heart, a young woman to fall in love with at every meal; but I despair of your finding one, even; and perhaps that accounts for the unreservedness of my wish!

My darling, believe me that I am taking the most cosseting care of your Tibby, and that she laps countless saucers of private sherry, and has every care that could mitigate a Tib-cat in a basket.

Only my paws come through and scratch savagely, and my lamenting *Waows* could be heard almost into Cornwall. Also, a Tib-cat, at last let out, stalks forth with dignity, and there will be no dignity, no moment of stretching each outraged leg, when I am let out and run to you. Yes, church me as much as you like (I am most penitently aware that I walked into the basket); in a white veil, if you please, or if you would rather a white sheet. And I promise to make all the proper responses in a voice of unmistakable devotion.

Because I have had your letter and because it is now past midnight and another day, my spirits have given a little leap and caper. But in your next letter, tell me ka-kas as well as temperatures. And your back ached, my sweet, and I was not there to rub it. And never, dare to say that you were ungracious in your sickness; for you have always been my stay and comfort in sickness; or in health. Goodnight, my dearest love, my Valentine, my sweet spouse.

Sylvia

---

1 She shamelessly snuffed out impending presents, and inspected them, so I took this opportunity to tantalise her. It was a writing-master's sampler of 1810, bordered with eight coloured vignette engravings.

1933

Inverness Terrace, W.2, 1 June 1933

My dearest Love,

How carefully I put these sad dates and places of parting.[1] In the time before you one day, one place, seemed as good as another to mope in; but now, on this day so like our love, so blue, so fervent, and yet so living and stirring, and in this room that still echoes with your presence, there is an odd unreality about being alone, and ready to mope. But mope I will not, I do not so easily forget the promises I made with your lips upon mine; and after I have written to you I shall go down into that placid empty kitchen, and sort out the dishes, the glasses, the cooking-pots which however they go, will go with our married estate.

If a bird does not know, when first the impulse to collect straws, sticks, grass-knots, thistledown, moves it, to what end of a nest it gathers, then I, when piece by piece I went on collecting household gear, was like a bird. And often I have supplied myself with the queerest blind reasons. Once, one unhappy day in a cold February, Mr Whiteley's White Sale window showed me a pair of fine linen sheets. I lusted for them. And I told myself how foolish it was to lust for sheets, so despairing of my bed. And then, suddenly, a defiant practical voice said within me – Well, one needs a handsome shroud – and I went in and bought them. But we must have lain in them many times since then, my darling, worn them thin, maybe.

So while I am looking over my cups and platters I shall not mope.

William has gone out to grieve in the garden; he reproached me with

---

1 She had gone to Norfolk about a house which we had fallen in love with and hoped to rent. In any case I should not write many more letters from 113 Inverness Terrace. Oliver and I had sold the remainder of the lease.

wails when I came in alone, and then rushed downstairs to tell his sorrows to the polygonum and the dustbins. The love bird sits staring at me, silenced by the silenced room. Sometimes when a breath of wind stirs in he half-lifts his wing. We must not leave him a widower long, Valentine. He does not say to me – As you are now, so am I; but how well he might.

Now I have chirruped to him; and suddenly, as though he gave me a diamond, his intact clear whistle has answered me. I don't think three days will make an accomplished whistler of me; but they should make a considerable difference. He has gone on from his whistle to a series of most eloquent remarks, and I believe he is assuring me that if I were to teach him to say 'Valentine' he would be pleased to learn.

It is like a change of scenery to him to see me alone. No wonder he has stared so, and has so much to say.

My dearest, my true falcon, at nine o'clock I shall look to hear your voice. There is a telephone poem in the Geraldy book, a long distance call, almost word for word like mine. No wonder. For it is a good love-book, except for its melancholy and fretting. Or I would say, a good love-book, but not to do with marriage. I read the poem last night, while you were in your bath, and meant to tell you of it; but you had better things for me to tell you, when you came upstairs so pale and shining, so sleek and tall and wilful on your long legs, so black-eyed and chafed and scented. You are in me always like the sound of the sea in a shell. And even tonight, when I lie down alone I shall resound with your love, my most loving, my most triumphing, my tenderised and most dear.

Be careful of yourself, of myself, as careful as I shall be. Do not tax yourself too hard, not at all. If you feel ill or tired tomorrow, stay in bed and let the rest rip. A house is so much to us, if we are to live and love in it. But what is any house to me, any world, any wilderness of a lovely world, or the least, rasping-without, sleek-within, beech-mast cap that may fall on our drive, except for you, my light and my gravity?

Care only for yourself, only for all I have.

My love, my dearest most-mated dear, I send you my love.

Sylvia

48: STW

London, 2 June 1933

My Heart,

Last night, after I had finished my letter to you and was just gathering up myself for bed, in came Oliver, with two glasses and a bottle of vermouth, and his flat-headed smile. And a document in his hand. I thought the flatness of head was rather beyond even what the pleasures of comforting warranted, and after the vermouth, he went on to pour out the gratifying fact that Mr Whiteley has estimated the value of our fixtures at sixty-two pounds.

We have been so near a rose, if we had but known it; though it is just to us to say that though we didn't know it was the rose we did think it an exceptionally nice dahlia. In less Oriental imagery, that nice Mr Dobell who came about the books is the son of the Dobell who found and edited Traherne. He loves to talk about it, Oliver says. So either we will go to his shop and ask him exactly how it all happened, and where the MS is, and if it really came off a stall in Farringdon Street; or he might come to 2 when you go through your books.

About the London Library books. Last night, just as I fell asleep, I remembered that one volume of pamphlets had African atrocities which you wanted me to read; and simultaneously I had a vision of a dark blue pamphlet binding in the w.c. of the flat. I don't think I omitted to go through that particular branch of our library when we left Winterton; but I may have done so. So would you just cast our eye around it, in case?

Nothing has come from Horner.[1] I am inclined to be slightly irate, for making every allowance for the tempo of a rural Bart and a family solicitor, I do think we might have heard something after a week's waiting. Unless Sirreginald is away. But you will be discovering all this, so I shall sit patient until you ring me up this evening. Even if they were to reject our kind offer of ten pounds less with contumely (theirs, not ours, of course) they should have done it by now.

I was so lank and lorn in bed last night, and the sound of London going on all round made my solitude so much worse, that I went down to the dining room, undid one of those cardboard archives which I had tied up with such firm care, and got out a collection of your letters. The early ones, written from Dorset in October '30, and during your two visits to

---

1 Horner: solicitor to the gentleman who owned the house we hoped to rent.

Winterton. I read them till two o'clock, and then looked at pictures of you; and when Keatsey walked in at nine this morning I was still asleep. Keatsey intensely voluble and prancing on the highest moral standards, for she had happened to meet Mrs Bowker[1] coming away from here after looking over, and consequently had chanced to overhear what Mrs Bowker was saying about the house, And would you believe it, Miss, Mrs Bowker had actually remarked, during Keatsey's protracted passing (unless she turned round and sleuthed them, which I suspect) that she knew how she'd manage to get round that bath room. Why, they were coming in for all the world as if the only thing they wanted the house for was to turn all my lady's arrangements upside down. And I'd thought her such a nice lady, too, at first sight. No better than a snake. etc. etc.

Short interregnum, during which I got out of pyjamas trousers into a skirt to interview the gas. Such a sweet gas, with pale grey eyes and a very soft voice. Gas is always so much politer than electricity; it is a pity that they can't emphasise this in their advertisements. Now a man has gone past the window in a Top hat (at eleven fifteen), and need I say that he was carrying a light raincoat over one arm?

It is boiling hot, I think of you in your inflexible flannel and wring my hands, my poor darling. I try to look on the bright side of things, and remember what a blessing it is that Lesbians don't have to carry light raincoats too; but this isn't much comfort when I consider your hideous day, Horner and Hospital, and everything, I forbode, in either brisk or sluggish tangles. And the car pouring out rusty tears. From which I imagine her radiator in trouble. O dear, O dear, why did I let you go alone?

It is the heat, I think, which makes the lovebird so merry. He has been chattering incessantly ever since he woke, jetting like a fountain, pouncing about his cage, dandling himself, scampering up and down his millet, the prettiest sight. He has a rapid nightingale trill on one note.

And about nightingales. I must be allowed some reward for my wifely meekness in letting you go to Winterton alone on all this hellish business of muffle and muddle. And what I should like to do would be to invite you to spend a night with me or a couple of nights at that nightingale hotel whose name I can't remember, on the way down to Chaldon. Where we would do nothing. Please let the idea smile to you. I do think it such a very good one. I have always wanted to see that cushiony black wood by night, and lie with you listening to that most amorous music. And poor Keats heard it alone.

1 Mrs Bowker: who had bought 113; my bathroom was a converted coal-cellar.

Only another night, I say to myself; and say it with confidence; for if you can't get back, then willy nilly, I come to you. I am doing everything that I should, I am perfectly well, at this moment I am drinking my elevenses of lager, and I should feel that I am dwelling under your beams of approbation. But that is only a deferred good. You must lighten on me close to. William lies waiting, curled comma-shape, his nose supported by his Lion and Unicorn paws. But he is not asleep, his little piggy eyes open and stare at me, his ears are pricked for your footsteps, your light step, your pretty whistle. He is waiting to run round after his tail, and the bird's wild frolicking rhetoric is only the music that waits for the curtain to go up. And I am wearing my little red heart with its patient pearls, its watchful diamond. I am so prick-eared, so sharpened to a point, that I feel as though you were coming today, as though it were possible that such expectancy could be stretched for another thirty hours.

Meanwhile, there sits Frankfort, that Belle au Bois dormant. If ever a house was got with a price. . . . But it is a beauty, a house like a ripe pear. Even my raging impatience stops foot on that mossy drive, admits sourly and grudgingly that perhaps there is some justification for this absence. But not enough, not nearly enough, while I sit cast out from you, my fair house of joy and bliss. And if, when you come back, you say that Frankfort is lost to us, I shall not even give you breath for a sigh, I shall hold you too close for any sighs but our own.

Sylvia

Narrative 5

But it was not lost to us: on a proviso that we would get the garden back into order, we rented Frankfort Manor for £50 a year. By mid-July we were in.

It was a beautifully proportioned house, with a Dutch gable and a reed-thatch roof – filled with the noise of trees. Valentine found it, exploring inland, but only because her quick eye caught sight of it behind its rampart of trees: backing to have another look, she saw it was to let. It stood in that stretch of Norfolk where the soil is deep and fertile: a soil for oaks and chestnuts to plunge their roots into. We never found time to count all our trees but there must have been nearly a hundred of them. Whoever planted them planted them very well, allowing space for their growth. The house was sheltered by them, but the sun bathed it, and seemed to have ripened it; its small 17th century bricks were tinted with pale ochre, faint rose, like a ripe pear. In front of it was a stretch of soft dense lawn, which had never been mown except with a scythe. Our lease stipulated that this should continue.

'We have a library now,' I wrote to Llewelyn Powys,[1] 'all Valentine's books and mine at last assembled and in order. The rest of the house is also furnished, perfectly to our satisfaction; though when I see strangers looking rather wistfully round the very large hall, it occurs to me that perhaps one horsehair sofa, two chairs, a bust and two guns is not quite all the furniture they would expect.'

The house was extravagantly too large for us — another reason for delighting in it.

Behind it was a corresponding amplitude of out-buildings: a stable with four loose-boxes, a harness room, a coach-house, a wash-house, several sheds, pigsties, and outdoor privy. One of the loose-boxes was heaped with chestnut logs; in another we found a rusty bayonet; and an apricot was trained on the stable wall. A path between trees led to the kitchen garden. At its entrance was a small vinery. The roof was broken, a renegade vine flaunted out from it. A penny note-book, bleached and cobwebbed, recorded the weather, day by day, for the summer of 1887. Beyond the kitchen garden was an orchard and a paddock. In the orchard was a vast leaning pear-tree, its limbs propped on crutches; it bore quantities of blunt-ended cooking pears, their rind dark as obsidian. I looked for it in Evelyn's *Compleat Gard'ner* — it was a tree of that quality. I never identified it, nor have I ever seen another like it.

William, grown old, failed soon after our arrival and had to be given his quietus. Valentine buried him in the paddock. This was my first experience of her capacity as a comforter: grave and encompassing, it had the quality of music. That evening, we played a long game of chess.

It was after William's death that the rough cats declared themselves. There was an indigenous tribe of them, thick-coated, low to the ground, moving with a swift slouching gait. They preyed on rats and birds, ate acorns and sweet chestnuts and grew familiar enough to come as far as the back door for scraps; but held no intercourse with our housecats, though when we domesticated one of the rough kittens it attached itself to me with intense affection.

Throughout the autumn we worked hard and honestly in the kitchen

1 Llewelyn Powys was then extremely ill with tuberculosis. Our letters, written to divert him, were returned after his death.

garden. There was about an acre of it, four square plots with flower-borders smothered in bindweed, two asparagus beds and a fruit wall. When we arrived, the ground was under potatoes. These we sold to a fish and chip shop on the Wroxham Road. The proprietor was amused to see sacks of potatoes delivered by an M.G. Midget. We made jams and conserves and pickles and sold them. We needed every penny we could raise if we were to stay on in this kind paradise where we were so happy, so hard-working, so good. Goodness is like a flower of the locality. We were never again so unimpededly good as we were at Frankfort Manor.

'We have dug up all our potatoes, gathered all our nuts, stored our apples and keeping pears,' I reported to Llewelyn. 'Now to saw and chop wood for the winter, the lantern hanging on a wooden peg, the stable very dusky and enlarged round us, and rustling with rats.' We had stored more than apples and pears. In November The Viking Press published *Whether a Dove or Seagull* (the English edition came out four months later). It opened with a

NOTE TO THE READER

Of the poems in this book fifty-four are by one writer, fifty-five by the other. No single poem is in any way the result of collaboration nor, beyond the fact that it contains the work of two writers, is the book collaborative. The authors believe that by issuing their separate work under one cover the element of contrast thus obtained will add to the pleasure of the reader; by withholding individual attributions they hope that the freshness of anonymity will be preserved. The book, therefore, is both an experiment in the presentation of poetry and a protest against the frame of mind, too common, which judges the poem by the poet, rather than the poet by the poem.

Valentine Ackland
Sylvia Townsend Warner

Since then, I have come to doubt whether Valentine gained or suffered by a joint book. It showed her poems on the printed page – an experience by which one learns and may be stimulated; but on the other hand it carried a sort of cadetship implication (fatally reinforced by an entry in the Chatto and Windus List for 1934: Ackland, Valentine – see Warner, S. T.). Probably, it would have been better to wait till she had sufficient poems to her liking for a book of her own. But at the time, we were pleased, even rather solemnly pleased.

After the turn of the year there was a heavy snowfall. The carpet of snow enlarged the dimensions of the place and gave the trees a new being. Patches of snow were still lying when the snowdrops came up. The house had its back to the north wind's steady rumble and slept the sounder for it; with its thatch roof and attics above, its cellars below, the house was dry and kept a core of warmth. It was a propitious house, and meant us well, we thought. Then, during a dreadful week in March, it became ill-lit, all shadows and obstacles and long cold passages. Our two kittens sickened and died. Out of doors, the rough cats lay dead or dying. It was murrain, killing all the cats in the neighbourhood: people talked of the cattle plague of 1866, which began, they said, among cats and squirrels.

Meep, our silver cypress (cypress is Norfolk for tabby) was a kit; hoping she might escape infection we took her to Winterton. Her spouse, one of the rough cats (I saw the mating), was among the dead but Meep came back in sleek health and gave birth to a litter of grey kittens. We kept three.

The house resumed its character of being propitious. There was a Victorian wire arch over a path in the kitchen garden, and I remember hanging grey kittens among its lolloping pink roses to get them out of my way as I thinned carrots, and thinking as I heard Valentine whistling nearby: 'It would not be possible to know greater happiness.'

It did not occur to me that such happiness might be too good to last.

In April another girl had run away from the lady at Chaldon. Llewelyn had drawn up a petition for an enquiry, had collected village signatures, asked for ours. We signed. He had been prudent, he said, and had consulted a law-minded friend of his who was a J.P. By some inadvertence, the petition had not been marked Confidential, Without Prejudice, etc. . . . , and went to the County authorities under whose licence the lady worked. One morning we had a letter from the lady's solicitors saying we would be sued for libel. We knew so little of the law that we were not much dashed by this till we consulted a solicitor ourselves. He pointed out that the petition, going to the lady's employers without those saving *et ceteras*, threatened her income and livelihood; it was damages, he said, she was after: of the many signatories to the petition she was citing the four of us (the fourth was a farmer) whom money could be got out of. We should need a skilled barrister: he recommended a K.C. We were foolish to agree to that K.C. who would for his dignity's sake require a Junior; but scared by talk about damages and costs, we let ourselves be rushed into an expensive defence (part of this was pique: we disliked the man too much to debate with him).

As the expenses mounted and mounted, we realised that whatever the upshot of the case, it would leave us too impoverished to go on living at Frankfort Manor.

In August we went to Chaldon to talk about the case with Llewelyn. The imperturbable familiar landscape, the landscape of our first love, called us back. Only Grannie Moxon was missing from it. She had died the year before; Miss Green was too small to live in permanently and we should be too poor to build on, but there was an empty house further up the valley, a solitary house with High Chaldon rising behind and the bare downs all around. There and then, we settled on it, and drove back to Frankfort to prepare our departure. At Martinmas we watched the removal van turn into the lane, locked doors behind us, got into the car and drove away.

> Here, where my wishes were, the leaves are lying
> Thinly upon the wet grass of the lawn,
> And the emptied house is creaking its bones and sighing,
> Dark in the evening, autumnal and forlorn.
> Between arrival day and day of leaving
> Time is unmarked; in years I shall not know
> That I came in hope and departed in bitter grieving
> Or whether the trees bore leaves or weight of snow.

1934

Frankfort, Wednesday 11 April 1934

My most dear,
    A brief letter. I saw your train trailing its white hair over the fields. I remembered that we had *not* remembered the flask.

    How foolishly and limply words hang when time is almost spent. I said nothing of love to you, only of care and sadness. But you, my Spring, my sweet May, you know how every breath I take and every movement and all stillness is yours. I am myself, without you, but how poor a thing that is when I think of how we are together.

    Your letter I read outside the Coltishall Great House, by that melancholy fair river. Bless you for it – poor little sad letter. It fitted me well.

    Take heed and care. Know that I love you. That you are mine and must not be given over to anything but to my love, my care and desire. Sweetheart – sleep well, we are never apart. Being in your flesh has made you be in my spirit. I love you always.

Valentine

Hotel Great Central, London, 11 April 1934

Room 333

My dearest, my most endeared,
    My telegram will have told you that I am arrived, and that the

Management knew instantly that I am but Half a Beast.[1] Ah, but such a poor limping half, so hollow and dazed and speechless. And tail-less. And but with half an ear, and that with no cock to it. Only my heart is whole. And that is in Norfolk, more good to me there than here.

Though I incline to think it is providential that I am cast into this most Odd Tank. It is the queerest place, enormous, and replete with all sorts of unexpected necessities, like mats in front of the w.c. seats. With terrifying endless corridors smelling of invisibly fried fish.

My mother is being nice. Terribly depressed, poor thing, by the consciousness of a scab on her nose. It is a horrid scab – right across the bridge. She is seeing the specialist tomorrow. She is rather frightened, and very like a dog that has seen the Bottle. It is a good thing I came, as far as any separation between us can be a good thing. I took her out to the Diner Français and collected a friend of hers to come too. A very nice waiter. Beaujolais, which I must have drunk half the bottle of, omelette Meyerbeer and a sweetbread I wanted to abscond into my drawers[2] and bring back to you.

I unpacked your sweet flowers and they sit beside the bed where I am writing. A nice bed – as single beds go; and everything very suitable and comfortable; but all in this fish-like dream.

I hope you are asleep, my long lorn one. Only I (and I say this baring my teeth with assurance at any others) can know how beautiful you are as you lie asleep. Often, often, for all I am so drowsy a cat, I have roused to look at you – to stare and stare, holding my breath, feeling almost impious to be staring at such beauty lying unguarded by consciousness.

Take care of yourself and do not distemper all day. There is that Apollo[3] . . . may be he is even now fitting an arrow. Walk sometimes into that danger, lie in wait for his wound. If you write a poem, you say, it is as though you lay with me. With all my heart I wish you a poem. Your coming from that bed is my greatest glory.

My love, my love, my love,

Sylvia

---

1 According to the Book of Revelation, the number of the Beast is six hundred and sixty six.
2 As a child, eating in the restaurant of St James's Court where her parents had a service flat, she used this method of conveying cutlet-bones to her Pekinese.
3 Apollo: Phoebus, not the canary.

51: VA

Frankfort Manor, 12 April 1934

Thursday – In the middle of an interminable afternoon

My most Dear –
    You will know soon that I AM COMING. Please God you will be glad
– I have had Wroothie here to lunch – Fish – halibut. Good. And then
rhubarb. Good. And disgusting bad faked cream which Wrooth brought.
The Peake family[1] seem to be congregated in the kitchen which is a
wilderness of white spots. Loathsome and not improved by yellow spots
from Mrs Peake's energetic distempering. But it may look all right later.
    Dyke[2] brought fourteen chrysanthemums (?) and I've planted them.
Willie washed the car and ate lunch here. Irene had to cook for six people
and did so, in a completely dismantled kitchen, without a murmur.
    We have since been distempering. She will not go out. I am taking her
to N. Walsham later on. She is a GOOD girl.
    I did not sleep with her. I slept with Bunny. There was a long
thunderstorm. Tonight I shall sleep lightly, I think – though tomorrow
night I shall not sleep at all – I shall spend hours of impatience. Even more
than now – These hours are bloody and prolonged.
    My darling – I love you more than ever I can tell you, whatever speech
I use, or whatever silence. I can't write now. I am restless and ill at ease.
You draw nearer to me, and I think of nothing but accidents and
punctures and gaskets blowing and evil geniuses and so on – But I got to
you through that ice and that fog. . . .
    I shall not expect to see you at a meal till we are together as we should
be. I shall wait for you –
    Bless you, my sweetheart. Forgive this most evil letter. I wish you
knew what is in my heart for you.

Valentine

P.S.
There is one slight good to be got from this separation, my beloved one,

---

1 Irene was the youngest Peake and our servant.
2 Dyke: our landlord's head gardener. He was sent to oversee our pruning of the orchard, took a
great liking to Valentine and did us many kindnesses – such as this bestowal of his employer's
chrysanthemums.

although it is far-fetched, of course, as goods always are! – The situation with regard to our book. It is easier to write it than to speak it, for we interrupt each other with such passionate denials and affirmations that there is no getting any sense out of it at all. But now I have the chance:

I have sometimes been gloomy about it, because I have been weighted down by a feeling that I should not have started on it at all. That I had injured you by having my poems with yours, and so on and so on. I have thought that the freak-fancy of having two poets in one book (mild frolic though it is!) had perhaps set many of your usual readers against you. And so on and so on.

I have thought that my poems were just the one kind of poems which should not have been put with yours – being not-so-different, and yet quite sub-standard. And so on and so on.

But I am sure of one thing, that I am *far more pleased* than sorry about the book – and – above all other things I am glad that we are together there.

Poems, after all, have always to wait their time. What happens now does not matter at all, except to one's own pride. But it doesn't affect the poems one way or another. I am sure of that. So we can dismiss them there. But that they will go on up for their test together is a thought which gives me intense pleasure. I love it. It is most extraordinarily pleasant to me to think of this child of our love. A neat, tidy, quiet child – but a child of passion and truth, and, I believe, of sturdy life.

That is what I truly feel. The scruples are true, but the satisfaction is far truer. And I love you more passionately and admiringly than you know.

52: STW

Hotel Great Central, London, 12 April 1934

My dearest Love,

I am wholly glad you are coming to London. I shall see you I do not know how many uncounted hours sooner.

Performances on my mother's nose have taken place, and on Saturday I see her off from Paddington at 12 noon. Immediately after this I am yours. We will lunch together and be off.

Tomorrow, Friday, my fixtures are thus. Morning, Dog's Home.[1]

---

1 Battersea Dogs' Home: we felt Irene should have a puppy to play with.

Afternoon, Keatesy (prancing and not to be postponed). Evening, dinner, with my uncle Robert.[1] By a little squeezing I will come to the Orange Cottage about 4.30. But the span from Portobello Road to Montpelier Street being what it is, do not be anxious (or enraged, prythee, sweet heart) if I am a little late.

But joy even among arrangements that you are coming, and that I shall see you tomorrow, even though but for a glance and a sniff at our true leisurely joy.

It is extraordinary – no it isn't, it is perfectly natural – how that joy and our life together makes every other pretexted existence a screeching vulgarity. I feel actually polluted by this day in which my heart has taken no part – as though I had been rolled in old dirty rags and had eaten from dubious dishes. There is nothing so ruthlessly aristocratic as joy . . . and every mattress but one has a peck of peas under it.

Though I have been assured that there are no round woollen puppies at Battersea I still do not despair – and I will do my best to steel myself against an elderly pug with his glazing eyes leaning from his grizzled face. No. It will not do for me to dwell on the vista of that elderly pug. I feel a weakening.

Nora's nose is a hypercallitosis, whatever that means; and will yield to treatment, and come forth again renewed. So that seems all right. However, she is still having a lovely time distributing brave farewells (mixed Barrie and Kipling) to all round. The fat-faced specialist looked singularly taken aback at her dignified thanks at having it broken so kindly when he assured her of a recovery. He reeled and laid a trembling paw on my shoulder – a paw of fellowship, no doubt. However, I deftly melted from under him, and left him reeling on his classical landing.

Like a good rain the thought that you are coming is beginning to penetrate me; and I am sending up green noses and encouraged sprouts, and have no order in my wits, only a centre to my heart again.

I have nothing whatever to recount, except that you are coming tomorrow, and that I am in a rapture; that I love you and am yours; and that I am even now chasing my Tib's tail to make time run faster. I am now going early to bed; and for all your kind wishes for a bad night, it will be – thanks to you – a better night than last night.

It seems so much sooner now, so much sooner that I will not descend out of my sky to check the actual hours and minutes. I thank you for this

1 [Robert Townsend Warner.]

good decision, my dear, which pleases both of us (and the one of us) so well.

Sylvia

Welcome to London!

Narrative 6

In letter 48, trying to track down a missing book from the London Library, I recalled that 'a volume of pamphlets had African atrocities which you wanted me to read' – and which obviously I did not read. This was characteristic. Neither of us had a stomach for such reading. I evaded; she read and compelled herself to comprehend. In November 1933, while I was telling Llewelyn about rats and potatoes she wrote to him:

Have you read the Brown Book of the Nazi Terror? If not, you should read it, and I will lend it to you. Apart from the consideration of my own fate, and others like me, if the Fascist State came to rule us in England, it is a Party I abhor so roundly that I can hardly contain myself when there is any discussion of it. And so many people are discussing them, so seriously and frequently now, that I think perhaps there is a true danger of the madness spreading to England. The book is so horrible that I am under a cloud still, from reading it lately. Though today I should not be, for I feel so well and so contented.

She went on reading and considering. In a day-book among drafts of poems, notes about birds, about the garden ('snowdrops like little princes', immediately revised to 'snowdrops like litter left by crowds') she wrote: After reading these men, Auden, Day Lewis, Spender, I plunged into an argument with myself, striving to find out where I stood, in what I differed from them, how I believe.

It comes out jerkily.

I instinctively dislike the ant-and-bee society.

But such arrangements of mass-society are the only ones that produce results.

It is collective action that I fear. I think we shall find ourselves reduced to being like the ants that walked in an unbroken circle round the rim of the basin, or we should be like them, if ever the *genuine* Bolshevik regime got us. Because we should have agreed to follow each other always, to behave always each like the next one.

All serving.

What? Each other. That gets you nowhere.

Comradeship.

Would cease to exist. As we have ceased to have tails. No use for it.

I once told her the only thing she never doubted was the necessity for doubt. There was no doubt in her abhorrence of Fascism; but she was not one of those tractable persons who, if they reject a party or an opinion, are automatically content with its opposite. Equally, she could not settle down in a cosy, something to be said for both sides Laodicianism. She went on reading and thinking, and I began to read too. Her seriousness made me reconsider the worth of my dislikes. Priests in their gowns, anti-Semitism, the white man who is the black man's burden, warmongers – I had long been sure of them but, beyond a refusal to give money to people who came collecting for missionary societies, my convictions remained unacted desires. Perhaps this was not enough.

For both of us there was one powerful persuasion. The *Times* correspondent had held on like a bulldog in his reporting of the Burning of the Reichstag trial. Whatever one might feel about Communism, whatever holes one might pick in the arguments of its adherents, Dimitrov's resolution and pugnacity and fighting cunning were fact, not theory.

After the move to Chaldon and the libel case (which went against the defendants; the damages were light, the costs heavy) we applied for membership in the Communist Party of Great Britain, were interviewed and accepted.

1935—1939

1935

West Chaldon, 8 April 1935

Monday afternoon 2 o'clock

My darling,

Already time has begun to drag. It was horrible when, passing the farm-house at Nethermoigne I realised that S T I L L your train had not started – that we might have been together for a whole quarter of an hour, and even half that time seems limitless now.

You did not see me as I stayed watching you until you went through that barrier, lugging your suit-case. A beastly brown woman came and blocked me out and when you turned you did not notice the MG's slender nose sticking out beyond her vile hips!

May[1] was gone when I got back. I started in to prepare the stew. I ate a sandwich of turkey and one of cucumber. Now I am boiling the stock and then going to wash-up. May does not make the copper hot.

I am nerving myself to be sympathetic to Ruth's be-parcelled arrival, and to enter into her inevitable pretence of being a Rescue Party, or a faithful St Bernard. I don't feel in the least imaginative.

Except about your mother. I can imagine quite freely about her.

My little Love. Take every heed of yourself, and do not be put upon, neither by bullying or by unexpected kindness or generosity. The 'unexpected' should castrate any burden of gratitude there!

I do so much love you. I cannot write more because of that. The wind blows and Thomas[2] has half-eaten his mouse and everything is beastly and I H A T E housework and the newspaper is full of war and terror and

---

1 May (née Hooper): a young woman who worked for us. She and her husband, Jim Pitman, were our tenants at Miss Green's Cottage.
2 Thomas: our cat, one of the grey Frankfort kittens.

CRASS stupidity. I'm glad that we're linked up with the only sanity there is abroad at present, but I wish we were not so far, so far apart. But don't worry. I am furious, but quite well. Passionately in love, cheated and angry. But loving you for ever.

Valentine

54: STW

Little Zeal, 9 April 1935

My dearest Love,

All day it has rained incessantly; and Nora has talked incessantly all day.

Did you, for Ruth's benefit, listen to the Holy wireless play from St Hilary's, Cornwall? It was the best of its kind I have ever heard; best for crass sancta stupiditas. This I nailed for your pleasure. B.V.M. calling.

'I saved him once. When he was a little child, Joseph and I carried him into a distant land. We had a donkey then!'

Scandal (true, I imagine) about Cyril Martindale. He was sent away from Harrow because his housemaster discovered that every night he had been regaling the little boy who shared his bedroom with stories about the pains of hell and the sufferings of martyrs. The unhappy child was a wreck. No wonder he became a Jesuit. (Faulty construction.)

Before this house is given to the Party we shall need a vacuum cleaner and a van. I have never seen such hordes of everything, a plenitude not only of junk (God alone knows how many fancy china tea-pots) but of use also: three small aluminium ones, in a row, like High mass. But the mattresses. And the blankets. And the plumbing.

It is a pity about the climate. Perhaps it might do for elevated scientists or deep thinkers, whom the party delighted to honour. I daresay Marx might be quite happy here, I don't think he went out much. Of course it would be ideal for any one making a special study of rain.

Your furious letter came here this morning, your rage must have winged it, I have never known a letter get here so quickly before.

I hope to bring back with me the *Pillars of the House*[1] as a loan, some

1 By Charlotte M. Yonge – to read as a change from Dialectical Materialism.

cooking-glass dishes as a gift; and a snapshot album full of young Tibs, if only I can find it, as a theft. One more day and a bit. Nora has made one good sized and one smallish try to keep me over the weekend, but I was adamant. So expect me on Thursday at the Dorchester G.W.R. at 2.55. It only leaves Exeter at 12.12, it must be the one good train there is, a special train for wives returning to husbands, for homecoming cats, their tails streaming out behind them with mental speed, their whiskers twitching, their eyes beady, their paws holding pillars and pyrexes.

Just to write down the dear good train makes me suddenly feel happy and excited, makes me begin to frisk and prance. I could almost believe it was tomorrow. *It will be your tomorrow.* Happy, happy Valentine, whose tomorrow is Thursday. I never notice how much I am pining (I just sink down like a soufflé) until something like writing down the 2.55 at Dorchester stabs me with happiness. At this moment everything between now and then is annihilated. I seem already started, halfway there, looking at the Martinstown wireless masts.

Before the reaction comes on, and tomorrow is only Wednesday, I shall be in bed with my Marsala, keeping my heart up.

My heart . . . You are my heart. Take care, take care. Do not let things be a worry to you, do not do any housework, do not cumber yourself with any arrangements. Keep warm. I wish I could say with the least confidence, keep dry. Keep the right way up, be careful on your ladder.[1]

Ah, my darling, I love you so! Tomorrow I shall wash my hair, the day after tomorrow I arrive in Dorchester by the 2.55. My tenderest love, I see you there, and feel your furious welcome, your pinches and fine bites, the cutting edge of your tenderness, which at my departure was all smooth and velvet-pawed, melancholy and pliable as a willow. The fat woman at the station – she blocked you from me. I thought you had gone.

Curse May Hooper for not being able to warm a copper.

Give my love to Ruth. I hope she is better, and comfortable in her room, and not kept awake by the telephone wires. They must be awful in this wind. Tell her how we cleared the bull from her path. I hope we did. If we didn't – be careful of the bull.

Ah, my darling, how I love you.

Sylvia

1 Her workroom, originally a loft, was only accessible by ladder.

55: STW

West Chaldon, 29 July 1935

My dearest,

I hear you up in your room, tapping away, and I sit here, also tapping at letters 'that ought to be done before I go away' . . . but this is the letter that ought most to be done.

My darling, I do beg and implore of you not to do too much in this hot weather. You are tired, and have jaggers,[1] and next week we must have Julius,[2] for short of a catastrophe like the roof falling off we positively cannot postpone him again. So I beg and implore you to take things easily now, and leave washing-up for May. And do not go out driving without your dark glasses, nor gardening without a hat. Anyhow, don't garden too much. It is a waste of labour while the ground is sunstruck.

And if Ruth talks too much about Brook Street entanglements,[3] turn her off on to something quieting, like slaughtered clergy or malnutrition. For no amount of talk can do any good, and if it works on your guts it can do any amount of harm. And try to drink some fruit juice, and not to eat tins. You could order some black currants, they are cheap now, and make blackcurrant juice. If you are only cooking them for the juice there is no need to snip off their tedious snouts, just boil them and put them through the peaked strainer.

As for the salt and the pepper, you know where they are now.[4] To think that I really went away from Miss Green indefinitely like that . . . the last of my indefinite acts, the last time I behaved as if chance would whisk me anywhere. But since then I have always acted with purpose, always swung on you, my magnetic one. And this exasperating jolt towards Devon is only a jolt, and all the time I shall feel your pull and know I am out of my true aim till I point to you again.

My sweetheart, my ringdove-voiced ringtailed cat, my embraced weasel, my true. Take care of yourself, don't let your melancholy foot fall on an adder, be careful of that gun . . . you forgot to uncock it once when we were out with Tom, be careful with that gun, I say.[5] Walk discreetly on the cement floor. Be wary on your ladder.

1 Indigestion.
2 Julius [Lipton]: Party comrade. He was a tailor-presser in an East End workshop.
3 Family finances.
4 See letter 3.
5 Valentine had leave to shoot rabbits, which were Tom's staple food.

This house, that seems so affable and familiar, suddenly yawns with dangers when I think of you in it without me.

On Friday, I come back. To Dorchester. I am sorry, but to Dorchester. For I don't think I can stand it if I think of you driving further than that alone. You drive like an angel but other people don't. And the roads will be crowded with them and the brakes aren't all that and the steering is slack, and I would rather dawdle peacefully to Dorchester and see your furious pale face (limpeted to the car by trousers) look its sharp greeting at me there.

Your Tib
(rhymes with rib.)

56: STW

Little Zeal, 30 July 1935

My dearest,

Well. I have had your letter, and a very good bath. And some good raspberries. And a heavenly cocktail. And a great deal of encouragement from Janet. Otherwise – dim. Except for the Browns (whose legal name is the Greens.[1] And Greens is exactly the right name for them too, for they are exactly like those vegetable messes, with a rank taste and a watery texture, served up in shapeless slabs on white dishes). They all came after dinner. The old woman, who is nice, and gentle, and erect, and would even have a slightly sub-acid quality if it weren't for piety smearing all. Then the middle one, Green par excellence. I spoke of her to Janet as 'that bellowing fondant'. And I don't think this paranymph, or whatever Jolas would call it, could be improved on for accuracy, except that she is more massive than most fondants. She is *enormous*; with a short thick neck and sow's shoulders, and a jaw which reaches half across the room. Her eyelashes rush out after the jaw, but don't get quite so far. I should think they are sewn on in a fringe: as in the cheaper dolls. And she has a stentorian voice, a laugh like an unmeaning earthquake and an incessant flow of platitudes, couched in languages such as I have never heard equalled. She talks about Whoopee and doodahs (under the doodahs by R. Kipling) and refers to her dead husband as hubby.

1 The Greens: friends of my mother's.

The sprouts are enormous. Jan and I, discussing them, think that they probably loathe her, but are too stunned to know it.

And there we sat in interminable clusters, in a salvo of platitudes, peals of laughter and hubbies. Jan remained like an inscrutable limpet. Every now and then her enormous clear eyes caught mine and rested on me for a moment with an expression of woe unspeakable nobly borne as far too deep for words.

Jan, I may say, is born for intrigue and would make a superb procuress. She is intensely observant, serene, tactful and a ruthless manager. She is being perfectly charming to me, and my opinion of her is rising in bounds.

She is delighted with the garnet brooch which suits her very well. Wore it at dinner and has laid it out beside her bed.

Now to turn to the cheerful topic of Friday trains. I reach Taunton at 12.50 and Yeovil at 3.29. The wait at Taunton I can dissipate with lunch – but if you would like to meet me at Yeovil?

I adore my earrings. And they become me and feel cool and airy, and comfort and support me as though they were a pair of your best, finest most intricate flatteries, permanently fastened to each delighted ear.

Fragment interesting to our Party minds. Nora told me how Hard the gardener spoke to her about another war, and what it would be like. She said to him that she supposed it would be much like the last (explaining to him that she had been well in the middle of that, living just outside London, and so could speak with authority); and added that of course people would join the army just as they had done then, because it would be the right thing to do. To which Hard replied, 'Well, I don't know about that. But I don't think many people from here mean to go.' She, I may say, did not even think this significant enough to be annoyed by it, and went on with her own part in the dialogue – experience, exertions, etc.

Unfortunately, I may not get a chance of a talk with him, since Friday, as you know, is dog's meat day. So I shall only be driven to Brent instead of Exeter. Still, I think Nora ought to make a reliable propagandist for our purposes, since she is so certain to emphasise the point that war is the perquisite of the upper classes.

And now, my darling, I am going to my cold bed to set you an example of being in bed soon after midnight. *Cold bed*. O, horrid dish to set before a Tib.

I love you with all my heart, always.

Sylvia

57: VA

West Chaldon, 30 July 1935

Tuesday Evening

My darling Dear,

I am a bloody bad Communist – I should be doing the N-B,[1] but somehow I can't make it go on. I lay me down to sleep a little this p.m., but the oil man came – Then I went down to the post, in the car, but even that was no saving, for I had to conduct Violet past the biggest dog in the world – The Bitche's bitch. It is spotted and enormous with big pink dugs, millions of them like centipede's legs.

It entertains me to think that perhaps they are being cunning and, having prized open this letter they are copying bits out, to compare with all the known and suspected codes – for we are famous for having many methods of trying to outwit the Police, and yet we somehow never do – But then again, it may be that you and I are not yet well-known enough, and our letters are only opened when they go to Tom.[2] Still – I hope.

It is nearly seven. Time C R A W L S. I have planted out two bucket-fulls of broccoli seed (undoubtedly a code) and corned and watered the hens. Old Doddy[3] has been letting off an enormous gun all round the house, and bellowing to his dogs. No rabbits have suffered as yet. He electrified Violet yesterday by shouting at her down the street 'Hey – hey! I've done a dreadful thing! I've been and shot the Old Man!' But it was only an old paternal hare that he shot in mistake for the hare's own child – the dead one – was so tough, he said, that he could not give it to Violet, it was unfit for human consumption, so he had given it to Miller.

I have only done one page of the N-B. and no more to our morning's job. I don't seem able to concentrate. I've drunken coffee for tea, so to speak, and eaten three cookies, lovely.

Your wire came, thank heaven – Dear Jan, I am glad she was there. I only pray and hope that you had something to eat. I felt a beast later on, when I thought of you scrambling about to buffets and things, and eating buns. Sweet bear – but even bears need something more than buns.

Drink, my little Love, and eat Cat's Tongues, and think of mine – and then sleep well and sweetly, without nightmares, and know that I love you

---

1 A News Bulletin, which she prepared and duplicated for Party Propaganda.
2 Tom Wintringham: a senior Party comrade.
3 Old Doddy: neighbour and semi-squire.

most tenderly and truly – and that I am pining in a more complimentary fashion than you'd believe without seeing it.

The air is busy with aeroplanes, and the valley full of voices. All sounding astir and happy, but Tom and I sit here and miaow to each other and feed respectively on rabbit-and-denny and on strong coffee and cookies.

You'll have to come back soon, or our digestions will be ruined for good.

Gray[1] has sent in his bill. It is awful. We must not get ill again for two years anyway. Thank heaven, doctors need not be paid at once, so we'll keep him waiting (he is rich enough) until my next quarter comes in and I shall not buy any more books at all and no more wine. It is nine pounds nineteen shillings and sixpence. In letters it looks less, I think. But he does know how to charge. For pity's sake don't eat any pips, in case you get appendicitis. And I am being careful not to get jaggers or a cold in my head or mumps. And we won't go to The Hill at all, ever – and only in the van[2] to Winterton if war comes!

But don't worry about this bill, sweetheart. I tell you of it so that it can be absorbed in the general misery of being parted. It is not a pressing one, you see, and Ruth is sure to give me something from the letting of The Hill, which is good of her and good that I know she is generous like that, dependably.

The mice have achieved an extraordinary piece of engineering – They have chewed a hole as big, almost, as my closed fist in the cement wall behind the cake-tin and the vestry![3] I shall leave it till you come back, to admire it, and then fill it up first with poison and then with cement begged from Miller – if he survives the hare.

There – now I've finished my kindness to the Police for today, and finished, alas – writing to you, my dearest little pretty – I cannot put off the N-B. any longer, with Vladimir scowling above my head. So I say goodnight and bid you remember your duty and your vows – be very wary, but be untroubled – Tell me if Gray is a shock to you, *truly*. My shot gun, popped to Doddy, would cover him easily, you see – and I don't believe I'd care a rap if it eased you of even an ant's load of care. Besides, there is only one thing now that penetrates me with worry – and that is apprehension that you may worry and not tell me. For God's sake don't do that to me, beloved.

Valentine
P.S. Thomas has just killed the engineer.

1 Gray: doctor.
2 A small canvas-topped caravan, bought to sleep out in when we had visitors.
3 Store-cupboard – an example of Victorian-Gothic wood-carving.

58: VA

Winterton, 8 December 1935

Sunday

My sweetheart,

This will be practically illegible because my hands are frozen. I got here at 3. Weather wet – then fine – then foggy. Car *appalling*. Bumping like hell. I got the tyres let down (that b. garage had pumped them all up to 40 and some over) but I had literally to hang on with one hand to my torso because I was shaken to bits! I think the springs must be flat. I'll see what I can do about this, but perhaps we'll have to leave it until Farnham.

I thought of you. The sun came out as I crossed Haddiscoe bridge and then St Olaves. The watery landscape was a curious mustard-yellow with elegant stripes of white water. Cotman, as it always is there, but the best I've ever seen.

Here – I was grumpy, as usual but the cats are lovely. Jubil:[1] just like dearest Tom, only still tiny. He is 1½ shades lighter, but all grey and very woolly. Tessa[2] is quite ravishing. Plump and large-headed; dark shadow gold and *brown*. Exquisitely beautiful and very conversable. The baby kitten is hideous and ill-tempered – perfectly solitary and up-standing; lean and ravening. It *roars* if you pick it up. . . . Clara has the sullens but astutely has 'em by the hall radiator.

I'm in my breeches and getting warmer. My cold is dormant BUT – I have a STYE growing in my right eye.

I've not dared to look at my fiddle yet.

Sunday Evening
My sweetheart,

I've collected some Radio Gems for you.

1. Pat McCormick: Jesus Christ is the right type of friend.

2. ,,   ,,   You will notice that we sing in the last verse Praise Him, Praise Him instead of Alleluia.

3. News Bulletin gave details of Hokey-Pokey at Geneva between

---

1 Jubil: Tom's nephew, born in Jubilee year. My suggestion that a later Hill House kitten should be called Abdication was not well received.
2 Tessa, Clara: other Hill House cats.

England and France to make up with Italy; details of further bombing at Dessaye; details of riots in Egypt yesterday and today – with proclamation to students that further meetings will be fired on. Details of a terrific and bloody outbreak of Jew-baiting in Budapest, where barristers, lawyers and students beat up all available Jews and including 'various world-famous Jewish lawyers'.

4. Ruth – in comment at end of news 'There's not much, is there?'

My cold is practically well, although I feel it a little in my back (that's probably the jolting in the car as much as anything) and the stye in my eye I will bathe in cold tea.

The fiddle is ruined. Sides caved in and the whole thing overgrown with seaweedish mildew.

You are not to get a booklet published by Martin Laurence and called '1936' as I've got it for your stocking and you'll adore it.

That is all – except, my lovely Love, that I think of you, solitary and with your face begrimed with ashes, and your hair as wild as a winter bramble-bush and your eyes tiny and bright; wrestling with the Corona and writing carefully in paw instead.

Keep well. Keep going. Keep happy and *faithful* and *true*. And by true I mean careful.

Valentine

It's 77 miles from me to you.[1] I shall start at 9.30.

59: STW

Lavenham, 8 December 1935

Sunday Night

Darling,

I have committed you to a little expert advice. For this evening I was talking to George and Mrs Parker about their garden, and about ours (it all began with the artichokes, which had excited George). And George saying, does Miss Ackland garden? I began to boast of you, saying that

---

1 To Lavenham, where we had been for a short holiday. I was left there to go on with my novel, *Summer Will Show*.

you could dig like a man and prune like an angel. George and Mrs P. simultaneously cried out that you must look at their pear tree and give them your advice. So I said that they could not do better than consult you, and that you particularly excelled at pear trees.

I have a great deal of commiseration on my widowed estate. And offers to sleep in the house if I should feel nervous. And the loan of an electric torch. So do not think of me groping about in the dark.

I have taken up my tent in the dining room. It is the best room to be literary in, and the warmest. Since you went an astonishing quantity of new draughts have sprung up in the lounge, melancholy draughts that snuffle round my legs and remind them that they are solitary legs. I am terribly afraid that this may be the last letter you will get on the Corona and that I shall not have time to learn that its L is where my Remington's K is – a discrepancy which I daresay you have diagnosed. For the spring that moves the rollbar round is sinking fast, and I daren't prod or twist in case I make it worse. I am so sorry. To my knowledge I have done nothing except fold it up into its case before tea and unfold it out after tea, both of which operations seemed to go smoothly enough. But the spring doesn't bite.

I am so sorry. And it is such a nice machine too. I have grown extremely attached to it, and it sits on a cushion like a cat and doesn't rattle at all. I am afraid I may have disconcerted it by trying to put in an envelope, though I didn't persist in trying when I saw it disliked envelopes. It is horrible that I should have damaged anything you lent me, and also I feel rather as if I had damaged an Old Master or Stephenson's Rocket. I am now moving it round by hand, to be on the safe side.

It is queer to be all alone in this house where I have so often been alone. It was here, lying on the lawn one summer evening with the coffee pot that I wrote 'How happy I can be with my love away'.[1] And meant it too. Teague[2] had just gone on one of his interminable tours to Africa, and I had come here feeling that Lavenham was a much better place. And spent all of a hot July day in silence except for topping and tailing some black currants with Mrs Parker and a short conversation with a very aged Salvationist and his donkey whom I found sitting by the roadside while I was out walking with William. It was he who told me of the sweep who broke into the meeting and said to Catherine Booth, What a handsome woman you are! You're a sight for sore eyes. And all the congregation

---

1 Published in 1928 in some weekly or other, where she read it, and speculated about me.
2 [Teague: Percy Buck.]

was horrified and tried to Hush him. But she only said, Sit down and listen. And what you'll hear will please you as much as what you see. And at the end of the meeting the sweep was a converted man.

He sat with his feet in the dry ditch, and his beard wagging, and his faithful donkey browsed around, and they were exactly like Joseph and his donkey having a merciful release from the virgin. And that evening I wrote 'How happy', a poem that I can actually remember writing because it came out like a ribbon and not like worms.

I don't see how you can have any idea how completely you have changed my days. Even I haven't except when some particular set of circumstances like this pricks it into me. It is as if I had always been in a half light, an esquimo existence of perpetual twilight. Carelessly, just now, I said to Mrs Parker, speaking of my arrangements for the evening, that I should be quite happy. 'No, you won't,' she said. 'You won't be happy, so don't you go about to say so. I saw your long face when Miss Ackland was going away.'

Sylvia

60: STW

Lavenham, 9 December 1935

Your letter came by the first post and your telegram soon after. I am sorry it was such an awful drive. I am afraid the tossed torso will be painful today. *And* a stye. Cold tea, or sour milk or a wedding-ring. You must persuade Ruth to take hers off because wedding-ring Knuckle has not the same effect. But I believe cold tea is the best of them.

You are horribly run down or you would not have got this.

I wrote till 1 a.m. last night, and got along quite tolerably though it is only a first draft. And slept well after I got to sleep, though there was an awful Owl just as I turned out the light. It wailed like a baby, a straight-on note with none of those feathering cadences an owl should have.

Your account of Jubilee and Teresa made me feel rather happier for you. How lovely they must look together.

It poured with rain all night, now it is lovely. A clear topaz-coloured morning. And great chrysanthemum puffs of silver bonfires smoke rising from the garden opposite, as though a primitive man were there signalling to me with a wet horse-hide.

Your pyjamas had been put round my bottle by mistake, so I slept in them. As I put them on warm and smelling of you I tried to pretend it was your warmth that I wrapped myself in.

One extraordinary stroke of luck. I wanted a dullish book in case I couldn't sleep, so I took R. L. Stevenson's memoir of Fleeming Jenkin. F.J. was an engineer, and when he was a boy his mother took him to Paris just before the outbreak of the 48 revolution. He has a whole letter describing the volley in the B. des Capucines which set things off. His account – a boy of sixteen with no political views – must be as good testimony as one can have. And it bears out in almost every detail the version of the incident which I decided must be the true one, and followed. Isn't that amazing? . . . my happening on it, I mean, choosing that particular blue and gold back of all others?

I love you with my whole heart. I beg you to take care of yourself as I am taking care of myself. I kiss my locket and my ring and love you, my falcon.

Sylvia

61: STW

Lavenham, 9 December 1935

My dearest Love,

It is late night, a timeless moonlight beyond the windows. I have been writing ever since dinner like an angel; and now I will drink a little glass of my Hollands and sit close to the fire, and write to you like a woman.

This morning I went for a little walk, posted your letter and the parcels, and took the films to Mr Ransom, who was pale and grand, and rolling rather aloofly in some fine frenzy. To my remarks of matte he asked me what degree of matte. I with female tact said I would leave it to him, he would know best. And slid off in a general agreement about the amateurs who prefer glossy. He is not sure that he can get them done by Wednesday, but hopes he will, I hope so too. I daresay his curiosity as to what sort of photographs you take may prod him on to be speedy.

I lunched early and finished off the pheasant; and put its bones and the woodcock's bones and an onion and the remains of the braised celery in a stewpan and left them to simmer on a bead of gas. All the afternoon the smell of stock growing better and better twitted me as I wrote worse and worse, committing a thousand words of mere mud.

After this I went for a walk round and round the church, resolved not to go home till I was in a better frame of mind, and alternatively wondering what you were doing and what Sophia[1] would do. Suddenly I saw a glorious light, and hurried back; and wrote: and had a grand thoughtful dinner of soup – woodcock-guts on toast – ah! and Mrs Parker's peculiar version of Welsh rabbit which is a Swiss rabbit really, a fondue in a little basin.

Since then, as afore-said.

Mrs Parker spent a long time singing me your praises. How handsome you are, and charming. What beautiful hair. And how much thinner you are. She is a good and sensible woman. She contrived to say how much thinner you are without making my blood run cold. This is rare, in fact, I cannot think of anyone else who can do it, but yourself. If I must be left, then Mrs Parker is the woman for me, just as Mrs Hooper is the woman for Tom.

There has been no letter from May, but I hope you may have had one at Winterton.

I am feeling extremely well and look extremely pale and sickly. It is inspiration, that as usual has covered my face with flour and coal-dust. I will try to wash off the coal-dust. I will try to wash off coal-dust at any rate before midday on Wednesday. But if I cannot wash off the livid light of inspiration, remember, when you see me, that it is that. I mention this now providently so that you may be on your guard.

If you have the sullens, I hope you will follow Clara's example and have them by the radiator.

It is past midnight now, so this morning I shall get a letter from you. Now I think I shall walk out and post this. It is a beautiful night – at least as beautiful as any night can be that is an empty one.

I am glad Ruth liked the cat.[2] It is a female, of course; tortoiseshells always are. And from its expression I should say it is a fallen female . . . but one can never tell. It may be a schoolmistress.

My love, I love you, now and always, before and behind. The wind is rising . . . foolish wind!

Sylvia

---

1 [Sophia: heroine of *Summer Will Show*.]
2 A china one, for the sake of variety.

1936

Rat's Barn,[1] 18 January 1936

Saturday

My darling Tib,

I'm all right. It isn't a bad house to type in. The room does not echo. There are one or two curses; the fire smokes abominably, and insists on having the window open A N D a door, if not two. It makes a perpetual cold draught. And the lamp is the very devil. How all the Powyses could eat their food by this light, God only knows. It is too high and too B A D. And, in the gale, candles flare and waste. I think I must have that reflector lamp, which is on the top of your china cupboard, mended. Farrows would do it. And Gabriel.[2]

Night-lights must be remembered, too, please. And there isn't a pig-tail. Maybe Jim[3] would bring one. I gave him 5/- today, which will cover tomorrow's oily journey, perhaps? You might give him a drink when he brings this.

Most fortunately, I found a copy of Montaigne here – Lulu's[4] – and all the best bits marked. I have been reading it with the greatest pleasure. Here is a bit for you: 'Yet those women of our times are not much out, according to their error, who protest they had rather burden their consciences with ten men than one mass.' Which leaves you four more. Or five – if you cavil at counting me.

---

1 *The Left Review* had published some articles of hers about village life. They were well thought of and she was asked to extend them into a book (*Country Conditions*, published 1936). In order to work undistracted, she borrowed Rat's Barn, a solitary cottage on the downs, used by visiting members of the Powys clan.
2 Farrows: the general store in the next village. Gabriel was their van-man.
3 Jim Pitman: who carried our letters etc.
4 Lulu: Llewelyn Powys.

My own most dear Love. I fuss a little about you. That bull, especially. You must be more discreet than you want to be about everything else! And, of all things, remember how more than precious you are to me – How, even here, so near to you, I feel anxious and uneasy and more than half-inclined to walk over – not to see you, but to see that all is well. I love you so very tenderly, my darling. Sleep well, eat well, be happy and industrious and be W I S E .

Valentine

P.S. My darling: The light is so formidably bad that I can't see to work – even using candles (draught blows 'em) so remember Gabriel and the lamp. Candles and handkerchiefs, please!

I have left behind my note book which has all the most important details of this bloody booklet. I think I have. If it did not come up with Katie's things, which I have not yet found. It is open and tousled.

I can't find *any* of the things Katie brought up.

Late evening.
Lovely snow! I went outside for a moment and was gently tickled by flakes. Heavenly and exciting!

Towser' waits patiently at the door to go home! WE could be very happy here – But he is right to pine a little, and to feel it is unnatural. I do now understand why it is so horrible to be unnatural – and also that I have never been so before, except the other times I'm away from you. But this is not so bad as they have been, because I am myself, unmolested by other people, and so I am anyhow a complete half.

Later
I'm playing at Siberia – Send up Krupskaya Vol. I because I want to verify the HARE.

63: VA

Rat's Barn, 21 January 1936

Lenin's Death-Day

---

1 Towser: a springer spaniel.

My own darling and D E A R Tib,

I hope you are all right. You went off in fine sunlight, looking so lovely
and so warm and fresh. You are the only person I know who can look
warm and not frowsty – but only the sweeter for your good warmth – like
new bread, or like fresh-cut hay in the sun. Last night was one of the
happiest we have yet had – and I shall not forget it, ever in my life. I love
you and thank you.

Do not worry a fraction about me. I am well and happy. It is doing me
a great deal of good, being up here – even though it still seems unreal, and
addles my brain a little. But it does my body good and I enjoy it. So long
as the stoats keep off and it doesn't thunder! The sheep are an immense
pleasure to me, and company of almost the nicest sort.

My love, my love. Keep warm and well. Write well (as I can see you
have been doing) and have no fear, for me or for yourself – only be wily,
remembering that *not* all the world loves a lover – the weather doesn't, the
evil ones don't and even a lover feels the cold if she isn't wily enough to
ward it off with rum.

Valentine

Here's a small love-present for you; unassuming, and not fit to carry all it
must.

> More true than tree or fruit
> The truth of the root;
> More keen than any gale,
> More resolute to hold,
> This, pliable and frail,
> Clings rigidly as cold.
>
> Love, rooted deep in us,
> By the gale's toss
> Deeper and deeper thrust;
> However high the tree
> Grows, its roots in dust
> (Our dust) hold steadily.

64: VA

West Chaldon, 14 July 1936

My darling,

Please bear with me, and do not allow my depression of spirit to weigh you down. This is difficult counsel, I know, but it is necessary to us both, although the weight of the burden falls on you, which is not what I would have if I could prevent it.

I believe my main trouble to be unavoidable. I do not think it will ever wholly pass, but I think it may well get better and lighter as time goes on (if it does go on for us). This 'black mood' is mine personally, but it is also part of the shadow which is on us all. Only I have got some kind of a natural tendency to wear my weeds very long and dark and perhaps to wear them far too showily. I will try my best (and I have tried) not to allow myself to exaggerate this mood; and I look to you to try that I shall not infect you.

I have been oppressed by doubts and fears and perfectly vain repinings. God knows what shape they all take, but it varies, and that is good anyhow! I have been filled with gloom at my own failure to reach some far-too-lovely vision of myself. Thirty is not a good age, I think, and I carry a very heavy weight of love for you (which I would not lay down for one moment, which I dread to lose even when I must, which is so dear to me that I could not comprehend even Queenie's[1] childlike delight at the prospect of being eased of life) and this weight makes me feel myself sometimes most bitterly, almost grotesquely, weak (in the sense of being unathletic) in comparison with what I love to carry. I have had for so long such a fine idea of myself (given me partly by hope and partly by other people's kindness) that when I come to look at it now, at my age, I feel as though I must be laughed at for having ever hoped and intended so much.

Our friends recently have not made it any easier. I am far, *far* too easily impressed by their obvious ideas of me. I have even suffered lately from some queer feeling which must, I think, be jealousy of your excellencies compared with my own, especially where you have them and I lack them. And immediately I lose my confidence I fall very far and very swiftly indeed, and each time I hit the ground it knocks me practically senseless. I think this is true and is not exaggerated. It is how I feel.

But I do not E N V Y you, in the sense that I do not (or have not ever

---

1 Queenie: engaged to Julius. They were staying with us.

yet) wished that you should not attain. I think you must know and believe that. I try very hard to serve you whenever and however I can, and I do it because I have a most deep respect for what you can do. For this reason I am often cast down if it appears that I have unwittingly deprived you of time or power to do what you want to do. That is why I lost my temper so deplorably about that wretched piano and music. I felt that I was accused by your genius (Socrates' sense) of keeping a richness from you, and felt that it was not just – I often, lately, feel what is, I think, an imaginary sense of injustice. I know that is sickness, but it is sometimes difficult to remember that one is sick and not perfectly reasonable! Even small things seem able to prick me very much as though I were stabbed to death, until I come to look seriously at the wound, and see the sword was a bodkin after all. The only thing to do is to L O O K at it, and I do, do that. Believe this, my sweetheart, and believe that I love you most passionately, most truly.

Believe, too, that this will pass and I shall be again what I should be to you. I feel very lonely sometimes, or anyhow something like lonely.

I'm very unused, even yet, to not A L W A Y S being in the front of the picture. I am violently arrogant, I think. Or something like it. And I don't know what is going to take its place. But something will. If the simple body can repair itself, and – as I have seen happen – a fine and proud young man have his face smashed, be disfigured, and yet assert himself so that he still looks almost as proudly as he did before – If that can happen the mind can repair itself and carry itself well and with assurance.

I heard what Julius said about my poems, too, and it came at the wrong moment![1] I'm glad I didn't hear what Queenie said. Two kinds of damning are worse than one, anyway! I don't know about poetry yet. I've tried very hard to keep my head above water, and to keep myself able to write if ever I get a chance to. But whether it's worth it is another matter. I have a lot to think about, but at present I can't think very well. As regards going away, we'll have to see about that. But remember that I genuinely misunderstood[2] what you said this morning, and thought you meant that you had been thinking you would be *better able to live* without me, except as an occasional lover – (And even in face of that I didn't think that we might stop loving. I have never thought that, E V E R). I genuinely misunderstood. Forgive me, but don't blame me for that.

1 Julius was Party-pious, and thought poetry should be simple and appealing.
2 We were feeling the strain of too many visitors, and I had spoken wistfully of our peace and quiet when she was at Rat's Barn. It shows how submerged we were in hospitality that she was reduced to writing this, though we were under the same roof.

And don't think of me, even now, my most Dear, as being hopelessly sodden by these storms. I know I am not. I am not even very wet! Don't (for God's sake) think me pitiful, or piteous, or anything disgusting or anything weakly and wet-chicken that would be a betrayal of my most deep love for you, and your deep love for me – In which I earnestly, most tenderly, believe. I love you absolutely. I am not very different from me as you first loved me. I won't get worse. But I want to know, T R U L Y , if you believe me?

Valentine

65: VA

West Chaldon, 2 September 1936

Wednesday, 6 p.m.

My love,

As you knew I should do, I sit down in this stuffy and incomprehensibly noisy room (it is rattling like a skeleton) to write to you almost before doing anything else in my desolate return.[1] I have read your letter and it made me weep – tears nearly related to those I wept beside a thorn bush in the cowslip field, during our first parting – That was a mirror of the last parting,[2] and then, as now, the sight of it made my heart stop.

I don't know what wanton-ness makes me determine to go to this trouble to reach danger; it is not exactly a wanton-ness, you know. It is not a compulsion either, in the superstitious sense of your fears. It is something I dare not define, because if I do I may well exaggerate it into a noble and disinterested reason, which it certainly is not. And anyway, you told me not to worry my head over these analyses, so I won't. But I want to clear myself from any accusation of your heart or mine that I am *senselessly* endangering our happiness. I don't think it is senseless.

When I came back I found Towser out, the back door open, the T W O bolts shot as though they were still holding the door shut. I experimented, and the door would not shut with them so, and would not, by any means,

1 From seeing me off to London, where I would join a delegation to a Peace Congress in Brussels.
2 She was bent on going to Spain – if possible, as a combatant. At the beginning of the Civil War the Loyalist forces included women fighters.

open when I had shut and bolted it again . . . It makes a pretty mystery.

I have shut up Towser again, to think it over. But my heart misgives me; I think he is, in this case, guiltless!

Tom has been in and had milk and meat. He is sweet but distant and melancholy. But so am I. So we are well matched. I cherish him for you and for me, because we D O dote!

Your letter was the most tender you have ever written me, and I know just how much that means. I love you most dearly, most deeply for it, and thank you, my sweetheart. And for the books and MS. I am saving that for this desolate night in that comfortless bed, which has hardly ever been comfortless before.

Love, and Love and Love – be wary and wise and remember me.

Always remember that no two people have ever loved *more* than we – but that many many, in Spain too – have loved as much – It is as well to remember that.

Valentine

66: VA

West Chaldon, 4 September 1936

Thursday Afternoon

My darling,

Your telegram has just come through, and although I have grave doubts as to the accuracy of the address, I am hopefully sending this letter to you.

I feel really very deeply jealous of Julius! It made me first of all very relieved, and then I felt a fury that he should be with you and I not, and I remembered how you always praise him for being so comforting and comfortable, and thought 'Aha! She would not think that about *me* if I were there!' and that sent me into a worse fury, and all my subsequent furies were mingled with the pleasure of knowing that you had a friend there whom you could rely upon and enjoy! So you see –

My mother has been here and is RETURNING! She has got the excuses of not liking me to be alone here at night when doors mysteriously open, and as luck would have it a stranger arrived to ask the way to somewhere lateish last evening, confirming her suspicions that this house is Not Safe! Also, if I argue at all, she weeps and says How Little Longer She May Have to Enjoy me . . . and when, goaded beyond politeness, I retorted that maybe I had very little longer to enjoy MYSELF, she at once wanged in with 'But you know I leave you alone – truly I will – I won't be any trouble – We needn't speak a word –' et patati et patata, and so there we are.

I read with disdain and dislike the N-C[1] reports of your Congress. They seem to have assented to the most absurd terms for restricting free discussion. *The Week* has an interesting paragraph on that, but you must wait to see it.

I heard from H.[2] today! Saying he thought you and I were fine workers and that he had spoken to the Unit ('Various people') and hoped I'd get taken on. Is he a liar?? I hope not, especially after having maintained his virtues to Ruth until 1.30 a.m. . . . A wild argument on the British Empire. Terrifically funny and infuriating. I had a good idea about staging a really exciting street meeting: get TWO speakers, one to impersonate Ruth's point-of-view, and dish up the ordinary dialogue used by her kind, and one to answer it as I do or Julius would or Tom would or Queenie would or TIB WOULD! The crowd would see a free show, and the bourgeois speaker could be masked, (how funnily my machine spelt that!) to give an added sense of pantomime . . . It's a good idea, if only you see it!

A.A. sent me their Continental Road Book which tells me that my distance will be, approximately, 850 miles. That is very small indeed. One snag is that I shall have to have a rear light fixed on the left, instead of the right side. I shall see about that.

I am so thankful that you so goodly took my macintosh. It is pouring with terrific rain and you would have got wet through. My roof is leaking already.

Tom is well; he did not sleep with me because he hated Ruth for yelling in his sensitive ear. He came up and had breakfast, however, and then stalked up the bed and sat on my shoulder and purred. He is rather miserable. He mieouwwwwws most of the time and looks for you. Towser is under the weather too.

Ruth brought the teaset and towel horse and a box of fine feathers for

---

1 *News Chronicle*, a Lib-Lab newspaper.
2 H.: Harry Pollitt, Party Secretary, to whom she had written about getting to Spain with the Medical Unit – a second-string expedient. A fortnight later I wrote to Alyse: 'I don't know exactly where we shall be on Monday – it never does to dogmatise where a car is concerned – but we shall not be able to walk up to Chydyok at half-past four or quarter to five. We are starting today for Barcelona. The Red Cross unit there wants supernumeraries for its office work, and we have been asked to go.'

you and the tool chest. The latter contained some fine things and provoked a very funny piece of dialogue: 'It is pre-Reformation. A bible-chest. That proves it is pre-Reformation –' Me: 'Why?' 'Oh – well, you see, it is fourteen hundred, or earlier –' Me: 'That is certainly pre-Reformation! because – well, you see, it stands to reason . . .'

I have packed my sack, and got everything in easily, with room for a few bits of your stuff.

No letters for you at all.

I paid A.A. the actual fees for papers etc. It was just £3 all told, including badge. May is making me a red-cross pennant. All this makes me childishly believe that I may go. A discussion with Ruth makes me perfectly clear-headed on the issues involved, and makes me persuaded beyond doubt that we should go. Not you, because you have a definite value, but for people of our class and of my sort of indecisive qualifications, the more the better – if only to shake the Ruths. And I T DOES SHAKE THEM! And I haven't yet turned on even a dribble of heroics! I played her the record we got, and it TERRIFIED her! Tell Julius that, it'll interest him. She got white and frightened and said it sounded HORRIBLE, most threatening, and why MUST we threaten!

She *liked* your note!

My dear – my darling Tib. I am too desolate to write to you as I should and would. Forgive me for this silly letter. You know how it is. . . . Be happy, but for pity's sake don't be too happy!

Valentine

P.S. Title of book by Ruth's bedside: *An Easy Method of Mental Prayer*.

67: STW

London, 19 November 1936

Bourne and Hollingsworth. Customers' Lounge.

Darling,

Your coat has gone to Chaldon, I – with much comfort – am once more an antelope. AND I have dared all and got you a hat. If you don't like it – tant pis! But (what an expressive fatalistic blot!) I saw it on a stand, black felt, flat at the back, high in the head and with a peak made of what appears to be shiny straw and really shiny plaited cord: jockey shape that, I know, suits you. It is being shrunk to your measure. It is small anyhow, I had some difficulty in persuading the damsel that any head could be smaller.

It is 2.5. I cannot tell you how cold I was, sitting beside your empty place at Bertorelli's. Love is a central heating, the moment you go the temperature falls. What a horrible departure! I *hated* the remains of the vin rosé, and the dregs of the coffee came straight from the lake of Sodom, and were ashes. Now I am already up to the knuckles in ink and in a morass of settled gloom. Take care of myself? My God, I am dreary, there is nothing else to do. Be assured that I will.

A German Jew is talking in Jewish German just behind me to a stout melancholy all-in-black wife. I remember our dear Austrians, and think how much better to be in a foreign land *à deux* than in one's own inhospitable country *à une*. Love is the only real patriation, and without one's dear one sits in a dreary and boring exile.

After posting this I shall take a bus to Woolworths and buy Christmas shrouds. I am in *exactly* the right frame of mind to contemplate Christmas. Then I shall have tea at Bea's,[1] and then go back to 32 to read the Anarchists. Then Oliver, then bed in your pyjamas. How odd to think that A.V. (*ante* Valentine) this would have seemed a tolerable, a well-filled day!

You may view R.[2] as objectively as you please, but she is a really valuable conquest, you can congratulate yourself on one of the best jobs you have done for the Party. To us her résumé of what she said on Tuesday may not be very convincing. But to the people to whom she spoke it was, you may be sure, extremely impressive. Please nourish this fire you have lit. I have an impression that R. may be a most valuable skirmisher on our right wing. Especially, did you note the grand and airy manner in which she spoke of 'Westminster being in such a state'? If you can get R. to talk like this, and in this airy accent, of Westminster, you have trained an Anglo-Cat battery in the right direction.

How strange that I sit in the bosom of B.H. writing you love and

---

1 Bea Lubbock [née Howe]: a London friend.
2 Ruth was in demand as a speaker at Anglo-Catholic functions. Now she began to mix politics with piety, and spoke out loud and bold against Hitler's persecution of the Jews, and assailed Bishops. This letter from Bishop Pollock, of Norwich, shows what she was up against. 'Thank you so much for your letter. Truly it is a shocking business in Germany. But I see in today's paper that the Archbishop has it in hand. And that is much better than any tiny interposition on my part. The only Bishop it might be worth while for you to write to, is the Bishop of Chichester who is the authority on these German subjects. Yours affly B.N.'

sedition. It just shows how, the moment we are apart, necessity compels desperate and unnatural situations. I love you with all my heart. You could never guess, from our tongue-tied parting, how much I love you. Do not be led into paths of sickness. Do not let your digestion be upset with talks of money. WE HAVE PLENTY. There is no need to fret, let the waves dash however wildly. Do not start on Saturday if there is a fog, or a bad forecast from the wireless. Trains run on rails, I can reach you by train however foggy it may be. Let your love be, for once, a BRAKE on your actions. Do not fall into the well under the lilacs, do not tempt fortune on the Snake piece of the road, however tempting it may be to corner the snakes at 40.[1] Remember how much I love you.

Sylvia

68: VA

London, 24 November 1936

My true Love,
   Most dear, most beloved – most lovely and lonely and stern-hearted tender one.
   I don't know what to say.[2] I can't yet endure to read your letter. I feel faint-hearted and childishly homesick and dare not even see your writing yet. 'Dick'[3] was in his black hat. He meant to be awfully nice, and was 'Up Guards, and at 'em!' which I hate. He praised my book, even – but he was ADAMANT about my going. T'other one (who was coming to stay with us) was really nicer, but he too was adamant. I don't think there's any chance of avoiding it. I would though, for I don't really think *my* presence at all necessary. There's to be a Frenchman for the journey across.[4] But letters are apparently very vital, tho' I've seen them and they could really go with any one. However: it does seem fairly clear, even to my reluctance-clouded eyes, that if I am told to go I *ought* to go. I have most

1 A series of sharp bends at close intervals.
2 A telephone call from Party Headquarters that morning summoned her to go there with what she would need for a journey – part of which would be cold. This plainly meant, over the Pyrenees. She was fending-off an attack of colitis but she started at once.
3 Dick: Harry Pollitt.
4 Across France, a neutral country which might question the two loaded lorries she was to conduct to the fighting line.

seriously presented to them what I really believe to be my INCOMPETENCE on this job. But they pay no heed at all. Dick said: 'By Christ! you *are* going.' And t'other said, later, 'We've made out all the papers in your name. Can't change now.'

Tom is said to be on his way back. If he arrives, I shan't be allowed to return, I think, but will be used either at A or V.[1] as something or other. In any case, the plans are naturally vague round about there.

I've told you all I know. I tried (and it seemed to me t'other tried too) to get you included – but Dick slammed off and would not even consider it. In one half of me I am glad, my Heart – for I think it would be so frightful a burden on my heart if you came. That is pure selfishness and very miserable, for it doesn't *comfort* me a bit. I have a leaden weight on me now, knowing your *load* of care. *I* could not endure it, but you M U S T try to. You *must*, all day and all night, you M U S T keep watch and ward over my dearest, my most unbearably precious treasure. If you feel ill, don't dismiss it as 'worry' but see Gray. For God's sake do this. I sweat with terror when I think of you ill, I can't endure the anguish it gives me. *Tib – my own love, be true to me in this, above all things.*

I am already a traitor. I love you far more than anything else. My whole heart stretches till it fills my body. I die when I think of you sick. Dear Heart, my True – be true.

And so, in all this, I haven't said a word of courage or comfort. Forgive me all I have ever left undone or done ill to you. My love for you has never, never diminished, never dimmed. Our dear love is the strongest, most loving of all life. I am inside you at this moment, as I sit in this comfortless bedroom alone, as you sit alone in our house. I am within you and around you every hour of the long, long hours, my Sweetheart. Remember me as I make love to you, as I strive to nourish and cherish you. Remember me always and forever as your lover, as the husband of your lovely body and your true heart and your intensely dear, beloved burrowing dark head.

Strive with yourself not to fret, don't let it get you down. Don't get ill and pine and dwindle. Eat and drink, be warm, be wary, nourish yourself because in that you nourish me. By *far* my greatest danger is that any ill should come to you. For pity's sake, remember that. For love's sake, my Sweetheart.

---

1 Almeria or Valencia. Entries in her pocket diary tell the rest. '24th to London. Telephoned for by W. 6pm at 16. To go out with two lorries. Nat only wounded. 25th Saw W. Shopped. Sick. Temp 103 at 2.30. Threw up job. 26th Saw lorries off. Sylvia CAME.'

I can't go on. But oh my God – I love you.

Valentine

I swear I'll take care, *all the time – do you.*

69: STW

West Chaldon, 25 November 1936

My dearest Love,

I feel tongue-tied with misery, anxiety, and exasperation. Chiefly exasperation, for this is a wicked piece of mismanagement, and it seems to me that this little helmet is the only practical step that any one is taking to keep you alive on the journey.

Take, if you can, the waterproof rug from the car, to wrap over your lap. The engine may keep your feet warm, indeed, with such a run will likely boil them; but if it snows, and the snow drives in, you will have a lapful of puddle, and be chilled through your middle.

Do not neglect my two ideas. The cap will go in your pocket, it is far more practical than a beret, and looks efficient and sensible; and the rug can go over your arm, or be fitted in anywhere, but best over your lap when you are not driving, if by any chance there is another relay driver found, or when you are relaying.

Please attend to me. I have often made very sensible suggestions, which we have been glad of afterwards (I am too distracted to call any instance to mind, but I know there have been such!) and these too are sensible suggestions.

Give the sensible man my name and telephone number, and tell him to wire me at once, and fully, if you get ill. He will not hate the idea of some one else to take the responsibility of an illness.

If your colitis comes on, please please try to stay on this side of the French frontier, again for a practical motive, because it will be quicker to reach you, and there is more likelihood of someone to look after you properly in a language you know.

How I can write these things and keep my reason I don't know. Because of the amiable liability of letters being read I will leave this sheet for you to tear up before you leave London, and go on to another one.

Poor Towzer feels it so much that he had to sleep in my room last night. He walked upstairs looking the picture of pine, but had a moment of revival when with a yell of joy he leaped on the bed and settled down in the middle of it. However, he slept on the floor.

May is very sympathetic, kind and concerned. I have sworn her to secrecy while I may to fend off enquiries and sympathies. She asked me to send you her love and her best wishes.

I promise to be careful and take care of myself. I shall work as much as I can, dig myself in as a machine that needs to be oiled. Do not worry about me, my dearest love, you will have plenty to worry about without thinking if a Tib has sneezed beside her fire. Tib must try to model herself on Thomas, will, as far as demeanour goes. I wish I could bring in a rat though, as he did yesterday, I feel a little ratting and mousing might mend my spirits.

I am perfectly well, no cold at all, it is almost disgusting how mechanically one's body plods on. I wish and pray that yours may too. Do take what care you can of yourself, do look at yourself objectively, and see when you are straining endurance beyond reason.

If love could do it, you should not be cold, even on the worst of the Pyrenees. It is astonishing what love can do. It can even make me prepare to endure this. I wear your ring. I looked at it this morning, and suddenly realised how beautiful it is. I simply had not seen it as a ring before. It is most beautiful, with its crimson drop of steadfast blood between the two faithful meditative pearls. It is so like you that I wear it on my finger, next to my wedding ring.

O my love, I know you take me with you, but I implore you and command you, when you think of me, think of me merry and contented, think of me happy as you have made me, think of me true and unvexed, think of me, even now, still brimful of all our happiness and security, though this turn of the world has turmoiled my clear content.

Putting by the reservation of my anxiety that you will attempt to endure more than you can endure, I trust you with my whole heart, as I love you. All the time you are away you will lighten upon me, there will not be a moment when I shall not be comforted because of you, because of our love for each other.

Always your true,

Tib

1937

In July 1937 the International Congress of Writers was held in Spain. This had been planned before the outbreak of the Civil War, but the Spanish Government stood by the invitation. We went as part of a depressingly puny and undistinguished British Delegation. Madrid was under siege, but the road from Valencia was still open and the main part of the Congress was held in Madrid. Much of the fighting was so near that people dusty from the battlefield came to address us. It was a proud affair. Those who attended were whole-heartedly engaged, from veterans of the fight against Fascism to the shining young, newly-married pair of poets from Argentina. Almost every one had hazarded something to be there (the British delegates forfeited their passports, a minor loss). We were sleepless, scorched, dusty and perpetually thirsty – I remember Pablo Neruda giving Valentine a lemon (very little fruit got into the city) and the fraternity in the giving and the accepting.

Endangered is too strong a word; but we lived at risk, reminded by shattered glass and destroyed buildings, a sort of curfew bombardment every evening (the Fascists had not much artillery, either), sudden rat-tat-tat of machine-gunning overhead, the thump, like some grotesque game, of a bomb. People in the streets, waiting in bread-lines, sitting in cafés, would turn their faces toward the sound and watch for the cloud of dust to billow into the sky. The Congress was admirably and humanely organised – by humanely, I mean there was no herding or dictation; we were looked after but never supervised. The delegates responded by being easy and concurring; and though the language difficulty inevitably drew them into bunches, with one exception they did not stiffen into cliques (the exception was the Soviet delegation who were invariably cleaner and better equipped than the rest of us, kept themselves to themselves and were ludicrously like the traditional British Raj).

Though there were so many of us, there was no sense of being in a crowd. It was a multitude of extreme individualities, sharing a common intention, a common hope. I remember the solemn incommunicable goodwill of the delegate from Iceland, the stately politeness of the Portuguese delegate inviting us to visit him in his native country when he was no longer an exile from it, the Chinese delegate, very young, smooth as porcelain, who at the noise of an aerial combat overhead, seized my arm, cried out in an ecstasy, 'C'est la guerre!' and tore up to the roof to see it better; I remember the affinity of mind which grouped the many exiles into a sort of internationality. Above all, I remember the hospitality of the Spanish people, the labourers isolated in the vast stony fields who reared up to wave and salute as we drove in cavalcade towards Madrid, the mechanic who changed a tire and, having nothing but courtesy to offer, pulled a walnut off a wayside tree and broke it in half to save me staining my hands, the crowds which gathered in towns and villages, the feasts they gave us out of their hunger, and the shouts of *Viva les Intelectuelles* (strange sentiment to English ears – and I have tried to justify that esteem ever since).

One never knows when a thing won't turn out to be useful. Valentine's 'finished in Paris' poise and unaffectedness eased some awkward moments of national incompatibilities and established her as a person to turn to – apart from her height: 'Meet at the tall English-woman.' The group of exiles, grave and sophisticated, accepted her as though she were one of themselves. After the years at Chaldon and the rather parochial outlook of our Party visitors she revived among these new acquaintances. The Valentine of letter 64 was cancelled; Madrid replaced her in herself. Some part of her, though, needed no replacing. Madrid was an eloquent experience but she never allowed it to become rhetorical. One day a group of delegates was taken to visit the front line in the Guadarramas. It was a quiet section and the hour of *siesta*. Even so, we were told to scatter and walk low to the ground while we were on the skyline. I remarked that if I drew a good shot it might have propaganda value in the English press. 'More waste,' said she. 'They'd not report it.'

A few days after our return we saw an advertisement in a local paper of a house to rent – a house by a river. We went to look at it. A month later, we moved there. For our house on the slope of High Chaldon had defeated us.

It had the outlook of a castle, it faced the south and winds smelling of the sea; we stepped out of it on to the untrammelled solitude of the downs. But it had no lighting, no sanitation, no damp-course, and eight dead rats were dredged from its well. There was no hope of bettering this; the farmer from whom we rented it was himself a tenant of the local land-owner.

Either party said repairs were the responsibility of the other, and our lawsuit had left us too impoverished to act ourselves. For the first two years we lived at full stretch and light-heartedly, admiring each other's devices, damning rural landlordism and sometimes remembering to boil our drinking water. I don't know whether it was the well or the damp (after wet weather the walls we had distempered so prettily ran with moisture), but as time went on we had a great many colds and stomach upsets. Our books, our clothes, all our belongings, were mildewing and deteriorating. So were we. Admitting that what we craved for was a little bourgeois comfort, we moved to the house by the river. Only for a while, we thought.

*

70: STW

Frome Vauchurch, 30 September 1937

My dearest Love,

I will say it for the pleasure of saying it, I will not rush at you bald-headed and sans cérémonie like Wobson[1]. My dearest Love, I repeat, it is queer to come back to this house for the first time, so to say, to find it so strange and yet ours. But it is a nice house to come back to, the river flows low-voiced and dusky under a sky of faint cloud and pale stars, and I can hare upstairs and send you my telegram, and find your letters on my pillow, and everywhere about the house signs of your love and care for me. Yes, I found the kitchen door barred, opened it to get a tray of crockery, and barred it again.

Thomas is deeply pained to see me alone; almost woundingly so. He insisted on going out, in order to see why you were so long in the garage; then he flounced in with a bang that made me think, Well, it's a large round burglar this time; he has demanded you with piercing mews, and not even the foie gras which he has supped off with me has consoled him. He roars and purrs – and then breaks off to search with mews.

Well now, my afternoon.[2] Amabel, Day L., Anand, Rose, Goronwy

---

1 'Wobson' [Geoffrey Webb] was an acquaintance who disdained such formalities of letter-writing as 'my dear so-and-so'.
2 A meeting to set up a committee of Left-minded writers. Present were Amabel Williams-Ellis, Cecil Day Lewis, Mulk Raj Anand, Rose Macaulay, Montague Slater.

Rhys[1] whom I supposed was a female but he's a rather foolish-faced young man with a lot of black curls and a turned-up nose, Calder Marshall, who is small and pale and hideous, and dear Montague. You can have Cecil if I can have Montague. He gave me the sweetest glance at parting, a rapid glance such as is exchanged by foxes. I am convinced that Montague is constantly playing at conspirators in shrubberies, with a hoarded guarded secret delight. Yes, I am to be secretary. And Amabel produced three addresses which may be useful, and everybody else just produced blessings, except Rose, who having dragged herself to second D.L.'s proposal, could do no more, and produced crabbings. However I bore them like a saint, and then got in one blameless prod at the end of my sufferings. For she had been going on like a vinegar barrel with a leaky tap about how one must be more cultural and less political, and say what was being done for culture on both sides. Lewis twitched her off that, but presently she went back to it again, and I said that it certainly showed how ignorant we all were in this country about Spanish culture that I, for myself, had not read or heard of any recent cultural developments on the right except that they had burned the works of Charles Dickens. Rose returned with a new thorn, saying grandly how extraordinary it was that people could never grasp the literature and culture of other nationalities. In her best Cambridge manner. So Tib, with a demure sigh, said, Yes indeed, how few of us would be able to know which Spanish books to burn and which not. And after that Rose chewed her paws for quite a while, and only returned to the attack when the agenda went on to school text-books, when she bit Lewis for a while. Any one could tell that woman was a total pacifist.

Well, they were still at it when I had to leave for SR.[2] And there he was, sitting in the corner of a perfectly deserted tea-shop à la Russe, ballets and samovars and Poloviestskis all round, and one stout waiter in another corner. He is middle-aged I suppose, or else he is just young and seamed with vice. He is small, with blue eyes and ashblond hair and an old ivory complexion, and a neat little brown paper parcel, and short, shorter than me. His voice is like embattled mice, small and shrill, I daresay it could be loud and shrill. He looks as though you could knock him down with a feather, and obviously has a most fiery and passionate temper. And he is the velvetiest pansy I have met in years.

We instantly coagulated, and had a lovely time, partly buttering each other, partly finding how simultaneously we felt about anarchists, partly

1 [Goronwy Rees].
2 SR: Stanley Robinson, a Hispaniolist.

deploring the vagaries of poor dear Stephen.[1] SR sent Stephen first to Spain, with all the introductions; and felt it acutely when Stephen returned telling him all about his (SR's) dear old friends under the guise of SS's dear old friends. 'Although he can't pronounce any of their names,' he added with plaintive venom.

All the really interesting things he said I will keep till I can tell you.

Then I went to Paddington, and caught a most curious train, that stopped about seventeen times and, except for Yeovil, all the stations were like Maiden Newton. It was like three and a half hours of a suburban train, curiously snug and dowdy. And when I got out here (tell Janet) I was instantly asked if I wanted to go to Bridport. I have never known a junction with such an obsession about being a junction.

Tell Janet also that I hope she is very happy and that I send her my love.

And you, my dearest, I hope you are being very happy, and gathering the sweetest pink china roses of that well-grown young bush, and enjoying yourself and your powers. I was thinking, this is the first time we have been parted when I have not been grieving to myself at your being happy, not shaking my head and thinking, now she mopes, now she pines, now she nips the hands that would feed her. And it is much nicer, I do assure you, to think of you being happy. And I look forward to admiring the white goose[2] when you return.

Lovelace, yes. But I cannot see you as Abelard. But then I do not like Abelard, I cannot stomach those cross hectoring mortify-the-fleshing letters he wrote from the Paraclete. No, no, I cannot see you in any kind of holy clothing. But I am sure that if one knew the Chinese lyrics better one could find you there. And Murasaki had more than a premonition of you, my handsome, my odorous, my conquering one. But how very silly to waste time comparing you with other people, trying you out even in Sappho's tire, when I can think of you as you, and never come to an end of loving and admiring and delighting. No, I will drink no mixed wine, won't adulterate you with any idling over comparisons.

It makes me so happy that you don't doubt my truth when I say to you, Be happy, gather your roses. I am, indeed, most true in this: at any rate, in the present instance. My truth compels me to admit that I might not always be the same. But even if I were jealous I think my jealousy would be always of a critical kind, and I would be possessive because of you and

1 Stephen Spender.
2 One of my names for her was Reynardine.

not because of myself. It is the base practical characters like mine which have these natural mitigating streaks of magnanimity, you will see exactly the same sort of thing in Janet, may be it is something to do with absence of conscience, for I have an idea that conscience impedes quite as many merits as faults, is a sort of alloy, a nickel which may prevent silver from bending but also prevents it from shining.

My heart's honey, don't for a moment worry about me. I have promised to take care of myself, and to let you know if the smallest thing goes wrong. And my bewasped hand is now perfectly all right, hard and thin and limber as ever, the only thing about it to even recall the wasp is a small fleck of sticking-plaster which I am too obedient to scratch off.

And now duly, since it is midnight, I am going to bed with Thos and a hot bottle, and your letter to lie under my pillow.

Tib

71: STW

Frome Vauchurch, 6 October 1937

My dearest Love,

I hear you upstairs, talking to Jan; and in my head rings that Brahms tune, alternatively so wheedling and so rough with love; and tomorrow you go;[1] and I cannot credit it.

I will look after myself, I promise and vow. Do not worry about that. But you. . . . Be even one half as careful as I will be. Be as careful. Be twice as careful, and even that won't suffice my fuss and care and anxiety and love.

Write to me often, I live by your letters. Write to me truly. I don't think I am clever enough to read between lines, or if I think I must, then I read volumes. Write to me truly. Tell me how you are, what your bed is like (I mean, what the mattress is like, the unembalmed mattress). What you are wearing, the colour of your eyes. Tell me the compliments you have, they please me better than they please you, though they may please you too. Tell me what is unpleasant, uncomfortable, annoying, for I shall imagine it anyhow, I would much rather you told me. The best thing you

---

1 To Tythrop House, near Thame, about to be opened by the Basque Children's Committee as a home for the children who had been got away from Bilbao. Janet was going with her; later, I went too and cooked.

can tell me in any letter is the date, for each date will bring you nearer back. Tell me the date, the hour, whether you are sitting in a straight or a curly chair, whether your window faces east or west.

This exile of yours among the exile of these unhappy children goes through me like a complicated arrow. The more sure I am, how I shall miss you, the more surely I see how you ought to be there. For on you, at any rate, I rely to tell the worst.[1] But most of all, you are so far more than duty to me – tell me of how you are, and tell me you take care.

My love, my handsome.

Sylvia

72: STW

In the train, 29 October 1937

My dearest Love,

I have a nice carriage all to myself, and there is Mr Gee's White Horse,[2] and I have just passed a colony of the happiest moorfowl imaginable. There was a large pond, with a rubbish-dump along its margin, and some of them were in the pond, and some were frisking over the rubbish, and all were in a paradise of contentment. In fact, they were behaving much as we should if we found a moated junk-shop.

No – your imagination runs away with you. I have no intention, no intention at all, of lying with anybody. I have always had a natural talent for faithfulness, at one time it was thwarted by circumstances, but from the moment I got into bed beside you, I have never wanted any other bed, my love, my darling.

There is a poor dog in the train, and at every stop it rouses up and yells. That is how I feel . . . resignedly acquiescent while the train carries me, but at each stop I begin to yell and think: if I got out here and crossed over to the other platform?

Your sweet letter, your dear letter. It shall stay with me all the time and all its commandments be observed. I will sleep, eat, observe, go to Grape St. – and think of you lovingly, my darling, my love.

1 There was a rumour that one of the helpers at Tythrop House was a Franco agent. If so, he was a mild one, and the children came to no harm from him. Their favourite game was playing at air-raids.
2 It was scraped clean and re-cut by an eighteenth-century antiquarian called Gee.

Don't dangle over the pit till I am by to hold the seat of your trousers. While I am holding I feel that I have no power, no strength to keep you – but when I think of you on that brink without me it seems to me that I have the most persuasive biceps, and a hand that is all that iron and velvet should be. Though alas! – it isn't.

What I said then is quite true. In Madrid, I never felt a flutter of fear; and yet, sitting in our own kind house, under the shadow of your black moods I become an abject coward, with all the vices of cowardice: peevishness, self-pity, loss of head, loss of temper, even down to that dreadful bodily clumsiness that goes with cowardice. Indeed, I think it is a marvel that we ever get through, you so clear-headed to perdition, able to argue the hindleg off a Jesuit, and I so hen-headed to reassure, so fatally fruitful to say the wrong thing.

There. It is because we so love each other, I suppose, that we do get through.

And because we so love each other, I am so glad to think you have Janet with you. Please, please be as happy with her as you possibly can be. Eat well of that wholesome young white goose, that is so well stuffed with shrewd sage and realistic onions.

My eye has just fallen on this remarkable advertisement: MEN LIKE YOU LIKE BOVRIL AND MILK. And all these years I have been making you bovril and milk, and never suspecting a sexual significance.

My dearest lovely darling Lesbian, my handsome and handsome-hearted – Take care of yourself, and know I love you with my whole true heart.

Tib

TELL ME EXACTLY HOW YOU ARE.

Narrative 8

I

It was the river which decided our move to Frome Vauchurch. It bounded house and garden. Sunlight reflected off its surface quivered on the ceilings, we fed trout and moorhens and visiting swans from our windows, a heron frequented the opposite bank. She gave me an E.M.G. Gramophone, then the Rolls Royce of Gramophones, as a moving-in present. Water is a sounding-board; our records had a purer sonority, as though the performers were somewhere in the house. We bought young trees and set willow-slips, and wondered what the spring would show in the garden. What the spring would show in Europe was a harsher conjecture.

Though our new landscape had not the grandeur of Chaldon, the curve of chalk persisted in the hillsides framing the river's valley of water meadows. A meadow isolated us from the village of Maiden Newton. The village was ugly but practical. It contained a railway station, some shops, and so many old women dressed in black that I said they must have lost their dear Sultan. I said it as a love-pat. She was so skilled in love that I never expected her to forego love-adventures. Each while it lasted (they were brief) was vehement and sincere. They left me unharmed and her unembarrassed.

We had been in our new house for little more than a year when a new love exploded in it.

I cannot trust myself to write a true account of the twelvemonth that followed. I know she began it in an amazement of passion and gratified desire and I with resolute good intentions to behave as I thought I should behave; that she truly believed she could love (as she said to me) in two directions at once; that in the end, drained of every vestige of joy, every illusion of good intentions, we still trusted each other enough to survive. But what I remember is so infected by what I felt that it comes back with the obsessive reality/unreality of delirium. There are no letters, no diaries; a few sharply impressed incidents and the witness of poems (hers and mine) written during that year is all I dare be sure of.

Elizabeth[1] was my doing. In 1929 when I was in New York as Guest Critic for the *Herald Tribune*, she introduced herself to me at a party. If it had not been for her New England twang, her Anglophilia, her piety about literary bigwigs, she might have been any well-brought-up young woman from the Shires who by some accident of pedigree had a mouth painted by Rossetti. She added me to her pieties, and wrote long letters at long intervals. We met twice, I think, when she was in England with her family. She was wealthy. When I was raising money for Spanish Medical Aid I asked her to contribute. Later she came to Europe meaning to attach herself to a pro-Republican organisation in Paris, and stayed here for a few days en route. From Paris she wrote saying that her courage had failed her, she had got nowhere, she must go home. We pitied her and suggested she should visit us. But it was not from pity that Valentine fell

---

1 Elizabeth [Wade White].

in love with her.

> Like whose kiss upon your hand
> the draught from door or window as you stand,
> so tall, so very white,
> tall and alone in the naked night?

> Like whose tread, that you so start
> to hear the hurried footsteps of your heart?
> Who but one waited for –
> My hand is on the latch of your door.

She said nothing about this new love, which alarmed me.

> It is the frost that lies
> Tonight upon the autumn meadow
> And will be gone soon after the sunrise;
> But later comes the snow
> And longer, longer lies.

I put this in the customary book of small poems which went into her Christmas stockings, and this:

> As the south wind
> Woos with the same note
> A wood in Dorset
> Or a wood in Kent,
> So yesterday
> I heard your grieving
> Love-note beguile her
> As though she were I;
> And heard such tones as mine reply.

In December I removed myself to the spare-room's single bed. That night I found the room scented with hyacinths, Tom the cat brought up from the kitchen, fruit and a sleeping-pill on the bedside table. And I could not run to thank her!

According to the lights of the day, I was behaving correctly in a quite usual situation. The only item by which I could have bettered my conduct would have been to take a lover. But I desired Valentine as sensually as ever, which saved me from that complication, as it saved me from any deviation into maternal kindness.

At Christmas all was duly merry till the middle of dinner, when at my too lighthearted acknowledgement of the new state of things, Elizabeth plunged into injured gloom. It was the first time I had seen her show real feeling. The sight was intimidating. In the morning she was still morose. Valentine announced that we would go out for the day.

> *A Mirror at Shaftesbury. Boxing Day 1938.*
> Something was left unsaid, undone,
> Something that I alone
> Could do or say –
>
> Harsh on that snowbound Boxing Day
> Time smoked itself away,
> While we were three.
>
> Grimly the guests wore finery
> Plucked from the Christmas Tree.
> We? we wore scorn.
>
> Shabby, the wear of faith foresworn.
> Love, beggarly and forlorn
> Then took fourth seat
>
> And so to feast our faint deceit
> We three did sit to eat,
> Then rise – and I
>
> Flaring like tow, at light of eye
> Burned in a kiss, to die
> Because, away
>
> Over her shoulder, hazed in the grey
> Mirror, a shadowy day,
> Mine own! Mine own
>
> Who stood very still, stood alone –
> Chill – heart fell like stone
> And lay still

This is a hindsight poem, of about a year later. Elizabeth's eyes were pale seawater blue; their colour intensified with excitement. I remember standing as she saw me. The mirror was near the lavatory where, safely alone, I had released myself into unhappiness, and coming out had waited, as I thought, unseen.

On the night of January 12th, I found a poem on my pillow.

> I do not forget,
> My Love, this is the bed
> In which we two were wed,
> So long ago, so long without regret.
>
> Lie here, most loved and warm,
> And in what winter of snow
> Year brings, securely know
> Me yours, you mine, and love-clad taking no harm.

Plain and awkward and with its crumpled ending, it was like a throw-back to the poems I had carried off to Inverness Terrace. The impulse to run and thank her was out of date. I had forfeited my spontaneity by that move to the spare-room.

I began to practise the idea of going away, almost making up my mind to it, unmaking it again. It was eight years since I had had to decide for myself. One evening in February I thought I would consult Beethoven, and put on the C sharp minor quartet. 'And you must go,' the entering voice said; and the other voices concurred, and the conversing voices flowed on in her room overhead. I heard her jump up, run downstairs, open my door. 'Why are you so unhappy?' she said. I fenced, asking her how she knew. 'I always know. Now you're thinking about going away.' A minute later I had given her my word I would stay.

When Elizabeth's visit had extended over four months her parents must have grown uneasy, for an emissary – a suitor of hers and another New Englander – rang up to say he was in London, and proposed coming to see her. Duly invited, he came to lunch, and immediately made it clear he had come to reclaim her. He was familiar and overbearing and she submitted to it. Instead of welcoming this gross Godsend, I moved in to attack. When I had provoked him into being rude to me, Valentine added her cold steel to my slings and arrows. We tossed him between us till the end of lunch, when Elizabeth took his mangled self-esteem for a country walk. Two days later, she followed him to London.

Valentine never discussed her with me. Whatever she felt about this, she kept to herself. When Elizabeth came back, plastered with gardenias, she took a sardonic pleasure in reminding me of the emissary's *pour prendre congé* to me: a very small bunch of the cheapest possible anemones. And we went on as usual. The situation was unchanged except for the added weight of time enforcing it, and the growth of Fascism overshadowing it.

In March 1939.

Strange to stand under the yew-tree and watch them working,
with the cat on a branch overhead and the dog running,
the two there I've loved so deeply and now am leaving
lonely while spring is here and the summer coming.

All pairs in the world, it seems, are now to forsaken
one-alone changed, into a bitter fashion
of the living bearing the dead one, forever burdened
by load of what once was light on arm, and lovely.

Alone up the narrow path, yet not unfriended,
I walked in this evening light, and ghost-companioned
by those in this twelvemonth slain saw the troubled glances
of these two live ones who did not know life was ending.

About this time, Louis Aragon wrote to ask if we would receive Ludwig Renn, one of those survivors of the International Brigade who crossed the frontier after the fall of Barcelona and were interned by the French Government. That afternoon he sat in the spring sunshine, collecting his scattered English. He had no passport, for he was a stateless person. He had no money, he had no future, he had sat starving behind barbed wire at Argelès, he had an unhealed wound, he had seen the bitter defeat of his cause. He had kept his interest in humankind and his slightly frivolous goodwill. His presence was so restorative that I wished he were coming to Norfolk with us – for Elizabeth was to be taken to Winterton. His refusal to cry over spilt blood would have admonished me not to cry over spilt milk, he would have managed Ruth as deftly as he managed Elizabeth when, seeing her in one of her fits of gloom, he said: 'Now we will dance,' bowed a court bow, put his arm round her waist and waltzed with her on the lawn. But he had to spend Easter in London where, among other engagements, he was to sit to Kokoschka.

Because it is a fine Easter bank-holiday,
With a blue sky and crisp waves flouncing the blonde

Beach, and like a heart the bell-buoy chiming,
And the larks singing over sea and over land,

Across the dunes and brushing through the marrom
Grass the holiday strangers loiter,
Happy and idle and a little solemn,
Sobered by so deep a sky and so straight a horizon;

And the black dog barking for joy
Casts himself again and again in the subsiding
Wave, and the lover spreads out his overcoat
And lies down with his young lady beside him.

I pretend
That I too am come here on a holiday
And have left my cares behind
In the pall of smoke that hangs over the city.

Like a visitor I stray
Hither and thither as the wind turns me,
And my heart is soft and light as a feather
Pretending that at the day's ending the wind will
    have blown me away.

Towards the end of May – a few days after Valentine's thirty-third
birthday - we sailed for New York: Ludwig, his passage aided by
Elizabeth, to try his fortune in a new continent, Valentine and I to attend
a Congress of Writers in Defence of Culture. On landing, we scattered.
Elizabeth went to her home in Connecticut, Ludwig to Ellis Island
whence he emerged a couple of days later saying it was the nicest
concentration camp he had ever been in.

I had been half-hearted about the Congress, thinking it would be small
beer after Madrid – as indeed it was; but I had the solace of introducing
myself to Benes and apologising for my government's part in the Munich
betrayal. 'It was the last chance for Europe,' he said. 'Now there is only
the hard way back.' There was no rhetoric in the statement, he spoke like
a teacher before a diagram on the blackboard.

Between Munich and the war we went to America: Sylvia and I, and
Elizabeth with whom I had by then fallen in love. If Sylvia had not stayed
by me then I should have been damned out and out. I was lecherous and
greedy and drunken, and yet I had two very serious loves in my heart,

even then – and poems, too, in my head.

This summary of almost six months is all she had to say of them in an apologia-autobiography written ten years later. It misrepresents one essential thing. It was not the fact of my staying which warded off that out and out damnation, but its quality. More fidelity could have become a bore and a reproach; it was my dependence on her which called back her sense of responsibility and steadied her footing.

After the Congress she went to stay in Elizabeth's home. I followed for a two day visit. I saw her looking gay, wicked and imperturbable, I delighted in the beauty of her neck and shoulders (it was a formal dress for dinner hospitality) and at seeing her outshine the rest of the company as a swan outshines a duckpond; but it was all at a remove. There was no remove about Elizabeth's mother's conviction that I was the procuress of the situation. Tall, sour-faced, white-skinned, with pale blue eyes, she was a solidly-corsetted threat of what her daughter might become. And the house matched her: it was overfilled with cautious good taste, and exhaled rapacity. It was no house to love in.

> Time on and on moving
> has little to say to loving
> except: 'on and on –'
> and under his breath, 'gone – none –'
>
> As in your house the clock
> deals its punctilious shock
> night-through behind your bed
> where more than hours are sped.

I went back to New York while Valentine was taken for a tour of Vermont and New Hampshire.

At Frome Vauchurch there had been talk of a stay in New England. This had come up again, and they made a second tour, inspecting houses for summer people. A house was found in Warren County. It was owned by a farming family called Kibbe and was the dullest they'd looked at, Valentine told me. But it was solitary and our share of the rent would be within our means. When she had deposited us at the Kibbe house, Elizabeth left us to settle in while she kept the family engagement.

We were by ourselves for two days, two long days of childish happiness. The house was badly equipped, but we forgot that in our pleasure over the cellar, cool and dusky, where a milk-snake slid down the steps from the burning greenery of the outside world. Behind the house was forest. There we saw Indian Pipes, unknown trees and butterflies, lost ourselves, and came out on a stony pasture and smelled sweetfern. We saw chipmunks and salamanders. We lived on wild raspberries and some biscuits we had happened to bring with us – there was no store within walking distance. At dusk there were fireflies and the forest rattled with cicadas. As we lay listening and snuffing up the odour of drowsy decay wafted out of the forest we heard a strange grunting and twanging noise. 'I believe it's a bear,' she said. 'Yes,' said I. 'It's a bear squeezing through a wire fence.' And we fell asleep to a chorus of bullfrogs.

I am glad we were so silly. It was no protection against what came afterwards. It glistened like dew and was gone. But while we had it, we had it.

Then Elizabeth drove up, bringing a New England Cookery book as a present to me, and herself to Valentine.

II

A bare hillside, and on it half a dozen tall gravestones, marking the graves of a mid-nineteenth-century family; and another gravestone to the memory of a brother 'buried in California, 1849'. I don't know why this should be my only unblurred recollection of the State of Connecticut; perhaps because I had wandered off alone, found it for myself, and did not have it explained to me.

Elizabeth had looked forward to showing us Connecticut. We were taken to birth-places, meeting-houses, historic taverns: all had traditions and were long distances apart. It was unfortunate that I was the good pupil; I admired while Valentine stared at the Contemporary scene. It was better when we explored for scenery. But by the end of the day, something usually had gone amiss. She had been too much absorbed to sound appreciative. Elizabeth had quarrelled over the charges at a filling station.

Dark Entry. Cornwall. Connecticut.

> I was named, as you were named, my love,
> Without a care how each of us might prove –
> Whether in voice, hands, gait or eyes or hair
> Either could match the colour our names wear.
>
> I was named, and this place was named, too:
> (Black as the lovely, lonely night of mountains,

Secretive as the landscape of your body,
Quiet and moody as a pool in the forest)
'Dark Entry' says the map, and we drive through.

Why did I think to see a large owl flying
Right up the tunnel-path? Relying
On what talk, guest or guidebook did I still
Look for darkness when we had topped the hill?

'Dark Entry', like any other, is a track
(Leads off the wide road, curls away up and climbs
Sleepily and then runs down, runs down to nothing;
And nothing is anywhere there from the beginning):
You can even go up Dark Entry and get back.

There was Valentine to show off, too; a number of people were invited to meet her. She had an intense aversion to being an exhibit. It was not possible for her to be ill-mannered, but she overcame the handicap by her talent for evasion. Thinking of something which would add to the visitor's pleasure she would go away to look for it. There was a lake near by, sometimes going for a swim was part of the entertainment. If the swimming became too social, Valentine disappeared in a dive and came up in some quite other place, like a dabchick.

If Elizabeth had loved her for what she was, none of this need have mattered. But love, which requires so little collaboration from circumstances, demands an agreement of tense. Valentine loved in the present. Elizabeth's love was pinned to a future conditional, to an amended Valentine she could safely call her own. If she noticed the discrepancy, she felt injured and sulked.

But at this time, her sulks were still part of her fascination.

One morning, a young man walked in and said: 'I had to come and tell you. I've allowed myself a bass tuba and now I haven't a wish left.'

He was Paul Nordoff, a composer. I had met him in New York, where we talked about the opera he had made from my novel, *Mr Fortune's Maggot*, and the problems of a restricted, money-saving orchestra. He was going to a cottage in Connecticut, to orchestrate and get away from the heat-wave. He knew the Kibbe house. With his entrance we were swept back to our own world, the world where a bass tuba, an adverb, the turn of a stanza, are things one lives by. Elizabeth, still dressing, heard our voices.

It was inevitable that she should be affronted. Rivers, meeting-houses, cousins, a festivity at Yale where a quantity of ageing men appeared in nightshirts – she had done her best to please Valentine with Connecticut. Except for a visit to a naturalist called Rex Braisher who led a Walden kind of life and knew a great deal about rattlesnakes, it had fallen rather flat. And here was Valentine, in full sail of animation because of this interloper. Her chagrin was so obvious that after Paul's second visit I was rebuked for ganging up with him. I complied by having him take me to his place. Setting out, I felt a craven relief; returning, dread of what I might not find. That harmless happy morning had toppled Elizabeth into the private hell of the tyrant. She forgot that she loved, that she was loved, and thought only of making sure of it.

The Kibbes had left behind in the kitchen a pamphlet about Loco Weed. I read again and again that loco weed grows on the prairies and the horses who eat it run mad. It seemed to me that if I escaped to the prairies, Elizabeth's possessiveness might be kinder, Valentine's love less careworn. But I had promised to stay. We kept up a sham of living in amity, a routine banality. As Elizabeth had discovered that she could use me as a stick to beat Valentine with I had to keep up my own particular sham of never feeling sick or sorry.

My cousin Janet arrived in New York (her passage aided by Elizabeth, who had the prerogative of the rich that she could be generous with large sums and niggardly over small ones), and we drove to fetch her for a visit to the Kibbe house. Valentine was driving, Elizabeth sat beside her. We had brought sandwiches for a picnic but forgot to bring drinks. We stopped at a wayside store to buy Coca-Cola. There wasn't any, so we bought a substitute. It was unbearably mawkish, and Valentine said so. I, from the back of the car, offered some making-the-best-of-it comment. Suddenly infuriated, she turned round and threw a sandwich at me. It was well-aimed and thrown hard. As we were staring at each other in horror, Elizabeth exclaimed, 'Well, that's no way to treat Sylvia.' Drenched in the same ignominy, we continued to stare at each other; and the stare became a recognition, and the recognition became a greeting. I felt my face relax into the ease of love. A moment later she had started the car, a flawless start, smooth as an otter's dive.

Janet, being young and wholesome, took an extrovert view of our set-up. It was reviving to hear her denounce the inconvenience of the Kibbe kitchen, damn the New England Cookery Book and say outright that Elizabeth was lazy and selfish. She was particularly resentful about the washing.

Elizabeth took her clothes to be washed at home. As it did not occur to her that Valentine also might like to look clean and spruce and not have to think twice about a change of linen, we did our own – I washing, Valentine ironing; for the Kibbe iron gave out blue sparks and she would not let me use it.

It was on a washing-day of Elizabeth's that we went for a desultory field-walk. Valentine noticed a large snake basking on the sloping roof of a shed. Listlessly mischievous, she took hold of it, grasping it just below the head, as she had picked up adders on the Winterton dunes when she was a child. It writhed itself round her naked arm. While we were struggling to unwind it, we were assaulted by a frightful smell. The snake was some kind of matrix, and had discharged its stink-gland. We got it off at last, and hurried back over the interminable fields we had crossed so idly. The smell went with us. It seemed the ultimate derision that Valentine, cleanly to the point of obsession, exquisite in choice of perfumes, should be conveying this foetor – and towards Elizabeth. I thought of her pride and was in agony.

There was no car by the house. Scrubbing her white skin as ruthlessly as though it were a chopping-board we got rid of the smell before Elizabeth returned. I heard Janet greeting her, and saying we had been for a nice walk. I was sorry when Janet left.

Every day, it grew hotter. The air was charged with electricity. There were constant dry thunderstorms, displays of the Aurora Borealis every night. Under the scorched turf the granite was hot to the foot, as though it lidded a furnace from which the Aurora spouted up in flaming gases. In the Kibbe house the party-line shrieked and jabbered. The screens didn't fit; moths and insects swarmed in, drawn to the naked electric light bulbs, and fell on us, sizzled corpses. Even people with minds at rest might have grown quarrelsome under such pressure.

We remained rigidly polite. After Valentine had gone down to the cellar to deal with the wood-burning stove (it was our only means of heating water) and I had washed up and put by the empty bottles, she and Elizabeth went to bed in the front room, and I, after finding a few more occupations for myself, went to the room where we had believed in the bear; and waited.

While I waited, I listened to the dog. Elizabeth had brought it with her, it slept in their room. It was a prize Sealyham and had eczema.

It scratched and whined, and when it scratched open a sore it yelped for pain. I was sorry for the dog, too. It should not have been imported from its native climate. From time to time, it got up, padded about the floor, cast itself down in a new place.

Then Elizabeth would begin to talk. She talked with perfect coherence, as the monomaniac does. I tried not to hear what she was saying, but I could not escape her voice. It went on and on, railing, reproaching, analysing, accusing. She never ran out of breath; but at intervals she made a pause. The pause extorted an answer – a weary half-sentence, a monosyllable of dissent. Valentine's voice, like a wounded viola; the voice I had heard from beyond the partition-wall at Chaldon. Then Elizabeth would begin again.

There was one night when her voice reached such a pitch of fury that I stood in the passage, waiting for her to attack Valentine. This time, I could hear what she was saying. She was appealing for consideration. Something must be settled, they must come to some definite agreement, she couldn't go on like this, all she asked was to know where she stood and not always to be put off and played with – and perhaps a little gratitude. Was that too much to ask?

'I never played.'

I knew it was true and would still be true.

In the mornings, Valentine would come downstairs to get Elizabeth's breakfast-tray and carry it up to her. That done, she came down again and we did the household chores together, drinking coffee in the kitchen and listening to the radio. By now the commentators were discussing the imminence of war in Europe. We were too drained for any hazard into intimacy; we talked of what might happen, not of what we should do. The tenancy of the Kibbe house was running out.

When it ended, she and I were going to North Carolina, where we had been promised a stay in a cabin halfway up the mountainside. I had counted the days to this respite; now I had left off believing in it, except as a hoarded explosive in Elizabeth's mind. She had become almost totally inert, sat blankly brooding, her eyes flicking like an accountant's. If I had hated her I might have pitied her; but dislike and dread are not enough to constitute hatred, and all my capacity for emotion was concentrated in a woe of pity for Valentine.

Warren. Connecticut. 31 August 1939.

For this a tree grew for fifty years,
Carrying leaves and fruit, shedding and bearing again,
Standing autumn and spring, drouth and rain;

To nourish the fire on this hearth, the red fire
That shudders its light on our faces and wavers and frightens

Itself with the shadows, the picture it lightens.

For these brief shadows a fire was kindled
Months ago now, that you in love should stand here
And I beside you, warming ourselves at our fear.

Our last night at the Kibbe house we heard that Britain was at war with
Germany. In the morning we heaped our luggage in the car – (there was
a great deal of it now, in overflow packages: already we looked like
refugees) – and were driven to the station. At New York Central the news
struck at us from all sides; from radio, placards, conversations. It did not
seem to refer to us. The taxi-driver who took us to the Pennsylvania
station was a Jew. He heard our English accent and refused to let us pay
him.

Celo, North Carolina, 1939

Not caring, we see that darkly under the mountain
shadows lie even after the sun has risen,
that the high sun drives them inward and not away,
for at evening again it is shadowed under the mountain.

Outworn, the warm rhythm of days and the seasons' turning,
smooth-running pattern of months for summer to summer;
these have been ours for an age. We lust for the crooked
stumble and jerk of beginning, creation returning.

It was at 3000 feet above sea-level, in the cabin halfway up Mount
Mitchell, that we decided to go back to England – more truly, knew that
we would do so. We were no patriots; but five hundred lives had been lost
in the sinking of the *Courageous* and it would be less painful to hear such
news in our own country.

Valentine travelled to Celo with a rising temperature. For several days
she was alarmingly ill, feverish with exhaustion and desolate craving. But
the mountain nights were cool and we had been warned to avoid a mound
of sawdust where there was a rattlesnake's tracks. She spent her first day
of convalescence beside it.

Our host had left us his car. This time, we saw contemporary things:
cotton-fields, a court-house, a revivalist meeting, the fleshless dehydrated
kitten she found in a throw-away pit, nursed back to life and named Curtis
Earl Dwight because it would live to be President (it lived to a

domineering old age in a good home). She had stayed indoors to de-flea Curtis when I was set upon by wild bees. Though I was only a stone's throw from the cabin, by the time I got there I was swelled stiff and turning blue. I remember her instant competence, and thinking as I lost consciousness 'What a moment to go and die in!' and coming back to an unrecognisable self, washed from all my cares, with nothing to worry about because she was there and looking after me. But nothing at Celo had the shine of those two first days at the Kibbe house. The shadow was driven inward, not away.

We went back to New York to apply for a passage. There was a spell of high humidity. We had been told of a cheap hotel near the station, and we set out for it, carrying our luggage. The hotel was picketed. I said I was too tired to go further, that one night could not make all that difference, that it was too hot to argue. She did not argue. She took a suitcase from me and walked on.

Within a day or two, Elizabeth joined us. She was friendly, sociable, in good shape: it was as though she neither resented nor remembered. She took us to a down-town hotel which she said was Bohemian. My bedroom there looked out on the back of a lodging-house whose windows at night were like a showcase of people in torments of heat and sleeplessness. Early one morning I was at my own window when Valentine came in, said, 'I'll tell you presently,' cast herself down on my bed and fell asleep. It was partly as I surmised. Night after night Elizabeth had tried to extort a promise to stay. With each attempt it was plainer that she had lost all conception of love except as something she could be sure of – like an annuity. But an obligation of pity and concern kept Valentine beside her, till she offered another inducement. This was what Valentine had come to tell me. '"Safer as an American citizen," she repeated. "Safer!" So I said, Damn your bloody United States! Now we must pack and go.' Suddenly, we were gay and laughing. We talked till it was time for her to go and dress. There was an interview; she did not speak of it, but it must have been brief for by that afternoon we were settled in another hotel. Presently, we heard that a stateroom booking on an American boat had been cancelled and could be ours. Elizabeth had moved to her club. We went there for a constrained autumnal meeting of goodbyes and parting gifts. She had equipped herself for it with a mutual acquaintance whom a few months later she took as a substitute.

We sailed without flowers in a boat without its proper ballast (pig-iron might expose it to a submarine commander's decision that it was carrying material of war). It was a rough sea, and the boat pitched so violently that it was almost impossible to keep one's footing. I was sitting in my bed with some mending when I saw her get up, come across to me and, as I thought, stagger. I put out my hand to steady her. She was kneeling beside me, clasping me in her arms, telling me we would recover.

1940—1949

1940

Frome Vauchurch, April 1940

My love,

I read your note and then wished to *god* I had you here so that I could kiss you for it, and to show you that it is not outdated by whatever happened this morning.[1] And I thought to send you a telegram but could not in case it reminded you of cables. That is one of the not-littlest evils arising out of the falsity of this position: things that were ordinary and necessary to do (and even WORDS LIKE THAT,[2] that I must use sometimes!) have become contaminated and can't be used for food any more.

So we are situated thus and we must wait by and wait for it to be better. That it will be I have no manner of doubt, but sometimes I am thrown off my balance by realising how all the main weight of it falls on you, mainly because I am too pusillanimous to cut my losses. I don't know how that has come about: it used not to be so. I have lost a great deal in my time and most of it cut – and far the most of it without spoiling the sound part of the joint.

Well, my dearest Love, we shall see how it works out, and meanwhile all is well and the World's Stores came and did not bring eggs but the dapper little man said he would try to catch the last carrier with them. And he won't because he can't. So I got 3 from Weston (Kit and Pat[3] eat breakfast). But the bacon is a good piece and is soaking. Tom had a greenfinch in the little sun-parlour and I got there in time and the bird got

---

1 I was going to Rat's Barn, at her insistence, to work on *The Cats' Cradle Book*; she had already gone out. A postscript to my note told her that after she left the house a cable from her to Elizabeth had been queried back.

2 Some endearment in the cable.

3 Kit and Pat [Dooley]: guests.

away. Quite well, but saddened. I pelted Tom with earth and he is eating worms in the field.

Jo is out and Mary[1] is still scrabbling. All therefore is well and you have no need to worry. D O N ' T   W O R R Y anyway. You have a spell of peace in front of you, if you can make it so, and I think you will be happy – I only fear that you may be so happy that it is a pain to you to return. Both you and I will always feel like that – being alone is so unostentatious and so decently grand. But it is not so good, probably, and anyway we have both practically announced our willingness to try for the more difficult success of living together. And for ten years we have been happy so. My Love, bear with me if you can, for indeed and indeed I love you. And I do not for a moment dislike the cuckoo,[2] although he calls me names now as well as you! He is a shrewd bird and better than his jokes suggest.

Sweetheart – take care of yourself.

If you will still consider yourself married to me, I think, still, you will not be deceived.

Love always, Work well and be V E R Y   H A P P Y, and not less so because we love each other: not less so, even, because I am a fool. It is not incurable.

Valentine

74: STW

Rat's Barn, April 1940

My darling one,

What you said in your letter, the last but one, about how the sending of telegrams, the use of certain words, has been invalidated, is partly true. And explanations and analyses, too, have been compromised, so that probably our instinct to behave with calm and reserve, like Thomas (or at any rate like Thomas thinks he behaves) has been a good instinct. But not now. I at any rate want to cast off my catskin, and tell you with the utmost plainness and truth that when I heard you say on the telephone that you had written to Elizabeth that it couldn't go on, though my first feeling was

---

1 Joseph and Mary were table-rabbits (Grow more Food campaign); we sold their progeny.
2 Soon after we left the States Elizabeth had taken a consolatory bed-fellow. Her frequent letters of reproachful self-justification did not make recovery easier.

just that I was most deeply sorry for you, and my next feeling a kind of despairing annoyance at seeing wine mismanaged into vinegar, yet after these began an unstanchable trickle of relief and a queer kind of happiness. No, not happiness. Happiness cannot fly on one wing, I cannot be happy while you are not. But satisfaction, or perhaps the best word is assent. Yes, that is the truest. Though I grieve for you, though I am furious that I have to grieve for you, and want to scratch the one and box the ears of the other, I *assent* to what has happened, I think it is the right thing, and the best thing, and I agree and am thankful. It did not need the sight of Alyse[1] to quicken my thankfulness. I have always known that if I lost you I should lose the core of my heart, and if I lost you to Elizabeth I should not even have the whaleboning of thinking you had changed for the better, for I should think it a change for the worse. And to lose even any part of you has been anguish; and made into something like madness by the thought, clattering on like a cheap instrument of torture, that I didn't consider her worth it, that it was all a bloody waste, a poem gone wrong, a lyric turning into a nuisance. And I suffered a great deal from fear. Because a love that gets arrested development turns into a greedy destroying cunning monster, a gamel-weed.

And don't suppose, my darling, that I am so dull and theoretical that I shall come home with a pleasant confident smile expecting to find 'everything all right again'. Because so much *is* right, because the foundations of our love have scarcely shifted at all, there will be even more complication and bewilderment in the superstructure. If we had been able to part and now to come together again it would be easier. But I am glad we did not part, that we were neither of us unfaithful to our love, and our belief in each other.

Do you remember a poem of mine that ends, 'that come back paired in spring as the cuckoos do'? That is what I really have got to say to you. And it is comfortable to find here so many people who take it for granted that we will. Philippa[2] and Alyse have both enquired a little, Philippa with the utmost delicacy and Alyse like a scrupulous gimlet, as you would expect of poetry and criticism; and each of them at my answer looked pleased and not surprised. And old Mrs Smith called me Dear with the utmost casualness, as she could never do to any one she felt to be in need of sympathy.

1 Alyse, returned from Switzerland where Llewelyn died in December 1939, had arrived at Chydyok that morning.
2 Philippa: Katie Powys's second name.

I had an insight into my own moral decisions while I was talking to Alyse. She was telling me about two Irishmen at Davos, one of them dying, the other his friend, and not dying. The friend fell in love with the night nurse of the dying man; and persuaded her to give him horse-doses of morphine, and then leave him and spend the night with the lover.

Alyse most earnestly asked me what I thought of it, did I think that passion would justify such an act. I said no, instantly; and found myself going on with decision to explain why I said no; that no passion gratified by such means could be a wholesome passion, a genuine honest-to-god passion; but must have an element of the pathological to be able to endure pleasure bought at such a price, and probably a very base variety of masochism, and dirt-eating. All this I said, with the air ringing with the name of Gamel.[1] And she listened like a cat at the mouse-hole, and said nothing, but looked for a moment alive and established. I don't think it did her anything but good. And I know now that is what I feel.

She is very melancholy, and I think it is irreparable, I smell no power to mend. However, she can talk about it, which is supposed to be a wholesome sign. I don't know. She arrived there this morning, and everything went wrong. Gertrude, who had been screwing herself up to the moment and laying the cloth, so to speak, all night, said to her how beautiful her complexion was looking. Alyse instantly burst into tears. Katie instantly burst into chivalry, and insisted on going down to the village to bring up a parcel that Mr. Trevis had forgotten to bring. Gertrude as instantly burst into defensiveness of a Powys, Katie had been ill, the walk would be far too much for her.

So this morning I saw Philippa coming down over the brow of the hill like a mad angel with vials of wrath in a knapsack. She came in here raging and trembling. I gave her rum, probably not good for her, but it made her much better, and very uprightly (p. training,[2] I suppose) persuaded her to see that Gertrude had not acted like a fiend from hell but only like a flustered and affectionate sister; and walked part of the way with her. And did the trick perhaps, or the lovely morning did; for when I saw her this afternoon she was calm again.

Remind me, when I come back to tell you about the poor P.s and the drama of the sergeant major and the canon's daughter. And as I shan't remember to tell you I will tell you now this fragment of the morning's conversation. *Tib*: Nervousness probably made Gertrude woolgathering.

1 [Gamel Woolsey, an American poet who had been Llewelyn Powys's lover.]
2 The Communist Party discountenanced emotional confusions.

Philippa, with violent conviction: Woolgathering, my dear? Far more than that! Ob-ob-obtruse.

It is exactly the word for Miss Powys. I saw in a flash that mystical performance with the hypodermic and the sofa cushion.[1]

My dearest love, to be writing to you, to be unbosoming myself to you, is such joy that as you see a letter which began in a mood of seriousness and sorrow for your sorrow has become as gay as a kitten. I love you always and always and in every mood and in all of them at once.

Sylvia

Narrative 9

> Into the war the poet is taken,
> Made one of, a comrade; returned
> Swift to a life he had slowly forsaken
> And for the duration interned.

When we disembarked at Southampton late in October 1939 we were issued with gasmasks, tried them on, saw ourselves as snouted pigs, heard each other's voices spectral and distorted; when we got home to a house smelling of mutton-fat (Mrs Keates and her family lived there during our absence) we groped in semi-darkness because of the black-out. And we had come back to the Phoney War.

As soon as the frost was out of the ground (it was a long, hard winter) we began to dig the garden for food-crops. The China roses we had brought from Frankfort Manor were in bloom when young men, still in the astonishment of Dunkirk, sat on the lawn offering daisies to our rabbits or watched the trout in the river. In July 1940 we moved to Norfolk. An invasion of the east coast was expected, The Hill House had been requisitioned for an Anti-Aircraft battery, and Ruth had to be helped to move into a small house in the village. The dunes and the beach were mined. The village was full of soldiers who listened to the news of the bombing of London and kicked their heels in idleness. Many of the Winterton young men had joined the Navy; one had gone down with his ship. We stayed in Winterton till after the New Year, hearing some

---

1 A demonstration with a hypodermic and an old sofa-cushion of her preparedness to give Llewelyn an emergency injection.

sporadic bombing and sandbagging an air-raid shelter for Ruth. It was a mutilation not to be able to cross the dunes to the sea.

One day we went to look at the stretch of country where the sea had broken in two years before. It was still a desolation. The ground was impotent; no life stirred in it, the salt had killed insects and earth-worms as it had killed the fish in the streams. Wisps of muddied dead grass hung on dead bushes. Here and there a stunted vegetation had struggled to the surface and died. It would take another five years, a man ditching told us, before a crop could be raised there or a beast pastured. He spoke with a dry patience, and my heart agreed. We had survived our inundation, were together, lay in the same bed, argued and were of one mind. But the salt was not out of our soil. We had lost confidence, not in each other but in our own capacities to nourish and support. I thought before I spoke. She doubted after she had acted. And she was still grieving over a love into which she had put so much truth. I remember thinking as we walked away that if we could leave those sick fields and walk by the true sea everything might come right. But the dunes were mined. On our last day at The Hill House, hearing an explosion, we looked out, and saw a soldier running like an automaton, holding a booted leg in his arms.

Winterton had adapted itself to war with a sort of rough composure. We came home to a buzz of compulsive activity. There was, in fact, very little real work to be done. With no illusion of importance, Valentine signed on as a clerk in the Dorset Territorial Army's headquarters in Dorchester where, after swearing to divulge no information, she was set to copy an untitled formula. As she knew nothing about knitting, she took the reiterations of K.2, p.2, slp 1, K.2. tog. to be code till the head clerk reproached her for using the wrong paper. 'Blue for Comforts, Miss Ackland. Pink for Welfare.'

To conform, to catch morning trains, to race for evening trains, to stand in corridors, to call Colonels Sir, to reason patiently, even respectfully, with fools and to listen to the whining complaints of people who, as far as I can see, have no need to complain at all, much less to whine . . . *and to have to combat in myself these revolting bouts of a similar whining* . . . I find all this to be most difficult. I am assured by those who know that it will be much worse before it gets better, and in myself I feel a most desperate dread that it won't 'get better' until I myself have been purged of the remembrance of what it is like to be free.

I've been happy once or twice, in a sharp delight and pleasure, because I could sit under a tree in the public gardens; and I've had keen interest in the passions and rivalries which toss all of us as though we were Balkan States. And I've had genuine happiness of heart because of the extraordinary kindness and chivalry of the other clerks towards me when I was new and totally ignorant, and they had so much they could despise in me, and so much vengeance to wreak on me as a symbol.

But I cannot accustom myself to wasting whole slabs of time. I sit for two hours and more with nothing in the world to do.

Time was precious because she knew what could be done with it:

. . . those long hours of time while a bird flies across the width of the window, and a hare stops short on the ploughed field on the side of the hill, time hesitates so long there that I think this pause more lasting than the life which contains it. It is as long as the life a bird lives in one phrase of its April song.

The next entry in her notebook was made nineteen days later.

23.3.1942. And now that I see, every day, individual effort – so unselfish and so *breathless* – being swept down the drain of incompetence and ignorance, it seems to me like another of those expensive, luxurious failures: Narvik, France, Greece, Crete, Lybia, Singapore – and so on. Every ounce one gives, every hour, is given to the very people who spend other hours like that.

And the next year there were wall-chalkings: Open the Second Front Now.

By then, she had been transferred to Civil Defence. I worked with the W.V.S. in the same building; on the ground floor was the National Salvage depot, where books for pulping were collected (there was a slight delicacy about the pulping of bibles and prayer books, and a soothing legend was put about that these were done in a separate vat). The W.V.S. was a libertine organisation; if I had nothing to do I slid into her office to see if I could be useful there. One day I found her glittering with fury. She had been visited by a breathless mother, boasting that she had carried in for salvage all the books of her fighting son. ('He won't want *them* when he comes back.') We revolted, and planned. Strings were pulled. In defiance of all regulations it was agreed that if Civil Defence would wink at losing a few books from National Salvage, Army Welfare would include them in the category of 'Blue for Comforts'.

Eventually, thirteen crates of books went to bombed libraries – perhaps the only significant result of our war-working careers.

Nothing resulted from an even more unregulated extension of Civil Defence. In the spring of 1942 invasion of the south coast was thought likely, and at official meetings we were told how to deal with it. ('Do not exasperate the enemy. Bury the dead. Boil water,' I noted on the back page of a book I happened to be carrying.) But the head of the Home Guard in Maiden Newton was the grandson of a poet. He had already recruited women to re-furbish an issue of begrimed machine-gun belts. Now his irresistible inheritance made him see a place for them in the Resistance. He organised Ladies Classes in rifle-shooting and throwing grenades. Valentine could throw a well-placed grenade, but she was surpassed by the quiet young woman from the grocery shop, who seemed to have come into the world for that special purpose.

This project must have been frowned on from above. But by the time we were disturbed, we had learned enough to be useful.

Teaching to Shoot

When we were first together as lover and beloved
We had nothing to learn; together we improved
On all the world's wide learning, and bettered it, and loved.

Now you stand on the summer lawn I am to show you
First how to raise gun to shoulder, bow head, stare quickly and fire;
Then to struggle with the clumsy bolt (outdated) withdraw, return, and
    again fire.
As the evening darkens, even this summer evening, and the trees
Bend down under the night wind and the leaves rush in a flaming fire,
I am to show you how to bend your body, take step lightly – and I hold
    your arm.

(Thin and sleek and cool as a willow wand fresh in my hand),
And in your hand you clasp fervently this dirty lump, this grenade.
This thing that you hold as you once held my hand is ready to kill.
We intend to finish those who would finish us – we who are not ill,
Are not old, are not mad; we who have been young and who still
Have reason to live, knowing that all is not told.

In your hand you hold iron, and iron is too old,
And steel, which breaks and shatters and is cold,
And our hands are together as always and know well what they hold.

Summer evenings were never long enough, nor Sundays. On Sundays we could lie late in bed, listen to music, stroll in the fields, pick flowers, gather mushrooms and blackberries, work in the garden, flow with the river. In 1944, river and garden had to mean more to us. One May morning I answered the telephone and heard Jim Pitman telling me that a German plane with a fighter on its tail had jettisoned a bomb behind Miss Green's Cottage. May Pitman, with the intuition of that date, common in cats, not uncommon in human beings, had heard the All Clear sounded in Dorchester, knew it for a warning and flailed the household out of their beds and out of the house. They were standing in the lane, laughing at her, when the bomb fell. They escaped with injuries. The cottage was a total wreck.

This must have been on a Sunday, for I remember sitting under a clump of hawthorns in full bloom – and how little we said and how calmly we spoke.

It was a time of destruction – so much destruction done, so much more to come. The invasion of France was preparing: lorries went by all night and screaming convoys, ammunition dumps squatted in woodlands. In this accumulation of metal, soldiers seemed intensely fragile, *objets de luxe*: one stared at the craftsmanship of their eyelashes and fingernails, their eyelids like flower-petals. It was a Restricted Area; no one could enter or leave it without a permit. This built up a remarkable bond of speechlessness and inattention. Convoys went through, trains ran all night, articulated dragons appeared in the sky. No interest was shown. Time went on, the grass grew tall – it would be a good hay crop if the spell of contrary weather didn't last too long. Early one morning, Valentine woke me. She had taken down the black-out and was standing at the window . . . It was like a steady drift of fireflies, for they were flying in such close formation that they used their port and starboard lights. The sound was continuous.

Later, she caught her usual train and went to work as usual. We were all so solidified in inattention that not on the platform, not in the train, not in the streets did she hear a word of comment until the man at the Salvage depot poked out his head and remarked: 'Well, seems something's going on.' Discipline, discretion – or flat indifference? We had waited for a long time.

5.5.1944. I have such a slight talent, so little power behind it, such self-mistrust (recently so much developed that it has become definitely a deformity in my mind) that I cannot take any advantage from this-and-that amount of unexpected time. I fritter; I dissipate and waste time; I don't even *spend* it. And at intervals my conscience burns me that I am feigning sick while Sylvia is working, and that *she* can use time and *I* cannot.

The days are lovely; they are beyond words lovely. As if I were a figure in an Italian painting, they throw into my lap such glories that I can only stare and worship. But every one of these things withers because I cannot 'do' anything with it. Today I saw the kingfisher. He sat on the bough of a tree stretching over the river and he groomed each of his bright feathers and I could see each one of them displayed; the sun shone down brilliantly and then the clouds raced overhead and then the sun struck again. It was very dramatic weather, very beautiful and keen, and the bird sat on the bough over the river, and then – after he had spread either wing separately so that I saw every feather, every shade of bright colour, he turned around and showed his strange, bright belly and his most delicately shaded feet. I could have killed myself after that.

It is not that I cannot sleep; I sleep like a stone. But I dream frantically and then awake to a regular, a punctual horror, no especial horror – but most often personal, worry about work, health, what will be done with me. And the fact that it is most often personal gives me an almost unbearable added horror, in which I remember, hear, visualise with distracting clarity all the horror in the world at large and then, with raging bitterness, realise that it is the weight of a straw to me – that foolish 'last straw' – and then I am overcome and overwhelmed by shame and I lie in my bed beside Sylvia and sweat and toss and ache with the rigidity of lying. And that is how most nights are – and I see no end to it because the situation cannot change.

The illnesses were never feigned; she had had a dragging infectious hepatitis; and ached the more with the rigidity of lying because she was increasingly arthritic. Her only feigning was to conceal her mental sickness by passing it off as boredom and stale irritation. The Civil Defence Office was a conservatory of pettifogging – and war-time pettifogging puffed itself up into petty tyranny. For eight hours a day for six days a week, she was at the beck and call of self-important nonentities, spluttering with provincial rivalries, scheming for petrol coupons, badges, ARP buckets, Red Cross safety-pins – each defending his own dunghill. From this, she came home with her extreme sensibility leaping at the stimulus of release, a poem dazzling before her; and was too jaded to secure it. A device of Nazi jailors was to bind the legs of a woman in labour so tightly together that she could not eject the child. A dozen poems can be mislaid and the poet be little the worse; but to frustrate the process of poetry is another matter. To be a poet was her deepest concern, her deepest obligation; to abdicate would be to sin against her light. The light had shone on the kingfisher – and she could have killed herself. She said nothing; as I worked in the same building and knew many of her frequenters, I could guess something of what she endured. But I was free to dispose of myself. She was in an age-group where, if she left a job, she could be 'directed' to factory work in some other part of England. There seemed to be nothing for it but to cling to the ills she had.

One evening in the late summer, she came home with such an acute pain in her midriff that I telephoned the doctor. He was an old man, who had come out of retirement to take up practice again, and was in Maiden Newton because the doctor before him was a Blackshirt and had been interned. He arrived. She was speechless with pain; instead of the orthodoxy of asking her where it hurt and punching her to find out, he gave her morphia. To me, he said it might be gall-stones, it might be nervous colic, the latter was the more serious. This, too, was unorthodox, nervous was a term of opprobrium by then, and overwork and malnutrition the accepted contra-indication. Seeing what the Civil Defence Office was doing to her, he resolved to get her out of it, and sent in weekly certificates of Not Fit to Return to Work, till the Controller lost patience and sacked her. He then engaged her on half-time as his dispenser. He probably saved her life, he certainly saved her reason. She worked in peace and quiet and knew she was doing something useful. He was a gainer, too, he had wanted her for a long time, as I knew when he engaged me six months previously. Of all the occupations I lent myself to during the war, being Dr Lander's unqualified dispenser had been immeasurably the most congenial; but when I had made up my last bottle of medicine and tested the last specimen of urine, I walked home like one in a dream, because the Lord had turned the captivity of Zion.

1941

Frome Vauchurch, for Valentine's Day, 1941

My love,

I want to write to you what I have just thought of: That I am so very glad to be free to love you again as *completely* as I had loved you for eight years, and more, before this almost-fatal interruption happened. I have talked so much of that, too much, and there is nothing new to be said about it, and I know the break may be there for a long time, even for always if we are lucky enough to have an always: but it will never now be worse than a scratch on the surface of the record, and I hope (and dare really to hope) that because the record is so lovely and so well-completed we shall not notice the scratch more than as a most brief trouble.

That depends so much on you, and if it were wholly depending on you I'd know for sure it would be all right. I do not know for sure because part depends on me and I am sure of very few things that depend on me. I am sure and certain of some, though; first, that I love you absolutely, for all time, and matchlessly: second, that whether I am bad or good at given times I am never bad with my own consent and that therefore I can be sure of giving you a very true love which will not spoil: third, that although I know quite well how much you have done by yourself to preserve our best treasure, my relief and happiness at its restoration is not at all tainted by gratitude or obligation – and that is so badly said that it sounds to be what it is not, but you must understand it.

What remains to be done is to restore the few damaged places very deftly and securely; you must try to trust me again as a character and as a person knowing what is and what is not. You *must* do that because even ordinarily each person is dependent upon the next person's view of him, and between lovers the dependence is more constant and more mortal. I have to regain my idea of you as not *a* person who loves me, but *the person who loves me for valid reasons*, (I didn't lose it ever, but it was overlaid by other people's interpretation of how and why you loved me, and sometimes still it goes out of sight in my mind). And we each have to restore the other's self-confidence. All of which is extremely difficult in wartime, especially when I have proved to be so much afraid of the trimmings of the war.

Of that it's no good to say much, but what I say here I hope I say for the last time because it is a pity to talk about it; I am not nearly so much afraid as I thought I'd be, and I am only afraid in two ways: One, narrowly and only physically (of noise and fright and blood and other people's hurt as well as my own – I rarely, really, think of my own hurt). Two, of losing our own dear life, of losing you, of losing the earth and the sky and peace together and night and day and things we see, and all that. I see ahead too clearly and often unnecessarily and always with too little control. I hope I shall continue to get better at blacking-out prophecy and clairvoyance and forward-looking. I am much better after only one year. If you can manage to believe I'm not as pale as I seem, I think I shan't be! (I'm not, anyway, I mean, I think I shall be able to stop seeming.)

If one of us had died before this confusion I put us into, the one left alive would have known F O R S U R E that however bad it was now, it had been perfectly good up to that moment of death. I want you to believe me, my Love, when I tell you that began to be true again, somewhere in November of this year,[1] for me anyway – and that so far as I know (and I know now a lot more than I used to know) it will be true right up to the time it's proved.

And I do love you, I do most truly and passionately love you. It was never a fantasy in my mind to know that on the twelfth of January 1931 something had happened which *really* happened. It must have been making itself long before, of course, but it showed itself then, finished and complete and as perfectly fitted and fixed as Miss Green was on the evening I arrived there and the duck was cooking, and the one enormous mushroom. That might have been a dream but it wasn't; and nor was the twelfth of January. And nor is it now, when it is all again as bright and rich as it was then. Because I love you with all my life, my Love, and that is how it is.

But I don't seem able to talk very well just now, probably because so many words have been used and jettisoned and fished up and re-used and jockeyed about and misused. I can't even write to you as I want to, and it

---

1 i.e. November 1940.

is like someone suffering from delayed shock, really. But this is to tell you (if only you can make sense of it) that it is *really* all right. After so many, many attempts to set it right and make it float again, we are so tired and unbelieving that we don't even know we've gone right down the river and out on to the sea and that it's sailing very nicely and doesn't any longer depend on favourable weather to keep afloat.

I hope this isn't nonsense. I know that what I mean to say is true. You must please understand what I mean, my beloved.

Valentine

1944

Little Zeal, 21 November 1944

My dearest Love,

So there you stand in your willow-mantle, being photographed in the most rubbishy bad secluded corner of the garden; but the camera saw you. You always pack most beautifully, and these two pictures of yourself will be a bosom-comfort (and I fancy I may need comfort rather badly). The Pomeranian seems to bark more than usual, it is raining, and Nora seems pretty much as usual, just as damnably active and fidgety and ill to forestall. If she would lie in bed and need waiting on hand and foot (how does one wait on a foot? exceedingly alabaster ointment and buttoning gaiters? it would be more rewarding.)

And I found your letter awaiting me. Be sure I will attend to every word of it. It was a pretty journey to begin with, while the sun shone on the yellow torches of the oaks, and the floods between Yeovil and Taunton. It was comfortable all the way except for a brief interim of women travelling with child, just to bear out Daily Needs for Daily Strength.[1] And S. Brent was looking so wonderfully the same, and I sent you a little telegram with such a lot of great love in it, and so many of the rather lonely feelings you will quite understand from the post-office. It cost 1/9.

Poor Nora! Her nose has a varicose *vein* in it. She is wonderfully brave about it all, but I can't help feeling it has changed her somehow. The nursing-home sounds really wonderfully kind, and gave her tea at 5.30 (a.m.!) even in wartime, and three meals a day, most considerate, and some marvellous celery soup, quite like cream, she says. But naturally she is so intensely grateful that it wasn't in her leg which would have been so much worse for such an active wee body. I'm afraid that is all I can manage just

1 *Daily Strength for Daily Needs* was a pious anthology much resorted to by Ruth.

now, darling, for though I am scarcely at all tired really, it is a long time since I got up (7.30 a.m.!) and not very much breakfast, though *of course* you did your best, how I do realise that. And then three changes, and having to look after that packing case, etc. etc. So I will snap out of it now before it gets a hold on me. I see it would soon turn to dram-drinking.

Vacquier[1] was a great success with Nora. So were all the things I brought. Reading dear Herrick in the train reminded me that we had a Herrick with epigrams in it (appendixed, of course, being indelicate). So I hunted them out, and most of them are dull, but I like this.

> Blanch swears her husband's lovely: when a scald
> Has bleared his eyes; besides, his head is bald.
> Next his wild ears, like leathern wings full spread,
> Flutter to fly, and bear away his head.

O Lord, I do so wish I were at home. When I was at home I was in a better place. I also feel I was a fool to come. Oh well, the first day is the worst . . . tomorrow I shall go for a walk, and start to make your slippers, and muse on how to make mine: I do not feel I have quite unravelled the purpose of those tapes; and take my serocalin, of course. I have already had one. But God! what a way to spend one's time, what a doting impotent drivelling way to spend one's time when one might be happy. And now I will go sullenly to bed, and gnaw chocolate.

My dearest, dearest love . . . I love you always and entirely. Try to remember this when you remember.

Your Tib

77: VA

Frome Vauchurch, 21 November 1944

My sweetest Love, (and this is carefully thought about – exactly true –) It's very early still but I have had supper and Cumquat[2] and Thomas have had what I suppose they think to be snacks. It is unfortunate that all the

1 Vacquier: a murderer.
2 Cumquat: our black Pekinese. Catering for our animals demanded a great deal of contrivance and some degree of self-abnegation.

rabbit was finished – or almost all: there is a little left but so little that it is only enough for Thomas. However, there is a silver side to this as to all situations – I am comforted (though they are not, which makes it all the more like a model Worker's Playtime[1] ballad) by reflecting that Cumquat doesn't know the story of 'Is that your darling?' 'No, mother, it's me' and if he did he wouldn't give a damn, unless for a passing moment he thought I was talking about Joseph and Increase.[2] So he will have bread-and-bovril-and-goat-soak and Thos. will have bones and bits and soak as well. That's for later. Just recently they had pickings of salmon which I opened, since I'd said I'd tin, and then couldn't eat all of (though I ate new bread and butter) and Cumquat sat for hours on his backside, and had snippets and then Thos. came mildly in and had the tin and then the dish – with a good deal of quite respectable fish in it still. Then the doorbell rang and I was furious, and armed myself as fast as I could in imitation of Rat and went to the door, and it was the drunken rascally postman, who has the dog that hoped to kill Joseph, and he brought your very odd telegram. It reads 'TELEPHONE IS DOUBLE TWO FIVE THREE THANK YOU FOR YOUR PICTURES AND HOPE PACKINGS'. I thought of Rope and Those and Most and other words that might sound like Hope, but it isn't any good because my mind ran off and thought perhaps it was really a word that rhymed with GREEN, because perhaps the telephone lady had read the same children's book that I miserably read when I was small which had a dreadful fairy sort of a woman in it who kept on saying, in and out of season, 'Green for hope, beloved – Green for Hope!' Not that that ever could be in season, come to think of it.

Beaumont[3] had a field day because the Red Cross rang up and said their Mr Wallis or Tibbits or something was coming at three; so I left Beaumont in charge. Mr W. or T. came, with a lady in uniform, who said the car would do splendidly, better than all their others, and Mr W. or T. said he knew Douglas Pennant (not a matter for boasting, I should have thought, but neither he nor Beaumont seem to have specified the sex and so it may be all right) and he also knew Tisbury or wherever Beaumont glorified God before he retired. Beaumont of course, I mean. And so everyone was very happy and they all went away and I was happy too. Then I rang up Ruth at Apsley and she sounded very tired and rather lank

1 A BBC feature.
2 Increase, Above Rubies, Show Forth and Peradventure were table-rabbits to whom we had given Pilgrim Father names (we were unsure of Peradventure Rabbit's sex).
3 Beaumont: our jobbing gardener. Ruth, sans chauffeur, had handed on her car to us; petrol was tightly rationed and we considered selling it.

but said, rather charmingly, that 'If they will give £250 then we must take it as the fortunes of war – but if they won't give that, then we can keep the car.' Which makes it clear enough, I should say. I read in Molly Panter-Downes that Lord Beaverbrook is campaigning for the restoration of the basic ration of petrol and so maybe we shall be able to get our hairs done by car, sometime or another.

Lander was profoundly morose after his sleep but I think that is because he has got four enormous lovely bacon-smelling wooden packing-cases from the US Army, which he is to cut up for firewood, and gladness is morosity after tea.

I found two dissimilar but equally happy recipes in Martindale,[1] which I will append.

Sylvia Rose (the little girl I feel worried about) has corns between her toes: a pleasant PAC young woman came in for some ointment for her and says that she suffers cruel. I expect she does. Horrible – and all that loathsome walking and standing one has to do in healthy schools. And bad shoes, and winter.

I was so pleased to have a reason to write your pretty name, twice – once in the book and once on the box – thrice – and once on the paper.

Going to work this morning everything was very handsome to see and I thought how odd it is, when we are apart, that I *see* very clearly and not especially plainly – through and not with, all right – but not in the least as though I were in the round. As a kind of inversion of the way animals are said not to see – This is clear really if you think about it. *I* am flat - I am less than I was and I am also not the same as I was. I suppose that is why any person with an ounce of shrewdity and a grain of self-preservation becomes terrified when he falls in love. The story of the young man who learned what fear is could have been made more accurate, I think. Not power and glory at all – but a wife.

There is no news at all! I met Mrs Edwards[2] and the Girl and the Brother-in-law (he in his car and cross: the others standing by it to see him off). Mrs Edwards was very tight and the girl was horrifyingly buxom. No prussic has come yet which is probably a good thing, one way or another.

It has flowed milk: I got a pint and a half of goat as well as our pint. Thomas has finished the Silver Cow and some goat but he is not very pleased with milk at the moment, of course. So I made a jorum of curry liquid which will do either as a curry or a soup for tomorrow when

---

1 *Martindale Pharmacopoeia.*
2 Mrs Edwards: an elderly neighbour.

Elizabeth Brims[1] comes.

Mrs Lander brought me in a whole heap of little trophies this morning – she'd been mousing about in her cupboard and she could hardly wait till he'd gone to bring them in – A funny little book with a hand-painted binding, flowers and knots and things, and a view. Poems about Tynemouth or somewhere. Very bad. An old copy of *Robinson Crusoe* with a pretty steel engraving and bountiful fat dark cats sitting around him and a very faithful parrot. I urged her to read it and she said she had looked at it and thought she might. And an older copy (about 1840) of *Gulliver*. She'd got Swift and Defoe mixed and thought Defoe was a Dean. She likes Defoe because he is buried in Islington – or died there – and she lived there once, which gives her an interest.

I shan't go on with this, my love, because it is getting rather dull and in any case it will make you feel odd, I expect, to read it directly after, or before, talking with your mother. Like switching from one station to another on the radio and hearing wild music in different keys. And there *is* nothing to tell you of any interest at all. Except that it is very silly for two people so deeply and so much in love to try to be apart, for it doesn't work at all well.

My love, my love –

Valentine

P.S. I'm going to be cunning about the envelope I send this in.

Did you remember your stockings?

Could you perhaps bring back our Havelock Ellis?[2] Or Bloch? Or Krafft-Ebing?

Aqua Mellis. Oils of bergamot, Lavender, clove and sandalwood, musk and saffron with triple rose-water, triple orange-flower-water, honey and alcohol 90%.

Mana. A saccharine exudation from Fraxinus Ormus. In flattish, somewhat three-sided pieces. A non-fermentable sugar, which does not reduce Fehling's solution. Has mild laxative properties.

1 Elizabeth Brims: a spirited Cockney evacuee, a clerk in the Dorset Territorial Army Office where Valentine worked before being transferred to Civil Defence.
2 In 1942 we had been told, confidentially, that in the event of an invasion our house would be requisitioned as a machine-gun post – in which case we would have to leave at short notice. So we packaged our smaller dear possessions and housed them with friends in less menaced places. One of these deposits was a crate of 17th cent. folios and Nonesuch editions with Havelock Ellis etc. squeezed in among them, which I had taken to Little Zeal.

1945

Frome Vauchurch, 28 February 1945

My dearest Dear,

There was one gleam of consolation as I saw you into your train;[1] you looked so very nice, so well dressed for travelling, that it seemed like a promise that we would go travelling again one day. Your little stuggy gloves looked so charming, and it is like a better world to see you in a hat of your own after all those deplorable Queen Betty's.[2] I wonder we have never met her in Braileys,[3] don't you?

Then I came home and read your notes. Of course I remember the blue squared paper.[4] What d'you take me for? Wot, I mean. I thought it was magic then, part of the same magic as the shells that came scented from the beach (was there ever a full-grown woman so head over ears silly? Lots, I hope). Now I know it is. How else can you still have it? Then I transferred my effects to the spare room, for I mean to widow it thoroughly; besides, dear spare-room bed, it is nice for it to be lain in, not wholly given over to guests. Then I went to Lander's.[5] He was extremely sorry to hear about Ruth, looked grave, then non-committal. Then all was overcome in a look of professional yearning. He would so like to be at her. He was not in the least perturbed about the car until I said that I

1 The day after she got back from Winterton we heard that Ruth had been in a bus accident and a cut in her forehead had needed stitching up. On November 27th she telephoned that the cut was septic.

2 Queen Betty: consort of George VI, now Queen Elizabeth the Queen Mother; her hats were deplorable.

3 Shop in Dorchester where war conditions had reduced Valentine to buying, only to discard, hats of necessity.

4 A hoarded supply of small square blue *billet-doux* sheets, which had accompanied bouquets from 1930 onward.

5 I had been his dispenser before he got Valentine, so I could stand in, but I could not drive his car, then in Dorchester for repair.

knew a young woman who was a good driver and whom I felt sure would
be delighted to bring it out. Then he instantly rang up Tilley's and it is
being brought out by one of Tilley's lads. I am really not sorry. I would
have welcomed Monica,[1] but I do not think she would have enjoyed the
drive. That car is better in the hands of a Tilly than in the hands of a
Willy. Monica, I mean, is so obviously one of those long pale green
nixies that pull you under the waterfall, and the Germans call them
Willys. I feel it is all for the best. So does Lander, no doubt of it. He
turned back from the telephone with a kind goblin grin, and if I had seen
the end of a chop-bone sticking out from his chops I would have felt it
natural and familiar.

A crate of drugs came from Wyleys, I took its lid off, but did not
unpack it, because I wanted to gallop home and begin writing to you.
Though as you see I have nothing much to write about. Unless I tell you
how sad it is for Mr Palmer[2] that he lost his clothing card last year and Mr
Wareham has not given him another yet, owing to his having filled up a
form for 1941 (given him at the WVS). As a result he has no summer
underclothes, no boots, no nothing, except what the lady he lodges with
(and who told me all this) has supplied him with out of her own book. She
was so discreet, and at the same time knew so much about his
underclothes that I think perhaps Mr Palmer has followed the example of
Mrs Palmer.

It has turned so cold. Je m'en rejouis de ton gilet. I hate to think how
damp your grey shawl will be. Try to air it.

The house is so bleak. Thos is poured out in dejection on the bed,
Cumquat is poured out with dejection on one of the dining room chairs
and I have not the heart to move him. We shall go on in a quiet way. You
need not worry about us, you will have enough to worry about without
that, my poor love. But at any rate, let us and Lander be off your mind.
He is quite easy now that he has saved his precious car from the hands of
harpies, and only concerned about your anxiety and your long journey.
Mrs L came in to say how nice it was I could come when Miss Warner
wasn't able to. Where are you now? You should be near Reading. Did
you see Mr Gee's dear horse on Bratton Camp Hill? A journey can't be
too bad, I mean the route of a journey, that passes the Revd. James
Woodforde[3] and King Alfred. At any rate, you had a window seat facing

---

1 Monica [Ring]: a friend of Valentine, daughter of a country family, she was beautiful and
ungainly, and I compared her to the Lady Gawky of Restoration comedies.
2 Mr Palmer: builder and plumber.
3 It took her past Castle Cary where James Woodforde of the *Diaries* held a curacy.

the engine, that was a good start; and a Nancy, I think opposite. Take care of yourself my dearest love, remember that you did have influenza, and smartly, and try to keep your feet dry; and don't do all the cooking for every one all the time. Trina would certainly help, either by coming over or by cooking something that could be sent with the meat.[1] Remember her sausage rolls. They might be a godsend.

Give my love to poor Ruth. I hope that things will be better when you arrive. I'm afraid her looks will be a great shock, I expect she bruises as blackly as you do. She will be so pleased to see you a day earlier, and pleasure is a very good medicine. I remember with some comfort that for the week before this infection she was mainly resting and keeping quiet; and that should stand her in some stead, much better than if the infection had caught her in full tilt. Thoughts of that wretched Mary[2] came into my mind and I can only shoo at them, they are too painful to be dwelt on. The goat's eyes of the scape-goat; for she will undoubtedly feel that her going precipitated the lorry into the 'bus, the stitches into Ruth, the sepsis into the stitches. O Ow! My mind wanders after you through a thornpatch. I did not like to see you start alone on this journey. If you want me, I can start at a moment's notice, and make it right with Lander. Anyway, if you want me, what is anything else? Alas!

Tib

79: STW

Little Zeal, 26 October 1945

My dearest Love,

There was a noise like a fire-alarm (Nora's telephone is reinforced with two gongs); both the dogs barked. Nora looked out of the window and said 'I suppose that's the butcher'; and I removed a flounced harlot off the receiver (Nora's taste is good enough up to 1900 but God knows what she won't adulterate with in the nineteenth century); and after the Post Office had got over its surprise at the call being answered, for usually in spite of

---

1 Trina was married to a butcher in the next village.
2 Mary: cook and sister to Trina. Mary's endurance had finally given out, and she had left Ruth's service just before the bus accident.

the extra gong Nora is only aware, from their mouths opening and shutting, that the dogs are barking, I got the glad news of your tooth. Oh what a weight off my heart! Instantly the clocks began to go twice as fast and my bristles lay down like tired children. All the same, I think you might take a bottle of Burgundy to our bedroom. It might ward off any more such attacks.

It has rained all day and is still raining. In the midst of this whirl of wet, the house has a water shortage, and Nora has a great deal of pettifogging pleasure in saving water: washing in a teacupful, only half filling the teapot, etc. At the same time she has developed a conviction that it is a dirty habit to wash all the same table crockery in a bowl, and each object has to be rinsed separately under the tap. This may be one reason of the watershortage. I am sure a psychologist would delight in her. She is a baker's dozen of phobias and at the same time perfectly rational in every selfregard. Remind me to tell you the story of the wedding veil. It is almost as fine as the emblems of the Passion, and in the same manner.

It is extraordinary to me to think that my father and Ronald both lived in the house. There is not a breath of a man in it now. Her devouring femaleness has eaten their very ghosts. All the way here, driving along the lanes, I can remember them perfectly, but the instant I am inside the house they are extinguished. Yet the one commissioned it, and the other made it, and both lived here. A wilderness of ghosts would be less alarming than this absolute vacuity.

Except for clinging to the thought of your tooth, today, as you can see, has been hard to endure, or more accurately hard to assimilate. But it is the first day, and it is over, and the first day is the worst. By mid-day tomorrow I shall begin to run down-hill, just as the train does after the Evershot tunnel.

I have found a book we must get from the London Library, *The Amberley Papers*. An aristocratic mid-vict. young couple from their youths up. They were Bertrand Russell's parents. There are some superb pages of a school-boy diary, the poor child riddled with religious jealousy of his boy-friends; and a very loveable letter from the same boy, rather older, to his mother, entirely taken up with religious differences except the last paragraph, which abruptly introduces the utilisation of sewage. And there is a daguerreotype of the young lady which I am sure you will fall in love with. Amidst all this nonsense they fall madly in love, and are suddenly transformed into being delightful, all their priggeries transmogrified into manias.

I am coming home on Tuesday. By the 4.10. If you are not at the station

I am to ring M.N. 206. Just in case you think I've forgotten! My darling, how I love you.

Sylvia

1946

80: STW

London, 2 April 1946

My dearest Love,

I am just back from the Barber[1] – and still in a rapture, unable to believe my ears that I understood so much of it, equally unable to believe my ears that on coming out of the theatre the spell continued: the same sharply-sloped voices all around me, crying out at the rain and then settling down to stand under the theatre's shelter and talk about the performance all night.

A thousand things to tell you – but most remarkable, most subversive (to my own conception, that is) the Don Basilio. Not the sleek round well-shaven well-oiled man of God, but a zany by El Greco, interminably lean, tufts of dejected bootlace hair, a long grey cassock like a hygienic dressing-gown, and the world admitted in pale green stockings. O lovely, O how I wish you could have seen him! It must be the tradition, it must have been Beaumarchais' nastiest insult to the C. of Jesus, to represent him, with all his baseness, his venality, his engulphing acceptance of bribes all round – and yet an idiot mystic, a Tom Bernadette, a gawk.

The house was crammed, I delight to say. All seats gone, and an audience of such silence, and on one side I had two young Frenchmen, and on the other, two old Englishwomen, governesses, perhaps, or cat-house keepers – and as quick as you please to enjoy.

The Figaro was a man called Dux, Pierre Dux – and he was also the Molière in the Impromptu de Versailles. A long sad rubber face, and ape's

1 The Comédie Française was having a London season, and she had given me tickets for two nights.

forehead, a look of preternatural monkey melancholy and wisdom and the most beautiful diction, and such a rubato in the phrasing of the tirades. O God, how good they are, how beautifully they move around, how the action swims and floats, and how grateful I am to you and How I would have enjoyed it a thousand times More if you had been there. They are coming back in September. We must see them together. London is old and new ... full of the strangest creatures, hordes of Poles, more soldiers than you can imagine, people dressed all anyhow, some with elegance, some in tatters. The most elegant a beauty I saw at the National Gallery, very tall and thin in the identical oyster-coloured trousers of Nancies in our twenties, golden hair in Van Dyke ringlets, and a short white coat. The air rings with Nancy voices. I kept on turning around thinking it must be Angus.[1]

And in the National Gallery almost the first thing I saw was your portrait with Hat by Rubens. You have been cleaned. You look lovely – indescribably wicked – and your red velvet sleeves have come up wonderful.

Everything in the three rooms has been cleaned.[2] Bacchus and Ariadne are a riot, and the ox in the P. della Francesca Nativity almost dominates the picture. There is a ravishing Wilson, presented by Eddie Marsh in VE day. A stiltonic Cader Idris with a lake sleeping in its crater, and such a grandly horizontal horizon beyond.

Some of the new Tate buys are grand. There is a Battersea Reach by Greaves I could cry my eyes out for, it is so tranquil, so consommée, so beautifully worked out in triangles of the ship in the foreground and the triangular perspective of the river: a Gertler, Duncan's portrait of Vanessa, and a *Bonnard*! It is a table, spread with a cherry and white checked cloth, a tea-pot, and at the further side two women and a dog with tea-cups. But the whole centre of the picture is just the painting of the chequered cloth, and it is terrific.

This house seems very nice.[3] It has nine cats in it, four grown up and five kittens. It is now raining a little, and the trees have that *bitter* smell only town trees ever have.

Your letter ... how can you think that I ever mix up in my mind dreariness (dreariness not cheeriness, but cheeriness equally neither) and Valentine?

---

1 Angus [Davidson].
2 Newly re-opened.
3 Where her cousin Alec [Robertson] lived with some other BBC musicians.

I do feel extremely pleased to be in London, and so to speak *back* – because at the moment the city side of me is boiling to the surface – but not liberated, unless you were with me. Then I would prance like a tigress – as it is I prance like a cat – more moderate bounds. The truth is, one can't really prance on one leg.

I have had two taxis![1] Almost as cleverly as if you had caught them. My legs look lovely. I *did* want to hang them over the dress-circle, but refrained. We need not worry about clothes for London – or hats. Very few hats. But I will go to Scotts[2] tomorrow all the same. My Love, my loved one.

Sylvia

81: VA

Frome Vauchurch, Wednesday 20 November 1946

I had a letter from Janet this morning, my Love, and she has not yet (or had not then, Monday) had the baby. She – I'll send it.

It rained and stormed and blew and raged all night. I went early to bed and then got a wild attack of toothache which became earache and then at last I went to sleep. You took my brown shawl by mistake and so I used your grey shawl, but felt sorry because the brown one is smaller and I am afraid you may have lacked around your toes. I hope you were not cold, my Love – I wasn't, but I was dismal.

I think Epictetus isn't at all bad, for a Stoic.

The lost parcel arrived from Elizabeth; I can wear the best thing in it, a dusty green dress, but only if ever we can get reasonable belly-belts and do not have to wear the fish-net I'm wearing now, which not only lets me out at odd places but squeezes me out through its mesh; and that looks unpleasant. It looks all right on a Spaniard – that odd intermittent bulging, but dreadful on a bloody Nord like me. There is a fine woollen[3] which will fit you and suit you very prettily; there is a grey coat-and-skirt which will do if we can get it buttonholed to be made into links and not do-ups in front. Blast my Scottish Grandmother's Bosom. Joan always

---

1 'Catch a falling star' – they were rarities.
2 Scotts: hatters, where I found her a severe sombrero to annul the period of Queen Betty's.
3 The W.V.S. supplied a grateful wearer for this.

said I'd get like it and I have. Blast Joan.[1]

I remember once travelling in a 'bus with Joan, when I was perhaps 11 or so, and an enormous woman opposite couldn't see into her hand-bag because of her bosom, and had to lift it up and look directly at it before she could see. Joan saw me watch that with horror and said when we got out, 'Tea on the Terrace – you'll have a front like that. You're like Daddy's side of the family. Aunt Lucy had.' I never forgot that. It made me scarlet with blushes then and it makes me pale with despair now. However – count no man happy till you see him dead.

My sweet Love – I wish I could think the river at L.Z. is being as great a pleasure as this river is to me here. It is making a very gentle and delighted noise and everything looks extraordinarily tired and pleased, as if all night the world had made love with the gale and the storm.

I'm sending Jan a large packet of N.Ys[2] and books (N O T the new N.Y.) and a long letter about Joan whatever-she-is-called and Monica's boat and you being at Nora's (I said N. had had some mishap but I didn't know what and seemed all right) and so on. And asking if her baby will like a little chair attached to a little table or else a carrying thing for week-ending. We shall have to give it something and I've seen these two things in Dorch: and so probably they'll be obtainable still by the time we have to get something. The animals are being rather boisterous, which doesn't suit my mood. They are both dreadfully greedy and have no hearts.

I've got to go out now to get some lavatory paper and a postal order for that silly football pool at which I did not win £1,000 for 1/-. It is odd that I can't when everyone else can.

I had a story (the one about the publishers) returned by your ineffable Mr Roland Gant, who is undoubtedly very, appallingly brave and whom I do admire theoretically but whom I know I cannot bear. I think it is impertinent of him to call you Sylvia. I wish we had arranged another name those people could call you – like Louisa or perhaps Cassandra, or – evilly – something that was a teaser to pronounce. I'm not feeling vicious towards the swelling crowd of innocent young men, but because he is called Roland and calls you Sylvia. It is so unsuitable.

My pretty Love – I can't think how you can endure me nor why you do even if you can. But come back soon: please come back sound and soon.

Valentine

1 Joan [Woollcombe]: her sister, eight years her senior.
2 [*New Yorker* magazines]

1947

Frome Vauchurch, 27 April 1947

My dearest Love,

My fingers are at this moment intensely crossed, for it is 10.30 and you are fetching John and Elspet.[1] I have been planting the Allwood pinks and throwing Shan's[2] ball. I did not put them in last night because the wireless said there might be a ground frost. There was, too. When I woke this morning everything was like the best aluminium; afterwards when the sun rose it was like the less best aluminium. There was a thick foggy cloud of exhalation rising from the valley behind the Mearns end of Visitor's Walk,[3] and the church bells began to ring and I thought how chilly poor Daniel would be and hoped the poor wretch would take an extra pull at his dive bouteille. Do you suppose, too, that loving clerics give an extra twirl to their wives on cold mornings? Twirl of sacrament, I mean. Sacramental wine, to be precise. One gets misled among these sacraments.

Since then it has become warm and very beautiful, and if it is like this at Winterton the garden alone should do the trick. I imagine the grape hyacinths and scyllas are flowering in the little orchard. I really don't think the dilapidations inside are so serious if the woodwork is still all right. I laughed at myself, though, last night, saying to you so gravely on the telephone, 'Ceilings always come down in bombardments.' Heavens, what a long way one gets floated on the ever-rolling stream, and to what odd banks and islands – and on the whole pretty unperceptiently.

You must have made my bed with a great deal of love, for I slept very

1 John and Elspet Robertson Scott, of *The Countryman*. They were looking for a house, and there was a hope they might buy The Hill House.
2 Shan: a Pekinese, successor to Cumquat.
3 A farm-track, steep and brambled, which we heartlessly recommended to visitors.

well. I carefully did not make it this morning, to keep the love in. Thomas closed my eyelids with kind paws, and then fell asleep on the second bottle, which had been meant for him anyhow, as it was a cold night. Though I did not make the bed, I have made the dough. I propose to have a pizza filled with sorrel and iced with Parmesan. I shall make some bread too, and cut down on the baker.

We had enough bread units left over from the last period to get another bag of flour, I have paid them in and the flour will come with the groceries. I ate two of your little cakes last night, and another this morning.

It pleases me to think how much broader Steven's[1] mind must be by now. Pleasantly broadened by the drive and seeing The Hill; searchingly broadened by first steps in the Anglo-Cat-Home. I wonder if it has occurred to him that the severe absence of plaster Jesuses in his own upbringing is only, as you would say, the other side of the wireless. His mother puts them in the soup,[2] yours on the mantelpiece. Now that he has a child of his own he had better think on these things, or he will begin to attach too much importance to them.

Though it is always agreeable to find kidneys, I imagine from the fact that you found and grilled them that you also found great slabs of Ruth's meat awaiting cooking. Just the sort of well-meant pole-axe one would find at the end of a day's driving. If I were really very rich, very very rockefeller rich, I think instead of endowing the Warner Prizes for Vice or something of that sort I would leave it all in a trust for supplying restaurants (with drinks) in every village with a population below two thousand. This would be convenient, and it would put an end to the church quicker than any other form of attack. When the church was ended the restaurants could move into the churches and so extend the lives of many deserving buildings – though one would have to do something about their acoustics. Will you ever forget the sacred shindy in the Brit. Rest.[3] at Weymouth.

I seem to have overlooked the churches in places where the population is over two thousand. But I expect they would die away naturally, cut at the root, and if not, then they would change their nature and become more like cinemas. Meanwhile I am going upstairs to paint the bathroom seat. It is an ideal day for art: dry and rather draughty.

---

1 Steven Clark: whom we first met in Barcelona in 1930.
2 She venerated her economies.
3 British Restaurants were a wartime expedient; this one was housed in a disused Victorian Gothic church.

I read some more in *Partisan Review* last night. Afterwards I had a moment of vision, and it becomes clear to me what will happen during the next seven years. Nature abhors a vacuum, and here are all these partisans and horizontalists and what-not all craving for a congenial literature and not able to produce one themselves (I couldn't find a page in either PR that was not written by a eunuch). The Vacuum will be filled by the new post-war German writers, who will produce a rather winsome Freud cum Kafka style of writing, but all very maerchen and dancing on light didactic toes. The Ps and the Hs will adore it, and totally forsake the classical French or English manner. I can't tell you yet, though, what the names of these new writers will be, except that one of them will be called Dott. Mark my words. Trotsky-Cattery, cut out of three-ply. Little men with big bombs. The Guinea-pig's suicide. A mosquito literature, gossamer wings, trills on the piccolo. Yellow Jack in the belly.

The other thing I have been musing about, though not so clearly, is the Pope's Film Rights, and the new Vatican Hollywood, with glamorous Mother Dolores and the boy Bishop and a whole Rin-tin-tin team of Saint Bernards.

But these speculations are very dull without you, my darling.

Sylvia

83: VA

Frome Vauchurch, 23 June 1947

Monday at about four

My love,

I arrived back in perfect safety – no, in safety – no, nothing whatever is perfect while you are away. Not even Thomas, whom I found sitting reproachfully on the doorstep, beside his emptied dish; he has ear-ache.

Shan looked well and squaked – no, squeaked – with pleasure because I had come back, and then dwined because I have mislaid you. Oh how I do hope I haven't! Did you get there comfortably? Did you see that they didn't lock those doors again? Did you travel alone? I saw no Royal Duchess; only the Royal Train with chaste blue curtians – no, curtains – half-drawn and a posse of police standing near it in case someone blew it up (I suppose): one policeman was smoking – in UNIFORM. . . . I looked at him in horror and then was flabbergasted to see another policeman, an old one too, bent double and prying roguishly through the Royal Train window, between the curtains. I fled in shame. I never knew British Police could stoop so low. It does go to prove that the R - - - D - - - - ss is what the common people say she is; otherwise, how should police behave so?

I found a letter from Janet when I got home. It is a sad letter. I will tell you about it when you return.

I stayed at the post-office because it came into my head that it might have slipped out of yours, to pay for the C.O.D. parcel. And it had. So I did. It was 7/8.

Returning via Yeovil I bought a pound of matchless fresh strawberries for 1/6. I have not tasted better. I shall go into Y. on my way to fetch you and try to get some more like them, then you can feast joyfully directly you dismount from the train. I have located the Stn. at Montacute but supposing the train runs through, don't panic but get out at Yeovil T O W N and I will meet you there.

There is nothing at all to say except what I have said, in every way I know, in every mood I have, during these bountiful years which have been all Junes. . . . Sweet dear heart — I love you.

Valentine

84: STW

Little Zeal, 23 June 1947

My dearest Love,

When I was at home I was in a better place.

I went on travelling just when you left me, quite uneventfully except for a man who got in at Exeter, and was so persecuted by an old gentleman who kept on asking him why the train didn't reach Plymouth at 4.30 as it ought to that I finally joined in and took my share of the explanations and consolations and exhortations to bear it bravely; and when the old gentleman had taken his grievances elsewhere we went on talking, and I heard how he and his brother had emigrated to Canada in 1920 and had been pioneer farmers in Alberta on the Peace River; and he had liked it very much, and especially fishing in lakes that were not marked on the map (you will understand this); and one fine day came a hailstorm, and hailstones as big as golf balls ruined their whole crop of corn in an hour and a half. So then he got into the timber business, and had got his affairs nicely into order when this war came; he came over to fight, and at the end of the year his timber business had folded up too: no means of getting the wood across, so no money to pay for felling, and if you don't fell, the woods (ah me!) decay and fall.

But he was very philosophic because, as he remarked frankly, he had no wives or children to get between him and his philosophy.

So then I got here, and Nora at first did not recognise me and when she did showed no particular interest. However, she was delighted with things I had brought, and instantly began to eat Turkish Delight and talk of Port Said.

The garden is full of weeds, all the borders are strangled with bindweed. It is strange to see our pink roses blooming here – and doing very well. But everything has an elegy in its hair. All the garden seems to be peering about from under its overgrown forelocks for Ronald.

Take the greatest care, and the tenderest care of yourself, my darling. Look after yourself as well as I would like to do, and never achieve. Don't lift great burdens, or work in the full sun, or be put upon, either by Mrs H.E.'s[1] hens or our own dear animals.

Oh what a waste of time lies between this letter and 3.2 p.m. on Thursday at Montacute!

With my love always and always and all-ways.

Your Tib

85: VA

Frome Vauchurch, 8 July 1947

Monday night

My only Love,

Do for God's sake keep care of yourself: I have always a sense of danger when it is a sick house – and I am troubled in my heart about you. Do be very wary of pitfalls – colds in the head, even; or too little food and too many draughts; or misery in your mind because of seeing misery in an

---

1 Mrs Hawley Edwards: she had to be helped with her hens.

old and sick mind. Do not let yourself be stampeded, even privily, my Love. And do remember to come back to me quickly as you can –

But don't worry, for there is nothing at all to worry about.

I kiss you, my sweetheart –

Valentine

The Dearest Child

Like the dearest child, the weakling, hardest to wean and rear,
My soul inhabits this house, wandering silent from room to room,
And when I call her comes only shyly near.
Sometimes all day she sits moping, until late evening gloom
Fills the tall house and the others grow tired and prepare for bed;
Then if I call her, then she will answer me gently, and lift her head.

(a poem I made last month)

86: STW

Little Zeal, 9 December 1947

My dearest Love,

I feel as if a thousand miles and a thousand hours were between us. It is *worse* to come here suddenly because one has not time to adjust one's mind, taper down one's appetites, inoculate oneself for the change of climate between being happy with you and unhappy with futility without you.

It is such nonsense. The smallest joint on your slenderest finger has more sense of me than the whole of this poor old crone. For about an hour after my arrival she was certainly pleased and aware of it – but it all ebbs back into the sort of muddled egoism which is the remains of her once extremely clear-minded egoism.

And the fidgets! The getting up for the dogs and the getting down for the dogs: the mislayings and changes of mind, and finally a protracted search for a short piece of candle to go to bed with. No use offering her a long candle - no, she had set her mind on a short piece of candle.

By tomorrow I expect I shall have inured myself, and be able to see more beauties in the landscape.

But only by shutting both eyes, alas!

Tomorrow, too, I shall see the doctor (opening one eye for the spectacle). But as far as I can make out there is nothing wrong except senility, and nothing that can be done. She has a bronchitis sort of cough, but only very occasionally, and a bruise on her elbow where she fell downstairs. Nothing like a stroke – and her main impression, the thing she noticed most, was the excitement of being picked up by Mr Evans'[1] gigantic strength, which she found very agreeable.

One thing may be significant. This morning, while she was still being kept in bed, she said to Mrs Kellow – Don't send for Sylvia. As Mrs Kellow herself remarked, don't might have implied *Do*: but another possible reading is that she is afraid of being be-doctored and chased out of her routine and her denny ways. So Mrs K. very prudently said she would not send for me, and when I arrived I came in as one who was expected, and said my letter must have gone astray, or Nora had not bothered to read it. After a little suspicion she settled down into believing this, and was, I am almost sure, glad to think so.

There seems to be plenty to eat – milk, eggs and butter abound.

But the things I brought were pleasant surprises (except the Brands essence. It doesn't seem cared for, so I am keeping it to bring home.)

I wish I could be kept in a glass jar and a cool place till then. O my darling, what Hell it is to be away from you. Soon I shall go to bed, and have some pleasure there, reading your story.

My love always and *all* and always.

Sylvia

87: STW

Little Zeal, 10 December 1947

My dearest Love,

Thanks to you I have been feeling much happier all day – because this morning I read your story[2] – no, not all of it, I am carefully spinning it out – but enough to feel a dayspring and laugh and tingle and be revived. It is – just as much as in the beginning – an extremely good story, and every inch of it is alive. There's not an ounce of fat about it, it is as prancing, as

1 Mr Evans: my mother's gardener and factotum.
2 A further instalment of *A Start in Life*.

well-knit, as prick-eared, as bright-whiskered as a young cat in his proud prime. And the characters are so bold and sharp. What they say is exactly what they should say, the rambling apologies of the Squire and the plumpness of China and the Laconics of Stinger. And the young man and Tandy are so beautifully in love – as much in love as we are. Oh I *am* so delighted with it. It is better than your short stories, you know: much as they improved. It is such a lovely texture, as crisp and airy and well-plimmed-up as a home-made loaf.

Then came your letter and that lovely poem. Which made me weep because it was so willow-wand and so pure.

Thanks to these I have got through a dreary day. Endless confabulations. First the unhappy Evans. I am extremely sorry for him. It is obvious that he has worked himself up into thinking that if something happens to Nora the skies will fall, a judge in a black cap will come down and hold an inquest, the village will point scorn at him and Mrs E. Then a friend of Nora's called Lefanu, a nice-enough woman, and she is intelligent, and has travelled; and she spent a happy constructive hour analysing the situation, suggesting various expedients, and then neatly demolishing them. Then Dr Creasy, who I must say I like, because he is a tall man, and wears good corduroy trousers, and has no sentiments, and says flat out that old persons are the devil and the bane of his life, and the only thing you can be sure of with Nora is that she isn't telling the truth; and that it would be far better not to throw good money after bad, so to speak, and that for his part he is perfectly prepared to run any risks of accidents and let her go on as she is. Then Mrs Kellow, who really is a very nice woman, and I feel great warmth towards her. She is, as you said, Elizabeth Brims, but with more consideration than Elizabeth, and a tenderness which Elizabeth hasn't at all. Then Veronica Ferguson, who I rang up to ask about a woman who had worked for her and whom Mrs Kellow thought might be able to endure living here (few could but this one was notably placid); but only to be told that she was in another job and wouldn't have done anyhow. Finally, Hugh Boucher, who also rang up, having heard I was here (the whole of Devonshire knows I am here) and he was very manly and limp and woe-begone – and could come on Friday and wanted to talk it all over with me. So there we are. Then I rang you up, and told you all this, like a lacklustre parrot, instead of hearing about you.

In between all this I have cooked and trayed, and fetched pillows; and performed a little house-building. For Nora, at some time or other, had dismantled all the fixings of her bedroom fireplace, so that in order to light a fire in her bedroom I had to take the spare-room grate to pieces and rebuild it in her room. By the grace of Ronald, it was the same pattern, and fitted.

It is curious how people live in their works. Nora has almost obliterated Ronald from the house he built and inhabited. His chest of drawers and some books of his languish in a dressing-room, along with all the things she doesn't use or never wants. Most of his furniture has been sold or given away. The house is flamboyant with her ideas, her devices, her taste. But when I refitted the grate and found how smoothly it adjusted itself, I felt as though Ronald's large deft hands had suddenly closed over mine, and were doing it for me.

Tomorrow is Thursday, Friday is Friday. On Saturday¹ unless the heavens fall before I can get away from under them, I come H O M E, I come to your arms, and my flesh will return to my bones. I don't know where it is now. I would like to think it is lying quietly in our bed. That is where I expect to find it. Or do you think it is in the lost property office at Maiden Newton GWR with Mr Trump finding it much in his way and only consoled by charging up a large bill for demurrage? 'Excuse me, Miss Warner. Here is your flesh,' he will say as he takes my ticket.

No! I will not receive my dear flesh at Mr Trump's hands. It is in our bed – and Thomas is sleeping on it, and thinking how much beds are improved by being left in a natural easy negligée. When I think of our bed – I can't really think of it till tomorrow evening. I will think of the electric cooker instead. I am glad you found the prunes in the oven. Did you know they were there, or did they burst on you like a thunderstorm. Then I will turn my mind to the top drawer in the spare-room. There you will find two Petersham belts and a coloured cotton handkerchief and you are welcome to them for Christmas presents if Christmas presents are biting

---

1 My mother's condition suddenly worsened. Her senility changed to insanity; her hoarded resentments and jealousies and furies came into the open, she was like a mad infant, pitiable and terrifying. I began to be afraid of her, as I had been in my youth. Others were afraid too, and kept away. Except for the District Nurse, who came once a day to help me wash her, I was unaided and alone. My hoarded fears came into the open. I had not the resolution to ask Valentine to come – I was afraid that Nora would recognise her, even attack her. But she came. Nora did not recognise her outright, though when they chanced to encounter, she stared at her with puzzled antagonism. Valentine, studying her compassionately, came to the conclusion that Nora's frenzies were a defence against fear: that she was afraid of the house, the river, imaginary or even real intruders, and must be moved – though I had promised her, many years before, she should never have to leave Little Zeal. On Christmas Eve I took my mother to a nursing home. Valentine returned to a cold house and two anxious animals, whose temporary caretaker had gone off to her own merry Christmas. I stayed in Devon long enough to see my mother growing more settled and even beginning to lord it over a very kind nurse. Then I went home.

you. But do not be bitten if you can avoid it. Go on with the story, that is much more important. And take care of yourself, my dearest one. And don't saw wood and give yourself a back-ache, and don't wind the car and give yourself a stomach-ache; and don't ever doubt me or doubt my love and give yourself a heart-ache.

If you could see me without you, you would never doubt my love again. I see myself in the mirror and I look like *hake*. Tinned hake at that; cramped and divorced from its natural being, and packed in a little brine.

Withal, I am perfectly well. So do not worry about me, either. At this moment my ghost is kissing the top of your head, your lovely scented and patterned Golden Cap.

O take care of yourself, my heart's delight, and my strength and my true love.

Sylvia

1948

88: VA

Frome Vauchurch, 31 March 1948

My Love,

Remember that you have all my love and all my life, and keep them carefully and cherish them in yourself warmly and wisely.

Please think of this, and drink wine, and eat well, and cover yourself snugly at night, and if you go to bed late sleep late into the morning: and nourish and cherish yourself and lavish care and kindness on my sweetheart, on my own dear love, on my best and dearest joy and treasure.

And shut the dining room window to keep out marauding cattles, and shut the doors and windows of your own house to keep out dreads and troubles, and to keep in our deep and private peace.

Valentine

89: STW

Frome Vauchurch, 1 April 1948

My dearest Love,

Yes, I will shut the dining room windows against marauding cats. Yes, I will keep all doors shut against Georginas.[1] Yes, I will eat and drink and keep warm. Yes, I will stay under the bedclothes at night. Yes, I will not undertake exhausting or giant works, only placid and pygmy ones. Yes, I

---

1 Georgina was one of a band of prevalent gipsies. To us she was amiability personified but she had knocked out a policeman with one blow.

will comb Shan, and concentrate at 11 p.m.,[1] and look out for the Fortnum Mason Hat, and shun strangers, and ever more industriously shun acquaintances, and do as little housework as possible, and remember my orange gin, and lock the box-room. Yes, to all that. The only qualified Yes, to shut out cares and troubles, for how can I do that with you at Winterton in this cold wind, with a belly in the offing, and no shawl, and no drinking (do remember that even your dear S. Paul, moderately dear perhaps, but you read him in the downstairs w.c., advised wine to bishops) and all those people coming in and leaving the door open, Miss-Molly-ing, and no Tibby-ing . . . how can I promise to shut out all cares? But I will do my best.

The sun is shining, and the gale is making an April Fool of it. What a cold journey you will have. And how much too early Mr Harwood was, for I was through with the post-office, and turning round into the straight of our lane before I saw the 9.25 puffing up the valley; and all that time you had been standing alone on that icy platform with nothing but Mr Trump's eye to warm yourself at. I was so cross to think I had left you there, and you had been there all that time.

I will not Vote for Haward.[2] He is that wicked man who put the cheap paint on the house and wore such genteel trousers. I am sure he is a Conservative Bandit.

I find to my disgust that my diary does not go back to Box Cottage and the Imber Foresight.[3] But I did discover some very nice bits of Arthur Machen in it, including his view that the mysterious little bits of iron fastened on to the outside of the church at Penally being put there to keep the air from entering the ventilators, and when we worked it out by tapping from outside and listening inside, they did.

Remember to tell Ruth how well the lilacs are doing, and that one of them is already showing its flowers.

I am in the long sun-parlour, because of the sun, with the fire full on. And even so it is not very warm; and the line of washing at the Brewery Inn has been steadily horizontal since I first began to notice it. Wind, I mean; not earthquakes or demoniacal possessions. Shan has been sitting

---

1 When I was to think with concentration of some object and she was to wait with a loose mind at the receiving end.
2 Parish Council election.
3 The Society for Psychical Research wanted cases of second-sight. She provided several, I could only raise my experience at Imber, a village on Salisbury Plain where, on a bland summer afternoon, I had the impression of a darkened sky, lightning striking the church tower, a loud clap of thunder, and immediately all the houses of the village falling in ruins. Over ten years later the War Office made the village an artillery target.

on the rocking-chair, wondering why it is so restless, and sometimes getting up to look sternly at its legs, and then sitting down again, dissatisfied, eppur si muove, you know.

Mrs Hawley Edwards has come to ask me if I will feed her hens tomorrow, and to repeat her offer to see to our animals on Tuesday, so I have shown her Shan's bed, and explained all. She plainly thinks the box-bed both brutal and eccentric, but I hope Shan's bedtime demeanour will set her mind at rest about the brutality.

But nothing can be done unless you take the greatest care of yourself, my love and my sweetheart. Tell me truly when you write or when we telephone how you are. You lie so well it would not be gentlemanly or fair to take advantage of it against poor Gullible. Besides, I might not to be taken in after all.

I am too distracted with your departure to write more. It seems too nonsensical to be writing and not talking, making crosses and not giving kisses. Conspuez les devoirs filiales!

Your true Tib

90: STW

Frome Vauchurch, 2 April 1948

My Darling,
    The ice-saints — no, they are in May. I was going to say they had come too soon; but what it is, right enough, is the good old-fashioned reliable Blackthorn Winter. The blackthorn blossoms are coming out, all along the lane. The buds seem to be *frowning* on the bough as the winds bang them. They look as furious as smacked kittens, they lower. I went to feed Mrs H.E.'s hens this afternoon, letting myself in her garden gate. It was curiously like going along some animal's private burrow, going along her path. It is just wide enough for her, up to her height; above that one has to avoid the branches. The hens looked much too large for the garden; they seemed to be spreading as one looked at them, like ink-blots.

After that I walked up to the station to fetch the cod I had ordered from Smith's for the dear animals. It was pouring with rain and unspeakably cold and melancholy, and the platform was empty except for your ghost in that thin flannel suit. Oh, how cold you will be. No shawl, no waistcoat, no warm boots, no nothing. And that cheerless kitchen with not even a hot pipe in it. I brought back the fish in a most cod-like frame of mind, damp and prosaic; but I did have the sense to make myself tea and cinnamon toast, and to wish to God you were having it too.

Both the dear animals are well and good. Shan managed to get himself shut on the further side of the gate by the postman (he was out between showers), and to be caught in one of them, and to get drenched to the skin; but I dried him well, and sat him down before the fire, in your room, and presently I heard him bounding about overhead with his toy, quite dry and restored. Thomas slept on my bosom all night, and was as insistent as you could be about having no windows open. It would have been impossible, anyway. Even with them shut there was an Arctic draught coming through the chinks.

No letters of any interest have come, and nothing for you except what I suppose is Mr Colley's receipt. It is a penny one from Weymouth. The only letter for me was the permit for the wood for our two windows. Except for the hens and the fish I have been totally secluded, doing proofs of *The Corner That Held Them*, and comforting my eyes with the grape hyacinths. The thought of Roy[1] works and scuttles in a corner of my mind like a rat behind the arras – I wish he could be as easily disposed of. The morning has brought me no good ideas, I am just as much as sourly at a loss as I was last night, though I still hold to the thought that if Janet wants to get out it would be the best thing for her. He looks so longevitous, too.

Large expanses of plaster have fallen off the Eyres' house. It has happened quite recently, the brick underneath has all its virginal tints. I cannot but connect it with that young man who came asking for them. Do you suppose that no one answered him when he rang the bell, and in desperation at the thought of having to make any more enquiries, he tried to fight his way in, like my grandmother's scotch terrier who bit his way into a mahogany wardrobe? Or perhaps he did get in, and sang to them, and the vibration was too much for the plaster.

Something must have happened I am sure; for Mrs Samways was standing near by with a glittering and well-fed glance. As usual, when I neared her she said, 'Miss Warner.' As usual, I had great self-restraint in not replying, instructively, 'No.' But one day I shall.

Now I must comb Shan, and put him to bed. As a result of being so well-washed by the blackthorn deluge, he is looking extremely beautiful, and like a meringue. More than I am. The remains of the scratches of last week-end's gardening on my hands look as if I had been tattooed by Klee.

1 [Roy Davis: husband of Janet (née Machen).]

That spider bite on my shin has quite disappeared and I feel rather sentimental about it. At least it was a token of spring.

I have not the impertinence to say to you, Keep warm. Casks, casks,[1] I can recommend nothing but casks. Do you remember that drawing-room song of Gounod's? Roulez, roulez, ma be-e-e-e-elle! Roulez, roule-e-ez toujours. The sun has suddenly flashed out a narrow spear, and lit up the glass bird. It is as if you had come into the room.

My Love,

Sylvia

91: VA

Winterton, 2 April 1948

My only Love,
(that looks reproachful, but it is not meant to be!).

Have you thought how pleasant it must be for the MI5 man who reads our correspondence, to have our innocent domestic bliss to study, instead of suspect letters from Howard Moorepark and Ben Huebsch[2] (something out-of-the-ordinary about that name – I expect they *soak* his letters in a bath of milk; like Cleopatra – felicitously asses' milk).

Well, we went to the Fair. It blew ferociously and we travelled in a jam-packed 'bus and had the new parson's wife sitting behind us and hundreds of lovely sharp-voiced, eagle-eyed children, who set up such yelps at sight of the Fair that I could have eaten them all in one mouthful: such whole-hearted, stout-stomached children there are in Norfolk!

And the Fair went down to St Nicholas and right over the road and flooded out across the bombed brewery. And there were groups of *lovely* small boys, each group with its handsome leader – lappets, shock-heads, starry eyes, yelping, snapping, passionate voices and hands so shrewd that I kept mine firmly clenched around the pen and silver in my pockets.

1 A reference to Brother Laurence (Nicholas Herman). 'That he had lately been sent into Burgandy to buy the provision of wine for the Society, which was a very unwelcome task to him, because he had no turn for business and because he was lame, and could not go about the boat but by rolling himself over the casks. That, however, he gave himself no uneasiness about it, nor about the purchase of the wine. That he said to God, *It was his business he was about*; and that he afterwards found it very well performed.' (*The Practice of the Presence of God*, 1692.) 'Rolling on casks' became a motto for times of adversity.
2 Ben Huebsch: of the Viking Press.

I gave a solemn little boy 4 celluloid balls @ 6d, to roll into grooves. He was about 9. He was alone and very alone and very shabby and poor. He stood for ages, calculating the exact 4 numbers he needed for the prize, and then rolled each ball straight into the right groove, and won a glass salt-cellar.

I treated Ruth to Hoop-la and dissuaded her from riding in a Dodge-'em, and attached her to a string which she had to jerk rather cunningly, to cause an electric contact and win a prize. She stood very contentedly for hours, holding it powerfully but perfectly motionless, until I took her away. She had no idea that she should have done more than just wait.

Then we bought popcorn and a present for Thomas and Shan, and then had ices and I bought a *very* fine 'Briton' broom for R. as the noble present (it *is* noble, too, and I wish we could have it!).

We came home in a car she had hired – to my confusion but also relief. It was driven by a Caister old man with a most lovely cherry-apple face; he had been a groom, a valet, a chauffeur. He told me lovely stories about being in France in 14–18, and spoke a bit in soldiers' French and said the French 'waar a nice, loving kind of people'. He had lived in Ireland for two years and adored it. He feels just like I do about driving cars. He knew John, from days before 1914, and when he met him here at the gate and they had greeted each other he said (with perfect, courteous seriousness) 'You *air* a good servant, John Powles – that you air; a good, faithful servant.' I felt as if I'd heard God speak at the Judgement Day – speak to John, I mean.

I think R. is glad to have me, so far. I am very glad I came, because the pre-fabs are being put up just beyond the window, and it is very unpleasant and troubling and a good thing I am here to distract her. But she has arranged such an expensive day to-morrow, which worries me a great deal. A hired car to *Norwich*, and for part-way back, too. However, it is all fixed and I won't expatiate, for it's too late.

I spoke to Mary on the telephone when R. was out. She is at Trina's. She sends you her dear love. T. is coming to tea on Monday, I hope. I have somehow a feeling I won't see her but I hope I will because it makes me very pleased when I do.

And that is all about me. R. has fallen asleep. She woke up with a jerk just now and said desperately 'Oh – my Christmas!' which horrified me – but it turns out to mean 'Oh my questions' and to refer to Twenty Questions[1] – and she thought it was after-dinner already.

1 A BBC feature.

She has said some riotous and lunatic things but, as always, I've forgotten them.

My Love – days D R A G – I can't read, or think, or even take in, except food. Meet me at 1.30 G.E. Hotel lounge (Waiter is called H A T T O N, remember it for me!) I daren't begin to look forward yet.

Trains are hell. I had to queue from 5 to 3 until 3.13 for the 3.40 . . . and people were jammed along corridors. I do hope we may book seats for we'll be exceedingly tired. *Please bring string bag.* And umbrella. Oh my Love – bring my Love.

Valentine

1949

Narrative 10

Living near the Asylum

When the madmen's cries sound nearer,
Blown on the wind and coming through the conifers
Flanking our front gate, as though the village dogs
Scuffled and yelped there, and no gardener now
To keep them off – Sometimes hearing the cries,
I turn to look at you, and feel my heart's slow bleeding start again,
Seeing in you all love and in myself all care.
As if our first Mother, the fierce Ape,
Had started out of sleep, and upright on her haunches
Had felt her angry pain, and moaned, and clutched her heart –
The old grief back again.

Note: Liverpool to New York is 3040 miles from door to door.

This was among a collection of poems written in 1948 which she gave me at the New Year. I recognised the old grief whose haggard face had recurred, though at longer intervals, ever since we came home from America. I did not know till several years later that in 1948 Elizabeth had written to say she was coming to England the following year with the intention of meeting her again; and that she had replied asking her very seriously not to.

Elizabeth disregarded it. In April she came briefly to Dorset.

11th April 1949. Elizabeth has been here. Towards her I feel a violent desire to possess, a profound obligation to love, a feeling of assertiveness and a dangerous excitement because of this. I can look at her with dislike, and feel bored by her, I can find time drag when I am with her and feel perfectly alien to her – and then, at a touch all that is blown away and all I need in the world is to *know* that she is mine. I could readily kill her, obviously, but not kill myself because of her – and I would die, I think, without Sylvia.

E. arrived at Yeovil and I met her. We scarcely spoke, and when at last we did it was with the utmost formality. But after we'd had tea and driven around the country, and returned to her bedroom at the Acorn Inn at Evershot, she gave me the signet ring she had had made for me, many years ago – and then she kissed me. And at once the love flowed back, like a stream returning to its old bed – and the river has run, but unusually smoothly and deeply ever since.

16th May. Elizabeth came back last Tuesday, May 10th. We stayed together in a large dark bedroom at the Kings Arms in Dorchester. We were there for three nights. On the first night everything happened; we were completely and irrevocably restored to each other, with greater happiness and completion than we had ever imagined. Everything happened – I do not know how anyone can believe man to be mortal, who has experienced how instantly, in joy, he becomes a god.

I know now that I love Elizabeth with all my heart and soul. She loves me like this. I do not know what we shall do, for she is at this moment crossing the sea on her return to America. But I, at least, love her with all my life.

As a result of being raised from the dead (meaning that my body has come alive again, after lying entombed for about 10 years) I am dissipated – scattered, 'sold into multiplicity' in my spirit. I am full of doubt, fears, uncontrolled desires, full of impatience and anguish, and I have scarcely any trust, even though without the extraordinary goodness and mercy of God these three days and nights could not have brought me to fulfilment – and unless I believed that God had ratified our pledge to each other, I could not have loved her in the way I did – not any longer as a mistress, not any longer with reservations.

During those three days and nights I tried not to think. Early on that fourth morning I was still in bed, clutching a wisp of sleep, when I heard her step on the stairs and turned my eyes to the door. She came in, young and beautiful and living. Her face had its expression, melancholy and remote, of a predatory animal. She told me she entirely loved Elizabeth, that Elizabeth needed her, that it had been settled between them that Elizabeth would return and that from then on they would live together.

One of the things I had learned during the war was the phosphorus bomb. Phosphorus bombs can be arrested by wet dressings; the moment the dressing dries, the burning resumes. This was what had happened.

We kept to the same pattern of living, slept in the same bed, spoke little, planned nothing. I found she was assuming that I would adjust to a joint household. Violently recollecting the falsehood and degradation of the Kibbe house, I refused. There was a missel thrush in the garden who sang 'Going to leave here! Going to leave here!' I took him as a prophet. With no notion where I would go, I decided I must take the pink-and-white coffee-cups.

4. VI. It is still not a month since I lay in love with Elizabeth; but in the days between, so much has happened that I feel as if I were a fruit-grower after ten days' storm, looking at the ruin of his blossomed trees and wondering how soon he will be able to tell if any of the fruit has survived or if indeed it is all as ruined as it looks.

Until yesterday, I think, I was in a state of confidence – even though it was threatened often by miserable letters, doubting letters, tormented and tormenting letters from Elizabeth; and by the deep woe and bitter grief I saw in Sylvia, and felt in and for her, and in and for myself in her. Compassion and protectiveness for Elizabeth, too. She turns to me to implement my promise of taking her to live with me; and I both long to, for I love her and am in love with her, and yet I feel I cannot conceive of life without being always in close, household contact with Sylvia. And in that state of extraordinary confusion and anguish, until yesterday I still felt secure and calm and full of confidence, at my centre. And I believed I could bring all three of us through to some pattern of serenity and happiness.

Yesterday Sylvia was so deeply unhappy and desperate; I had terrible letters from Elizabeth; I myself became somewhat ill; and suddenly it was as if some contact wire had snapped – and I was out of touch. Like an airplane whose radio breaks when the rest of the machine is falling, and he loses contact at the same moment as he loses height. All yesterday and most of today I have been in a state of desperate feeling – dream-like and yet quite real.

And now comes a quite different development.

That morning she had been told by Dr Gaster that an enlargement of her right breast might be cancerous.

The practical difficulties are appalling. I should not tell S. until at least I know what the surgeon says. But I should tell Elizabeth as soon as I can because somehow she must be prevented from cutting adrift from her home to come to where I could not give her what she most needs from me.

She did not tell me. But she called me into her room and asked if I would come back to her if she fell ill. As instantly as I had refused to live with her and Elizabeth, I promised I would. Still in ignorance, I drove with her to the consultation with a surgeon in Sherborne (she had made some pretext for seeing him). It was a serenely beautiful day; too beautiful to sit waiting in the car. I was standing under a lime tree remembering another wait in Sherborne, seven years before, when she was called to an interview which would determine whether or not she should be 'directed to work of national importance' – factory, lorry-driving – when I saw her come towards me. She told me what she had feared; and that the surgeon had said it was mastitis. She was trembling with the shock of relief. I was dizzied by the shock of knowing I had not known: it was as though we were already apart. That moment under the lime tree compelled me out of the irresponsibility of despair into being humanly unhappy and practical. A visit from Ruth impended during which we must keep up appearances – the prospect of being discussed, becoming subjects of partisanship, was horrible; and the question of whether Valentine and Elizabeth should stay in the house or move elsewhere had to be considered. In either case, she wanted to keep me within reach. We went to Wareham, further down the river, and thought it might do. A calm unreality accompanied these decisions, but imagining myself at Wareham I faced what would be true for both of us.

> And past the quay the river flowing:
> And I not knowing
> In what gay ripple ambling and sidling
> The tears you shed for me go by me.

> And in the ripples the bridge flaking:
> Making and unmaking
> Its grey parapet, and I not knowing
> How in your mind I am coming and going.

> And to my heart the wise river
> Murmuring, Oh, never
> Under the same bridge of any river
> Does the wave flow twice over.

Realising how shaken I had been at not knowing why she went to the surgeon, she decided she would not part from me taking a secret with her. One night she told me there was something I ought to know, something which at the onset of our love she had resolved to keep from me: that even then she was a drinker. It had begun by drinking for reassurance – to muffle a pain, to overcome shyness or boredom, to release a poem, to be the social asset she was expected to be. She had a good head and enjoyed wine. During her ill-starred marriage, she drank more purposefully – not for assurance, but to disassociate herself from a state of loathing and misery; and turned to spirits. Her good head was her undoing; she was caught before she knew. She tried again and again to free herself, entering in pocket diaries D.D. – for devoid of drink – sometimes up to a hundred days, but always to be toppled back. She asked doctors to help her; they said it lay in her own hands. She bought advertised cures, which were very expensive and did not cure. Fighting this losing battle, she still kept me unaware of it. Dragging herself out of drunken stupors, she would plead a migraine and demand to be left alone. Craving and concealing she would drink wine with me and be festive, and then go off to her grim colloquy with a whiskey bottle. In the autumn of 1947, after an untroubled undrinking holiday in Dublin, she began to drink more besottedly than ever. In desperation, she tried to pray, and felt an unhearing silence. Declaring her disbelief in any power which could help her, she tossed into this vacancy an oath never to drink again. In the morning she woke to the familiar hangover and by the end of the day knew she was cured.

I believed because she told me. Overcome by amazement at this heroic deception, compassion for that long loneliness, admiration for her fortitude and good manners, I accepted the end of her story as the end of her story – the crown of an explicit, her due. 'I think you might spare a kind word for God,' she said in her voice of gentle teasing. But to me, she was the miracle.

As though with other completions in mind we went for several long drives, to places we had always meant to go back to or places she knew and had promised to show me. One of the promises was Kingley Vale – a cleft in the Sussex downs with an ancient population of yews. We stayed so long that summer dusk was turning to darkness when, a few miles from home, she abruptly halted the car. I asked why. 'Dread,' she answered. 'I dread going home. We have been so happy. And when I get back there will be another letter from Elizabeth.' I said – it was the best I could do – that perhaps this would be a kind one. By now she had shown me a letter, asking me what I thought of it. What I thought of it made me write privily to Elizabeth, asking her to remember that Valentine loved her, and to show more mercy. Not that I had much hope. Gibes, recriminations, mistrust – these can be impulses of love. What appalled me in the letter was its deliberation. It dunned, as though it had been written by a money-lender.

Meanwhile, as though we were trapped in a novel by Balzac, everything hung on the death of Elizabeth's mother. Thought to be dying when Elizabeth came to England in April, she was dying still. When she died, the situation of mid-May would be resumed: Elizabeth would come to live with Valentine, and I would go. Her death removed a grisly embarrassment, but the situation of mid-May had lost its straightforwardness; Elizabeth would come, but not yet – there was a great deal she must see to first; and though I would go, it would only be for a while. Elizabeth was coming 'for a trip'.

It was a come-down, and an affront – such an affront that I could hardly look Valentine in the face.

Before the end of July, Elizabeth's return ticket had whittled down the trip to a month, and the month had been postponed to September. I would spend it in Yeovil – a dull town, with no river and no poetry, but with a good train service and within easy reach. I would stay at a hotel which Valentine, posing as my secretary, had inspected. It was small and unpretentious. I would have a room with a view of a hillside and some trees. We agreed that we would not meet or write to each other, except in necessity.

*

92: VA

Frome Vauchurch, 27 July 1949

My Love,

This day you are away visiting Nora. I know I could not write this to you when you were in the house with me, and I do not know whether I can write it now; but it is like being without you, being here today, and so perhaps I can.

It's a kind of arrogance that snatches at any guilt that's going: I don't want to do that, so I don't say that *I* have brought all this down on us, but it has all come down, one way and another, and although I sometimes – often – think I can see daylight and a clear way out, I know that for you it is still a case of being buried in darkness and dust, and nothing but unidentifiable rubble and corpses all round you.

But, my Love, everything has been 'settling' from day to day, since the explosion: sometimes more bits have dropped on us and sometimes some bits have shifted their weight, and for me at any rate, one or two times quite large pieces have been tilted off me. Or so it seems to me; and I do think I can see light and often I think I can see which way out we'll have to go.

I hate similes. I shall leave this one.

The fact is that the way we love each other is different from the way either of us has ever loved or ever can love again, Sylvia: that may be why I thought I could easily love Elizabeth alongside you – because it was different in every way. If I did think: *when* I did think. For I had no thought at all in my head at first. I had, my darling, done you the grievous wrong of ceasing to realise *vitally* that you love me *vitally*: this was not only, or chiefly, I think, because of having been choked-up by Elizabeth . . . it may have been a result of my own private misery over drink. And I must talk about that a little: –

I am so afraid that while we are separated by 12 miles or so, you will come to think – if you haven't already – that the fact for all our years I kept that from you, and the fact that I kept that brief fright about cancer from you, together with what you think to be the fact that I was consciously loving and wanting Elizabeth all the ten years between having her – That all these things will make you think our love was *unreal*. My Love – do you think that?

I do not know how to tell you violently and solemnly enough that if you think this you will be as wrong in every way as you would be in hell. If you think this and believe it you will be as far out of line as the damned are. (I have to use Wm. Law's view of things for that is the way I am seeing them just now: do you understand it?)

They are all separate things, my darling: *perfectly unrelated* . . . except insofar as they happened in me or to me and so are expressions of my character: but they are only separate expressions of separate facets of my character.

I told you why I did not tell you about drink. I still think I did right, and it seemed proven to me when, as I believe, it did give you some support when I could tell you that *that* (never-to-be-belittled) bogey had been overcome.

The cancer fright was something which, as I was then, I felt I must look at by myself, because it was very important to me *in* myself, and had to be looked at first like that. But I should have told you – so gladly too – within a day at most, I am sure, if it had not been for this other business. As it was, I dared not put that added strain *of waiting* on you, my Love; and you will surely understand that? I did not think it was as much selfishness as I now see that it was – I did truly believe that I was doing it chiefly and almost wholly to save you: but that can never be true between us, for anything that saves or spares or pleases or makes you happy must do the same for me, exactly the same – and so I can't be 'unselfish' towards you, ever.

As for loving Elizabeth – Oh my Love, surely you could understand it if you could clear away the phantoms for a moment? I was thwarted in my *desire*: and it had been a very compelling and violent *desire*: and I was angry and ragingly jealous; and I was sick from other reasons – of drink and war and self-disgust. So I became paralysed: and then for a long, long time I scarcely thought of her except in occasional rages and miseries. The romantic love I had for her had been forgotten for a long, long time. But, as you know, it came back when I saw that she still had it for me. And then I lay with her and felt that old, strange, almost-quite forgotten UNTHINKING pleasure. Whatever there is here of continuity I do not yet know; I must know. In her I think it is truly continuity: but for me I think it is not, although I have said at times that I thought it was. I simply do not know.

I do know *for sure* that I was not cherishing that love for her during the last years of the war, during the next years, during Ireland and Rome . . . I know for sure, and you MUST know too, my Love, that my love for you and our love for each other has never been invalidated by any thing that has happened to either of us, in almost twenty years. And that is a fixed certainty in my heart and soul and nothing in life or death can change it for me.

As for analysing the way I love Elizabeth: I could do that for a long time, and I wish I might because what emerged would give you an absolute reassurance – if you believed it. But you would not be able to believe it, and I know that, until something more has been added to the story.

It is because that has got to be done that I have said all along that I *must* have Elizabeth alone with me for a time. The only thing I fear is my own re-awakened desires which blind and batter me and make judgement difficult. But *not* impossible: and I am not at all seriously afraid that I shan't be able to make sense come out of this month of September.

I said to you, and I say it again very seriously, that if it comes to a flat choice, you are my *whole life*. Perhaps it was a choice in May, but it did not declare itself to be, and I was tossed straight over the precipice because of what I still think to have been a *pure joy*. I felt blessedly happy to feel like that. That is how the word 'marriage' came to be spoken: it is the word that fits that complete and blinding rush of light into darkness. It could not be otherwise, Sylvia my Love, and when I spoke ruefully of 'bigamy' afterwards it was because I could never in my life, go back on my absolute knowledge of how you and I love each other.

So it *is* an *impasse*, and now that the thing I thought possible (some kind of duality) has become totally impossible, I am faced with an apparently inevitable choice: and if it is so, there is no doubt at all but that you and I must – if you will – live our joint life together: *and not as a second-best*. If I felt it to be that, for one moment, during this month of trial, then I should (for I do not think it possible to happen) throw away my whole and true joy and keep the other one as long as may be – rather than degrade what you and I had had, my Love, my true Love. I say that because it is what I know I should do: I do not know whether I dare to, but I think and most constantly pray and wish that I would dare to. For everything that is our love is first-best: it is whole and perfect and even though I have become maimed and so bitterly defrauded you, still because of your truth and integrity (in you and in loving me) it has always kept that quality of being perfect and whole. And I could not endure to do it a wrong – Oh it would be much more than that – I *could not* let it in anything dwindle. I have said this NOT because I think any of it could happen, but because I have been trying to anticipate your worst imaginings when you are away from me. I have often and often thought that I'd be best by myself; but it is because of me that all happened, and I should not run away and leave chaos behind me. But if, when Elizabeth has gone you feel you cannot endure me – even if you still love me you cd. feel that – then *tell me*, and I will go away by myself, for a time or for ever: or let you go: or do anything I should that might redeem something for you –

But my Love, I do not think it need be so bad. If you can somehow manage to endure this exile for my sake – and it is so hideous to think of that I cannot get it out of my mind for one moment – but if you can, somehow, draw on me for the infinite love that is all yours, inside me; and draw strength and assurance from it, and *know* that it is there as it always has been, not one whit diminished in kind or in mass . . . if you can only last out this month without getting so ill and tired that you lose touch with me – then I do most truly think we shall survive: *and by 'survive' I mean in our whole state* not diminished and not degraded.

I cannot think it is wrong to want to lie with Elizabeth – except that it hurts you so much. I did not know it would do that. It seems fantastic that I did not but it is true. I never for a moment thought, even when I did think, that you would feel *that* pang. I cannot ask you to forgive me, my Love, for it is far too much to be capable of forgiveness: but because I know your love and love you so profoundly to the depth of my being, I do ask you to bear with me in this return to my body! Bear with me and above all, even in the teeth of this strange infidelity, *trust me*; it is true that I love Elizabeth, but the whole truth – all the truth I have ever seen and known and all the loves and desires and recognitions of my life, and all my happiness and endeavours to be good (in the sense of being whole) are all planted in you and growing out of you, and have their daily life and light solely from this steady and sure love of you, and your love of me.

Perhaps, indeed, it is all in that: That when I love you it is also you loving me: that, as I have tried to explain to you, in some manner I always take you with me and I am always with you: so that you came with me into bed with Elizabeth, and you came with me into my drunkenness and into all my ill-being, because you are quite literally bone of my bone and flesh of my flesh and one heart and one spirit with me. In all other loves it is 'My love for you and your love for me –' but in this it is love, and indivisible.

I could not help making a long letter. It is not in the least like any other long letter I have ever made or ever will. I feel a curious jealousy about using words to anyone else that are words I use to you, but even in our language I have to . . . and only the capital L of 'My Love' can reliably be held on to! But because I am childish in such matters I do hold on to it – And it is so in everything, my Love. . . . I am jealous for us.

Can you make any sense out of this? It is so muddled, but there is truth here, as well as sense and all my heart's life. I should be in front of you asking forgiveness but I am somehow not: I am altogether yours and you know that well: and I hold you most safely, and for ever, inside me.

And if this seems odd, being written on a day when I shall send a letter to Elizabeth – it is odd, and it is appalling and it is desperate – but every word I have said to you, and everything I mean by these words is exact, absolute truth.

And I love you, my Love.

Valentine

93: STW

Frome Vauchurch, 31 July 1949

My Love,

Today it became possible for me to write you a letter; partly an answer to yours, partly a letter of my own. For at last I know the quality of our love, and why it is beyond all other loves and considerations.

You will say, how often have I told you this? Why don't you listen to me? And you have told me, and I have listened, and I have known you were speaking truth. But still I did not know why. When you came back from the King's Arms, and told me that you loved Elizabeth, and had an understanding that you would live with her it seemed as straight forward as the headsman's block. You would go, and I would die or be as dead. And if during those first ten days you had gone, it would have been a simple pattern. 'Time goes on,' you wrote to Elizabeth on the 24th May, 'and she has no wish to turn elsewhere, but grieves bitterly and bitterly in case she is checking or preventing my happiness.' Often reading that part of your letter which you gave me to keep, and time going on, and seeing you ravaged, as I thought, between the past and the future, I felt that the only way left for me to love you was to let go more, was to impel you to go. When I suggested that she should live in this house, I had that in mind. You would slide more easily into a life with her, I thought, if the routine and aspect of living were unchanged; and I thought, too, that this suggestion was a relief to your mind. It did not work out as I supposed it would: partly because of her changes, and partly because of yours – your proposal to adopt my sitting-room, your dislike of my suggestion that she should make over the new garden for growing her herbs; but it began as a means of clearing your path towards her. And when you showed me those two letters, though they seemed baleful and hellish, and the word 'marriage' in hers (I think) but implicit in both, was like a splash of vitriol in my eyes, I still thought I must clear your path to her, and wrote her that letter begging her to show you more loving-kindness. And things like this were not idle self-immolation. I thought I was following the right course, the only honest course for me to take. I thought of you being wing-cramped, of how a falsified life continued with me would harm your poetry, I thought of your love of loving, and I thought a great deal of what you said about Elizabeth restoring your physical life. Remembering the joy of the body we have had together, it was inevitable that I should think deeply and passionately of that.

And yet every time that I made a movement towards freeing you I had the most extraordinary sensation of guilt, *of guilt towards you.* And whenever we re-attached ourselves, or whenever I asserted myself as oned with you, as I did in the garden among the leeks, saying, so definitely that it even surprised me, that I could never be reconciled to the idea of you living with Elizabeth, I felt no guilt at all. And that was not just brazen self-justification, but a plain whole-hearted assurance that what I had done was right for you as well as true for myself.

But not till today did I know why.

When you were walking about the garden of Miss Green I stood looking at the remains of the hearth, asking myself what it was that you lit with the first fire. Not only our perfection of bodily love, not only our intensity of joy in each other, not only our innocence, our paradisal innocence; all these things you might have, and perhaps have already, with Elizabeth. But there was something else, I thought: something rarer, and yet more durable, some especial virtue, some blessing that had been given. And then I knew. The word, I suppose, is trust. From the moment you spoke from your side of the wall and I came in to you, we have been sure of each other, as sure as fish are of water, as birds are of air. We are each other's element.

That is what I knew all the time, though I did not know it. That was why I felt this deep guilt towards you, every time my compunction about your happiness with Elizabeth, your unhappiness with me, drove me to what seemed your release. That is why every re-attachment and self-assertion left me feeling that I had done rightly. We are each other's element. There is a quality in our love which we *only* can give each other. That is something, perhaps the only thing, that Elizabeth does not give you, nor you, her; and the lack of it is why there are these uneasy compulsions of bargaining and contracting, these legalistic anxieties of what and how and how much, all tangled up in a love that would seem by its romance and vehemence to be the antithesis of bargaining. And that is why, too, you feel as you do about Evelyn.[1] If you were jealous about me, you would feel a different kind of jealousy. You would feel despairing grief, and bewilderment almost to stupor, almost to lifelessness, instead of fury and emulation.

I know this, for it is the nature of the jealousy I have felt, the anguish of the fish out of water.

And that is why, my Love, in all these weeks of torment and perplexity,

1 [Evelyn Holahan.]

and in the misery of ten years ago, and in the long iron frost when we were back from America, we have turned to each other for comfort, even while we thought we were trying to be the comforter.

That is why we make each other's heaven in hell's despite. And that is why, when I saw the blackthorn, I burst into tears. It was not grief, or regret, or comparison of then or now. I wept from illumination, I wept with acceptance. I accept. I take you back again in my heart, you are as much mine as I am yours. Not only can I have no doubt of your love for me, I have no doubt of my love for you, no doubt that it is right, no doubt that you demand it and require it. We are each other's element, we are what we live by, and such a love is beyond every other consideration. Yes, I will go to Pen Mill. Yes, I will come back. Yes, if you ask me, I will go away again, and come back again when you ask me. But going, and returning, and whatever I do and whenever I go, I will unwaveringly and sternly and completely hold you in my love, and hold you to your love for me, and follow no other intention but that we may completely live and love together again. Any other way, I wrong you.

Sylvia

94: VA

Frome Vauchurch, 31 August 1949 / 1 September 1949

My Love, I am doing what I should not — but I could not *not* do this.

I have had 'Dover Beach' in my mind for days and nights, and now it is in the forefront of my mind, in that one cry — And that is from my heart to yours. Because of what is true, and what I said to you this dreadful evening:[1] My Love — in my pride, and perhaps for both our credits'-sake, I would wish to liberate myself, but if I cannot, then you must do it for me, *and you can*. For what I told you is true; do not ever for one moment forget it.

I do not know if I have done very wrong; I know it is not right; but there is a great deal going on between the extremes. And whatever position this act is in, I do know that it has shown me beyond all doubt and all forgetting (and I, in my peculiar way, think beyond all harassment of

1 She had left me in the Yeovil hotel where I was to spend my month's exile.

time) that you fill all my need, my most need, beyond anything I would have known how to ask, and in my most need to be at my side, my Love, is what I ask now.

Not without repaying, though: but nothing could tell you that. And I know that so many words of mine have been apparently invalidated by this same blight which makes the leaves fall off even in mid-summer. But it has never, never come near to killing the tree. Even if you can't believe that now, my Love, at least wait in hope – for it is true.

I am going to be as happy as I can: if I am happy, I will do my damnedest that it is in the right way and not for nothing. That is as far as I can safely say. And I'm not raising false hopes or making rash promises: I am only promising what I promised at about the same time that you promised the thorn-tree at Chaldon: something that I have never broken and never had will or power to break: To love and cherish and love and cherish and with all my being to love and cherish you, my Love.

Valentine

(She left the book open at the last stanza of 'Dover Beach')

> Ah, love, let us be true
> To one another! for the world, which seems
> To lie before us like a land of dreams,
> So various, so beautiful, so new,
> Hath really neither joy, nor love, nor light,
> Nor certitude, nor peace, nor help for pain;
> And we are here as on a darkling plain
> Swept with confused alarms of struggle and flight,
> Where ignorant armies clash by night.

Narrative 11

'We are older but we are not much wiser,' she said as we drove away from East Chaldon. By measure of time, we were not three full months older than on that morning when she told me that Elizabeth was coming to her, and I made ready for exile, and both of us were entirely sincere.

During August, we prepared the house for the month Elizabeth proposed to spend in it.

As sincerely as we had been about to separate, we returned – not to our past, for the wave does not flow twice under the same bridge, but to each other. We accepted the restoration without embarrassment, almost without surprise; events had not so much propelled us as set us free to follow our course. It was nothing like a happy ending. We went on towards September, she in a trance of desire, a stoicism of disillusionment.

> Accept the cold content and in the comfort
> Of an unbending winter lie you down;
> Receive the sure embrace of no-love, lying
> Easy within the solace of a frown.
>
> The northern darkness blanketing your sight
> Carries no moon, puts on no worn device
> To herald a soon-rising sun; in stealth
> Your long life bleeds away, and turns to ice.
>
> The sure and certain stronghold of that North
> Withstands all foes that beat upon its wall;
> No joy, no season's change, no spring to come
> Can storm or charm you now; no love at all.
>
> Deep in your cold content, sleep in the comfort
> Of the unchanging winter of her frown;
> And in the quiet embrace of darkness lying
> Confide your soul, and lay your body down.

The house was shabby, and cluttered with a post-war accumulation of things which might come in useful. Our first intentions did not go beyond bonfires and licks of paint. Then, without consulting, we adopted a policy. She put away the familiar china and belongings of daily use, and made over my sitting-room to serve as her own; I submerged all traces of myself, even to unpicking initials embroidered on household linen. It was as though we were impelled to look to our defences, to raise fortifications of anonymity round our love. Fortifications against whom it would be hard to say. Elizabeth was singularly unobservant – so much so that 'Sylvia at a hotel' was included in a list of hardships imposed on her by Valentine: she would scarcely have been disturbed by my initials on a pillow-case. Fortifications against ourselves, perhaps; perhaps a resort to an ancestry which buried its nail-parings and shorn locks of hair to baffle witchcrafts.

In almost unrecognisable tidy surroundings, with nothing more to do and the apple crop gathered, we began to exchange parting presents, parting recommendations – she begging me not to pine, I urging her to enjoy. Late on a sultry afternoon she drove me to my hotel. We went on sparing each other's feelings till the last moment, the horrified, incredulous embrace of parting.

*

95: STW

Frome Vauchurch, 1 September 1949

My Love,

I was happy to be back:[1] to your kind carefulnesses and provisions on every side, the key looking out for me so watchfully, and the tray, and Shan's impassioned wet-headed welcome (He told me that things had been very Odd, and that he didn't like them, and that Thomas would say nothing to him but proverbs in Spanish).

And then I went upstairs, to the room looking so welcomingly yours,[2] and to Thos. reclining, and found the letter you had left for me in that book which I shall have to review as a good one, whatever it is really like. And then I came to my room and saw Matthew Arnold, and guessed why at that page, and took off the lid of the typewriter.

I will, I said. O My Love, do not doubt, do not fear. You shall be freed. By your own strength, I trust and believe, and if not, then by mine, which for you is limitless, and which is yours, really, since our love gives it to me. Rely on this, rest on it; and so, feel enabled to be happy, to roll on joy and pleasures as securely as though they were casks. Joy is an innocent thing, when time blows through it and keeps it sweet, it is only when crumpled into a possession that it grows sour. And there is no malice in the body, that brief imperilled creature, that for all the misunderstanding and scorn and ill-usage that mankind lays on it, is still good, willing, artless, enduring all things, hoping all things, and surely much more congenial to God than St. Paul could be.

1 I had come home for twenty-four hours to feed the animals and do final tidyings.
2 The lesser bedroom, made over for her dressing-room.

If you can roll so, then everything will be much better and easier than we dare think. Only today I read in la Bruyère that love grows by kindness but passion is fuelled by vexation and crosses. I do not think that what you have done is very wrong. It is only very dangerous, like a sudden change of diet or of climate. Five months ago we were thrown into a burning fiery furnace; but now it seems to me that we were walking in the midst of it, and that, hand in hand. And so, my Love, I think we shall be able to walk out, neither pulling the other, but together, and step for step.

Take care of yourself, my Love. More than I will allow myself to think, depends on that. Trust me. Trust my strength to come to your help, and trust my weakness, to need your love and cherishing. I am nothing without you, you know that now, it is my comfort that you know it, that you know you are my life as well as my love. I will do well at Pen Mill, I promise you. It is very comfortable, and the proprietress is kind. She brought me a cup of early morning tea. The edition of the Anatomy[1] is in three volumes, and bound in light red.

I thank you for ever for leaving me that letter. I feel it has changed the colour of the blood in my veins.

Sylvia

96: STW

Yeovil, 3 September 1949

My Love,

Here is something from Mme. de Sévigné, writing to her daughter. 'I am going to tell you something funny. Corbinelli will bear me out. I said to him on Monday morning that I had been dreaming all night of a Mme. de Rus: that I couldn't think what had put her into my head, and that I meant to ask you to account for this sorceress. Thereupon, I got your letter, and lo and behold, you told me about her, just as if you had heard me.'

So you see, it could be done in the 17th. cent. too.[2] It's not clear to me why she calls Mme. de R. a sorcière, but I daresay it may be a glance at the

---

1 *The Anatomy of Melancholy*: I had forgotten to pack it.
2 Precognition.

sort of thing that happened to Mrs Rockett,[1] who belonged to much the same date.

This morning, walking advisedly, I went into the town to buy some grapes and a *Radio Times*, and saw a bus called Sparkford, and remembered how much we had liked Mudford. So I got in, and spent an hour there. The pew reserved for Quiet Reading was still unoccupied, and worm has got into John Gardiner's plank,[2] which is a pity. Then I found something so lovely that you must see it; and if you should decide that there is enough petrol to take Elizabeth to Cadbury Castle as well as to the Quaker Burial Ground (it is between Milverton and Wiveliscombe, by the way, on A 361) you could do it en route, if you routed by Mudford. Just opposite the churchyard gate there are some stone steps leading up into a field. You walk straight across the field to the row of willows along the bank of the Yeo river; and follow the river along till it comes to a weir. It is one of the grandest weirs I have ever seen, and the pool below it indescribably noble and solitary: one of those nothing and everything scenes, like a Monet. And I was impressed, too, to see the summer river lying along the bottom of its deep channel, remembering how we have seen its acres of fields under flood-water.

It's no more than five minutes walk; and the caravan in the field is nothing to dread, its dogs are harmless, and its occupants (I saw them in the village, and identified them by the dogs) were stalking unashamed, and looked very happy.

I must have been under the impression, when I said it would be better not to write to each other, that I should cease to exist during the month of September. It is impossible not to tell you all the things I see in Mme. de Sévigné and Somerset. Or that I have got a silver threepenny bit for you.

Now I must tell you something funny, like Mme. de S. Yesterday afternoon, while my mind was entirely engaged in looking round on the kitchen to see if everything was tidy, I was transfixed by a violent impression of you and Elizabeth in passionate contact, looking at each other with intense contained excitement. It was like an electric storm sweeping through the kitchen, it was so sudden and so compelling (I may say it did not in the slightest distress me, for it had an arbitrary quality, like a work of art, a musical performance, and my reaction was to take up the remains of my claret and drink it off to your happiness). They must have stopped the car, I thought, being out of London by now, and be

1 Mrs Rockett: a village woman who believed she had been bewitched.
2 A pew-back, on which John Gardiner must have passed many sermons carving his name.

looking at each other. The time was just after four o'clock.

It really would be a slight relief to my mind to know that the plane did not arrive till four thirty: but I think you said four. But then according to your distracting theory that one can be en rapport with something that hasn't happened yet, this would be no remedy.

Now that it is over, I can tell you that on my first evening here I thought I could not endure it.

I have never known such a vacuity of time. One talks of time going slowly, of time dragging: but this was like no time at all, as though time has ebbed out of the texture of existence. I sat on the window-sill and looked at the laundry, and wondered if I should go mad. I thought I would read your autobiography,[1] but I could not, all I knew was that whenever I turned a page I thought, there's a page less. And what shall I do when I have finished it? I tried to write. I even tried to darn a stocking. I turned on the wireless, and couldn't hear. When you rang up I must have sounded drunk, I think; but really I was stupefied. In the end, about eleven, I knew I must compel myself to something, and I remembered that providential list of Gaster's drugs;[2] and indexed the ointments. I have often been grateful for the alphabet, but never more than that evening; for it gave me enough courage to go to bed.

But I do think this is really a very good place to have come to. The bed is marrowy, I don't mind the room being noisy, for it is a mechanical, not a human noise. The cook makes very good Violet soups,[3] and there is plenty to eat: so much meat that I think you ought to come and stay here during the winter, to keep your strength up. I suppose it is because it is a hotel for men. There is, I discover, one woman, but she is in bed with a chill. (No, it doesn't sound in the least like polio. A doctor sees her, and says it is chill, I know all this because I listened to her husband answering kind enquiries, mingled (they were from another man) with commiserations on having to carry up trays.)

And there are quantities of buses, raging out in all directions. And Mrs. Patrick is friendly, but not talkative. I am feeling perfectly well, and I have not had another Soneryl, or needed one.

And as for the upshot, O my Love, I am trying very hard not to think about it yet. This is partly foresight, *ménager la voix*; since there is such an

---

1 [*For Sylvia, an Honest Account*, 1985.]

2 A list of surgery stock which she had not had time to type. Dr Gaster, at Evershot, about six miles away, for whom she worked as secretary and dispenser after Dr Lander retired. It was not such a congenial post but it ensured petrol and salary.

3 Violet Powys excelled at omnium-gatherum soups.

extent of *yet*, and I do not want to become breathless too soon; and it is partly a queer scruple of honour, as though by thinking of it I should prejudice what I hope is a happiness in being. But I trust you, my Love, and whenever you need me, here I am. I am sure you are right not to make plans. Plans are ridiculous, encumbering, and ruinous. One makes a plan, and it miscarries; and in one's attempt to retrieve the plan one miscarries of the object. I ought to know. I make far too many. But perhaps I will give them up from henceforth. For I have been rescued, quite as surprisingly as you were, from despair – and, as you say, it gives one a strange new feeling of letting the sea do most of the swimming. I can't promise you that I won't sometimes be in agonies: but I have No Fear.

Sylvia

97: VA

Frome Vauchurch, 4 September 1949

My Love,

This will be a short letter (?). It is to tell you the strange news (or you will think it so) that I have missed you steadily and without any diminishing and without forgetting.

I have taken your advice – or it came naturally to me to behave so – and enjoyed, and been happy, and I am extremely tired as a result: but I am profoundly lonely and astray and I am as I always am apart from you – a little half-witted and more than a little inclined to quarrel with any alternative good.

I find *so far*, and by the grace of God which is, to my mind, a most reliable source of supply, that I am not in the least moved by jealousy or sense of power. Perhaps that is an exaggeration – but only insofar as it is an exaggeration to say that when I stopped drinking I never again wanted to drink: the thing came within touching distance, and so has this sense of violence of various kinds about Evelyn, but not nearer. I hope it may go on like that: it will be inexplicable (although no doubt some correspondent to the *New Statesman* could explain it readily enough) and I should be very glad.

But I AM tired! Belly and natural fatigue of strain and sleeplessness and the necessity to do what cannot be left undone like feeding animals and washing myself – these things, and trying to remember what I have to do, tire me enormously; and today I am enforcing a regime of segregation, because I am irrevocably spoiled for society, and I cannot endure a conversational life. And why should I at my age? I have been forty-eight hours and more without reading or writing and I can't do that for another four.

But I have been, and I am, enjoying myself: if I were not rather below-par in physical endurance, and I suppose practise (I think that should be c) has something to do with it, I should be extremely pleased with my temporary situation – given that qualifying adjective – I think. And Elizabeth is being extremely virtuous and willing and hard-working, within the limits of my patience in telling her how to be! She makes the big bed and carries coal and of her own volition and, I suppose, observation (for I could not make my pride consent to whine to her). She carries and fetches and picks things up. And she has cut some of the lawn (but I stopped her for she looked very tired) and is going to do great deeds of gardening: and will, I think. And she submits very sweetly to my impatient commands to shut up and stop talking like Henry James (I always feel a misgiving about that: do I mean some other James?) and so far has scarcely once slumped into her oppression. And she has answered my enquiries and I know a great deal more to fill in the gaps in what I knew about things, which eases my imagination a good deal.

And she knows that she is not to see you, and took it very well and without more than a decent reticence, which I was most glad of and is much to her credit.

I am coming on Tuesday,[1] if that is still right, my Love: I shall come, I hope, at about 2.30–2.45: depending on how I succeed in getting things working to time (so far I have got it down to a time-lag of ¼ hr., which is good if it will last) and I think Elizabeth will come as far as Mr Whitby, which means that I should probably fetch her there at about 4.30 unless that disturbs plans in your mind. You will tell me that on the telephone at Gaster's on Tuesday morning at between 10.45 and 12.15 if you possibly can?

And that is all I can say now, because I am so tired and it is 11.45 a.m. and I must devise about the pork and meat so as not to waste; and I have washing in the basin too.

I have said definitely that she must return to Evelyn and for various reasons to be explained later it is an easy thing to say and for her to hear,

1 We had agreed that it would be wiser not to write or meet – and threw wisdom to the winds.

although as yet she does not, *perhaps*, feel able to think of it as anything final. But it wd. take long to explain why I have not said more as yet: I have only refused to make a date for her coming to England next year: saying, what is indeed most true, that it is not for me nor yet for her to make engagements of that kind at the beginning of her stay with me this time; and that I do not feel in myself that I shall be able to make engagements of that kind later on: but that such matters must not be mooted until we are much less confused than we are at present. Elizabeth says she is not tired but she must be – although she has infinite stamina compared with mine! I am become, apparently, only able to do one thing at a time. I suppose you have known that for years, about me, my Love? I did not. I've got V E R Y one-track. Not a 'bus, not a 'bus but a tram.

I hope to bring you a pork pie: and maybe a jug of strong Cooper coffee to take out on a Nic with you.

My love – if there is anything in this letter that is woebegone or bad, discount most of it: it is fatigue and a certain melancholy, Not (alas) just *post-coitus*: but age, or difference – divergence, more truly. 'Miles to go before I sleep –' and some of the miles travelled already. I am glad, but it is sorrowful too, for Housman links on there, and it was a beautiful country and I loved it, but I have left it.

My dearest, true Love: I wait for your letter with extraordinary impatience: I think of Norfolk:[1] I warn you that I may be (if things are still as they are now in my own mind) very silent and that won't be pining – it will be something that my mind does without my being able to stop it. It *withdraws*: not into stupor, but into a conversation with itself, or something else, which it loves and will *not* leave. And it will be, I think, colossal fatigue!

But Elizabeth is being infinitely more docile, gentle and 'thoughtful' than you, or even I, thought she would or could be. Does that sound like Ruth about one of Joan's? GOD FORBID.

I love you interminably.

Valentine

P.S. She *knows* her mother was a Vampire. *Really* knows it.

---

1 We planned to spend October there.

Yeovil, 6 September 1949

My Love,

In ten minutes I shall be listening to Margarita Grandi (only the first act, alas! But have you noticed that on Saturday they are doing the whole of *Il Ballo* on the third? She will be superb in the first scene of the second act, and the first scene of the third act. Do try to listen to it). And here I come naturally out of my parenthesis, for one of the possible ameliorations of your fatigue (I have been Racking my brains) could be music. One can hush talk for that without having to assume the Robert, or for that matter, the Flora Jane Warner[1] (have you used Have Done yet?), painlessly, and almost complimentarily; and I think if you would let yourself sit back and allow the music to do the rest it would carry away a great deal of mental and physical fatigue. There are states, and I think you are in one of them, when music is like oil to Thomas. Do, if you possibly can, hear the 1st. scene of act 3 where she has an aria about loving and leaving her child. It is exquisite, pure feeling and no sentimentality. It is as natural and as noble as seeing an Italian woman pick up a child, with exactly the same slight frost of fatalism: My nature to love you, and I do. You know: that look of responsible joy, without a vestige of the self-conscious smirk of pleasure. Cows and monkeys, too, have it in the same perfection.

(A very large bus labelled R.N. has drawn up outside, totally empty. And now it has gone on, in the same condition. Thank God and the British Navy for my good petrol ration.)

If you could bring yourself into the habit of sitting with your feet up, or even on my little footstool, you would learn how extremely reposing it is. Mme. Recamier did, and her legs were quite as long as yours, or at any rate David thought so. A fan can do a great deal to compose the mind, so can face-cream, so can rose-water, so can a smelling-bottle. Believe me, all these small female ceremonies, the fan, the footstool, the wrap round the shoulders, have been turned into graces because they were discovered as necessities and practised (S, not C. Your query. I make a practice of practising on the piano) as arts. I am sure this is right, because I learned it from Colette. There are passages in *Chéri* on healthy living and lying that,

---

1 Robert was her father, Flora Jane my grandmother. Both had a stern talent for quelling needless conversations.

if I had had a daughter, she should have embroidered in her sampler along with the alphabet and square cats. As for Mr Whittard's little gift of Mandarin Tea, I am positive it was Sent for the Purpose. And the sex of your body, without prejudice to the rest of you, is female.

But I suspect and hope that part of your fatigue and nervous racket is the echo of those five hours at that ever-to-be-except-for-the-porter-accursed Heath Row. And if you will be reasonably *douce envers soi*[1] (S.F. de S. so pray, mark it) I hope you will feel better quite soon. If you don't, I shall begin to fidget quite seriously about moving to the Acorn[2] and coming in by the day to oblige. It would be ignominious; but ignominy would be better than becoming ill while Elizabeth is still here to be appalled and stricken.

After you had gone I re-read Ruth's letter. It is indeed a stinker. It forced me to the hypothesis that the reason why so many people believe your mother to be the soul of Christian charity and long-sufferingness is that so few can read her handwriting.

Truth sheds a livid light on passages in your autobiography. Indeed, if I did not read them in that light, they might make me a little angry with you. Knowing her, I know that it is impossible to be with her for twenty-four hours on end without a sense of guilt beginning to ferment in one, like the sense of a cold beginning to ferment in the back of one's throat. Her insistence on self-sacrifice turns all goodness and kindness into a dreadful mercantilism. She cannot be so good without other people necessarily being bad. She turns figs into thistles, harmless figgy pleasures have to be ungrateful selfishness and vileness. That is why I am not a little angry with you, my love, for writing as you do of 'blundering from shame to shame', and in places in your day-book with such violent self-reproach, and with what you provoke me to qualify as a satanic mortification. It is not natural in you, I know you too well to think that; but it was dribbled into your open heart, your extremely candid and receiving disposition, as much as though the Jesuits had got hold of you in your first seven years. But indeed, my Love, you should not let yourself feel like this. It is a dangerous ingratitude to think oneself worse than one is; even, I suspect, to think oneself as bad as one is. And it is dangerous, not only to oneself, but to others. If one falls into the way of thinking oneself bad, the next step is to begin to suspect that those who think well of one are fools, and that those who love one must be blind, or besotted, or supernatural. I love

1 'Il faut être doux envers soi' – a recommendation by St François de Sales.
2 An inn near our house.

you with my whole heart, I deeply honour and respect you, and since the night you told me of the black road you had walked in for so long, I have honoured and respected you more. Loved you more? If it were possible, yes.

But I will not have you think me besotted or supernatural; or blind, except for the bandage you so tenderly and faithfully laid across my eyes. I am an ordinary human being, my Love, you could pick me off any bramble-bush in Europe. The only thing that makes me extraordinary is that I have had the incredible good fortune, the crowning mercy if you prefer, of loving the person whom, in the whole world, I would choose to love. I don't want to be a person from Porlock in your spiritual colloquies, I don't above all things want to show a little common-sense. But *teste David cum Sibilla.* And from my heathen thicket I remark that it is impious to the gods to slight the graces. Do not slight your graces, do not be ungrateful to yourself. If you could read your autobiography with the pure eyes of all-seeing Jove you would be thankful that you have been so good, that you have kept such integrity and sensibility and have been *Inébranlable* through such black gusts of tempest, and so quick to feel the sun and light and relish versing on the morrow of tempests.

My Love, I beseech you in the bowels of Christ to think that I may *not* be mistaken.

And to remind you that I am from an ordinary bramble, I am your Tibby.

99: STW

Chaldon, 10 September 1949

My love

There was a letter waiting for me, and another came this morning. I will write to Miss Rintoul – artists are best, as you say, and Rintoul is a very respectable name, I would expect a Rintoul to be clean and orderly. Besides, if one were an artist, our house would be a pleasurable house to come to. I am never quite easy about Janet, because of her bad star in the matter of machinery.

And as for annotating your day-book, I have already begun to do so. And I can bring back what might be an addenda to it; for among my bedbooks Alyse put a review with an article in it about Gourjieff's theory of consciousness and the 5th dimension. It must be clearer than usual, for

I can almost understand it, and there is a neat diagram. I will copy what I suppose to be the crux of it.

You *must* stay here, and sleep in the shelter, under ancestral Powysian blankets and on the grandest Dunlopillo mattress. Enormous windows, larger than those of a French train, on either side. I woke this morning between the moon and sunrise. Alyse when she brought me to bed pointed out the anubis (I *think*: sharp ears and long nose) head you gave to Llewelyn. It is fastened on the wall with an ankh framing it. I slept under your protection, and very happily, and well, sometimes opening my eyes to a bramble wand, sometimes my ears to a sheep's baa.

She is very kind. It is clear that as a hostess she intensely foresees everything, in an agony of lest it should go wrong. 'You sit there,' she said at tea; and hearing the commanding urgency of her voice, began to blush.

A sea-mist covers everything. The man ploughing on a tractor appears through it exactly as though he were the appearance of his sound. Mr Miller is here but Gertrude has him. I looked from the bathroom window, and watched her conveying him. As usual, he stopped for great thoughts and speeches; and Gertrude, blandly agreeing with every appearance of consent, swept round and on with him, like a calm swelling tide conveying a child's boat. There was a little struggle – something about plastic, its inferiority to wooden door-knobs – on the threshold; but only for an instant. I have never seen anyone crossing the bar more smoothly and painlessly than he.

I visited her yesterday evening, and drank a little glass of her mead. It reminded me to tell you that in Yeovil mead (made in Cornwall) is on sale 11/- a bottle. Would you like me to get a bottle for Eliz.'s drinking? It is Gertrude who will get my arrival-figs. Alyse cannot eat fruit. Gertrude is very fond of figs, as I would suppose. She is in a very fond of figs state, because she looks forward to Africa. 'Goldie,' she said to one of the old cats 'you must not *growl* at your grand-child.' It was said in a voice of such floating hypocrisy that I laughed: and instantly she laughed too, with delighted recognition for her insincerity. The kitten is such a kitten! Alyse detached it from the shoulder of a heap of Gertrude-coats hanging on the door, and gave it to me. And instantly it roared with purr, and patted my face with pinless paws. It is just where brook and river meet, standing there with pinless feet, very compact and tenderly muscular.

I am determined to get two light wickerish chairs and cushion them, and make our sun-parlour a more comfortable sitting-place, on the model of this shelter of Llewelyn's. This winter I shall devote my mind to cushions.

Alyse gave me your letter this morning with a look of such pleasure and wistful congratulation that if you had seen it you could have had no doubt as to the state of her mind towards you, and towards us. I think her imagination, as well as her analytical curiosity, has been deeply engaged in our love; the threat to it must in some way have come as a threat to something of her personal cherishing. You have a deeply romantic quality in her mind, and I, by conjunction with you, have acquired something of the same quality, in spite of her old mistrust and censure (those letters!), and seeing our love threatened she seems to have felt rather as she would feel at the news that the army was taking over High Chaldon for a tank-ground. She said, of you, and it pleased me so much (we were talking of how country life blunts one's self-respect, one's original standards of distinction) 'Valentine is *always* elegant.' For it was said as a tribute, not to your clothes but to the discipline of mind that makes you put them on so well.

So I am very happy here, my Love, talking about you to someone who loves and admires you.

Sylvia

100: STW

Chaldon, 11 September 1949

My love,

I am thinking of you driving to Weymouth to fetch Janet. It is such an exquisite morning. There is an enormous hayrick behind the Chydyock barn – taller than the barn; and Mr Mackintosh's sheep step delicately down the bank and eat away at its foundations with looks of ineffable condescension. Poor creatures, there is not much else for them. The turf is as dry as Spain.

I am living in the extreme of luxury. Alyse brings me my breakfast tray to the shelter, with an outdoor peach on it. In the evening I have an apéritif of mead chez Gertrude. She said that when she saw Katie and Lucy walking together it was as though she saw her father and mother.

Yesterday I went down to visit May and Jim. May's good lung is now affected. It is a story straight out of Theodore, but I must tell it to you. Remind me also to tell you about young Oram's wedding – another T.F.P.

Alyse is talking with the greatest freedom, and is very amusing. I told her how I had visited a church last Sunday and added an eighth person to the congregation. In return she told me of how, when she was at Mappowder at a weekend, Theodore had spoken to her of how sad it was for Mr Jackson (his Good Parson) that no one went to communion. He so worked on her feelings that at last she consented to his proposal: that he and she should go to communion together in order to comfort Mr Jackson. That was overnight. All night Alyse pondered and fretted and worked herself into a fever of scruples, and meeting Theodore in the morning told him that she felt she really could not go through with it; it was so false, so confusing, etc. etc. Theodore took her hand and began to lead her towards the church, saying, 'You must pretend to yourself that you are in Africa, in darkest Africa, among simple savages worshipping a black God. You would think nothing of it then, dearest Alyse.' And with these consolations prevailed.

But indeed it distressed her, Alyse added, to think of all these village churches falling into disuse, and all these parsons with their neglected rites. I said that I foresee the formation of a League of Church-Goers, drawn entirely from the ranks of compassionate free-thinkers.

I have written to Miss Rintoul, asking to let us know as soon as she conveniently can.

I did not go to Miss Green yesterday – I was half-minded to, but found that really I did not want to break the spell and seal of that early morning visit yet. I was not in the least homesick for the *village*; indeed, as the curve of the hill rose between, I was rather glad to feel it lay behind me. For the downs, and the view from here, and the smell and silence of the place, yes. Chydyok has taken a new colour since we saw it last. Projects have become performances, seedlings are trees. It is strangely romantic to see Llewelyn's medlar-tree, in its tapestry of dark fruit and dark leaves, against the bare sweep of the field, and to turn one's eyes from the old barn to the clusters of grapes on the vine. I am so glad to think that Willie's[1] children will have this place to remember as they grow old. It is so deeply poetic, so deeply English, and most English of all in being like no other place.

Kiss my Tom for me. I am glad he has adopted your narrow bed, and I am glad, too, that he adapts himself to Elizabeth. He is a wise cat, steering his course among ports and happy havens, and I hope he will adapt himself as kindly to Miss Rintoul. Of course, if she were a feline

1 William, the youngest of the Powys brothers.

portraitist – Tomorrow I shall hear of you from Janet, and the day after I shall see you.

My Love

Sylvia

IOI: VA

Frome Vauchurch, 13 September 1949

My Love – I do not know *any* worse pain in the world than the pain of leaving you in exile: the pain of leaving you at any time is almost too much to bear, but to leave you as I did today makes my heart faint and die within me.

And it is not pity –

It is love and horror at what I do; and a dreadful sense that to everyone but me it is lunatic; while to me it is an extremity of anguish and yet in its essential it is both clear and not-wrong. And I am physically very happy and I often enjoy myself considerably in many, in sometimes most ways. But all this – this not-more-than-half-way-through-time – is a build-up, and we both know it (E. and I) and it is to establish a quietened unhurried mood between us. Which it is doing. So that when we come to say what must be said, it will be said not harshly. I hope that will be what happens. Many, many straws blow the way of the wind, but the time of the day is not yet come for announcing the quarter it blows from.

She is being good and very kind. She truly loves me and while she is with me she trusts me almost completely. I strive at times not to feel shamed by this, for whenever I can get my mind to itself, free from Ruth and Kipling and my own self-mistrust, I know that I should not be shamed.

But the whole matter is, my Love, that there is no sign yet, and may never be, of *the thing we feared*:[1] but I also fear inflicting and receiving pain, and Elizabeth can give me very sorrowful pain to bear. I hope she will not and if she does it will be because she is driven to it, so that, somewhat at least, it lies in my hands whether she does or no. And with your truth and steadfast help to me, my Love, and my own certainty within my mind, I think it will be all right.

1 That she might take some desperate step in order to prolong her stay.

Alyse is wrong[1] and you are right: it is in its nature true. But you are wrong and she is right, as I understand her to have been, when she says that I cannot under any circumstances be alive in life without being literally with you. There is nothing pseudo-Platonic about any part of my love for you. It is the love we said it was on the 12th January at 113, and it is the love we knew it was when we stood beside Miss Green, – and the love that I, at least, recognise with joy and profound relief and pride whenever I see you in what is only a pretence of exile. Please, my dear Love, believe this. I have two people believing me in what are not conflicting truths: not conflicting when they are with me but for ever in total war when they are with you or with her. I know this and accept it – with deep sadness but without any sort of pretence that it isn't so. And without any wavering about what it means.

My Love: please do not let any word in this letter overthrow you. It is sad because I am sad and tired tonight and my heart is dragged out of my body and is with you; and my body is grieved and that is all there is to it. But the truth of the matter is that I love you both with my body, which is wholly unregenerate, I suppose, and in total rebellion at not being able to have all, always. Please do not think that in this situation it is that I love Elizabeth with my body to the exclusion of my body's fealty to you; I do not know in the least about all this if it were in a text-book, but in me it seems to be working most beautifully like a machine that is got running again – I think a Sunbeam or a Rolls would run like this even after being laid up for a very very long war. You must bear with me in love, in my love for you and yours for me, and whatever emerges from this it will not be LESS than went in: and whatever emerges is your true and unfailing and unchanging Valentine who loved you and loves you and will have no life at all when that love ceases. I have to talk as if I thought it could cease because you don't like to think it won't! But I know it won't. And so, my Love – till Friday. I SHALL COME ON IN THE CAR TO FETCH YOU: BE READY ANY TIME AFTER 9.30. *Soit.*

Valentine

Bring this letter with you on Friday in case there is anything wrong with it.

---

[1] Alyse had used the word 'infatuation'. I had rejected it.

Yeovil, 17 September 1949

My Love,

I shall see you before you get this; but I do not like to think of you having a Monday morning without a letter.

Please thank Thomas for today's cats. He must have known better than I did where I was going. When I tried to take my train for Athelney it did not start for another three hours because it was Saturday. So scorning British Railways with my heels I got on the bus outside the station which was going to Odcombe. Odcombe churchyard has just such views as I remembered. I lay on a flat stone in company with several grasshoppers for some time. Then I went into the church, because though I remembered it as unproductive, one can never be sure a church is not keeping something up its sleeve. Odcombe was keeping one of its rectors up its sleeve. *1606 Gibbesius Gollop.*

Coming away I met the first cat, a dark O'Toady-coated tabby, sitting mousing-still on a low headstone, as if it were a darker outcrop of Ham stone carved into a family crest. Its stillness and decisive dark colouring among the long pale waving grasses was exquisite. Then I went to The Rising Sun for a drink of cider, and found a charming Madonna and child. By Raphael. The mother young and plump, the child grown into a handsome little marmalade Jesus. It was hair for hair the colour of my cider. The landlord, who had cut me some admirable cheese sandwiches to eat with my cider, answered my question about the lane to Hamdon Hill by saying 'It is a narrow road but very pleasant' – Straight out of Bunyan. So it is. Wonderful blackberries, the oddest view of the hindquarters of the Montacute mont, reared up all tufted out of stubble fields; and then Thomas's last cat. I had come into the shadow of the wooded hill called, I think, Hedgecock.

The road had suddenly become cool and damp under a grove of beech trees; and then looking down a cart track that led to a barton, I saw Artemis. She was pure white, long-legged, rather small-headed, short-furred, and her figure was as graceful as yours and as full of implicit pounce. What she looked like, standing in that green-shaded tunnel, no words can tell. She was so beautiful that I was half-persuaded that I had really seen a nymph. Then she gave a spring, and disappeared into a thicket of weeds and elder-bushes.

Then the road came out into a stretch of bare, stone-walled country, exalted, like the Mendips. And the next thing I knew I was in Rome, about a hundred years ago or so, looking at the Capitoline Hill. The road skirts the edge of a very old quarry, very old and very deep. This great wall of golden stone with its feet in a fleece of bushes and small trees was so like Rome that it seemed to me that it *smelt* like the forum, too.

You must see it. Fortunately the narrow road but very pleasant has a perfectly good newishly-metalled surface; and then I sat, wishing you were beside me and looking down from the western escarpment of the hill. Do you remember, we drove along under it, once, and came to a small village with a brook running through it? Incidentally, there is enough good Ham stone lying about the disused workings to edge every path in our garden. Then I walked back eating blackberries and looking for adders (I have never seen such good adder terrain, but not one did I see) all across the top of Hamdon Hill, and down the side of the old camp by an exceedingly steep and narrow path through a ferny copse that Master Llewelyn must have trodden many a time to East Stoke. Did you notice, when you were there with Eliz. the marble tablet in the chancel with a very noble relation of the gentleman who tutored Alfred Duke of Edinburgh while he was in the royal navy? (You remember Alfred – he was the *mauvais sujet* of the family, and caused the Prince Consort to despair by putting his hands in his trouser pockets at the family breakfast table.)

It is a very polished and *non nobis domine* and marmoreally toady epitaph: but the truth seems to creep out in the final detached line *in caelo quies*.

Then I walked to Montacute and caught a nice bus. It was a lovely outing, and I was so refreshed to see cats again, especially the unforgettable cat among the beech trees. Perhaps they were penitentially sent; for when I came to look in the basket for my cold grouse, though everything else was there the cold grouse wasn't. I suppose it may have gladdened one or other of our dear animals . . . and I can't grudge it to either of them, though I would have liked it myself.

I am so sorry that your evening and morning were overcast by Elizabeth in gloom. It worries me to think of you left all alone with it, as if you were shut up in the house with a gigantic toadstool, filling the house from floor to roof and distilling a cold venom. You are doing so much that even with a cheerful Elizabeth you are on the margin of fatigue all the time; and to have to go on doing all that against that force-of-gravity-gloom will be very hard for you, and bad for you. I hope to God that when I see you tomorrow you will be able to tell me the cloud has lifted, and that you can be happy again. I think I tell two rosaries, for at once I count the days you are happy, and the days to when I shall be with you again.

Yesterday was so lovely that I am still basking in it. O my Love, whatever else may be *annulled*,[1] never the delight I gather from you, nor the comfort you give me. Oh, how melting you were as you said that. Blessed be the apple!

My Love.

Sylvia

103: VA

Frome Vauchurch, 19 September 1949

My Love,

I have had a tiring, trying day, and I have been weighed down during most of it, since early morning waking, by a great fear for you. I am hoping to telephone you in a moment to hear if all is well. It was dreadful to pass through Yeovil this evening, not long ago, and not to see you. Worse than I can tell you now.

A letter from Evelyn this morning precipitated a profound and miserable gloom. My offer of Dexedrine was refused, and I felt it illegitimate to press it, since I suppose one should not expose anyone, under any circumstances, to the possibility of an obsession: and with such a tendency to melancholy attacks that drug might well become like drink or morphia. But it was a pity –

I had designed a drive to Nunney and Norton St. P. and Wells, Glastonbury, Somerton, Ilchester – and this was undertaken, and undertaken is the word – it is almost a grisly play upon a word.

I was helpless, and would have been so if I had been a renegade monk or an unmarried middle-aged eligible gentleman. It is not – or not wholly – or not more than most partially – a feeling of grief and woe because we, she and I, are not likely to live together; that is the *sharpness* that is sometimes added to the mood; but the mood itself is a dragging, sick depression of mind – a fog over the whole creature, which cannot be dispersed, I *think*, except artificially – or by someone not yet found. (I do not mean someone in love: just someone who could manage it.)

1 'I thought it was annulled' – her promise not to read a letter.

I don't know what Evelyn has said, but that the letter is furious, abusive of me and pleading and threatening with Elizabeth, I have gathered, without any positive certainty: but I do not think I am far out in my supposition. I do not expect that it says anything definite (except about me); but Evelyn, in her relationship with Elizabeth, is not definite – except that I think she loves her angrily, possessively and clingingly: their positions vis-à-vis have not ever been clearly defined, and it is not that kind of relationship. That would not matter except that in a crisis it means that neither is quite sure of what position to take – and that uncertainty makes for panic fear, like the fears I had in the war when I did not know positively WHAT *I* should do – how to run or sit or stand or *what* – if the house were hit and you buried in it.

I shan't go on, because I feel sure that this night (it is now only eight-thirty or so) will be a long one and almost all full of repetitive talk: a monologue after the first half-hour at most, because I find that I simply run out of words. It is not boredom, for that is cold-hearted, but it is fatigue and a kind of wonder that things can go on and on so, when there are one or two facts and one or two beloved fancies and one or two familiar griefs and regrets – but all of them very clear and precisely defined. However, that is only my view of it and it is not possible for Elizabeth to run anything down to a conclusion until she herself is completely run-out and run-down and voided.

I am profoundly thankful for Eckhart; in spite of his middle-ages decorations and rough flourishes and scrawls, he is 'steeped in the Classics' and that sharp chisel-line comes out on the material invariably, and is a great sustenance. And the innocence and candour that he has is nourishing to me in this sort of fatigue, and gives me patience, and makes me suent (suants?) where otherwise I become dry and unsympathetic.

But I am most of all profoundly, endlessly, forever thankful for you, and for us, my Love: for the good manners and the self-restraint and gentleness we (I too, I think) show in loving and even in horror of separation and confusion and appalling bogeys and fears. 'Never heed,' said the girl. 'I will stand by you –'

I think this cloud will pass; I pray God it will: for I have my mind set to complete this month smoothly and as I like to drive a car. It has been a matter of pride to me that I have made Elizabeth very happy and contented and quiet; and that she has managed to make herself so has made me respect her. I hope I shall not spoil all that by becoming what she calls 'detached' which is – after all – something I dare not throw away, so far as I can manage to make it be true: but it should not be a detachment of the heart, at least not so far as to cut out compassion and patience.

And I shall rest my case, as Paul said, as soon as may be: insisting that things, for my part anyway, are left unsaid and unimplied; and yet keeping it clear that I am as I am and may not be changed, nor will accept a change.

For it is clear and it has never faltered nor become dimmed at all to me during all this time since – when? – Miss Green, I think – that you and I can communicate together and I at any rate cannot communicate with any other person alive on the earth: except by gestures and tappings on the glass and rudimentary languages of signs and indications – But with you, my Love, I can make Shakespeare's plays and Beethoven's music quite easily and naturally, and build Rome in a day and live at home in the whole of Greece, and argue in Paris and inhabit naturally the palace of the MerKing, or stroll about on the pink plain that Dear Monkey found so interesting, and with you I can walk up to the five tall pink columns and recognise them quite easily as the four fingers and the thumb of Bramah.

No more: all's said. I love you.

Valentine

104: STW

Yeovil, 21 September 1949

My Love,

I came here[1] early to get letters from you; and now it is halfway through the morning, and I have been reading and thinking over your letters ever since . . . all that is in the long term establishing and dear, but so much in the short term that is worrying and melancholy. I was so much agitated that I forgot the day of the week (I know only Friday and Tuesday and Friday again) and rang up the Gasters – and apologised, and said I would ring tomorrow. It was Mrs. Gaster.

Alyse said, 'It is Evelyn I pity most. In comparison with Valentine she has nothing. And she must realise it and feel destitute.' 'She has love,' I said, 'and love is an incalculable asset.' And I said that from new depths in my heart. But Alyse sunk her chin into her ruff, and was not convinced.

I hold by what I said then. If I were Balzac or some other author of

---

1 To the Hillside Hotel.

universes I would now be warming Evelyn in the palm of my hand, thinking forward to the chapter where she will emerge in a grimy glory. You say she is not definite in her relationship with Eliz.: That is true. But is any one? Elizabeth is water, she saps and undermines and dissolves and re-makes every relationship. Even the relationship with her mother turned out to be of this kind. Mrs White, with all her will to contain and possess was water-worked into rejecting and casting away.

But Evelyn must be definite in her relationship to the love she feels – so definite that she throws away all her advantages, conversion to the Congregational Church, adoption into good old New England society, assumption of culture, throws away all this righteousness like filthy rags and comes out herself, yowling and glaring, scratching and spitting, the authentic alley-cat. I don't doubt the letter was abominable, but I have to admire the uprightness in vileness that wrote it.

If you can teach Elizabeth to be grateful for such a degree of love I think it would be more substantial than all the understanding and compassion and wisdom that you hope may develop. Even gratitude is not a sufficient word. There is too much *de haut en bas* about it. What she should feel is something with astonishment in it, something like awe. It is as if the ratel,[1] poor graceless shabby animal, suddenly thrust away the brush it had been so servilely appreciating, and stood on its hind legs crying out, screaming articulately to be let out of its cage and treated as a real wild animal. My worldly wisdom has to agree with Alyse. Evelyn has nothing, not even a chance. But in my heart, and in my creative mind I think she has what might become everything.

Though whether the poor alley-cat can ever learn to swim in water is another matter.

I am very sorry that the letter came (that you did not impound it because of regeneration is just one of those squibs thrown down to astonish palmers), because I fear it will impoverish all the rest of Elizabeth's stay, and untune the harmony that you had been at such pains to establish. And it has brought on an interview that need not have been gone through at all, perhaps, and anyhow could have been gone through with less confusion and misery and strain. I won't think that everything has been lost, but I'm afraid a great deal must be endangered. But if you are not shaken yourself, then all is well and all will be well. Only, remember that if things suddenly get worse and you think I could help, here I am and I would come at once, and do all I could to allay and set in order.

---

1 Seen at the Dublin Zoo.

Your telegram about the telephone has just come. Of course it would go and break just now. So would the weather. And all that lovely drive going unenjoyed: that grieves me. But I think that perhaps you and I have set up an inordinate standard of enjoying, so that we are unduly shocked to see pleasures half-eaten and then thrown into the gutter, just as we were with the American's buns during the war. I, at any rate, have enjoyed it, since I have the postcard of that exquisite miserere carving. The pattern of those hoofs! – and the solicitude and duty of that heavy head.

This is not such a nice room as the other. It is higher and smaller, and a large bed in the middle of it makes it awkward to move about in. But it is very clean, the pillows are soft, the hot water seems willing to be hot, and outside the window (which is a large Victorian sash window with a rounded top, a charming shape) I look into classical bowers of magnolia. There are no pictures, only a little admonition in old English lettering about not washing clothes in the basin. There are three mats; but I can fold them up while I am using the room and put them back when I go out. And I can lunch and dine with Mrs Patrick whenever I please. So I shall do very well – if you do.

Thank you so much for taking my coat to Wakely. I do hope he was not too loquacious – on that morning too! Did you tell him that I should be like a lioness robbed of her whelps if it is not ready in time?

Yes, I do want to hear everything. In Norfolk perhaps, or while we are driving there – or whenever you feel yourself inclined to it. I have complete trust that you will walk, swim, fly, or roll over mountains and crags that may rise up, and that your heart will be strengthened – no, not hardened – and if anything can exorcise Elizabeth's bog-water melancholy, you will have it in your power. Only for God's sake take care of yourself – and *be to yourself* as much as you can. Not only by getting up early (and then writing to me) but in moments and flowerings of solitude, of going out on to the deck to look at the willows, or standing arm in arm with Eckhart under a tree planted in the country of non-existence. For when people are as tired as you must be they should have solitude given them at short intervals, like sips of champagne and spoonfuls of chicken jelly. I cannot begrudge the time you spend in writing to me. Your letters are my meat and drink, and beyond that, I come to life as I think of you writing to me with love and trust in your heart.

Yes, we may well be thankful for us, my Love. Learning all this in your letter today I thought how extraordinarily blessed and fortunate we are that our love, almost in its first hours, outgrew the desire to wound. I think that may be something to do with the gap of years between us; we had to start on a footing of consideration and mutual compliance, we were protected from any impulse to contest or impose ourselves. But you, my Love, have the most beautiful manners in the world, and how could I live with you in Love for so long, and not learn some of them? And then we do not need to be forever explaining or making ourselves clearer than we are.

I do not think for a moment that you are in any great danger of becoming *detached*; fatigue might make you only semi-conscious, but that is not the same thing, and I hope it is in your power to avert being driven into such a state. If I were you, and she inclines towards it again, I should not scruple to give Elizabeth more Dexedrine. It is not a serious likelihood of bringing on an obsession. The obsession is there already. She is an addict to her melancholy: 'A dragging sick depression, a fog over the whole creature' as you say. And she has all the addict's piteous pride and wonder and cherishing of her obsession. To discover that this black dog deity of hers could be routed by a humble little pill might go a long way towards freeing her from believing the black dog irrevocably bound on her back. One doesn't know, Dexedrine might turn out to be no better than a Turkey; but I can't think there would be any harm in trying it, and it might be the little horn that blew down the whole castle.

As for detached in the sense she doesn't mean it, it is, of all the things that you have, what has done most to make her happy and contented up to now, and the most likely to work that way again.

Half a day, and a night, and a day and a night, and then we are together and at home. I will offer up some of his own poems to Thomas Hardy to placate him; and I will also watch his squinny eye. Besides, it is too simple for him. He would madden the driver of the 10.56 with love or a hornet, so that he swept through Maiden Newton without stopping. Elizabeth would proceed to Weymouth by the next train, which would collide with the train bringing me back from wherever the maddened driver allowed me to stop – unless he got into reverse, and did it that way. Meanwhile Mr Trump would be pouring out his unrequited passion to you in the waiting-room.

My Love, my Love

Sylvia

105: VA

Frome Vauchurch, 21 September 1949

My Love,

I really do feel tired now, after the rain and a day in Dorchester. But when tomorrow is gone I shall see you and feel restored.

This B L O O D Y telephone . . . I feel desperate with anxiety every time I let myself remember that you can't get hold of me at need. And you may need so desperately in this weather, in your strange place of call.

I have told the people but they have not come to mend it. The weather has put them off, I suppose. It would me. But not if I knew the owner of the broken telephone was sick with anxiety –

I got myself a pair of lined boots in D. today, frightening myself considerably by doing so because they cost £4-10-0. But they are made by Burberry and they come up quite high and they are plain and made of excellent leather: and they were almost half the price of their kind today, because they are two years' old stock: and I think it most likely that such things as that will be beyond our reach for some time to come, in a very few weeks from now. They will replace the very-nearly-dead ones you got me in 1940. I do not think it was rash, nor that I have been rash to order two pairs of stockings of chiffon lisle and two all-wool light vests from Gamages: against the winter. These cost respectively 7/- a pair and 8/- each O.S. (for shrinkage: I am no longer O.S., I am glad to say) and are not very dear, I think. The boots will be reasonably water-proof and they fit with a zip and look all right. I hope I have not been wicked. I was driven into despair because I found a pair of dark blue Sealskin leather lined boots (the only remaining pair of old stock) at size 5½. Wonderful with your new suit. But would they fit? I tried them on (they are cheap) and they fitted me perfectly. They will stretch, of course, as lined ones always do. And wear for *ever*. The nice woman said she would do her best to keep them against Friday IF you wd. go in with me, and if not, against Wed: if you thought them worth taking a chance on. They are extremely cheap. I will talk to you about them.

Five p.m. In the interval I started a partridge stew and a nice young man came and mended the telephone and now I have talked to you and I feel my heart lighter. My Love – how miraculously you and I avoid stating the obvious, don't we, in our daily conversation? Or do you not realise this? I assure you it is little, if anything, short of a miracle.

I hope you may consider the blue boots: so far, at least, as trying them on, for they are exquisitely made and pretty, and with dark grey ravishing. And they would last for aeons.

The house has three leaks; and the car has two at least. But Mr King is going to mend the petrol consumption, he hopes and thinks, on Monday Oct. 3rd.

I wore my brown cape and brown beret in D. and looked wonderful. But people stared and I felt ashamed. Still, I did look grandiose. After lunch the train R O A R E D down; and Mrs Oleranshaw told me that there was going to be a Procession of all the shop people down the main streets, with set pieces and that theirs was to be Noah's Ark with animals made of flowers and Young Pug as Mr Noah. But he had said he wouldn't be Mr Noah unless someone lent him a beard . . . I thought of waiting to see this but it was going to be so horribly tragic, in the rain and dismality of the day that I drove out of the town without a backward glance.

I cannot write more. Your letters are enormously important to me and I race downstairs every morning directly the postman comes. If you do not know that I love you with all my soul, you should not know anything, for you would be unable to know anything at all. But you do know.

My Love, my Love –

Valentine

106: STW

Yeovil, 23 September 1949

My Love,

I have just come back from my dinner at Pen Mill Hotel, and on my way I paused to continue my amours with a little black and white cat, who is too young to have got Yeovil manners. This time he pranced towards me, and sat on the edge of his hanging garden of this Babylon, advancing first one very large ear and then the other with the expression of a tea-taster. He was so very young and innocent that I remembered Keatesy turning on the little Keatesies, every night regular, Miss; and so I asked him to join paws with Thomas and pray for your welfare. Then a little girl came out, and entered into conversation thus: 'He's my kitten. He's had a little baby.' I could have eaten the pair of them.

You are night and day to me, my Love, rain and fine. I come away from you with a whole new load of cares, and feeling so much better, ravaged and revived, ploughed up and with the young corn springing. How we are to get through this next I do not know, and yet you have made me feel confident that we shall, and that we shall go to Norfolk, and that all will be well. I am the most suspicious cat alive, and yet I trust you to take what good care you can of yourself, as I shall of myself. Indeed, I never cross the road without thinking, This is Valentine's Tib I am conveying.

But do not, *do not*, waste a jot of your strength on tidying the house; for ever so many reasons: that it will be a solace and distraction to me to have something to do while I wait there for you; that it is very tidy as it is (and how you get it so marvels me); that it would be a waste of time anyhow, for packing would re-dishevel it all over again; but mostly, because I beg you not to. To see you on the station today looking so deadly tired scourged all the gaiety of my exploit out of me, though a moment before I had been as gay as Figaro. It may be that one of your feet is in a serious illness – but then, there is the other foot; where is that? Will you at least try to go to bed early? There is a good, a natural, an unexceptionable plea for that; it could not and would not be discourteous, and at least it would put you a few miles nearer the covert of sleep, whether or no you got to it, at least you would be in a likelier state of getting to it.

Poor Janet! I found a letter from her at Pen Mill Hotel. Roy is coming back from Ireland earlier than she expected, tomorrow, no less; and she has written to put me off. O poor poor Janet, most destitute of Janets, who has no joy because her husband is coming back earlier than expected. And if your train brought you in ten minutes before time I would be on my knees thanking heaven for it, or biting the earth with rage because I did not know, and missed a whole ten minutes of knowing you were back.

And now I will re-read Ruth's sybilline leaves, and ring her up.

She has written you a long letter, and God knows what's in it. But we are to go to her on the original date. At first she said that she did really mean the second postcard (the taxi one) and was going on that. Then, when I said, good, then we would hold to the original arrangement also, she began to heave and mump a little, and say, yes, yes, of course she could manage it, she would find someone – but I am sure from the way she did it that it was just one of her funeral dances, for the impressing of Bessie, or Nora-and-Bailey.[1] So then I said I was so glad, because I had seen you today, and I thought you looked very tired, and in my opinion

---

1 Nora-and-Bailey: Ruth was visiting her sick sister, whose cook and gardener were habitually spoken of as a compound noun.

the first thing to do with you when we got to Norfolk was to keep you in bed for at least three days. I think this sank in. I then asked after Bessie, and sent our loves and then I asked after Ruth, and she said she was so-so, with implications (N. and B. again, I think, for it was a totally different manner, a platform bib). Then she said she was sorry you were not looking well, and then, like one leaping gallantly on to the one spar in the black ocean, remarked, 'I'm so glad you're having *such* a splendid time!' The spar must have lurched under her spontaneous bound, for she added, with the mechanical but failing spirit of a top just beginning to die, 'Q U I T E quite . . . splendid.'

She certainly has a hate on against me: if it is because she thinks I have deserted you in the hour of need, I think the better of her for it.

I felt I had to clear my mind of cant, so I rang up Janet. She is, I think, really disappointed that we can't meet; so I said, couldn't Roy look after Catherine on Tuesday afternoon, and let Janet get away for a little to play with me. She jumped at it. To save time, I am going to meet her *in Dorchester*. Her train gets her there at 2.45 (it is the only one that coincides with a train from here) and we shall be in Dorchester until I catch the 4.26 to Yeovil. I hope this won't upset any plans of yours. If it seems likely to, you must ring me up, and I will fix it so that our paths don't cross. She and I could entertain ourselves with the dolls house in the Museum for an hour at least. Poor Janet, I think she would sit in the gutter with pleasure, just to get a few hours away from being wife and mother. I do hope this won't embroil you. If you had heard how pleased she sounded, and how her spirits instantly leaped, you would have arranged it so yourself, however and whatever.

Whatever there is in Ruth's letter, hold on to the plan that we go to Mrs Howlett[1] first. If she were anything like what she was this evening she would kill you and then I should kill her – which would be a very bad shot, for I don't want to. Not consistently, that is. Though when she is doing her *valse des morts* or whatever that popular piece by Sibelius is called, I do hanker to let off a gun somewhere in her direction. Deaths do something to your mother's Adrenalin gland.

Woe's me that I must dwell in the tents of Kedar, and have my habitation among the children of Mesech! I wonder why our lot is always being cast among such rumbustious grievers – not a silent tear among 'em. Though at the moment I write that, Katten's[2] composed shade comes into the room.

Diderot's letters are delightful. They must come to Norfolk with us.

1 Where we would lodge in Norfolk.
2 Katten [Hallward]: A friend of Ruth's, a friend to us.

They are a series of letters written to Sophie Volland. She was forty when he met her and he was forty three and they fell in love and loved each other till the end of their lives. He writes the kind of letters that you do – the best, the most living kind of letters, letters of a man with a pen in one hand, but in the other the hand of the loved one he is writing to. They are so entirely written to the person they are written to, that one has the impression of her almost as strongly as of him. And he is adult, in the best Latin way, and so must she have been, for he says, apropos of a witty and indecent talker that she would have enjoyed the talk because when needs was she was man as well as woman. They are going to be the greatest comfort and solace to me, bless you and the London Library for putting this good stuff in my hand for the last stretch of the road. And I think, without affectation, that when we are together I shall be a better creature for the comradeship of this good and wise and free-spirited man. And a good sociologist. He notices that cats in the provinces are afraid to eat off plates.

O my Love, my Love, my Love . . . walk warily for my heart hangs on the destination!

Sylvia

I did not thank you as I meant to for my tomorrow's lunch. I do now.

107: VA

Frome Vauchurch, 26 September 1949

My dearest Love,

This is the usual early morning letter, but this a.m. Mrs Lambert[1] comes and so I must hurry. There have been a great many letters, too, and these are your share. I hope none are nasty.

I had several from Ruth and some conversations. She seems to be temporarily placated by me being thrown to her for Friday lunch and so on. I hope this may do some good but alas she digests so quickly.

I have a wonderful letter from Mungo Park who writes exactly like G. Stein and not, I T H I N K, of intention.

So you were probably at Yeovil all yesterday and I was here all yesterday and cd. have come to you if you had wanted me and I never

1 Mrs Lambert: charwoman.

knew but thought all the time that you were happily on the damp and Sunday sands with Janet. Curse that little hog's eye, Roy. . . .

I found an appalling letter from your mother about Janet's marriage. Do you remember that one? (I was looking for the Upright and Godly letter and found it and another equally good or better. I must copy them into a book to keep for ever.)

I do not feel nearly as tired, my Love, thank you; but it is being heavy on the spirits (mine) and so I am at times a little downcast but that will pass. I shall not be pining, I hope and think. There is another letter from Evelyn today. I hope it is all about practical matters. They are having a very grand new car and I expect it is about that. I do not in the lewast envy them. I meant L E A S T but my machine went one better.

Every paragraph in this letter begins with 'I'. There was a calendar on the wall of a room at Winterton when I was little which R U T H put there and which had a little quotation from a saint on it about how the Alphabet shd. not contain I – or not at least as a personal pronoun. I took it very seriously and tried hard to cut it out but in fact one cannot without being (like the Quakers) an ungrammatical nuisance. Still – it had an effect on me and even now I become uneasy when I happen to notice the word. And R U T H put that calendar there . . .

My Love – you have no idea how profoundly thankful I am for your letters, each day, this day especially. Come back without a moment's hesitation in your mind or heart. To a dirty untidy house and god knows what not to make you feel hurt and angry with me. D O N O T F E E L H U R T O R A N G R Y (I cannot think it should be 'nor') because nothing whatever comes between thee and me.

Valentine

108: STW

Yeovil, 26 September 1949

My Love,

Here I am, still quite dazed with such an unexpected day;[1] that modulated into the relative minor after you had driven off, but still explored the same

---

1 Between leaving work and following Elizabeth to Weymouth she carried me off to spend an afternoon at home.

tunes. After I had eaten my hare (I really did eat a great deal of hare, how could I not? – it was so extremely good; but it may not seem so owing to the vastness of the pot) and drunk my coffee and done a few small chores to the house, I let myself loose in the garden; and had a lovely weed. The robin sang, Thomas and Shan gavotted, and I admired to see how the rain has made plants that were still small when I left now large and virtuous. If the weather holds up, it seems to me that we shall have pinks and carnations right on till Christmas, as well as anemones. I also – as a form of unobtrusive browning[1] – cleaned Tom's ears. They were not at all bad, but I noticed he was inclined to shake them. I saw the postman but he did not see me, for I was sunk behind the large majenta Michaelmas. Have you noticed the small crimson one beside it? It is charming; and a more amenable size than usual. It was a cutting from Mrs H. E. last year.

I do think we've got a nice garden. And next year, I promise, it shall be more orderly (though to my eye it is already more orderly) with a straight row of auriculas where now the gladioli are. I have considered them (the auriculas) and there is enough, because all the original plants are now parents of fine families. I also have a majestic project for continuing that new mass of M. daisies along the outside of the wall.

Grubbing in our garden has done me a great deal of good, my Love. I look at the verbenas,[2] and remember the psalm that begins When the Lord turned again the captivity of Zion then were we like them that dream. Which reminds me, that worthless Mr. Whitby has never sent Chaim Weizman's book that I ordered for you. Another book is on its way to us, for I had a letter from that amiable Miss Hoggenstogger to say that she is sending me (by which I understand she has made the firm do so) a collection oddly called *The Portable Medieval Library*. Of course it may be only all the things everyone knows; but there might be something in it to your purpose.

One day you must read the first story in the *Illustres Angloises* (the little book from Weymouth). It is extremely interesting, for the plot winds and unwinds like one of those magical clocks, cups are always being dashed from lips, each accident propels the story further; yet none of them is out of probability, and the characterisation is really distinguished. And as a study of love and jealousy it is as fine as *la Princesse de Clèves*. Whoever wrote it knew a great deal about novel writing, and there is a kind of Stendhalien dryness and perspicacity in the way that the matter of the

1 Brownies are house-spirits, who privily sweep, etc.
2 Planted at a time of great unhappiness.

story is made to affect the moods of the characters. For instance, when Helena (the she-villain) is abandoned by Cesar, who has been keeping her, but on a suspicion of H's infidelity has returned to his wife, Helena decides to get him back by the embarrassment of a semi-public repentance. She works on her confessor to apply to Cesar for enough money to enable her to enter an austere convent (I think this may be unconscious, but it is pleasing). He comes back to see her. Her house is much barer than when he left her, because she has been selling things to make up for the fact that he is no longer keeping her; but he sees the bareness, and it convinces him that she has really turned to the austerities of repentance. Though he was able to leave her on his own initiative, he cannot endure that she on her initiative should be able to leave him; so she gets hold of him again.

Now isn't that admirably worked out?

My Love, do you think you know how to find this hotel? It is on the summit of the hill that you come up from Yeovil to Pen Mill; and on the same side as the Pen Mill hotel. It is a red brick house with stone quoins, there is a large magnolia on either side of the door, and the name of the hotel is on a large board on posts in the front garden. And on the Pen Mill side of the house there is a drive-in towards a garage, where you could leave the car; at least, my taxi driver did, and no one said him Nay. I will be looking out for you, to convey you through the dainty touches.

The same Sherborne road as usual, just as though you were coming to the other hotel, but before you begin to go downhill towards it.

That will be the day after tomorrow; and tomorrow I shall be talking about you to Janet. And then at the end of two days when I shall sit at home with my fingers crossed, adjuring Thos. to do his utmost, his really utmost for you, and bidding Shan to be his obedient acolyte, we shall be together.

My Love

Sylvia

109: STW

Yeovil, 27 September 1949

My Love,
  When you rang up this morning I had gone to Thorney, pursuing baskets.

It was a delightful pursuit. I began with a grey haired woman with a mahogany cat (just about that shade really, with some hogogany tooral-looral auburn tints thrown in); and she was so emphatic about the other end of the village that I went too far, and then on the assurance of another woman that Mr Rogers lived in the very next house, standing back from the road, I went to it, but postponed Mr R in order to watch a mill-leat just being worked by a silent old gentleman. So lovely: the smell of churned water, the smooth brimming lock with bunches of steeping osiers bobbing about in it, the water sliding through as fine as oiled silk and a great mountain of whipped-up foam swelling to meet it. All this worked a real mill. The old gentleman was the miller and said sadly that he was almost the last miller in Somerset, but he kept it going because some of the local farmers preferred to send their stuff to him rather than the combine in Bristol. All the time there was the solemn lumber of the mill-wheel shaking the low dusty room, and a Caldecott sack was lying in a wheel-barrow waiting to be fetched away.

From him I discovered that Mr Rogers was again the next house standing back etc. . . . . A pretty house, too, with a great swag of honeysuckle on its porch, and a black cat keeping house, a young one, who stretched and fawned and wound about my legs, and thrust its wonderful new claws into the grass to show me how lovely and terrible they were. And I was there some time, sometimes remembering to knock on the door, when one of the people in the miller's yard asked me who I wanted, and I called back that I was looking for Mr Rogers – as though he might come out of the honeysuckle presently if I did not alarm him. So I was told to go round the back and through a little gate and I'd find him in his orchard.

Actually he was in a little shed, being a prawn.[1] A forecast, a good augury, a Norfolk-looking man, with a neat solid barrel, and brilliant blue eyes and a small head on a long neck. And with Mr Rogers I spent the next half hour or may be three-quarters. For when I had admired his baskets, and ordered an apple basket of his personal devising with all the rough ends turned to the outside, so there is nothing to bruise the apples or scratch them, and conversed a little about withies, he took me from shed to the machine for stripping them, and the tank where a bunch of white wands lay steeping, and looking like Ophelia, and a clothes-basket he'd made twenty-five years ago, and which is still a very sturdy container for potatoes; and out of each shed poured a cat,

1 Weaving a basket from long withy wands.

the black one being his own and the others neighbours. You couldn't have a better locality for cats, for when they grow tired of the mill they move over to Mr Rogers, and when they are hungry again they return to the mill.

Mr Rogers does the whole thing from start to finish. He has an osier bed (it came to him through his wife's mother), he re-plants, and cleans in spring and summer, in the autumn he cuts; in the winter he goes out when it looks likely to be a flood to haul in his boat. And all the year round, in between the osier bed, he makes baskets.

He is one of the nicest men you could meet. We parted devoted friends (at least I did, and he kept on hoping I'd come again); and I have ordered an apple-basket for us, which will relieve one of our current baskets for logs: a log basket for Janet; two quarter bushel baskets, very sturdy with handles; and a cat's basket.

After all this I still had half an hour before I need catch the train to get me back to lunch before I set out for Janet. So I went down a chaseway to the moor, and sat on a little bridge, looking at two straight green lines, stretching away through the mist in a V for Valentine.

Janet and I had a thorough tour of the dolls' house, and were pleased to see that the curly-cue 18th. cent. mirror was in the housekeeper's room, whereas the grand rooms had large dull plain ones. And Janet was justified in saying that a mysterious cylinder in the same room was a spicebox because we found an identical life-size one a few cases further on. Then we had a long gossiping tea at the Wessex; and she told me that when Elizabeth was there (at Weymouth) yesterday, she had talked of getting a house in Ireland, and asked Janet to ask Hilary[1] to send local papers. So your seed seems to have struck root.

Two nights and a day in Yeovil; and then a day and a night and a day; and then, O My Love, we meet!

Sylvia

I presume that the saint in your mother's calendar was an English saint, in the second half of the Christian era.

---

1 [Hilary Machen, Janet's brother.]

110: STW

Yeovil, 27 September 1949[1]

My Love,

You will not have time to read a long letter; but since I can't discreetly order flowers to meet you, or arrange for a poodle proud to be wearing a harness to be awaiting you with a basket of grapes in its mouth (*oui, je me suis reconnue dans ta caniche*), I must be content to write a letter; for I do not want you to arrive at a cold door.

My Love, I hope that after you have guided a difficult situation so gently and so compassionately, and at such cost to your own heart and spirit, the close will not be too painful to you, and that you will not be left feeling frustrated or derided. You should not, however things go. But I hope they will go well.

And remember that other autumn evening, and that other autumn departure, when you took me to Winterton for the first time; and remember that you are as deeply romantic to me as you were then, and far more deeply loved and trusted. And let my love be a comfort to you, as yours is to me, and has been all through this summer, and this exile which you have made no exile at all, only a *sala de esperanza*.

I thank you and I love you with all my heart, My Love, My True and Only Love.

Sylvia

111: VA

Frome Vauchurch, 28 September 1949

Evening[2]

My Love,

Be happy tonight, and settle down in safety in your own bed; and meet me on Friday, and love me all the time.

I feel very angry that I leave the house so dirty and dishevelled; it is not lack of will nor yet laziness, my Love. It is sheer lack of time and a

---

1 Posted to meet her in London.
2 Left for me to find when I got home.

considerable amount of self-control that I have employed to make myself *not* strive officiously – rather to conserve as much as I can of my wits, so that I may not be a heavier burden than the dirty house will be, to you.

But if you love me and understand that I do truly feel bad about this, you will leave the shifting of furniture and as much as you can possibly bear to of the tidying, so that we may do it together when I get back. And cosset Thos. and poor little Shan, who feels rather low and unloved just now, and who should not, for he has a warm heart and a very ready affection and he is self-reliant . . . but for all that he does like to be talked to and combed, and I have been too busy for the last 2–4 days.

I am sad but I am not any of the things you dreaded I should be. And I do most truly, and with all my heart, love you, my love.

Valentine

Narrative 12

It was dusk and the moon was rising when we turned up the track leading across the marsh to Mrs Howlett's house. An owl flew towards us, and I remembered the letter where Valentine said, 'Do you think she hunts mice at night, flying low over the sand-dunes and crying Mew-mew? I long and long and long to walk with you on that rough grass, although it will break my heart to be there again. But I don't mind that.'

It was a sturdy little house, brick-built, reed-thatched, lying close under a massive rampart of sand-hills. As we got out of the car we heard the sea, the powdering explosion of a wave falling on sand – which gives a fuller, yet gentler resonance than a pebble beach. Childishly acquiescing in this arrival at a place unknown to us, we went in and were glad to see a fire and Mrs Howlett bringing our supper. The second course was a milk pudding, a bowl for each of us. I detest milk puddings, yet I did not want to hurt her feelings by leaving mine untouched. Valentine heroically ate part of it for me. We went up a very steep stair to a raftered bedroom. I regretted the steep stair because Valentine's back had hurt her all day. The beds were not very comfortable either. We agreed it was heaven to be there.

In the morning we climbed the rampart, hauling ourselves up by clutching the marram grass, and saw the long stretch of beach, empty, with no print but the sea's on it. We paddled, and gathered driftwood for our evening fire; and that afternoon we walked together on the rough grass, eating blackberries to the placid thunder of the waves.

We spoke little and said nothing of our own affair. 'I must wait for the dust to settle,' she had said. It was a kind place to recover in, sufficiently like the Winterton of old days to be familiar and endeared, different enough to be unreproachful. The days were warm and windless; the waves came to the shore by their own momentum. We saw a sleek iron-coloured object bobbing in the surf, and took it for a mine till it turned its profile and was a seal. It was restorative to find we could be silly as ever. On our first evening, thinking that it was a long time since she had been left to herself, I went for a solitary walk, trying not to associate it with the solitary walks of exile. Coming back, I heard her typewriter and my heart clenched. But she was pleased, because she had begun to work on her Norfolk story again. A couple of evenings later a thunderclap on the heels of a brief rainstorm fetched us out to the sight of a double rainbow, with the air washed so clean that we counted seven church towers under its span; and she suddenly spoke of buying the house, or at any rate, of spending the winter in it.

Then Elizabeth's letters began to arrive and she left the Norfolk story to answer them, and if we went out in the car, it was to send cables. Yet in between we still aimed at happiness.

After Horsey, we had to visit Ruth, who welcomed us as though she had been rolling in catnip. There was a letter for Valentine. That night she told me how things were. She could not live apart from me, she said, though during September she had loved and delighted, felt renewed, been confident. All she then tried to establish was in ruins. After making a good departure, Elizabeth had relapsed into a black fury, a determination to get her own back, to cling and to wound. The letters had been so frightful that she dreaded reading them. But she felt a lover's responsibility; and she was desperate with desire.

What shall lost Aeneas do? We walked till morning and could find no answer. I was shown the latest letter. 'All I have sacrificed . . . the least I might expect . . .' Impatience gave me a gambler's courage. I drafted a proposal to Elizabeth: that I would go away for a year, or years, while conceding nothing of my right to hope; with a proviso that if I became ill or crazy Valentine must be free to come to see me. She typed it, I signed it. It went off that day.

We drove home through a weeping gale. We waited to hear that my proposal had been accepted. We waited. Some weeks later it was acknowledged, with a statement that it would need consideration – and prayer.

It was a grotesque relief, a flouting redemption. It freed me to speak out and say what I thought of such behaviour. Valentine said nothing. That evening she showed me her answer: there could be no further possibility of living with Elizabeth. She still loved, still desired, still hoped for meetings; but she could not mate with a heart that felt no impulse of reply, even an impulse of abuse and anger, but only its need to consider.

With astonishment, we went on living as usual. But she was still tied to the stake. Letters flailed on and on, and had to be answered. I fretted, and had to be comforted. And through all these months she had never escaped into the regions of the mind, never been able to call her soul her own. Meanwhile, I was going to London to companion Monica in the last week of her pregnancy. She had wanted Valentine who sent me instead.

*

112: VA

Frome Vauchurch, 21 November 1949

Monday night

My Love,
    My Love, it is such a stormy evening; gusts of furious wind and beating rain. Thomas is on my chair. He would not eat his rabbit but he ate a few pieces of my cold pork. He looks rather sad. I think I shall get Thornton tomorrow. I did not want to, because I think when a cat is so old as Thos. it is better for him if we are not told he is ill. If he and we know it together it is all right; but to be told it is not so good. Or so I felt in the case of Cumquat. But it is a little different with Thomas, for he has lived longer and he is more self-sufficient, and he is very knowledgeable in matters concerning life, so I expect he is in matters concerning death. I think he is ill, but I have no means of knowing whether he has anything wrong with him, other than running down, which I suspect it to be. He is happy now, however, for he is asleep on the cushion on my green chair and there is a pleasant fire and he has drunk a bowl of milk. Do not grieve about him more than you can help, my Love; he is not distressed in any way and it does not seem to trouble him at all that he sometimes makes messes in rooms, fortunately. I shall, I think, put him to sleep in the kitchen tonight

because I feel very tired myself, and the kitchen is reliably warm and the floor can be washed, and there are mice to amuse him if he wants amusement. Unless the mice are all in the larder, where they have already made the little bowl of fat their own . . .

Ruth has just telephoned. I was confident it was you, which was unfortunate for me and might have been for Ruth, except I managed to be nice, for once. It was very good of her to telephone.

I had a letter from Elizabeth this afternoon. It made me sad because it was written when she was alone and had been alone for a while (an hour or so) and so had resumed some of the manner she has with me. She talked very happily about what she supposes has happened inside her; a change of mind, or at least – something that has changed and enabled her, as she believes, to 'accept' some new manner of living. I think she is *en l'air*, and has a notion that her proposal of coming over here at more or less regular times is the same as my earlier suggestion of her living here. I do not think that she truly believes it is the same, but I think she has exalted herself so as to be able to seem to herself to believe it. If you see what I mean? She says she's had a talk with Evelyn, who has said that she doesn't think Elizabeth could possibly separate herself from me, and has said that she will stay in America for 3 months next spring while Elizabeth comes here, if I agree to her suggestions (it is the first mention of a length of time) and will do it also for 'unspecified times after that'. Elizabeth also says that she dreads to think I may have told you that she and I are going to separate completely and never see one another again. And adds 'Because she did say that we might be together sometimes, that she would try her best to adjust herself to that, and if she has not revoked the written words she gave you, then *might* we not try?'

Except that I think she has succeeded in deluding herself in the matter of having a 'change of heart' when in fact she has conceived a plan quite different from mine and accepted *that*: this letter is not insincere. It is painfully outpouring and very immature and – strangely foundationed on self-deception, it is truthful and from the heart.

I would not have answered it or referred to it at all, but that I had to acknowledge a large parcel which came this morning, and contained among other things a suit of brown wool which fits me perfectly and will be an absolute god-send to wear to work and to Dorchester and on occasions in winter which are like summer occasions when I wear the grey suit. And 2 shirts and stockings and soap and fougère powder and food. So I had to write, and found it difficult indeed to do it gracefully; for all that I am providentially and constitutionally able to receive presents and enjoy them, and in the case of things like this suit, thank God for them, with less embarrassment than most people – with perhaps abnormally and unpleasantly little revulsion of pride. But still, even I felt it to be a difficult situation and heaven only knows, since only heaven could direct it, what sort of a shift I have made in saying thank-you. And so the letter had to be referred to: but I reiterated the refusal categorically, and only said that I did not know any more at present than that I could not possibly live like that, and would find it quite unendurable. And that I had told you the contents of my yesterday's letter, and you had said that what I told her of your probable reaction to the proposal was, in fact, correct. I also said that you had all along maintained that the physical desire between Elizabeth and me was (by implication I made it clear that you meant it was *the only*) wholesome thing: and that you had never done anything against it. I said no more of that or anything else, I think; but wrote chiefly about the presents and what I would send her for Xmas.

Today has been interrupted by Mr Edmonds, who came in and sat down and had some Breakfast Bun that I had just made myself; and by the postman who would talk about foreign stamps and his nasty little daughters. I had cold pork and cold peas and apricots and cream for supper, and 3 slices of bread and butter; I had two date biscuits and 4 ginger-nuts and black coffee for lunch. I may try to listen to Goethe's *Faust*, part 2, soon.

I wish you would telephone – I thank GOD for your telegram, and that you had lunch. Ruth says London is warm and fine: for that too I thank God. But if this gale reaches you, my Love, take care of SLATES. And if M's baby starts in the middle of the night, don't RUN or PANIC. But if you go out, remember to take the key or snib the front-door! And DON'T rush across dark roads without looking right and left! Oh dear – I wish you hadn't gone. No. I don't. But I wish I were with you. I always, always want that and there is no other place I want to be, but with you.

Valentine

10.10 p.m. I miss you bitterly: I am lost without you. I am going to bed – eheu!

113: STW

London, 23 November 1949

Good morning, my Love. This is the 23rd. November – a little foggy, very London. Monica is eating her breakfast. It will be a strange thing if that baby is not born soon, for the poor little thing is continually jolted and alarmed by Badger[1] leaping on her womb. It cannot be good for anyone – not even very good for Badger – but she seems to enjoy it, and looks mildly grieved when I interpose. I have to be very tactful about interposing, or she would think me a midwife and mistrust me. As it is, I think we get on very nicely and yesterday from tea to bedtime we talked of – if I were clever I would go on till over the page, but I am not clever – we talked of nothing but poetry.

When she has learned to buy poetry herself she will begin to lead a fairly happy life. But she has yet to learn. I discovered she was longing to go to Wards, and had not dared to, because of the sellers. She came in with me and I gave her over an hour there, to poke and prowl. She pulled down branches, she fingered the fruit; but came away with not so much as a currant.

Flatter is not the word: to smooth, to tickle behind the ears, caresser; none of these are quite the word. Whatever it is, I realise here what an extreme development of technique you have brought me to in that pleasant pursuit. It is charming to find how easy it is to find the right place behind Monica's ears, and the right pressure, and the right duration. She shuts her eyes, lies down, and faints with pleasure. Not like you, my Love, who are as apt to bite my finger off or walk disdainfully away. But though it is nice to please so easily, I am spoilt for it. I fly at higher game. I do not really care much to please easily. I set my mind to please you, and when I do that I am contented with my talents.

Now the post has brought me your two letters – Monday evening and Tuesday morning.

Yes, I expect you are right about Elizabeth. She has very strong powers of self-delusion, it is because she feels she *ought* to be right that she so constantly convinces herself that she *is* right; and I suppose that now she has come to feel that she has had a change of heart, that she has accepted with a good grace and can now enter into her reward – besides, *she is in Love*. But I wish it were not always how *she* feels, what *she* has accepted or not accepted. She has, it now strikes me, no sense, or very, very little, of

1 A Sealyham.

the situation, no sense of what has really happened or is happening. That is a most hazardous variety of love – for love is a *responsible passion*, and a love not mixed through with responsibility is always a sort of ether. It drugs and anaesthetises, and the next instant it explodes.

But if you think of the look on the faces of copulating animals, so deadly serious, you see that love without responsibility is always open to being disastrous. I don't mean light or fleeting; hers would be neither; but somehow I think she has no sense of what she is doing, what you are doing, what any of us are feeling, what any of us are. We might all be angels dancing on that needle.

No wonder you had that headache.

I wish to God I were not here just now, being so acceptable. My heart just vanishes out of my breast when I think of you with all this sorrow and care, and alone. It gives a leap and vanishes like a grasshopper. I am grateful that you wrote as you did about me. It is true. Though I have often been riven with jealousy and sexual despair, I have never for an instant felt anything but trust and approbation (odd word!) for your bedding with her; and by that I mean all your amorous pleasures of sight and touch. And she ought to believe this. I hope she will.

I have to keep on breaking off – the dustman and so on – and heaven alone knows if you will be able to make out what I have been meaning to say. But the heart of it is love and compassion – and I am sternly withholding myself from any thought that begins *if only I*.

Alas, alas, my dear Love, how nearly we were lost. But not all your doing, and never infidelity. I had a hand in it, I must have had. For seeing you so ravaged after U.S.A. and knowing that your physical love for me was blighted, a kind of frost fell on me too. I did not want to remind *either of us* how it had been. And telling myself that the best way to heal (I was always somehow sure it would heal) is not to lift the scab and not to press or fidget, I thought that by just going on, by just dormousing that winter, we would survive. I see now that I was wrong – though wise. Sometimes it is wrong to be wise. For what it seemed to you was a habit of love, a dull drowsy thing; and really it was the dormouse sleep, that shuts its eyes and ears and whiskers to everything but a determination towards spring. But I was wrong. I should have taken the risk, and *woken*. It kills dormice, but it would not have killed love.

Of course I saw you were unhappy. But that I saw for so many other reasons. Elizabeth, the war, your health, and above all, your poetry. I did not think you were unhappy beyond what could be accounted for by these things. They were enough, God knows; and you had them all.

I won't go on. I begin to think how nearly this lost us all. It frightens me too much, and I won't go on.

O my Love.

Sylvia

114: VA

Frome Vauchurch, 24 November 1949

My Love,

I am so glad you are being such a good success. I had a note from Monica today in which she says with obvious feeling: 'If virtue is at all a comfort to you I cannot tell you what it means to me to have S. here; I am extremely grateful.' And then as abruptly ends. That 'if' is either very profound or very foolish! But you see, that Lady Gawky is stiff with gawk about it, and genuinely and manifestly and certainly relieved *and* enjoying herself – I hope you are too. It will be good for you, comely and reviving, to comfort someone who does not be ungracious about it – that part of your letter reproached me sadly and made me very pensive.

I woke to the king of all headaches, and no doubt will have the pope of 'em tomorrow. I had done nothing to deserve it: I had had a bath and gone to bed by 11 or so and slept the night through apparently quite stilly, and overslept, too – and had no fever when I woke. But simply was stricken with the most blinding of headaches. I have had two Edrisal and an alka and an aspirin and it has not abated. I shall have to go to bed shortly, I think. Even though Mrs H.E. brought me a loving parcel of o x b r a i n s – god save us.

Thos. had his pill this morning. He had not messed in the night. But he had messed in my sitting room by the time I got back from work. I had put him out before I went. But his mess was healthier and he is not at all troubled in his mind about doing it in the house. He is a true philosopher: may we learn of him how to support our infirmities! I have borrowed a pair of blunt forceps from Gaster, to try whether it is not better to pill Thos. with them, rather than struggle with him – which is perhaps bad for him and certainly bad for me. I do not think he cares very much (for I do not hurt him) because he swears a great deal, and I expect that eases him. I shall have to re-learn to swear, if this headache goes on; but it is rather late for that.

Your letter came this morning and I was glad; for I felt very sad and bleak. But – I hasten to assure you, my Love – nothing could have been done for me. I am N O T pining for Elizabeth, or for anything or anyone except for my own wits. You know how that feels. Nothing can be done for it – short of death or an island in the Pacific with you and a Siamese cat and ten snakes and two young, *speechless* and beautiful native girls – one to amuse the other – and a few bright and also speechless parrots. And fruit and champagne and plenty, plenty of time, and some books of poetry and twenty years off my age.

Meanwhile, Christmas comes but once a year and it's getting bloody near. Ruth says I shd. send off American presents at once and I haven't got anything to send Elizabeth and what C A N I send. And I am working on little books and you must be prepared to bind and bind and B I N D : and then I can polish off several people and they will never know or care what hit them.

I can't do anything at all; not even write a letter. Fortunately I'm still all right at work – even today when Gaster was in the worst mood of exaltation and over-stimulation I have yet seen him in – which is indeed saying a good deal. And he stayed in and chattered and dictated letters and talked down the telephone (driving hard-working people M A D by being cheerful at them) and I had to keep pace and turn a smiling cheek and get off no less than 13 letters, some of which needed research into files and so on: and I think I did not make one mistake. It is curious how one can do that. Like passing exams, I suppose.

But I shan't try to write any more, for evidently it is not Meant. But whatever looks dry and stupid in this letter isn't lack of love and of wanting you, my dearest and truest Love – if you were not with Monica, who does truly not only need but appreciate you, I should have sent you a telegram yesterday asking you to hasten return – or I think I should – but not if it had been clear that you are having a good time. It is clear that you are doing a good job and enjoying that; and enjoying London; and so on; yet I feel in my bones, my wise bones, my last wisdom, that you have a shadow on you like the foggier one I have on me, my Love – which is there always when we are apart. Never mind: we will go to France or Dublin or somewhere soon. And – best of all – this is mid-way or nearly mid-way, and you will be home again . . . Oh remember to take care of those long skirts and those steep stairs: and of fogs: and of murderers: and do not come unless you feel it is what you *want* to do – and what you *should* do – but when you feel those things, then, my Love – come –

Valentine

1950—1959

1950

Frome Vauchurch, 14 February 1950

My true Love,

It is dreadful to be writing to you on St. Valentine's Day, and to address it away from me – and I loathe you to go to Little Zeal without me, even though there is a happy, abounding family[1] there now. And you will feel strange and I'm afraid you will feel desolate this time, for whatever there was not between you and your mother there also *was*, and it is a strong tie and when it is broken you must feel shocked and lost for a while. I should be with you, my Love – Please forgive me and the circumstances that I am not – I find it hard to.

And think of how I kissed the pillow of your bed, my beloved, when I first went into that inhospitable house which, last time I was there, was good to both of us and was not inhospitable at all. And remember that I love you in all ways and in all places and for ever, and that I am *true*.

Sleep quietly and well, dear heart, and come back as soon as you possibly can; for I am terribly lost without you and I do not want to be lost.

I will kiss you on your pillow tonight and do my best to sleep beside you and keep you warm. I count you most truly my dearest Love –

Valentine

---

1 The tenants at Little Zeal. My mother had died. I was going to Devonshire for her cremation and to bury her ashes in the Little Zeal garden.

116: STW

Little Zeal, 15 February 1950

My Love,

A fire in my bedroom; two hotwater bottles in my bed. The young woman has an excellent idea of hospitality and you must esteem her for that. And another grace is that she has re-arranged the house so thoroughly that it scarcely bogeys at all, and there has been very little of what I had rather dreaded: the husk of a dead person's house, Nora's caddis-worm shell motionless and echoing.

I called at the lawyer's office in Totnes. He was out – but I saw his confidential rascal and got a copy of Nora's will.

The legacies and death-duties (so I feel at present) will be a directing shove towards selling the house. But I won't *make up my mind* to do anything. There will not be much to show immediately, because of all the settling up and death-duties and so on; but as far as I can see it will be reasonable to expect £500 p.a.

Enough, anyhow, to shake off your fetters[1] when you feel the day has come for it – that is what pleases and eases me, my Love. For though it is dear and natural to me to depend on you, and your shoulder to the wheel endears the shoulder I lean on (and I have been quite conscious of your reason for working) yet it appalled me to think of you becoming a routined animal. A hop and a frisk will be good for you now.

And we will have the kitchen done up proper. *And* we will have some sort of carpeting in your room. And we will see about that motor-mower. And when we go abroad we will have another wagon-lit journey. I feel great stirrings towards luxury. And we need not wait for these things, because with this new income *in petto* there need be no conscience about some raids on our post-office savings here and now.

WE WILL NOT PROCRASTINATE.

(Did you know that Dr Johnson probably wrote Goody Two-Shoes?)

There are a great many improvements in this house. The new-painted and distempered passage looks twice as large being light. On the long stair wall there hangs David Deuchar's great-grandfather's equipment as

---

1 Her job as Dr Gaster's secretary. I did not know I would be my mother's residuary legatee (she had told me at an earlier date that she was cutting me out of her will). Had I known, I would have post-obitted and raised enough to cover her nursing-home expenses. It was to help me through these lean years that Valentine continued to work.

Royal Archer of Scotland: the heavy baldric, the bonnet with the eagle's feather, the six-foot bow; there are new small lamps, solid and non-inflammable.

But the greatest improvement is: that now this house reminds me of you. You stand in the window. You sit reading by the fire. You lie in this bed. Your love and your protection encompass me here, too.

My Love – I shall soon be home.

Sylvia

117: VA

Frome Vauchurch, 18 March 1950

My Love, as I sit here filing, and know that today I am going to London[1] and leaving you unhappy, I cannot endure not to write down that I love you, with the *whole* of my heart. I am trying very hard not to get in the way: I don't want to be stupid and selfish and gross and make it worse. It is much harder than anything else – not to comfort you, my Love – even when you frighten me by thinking that I can't.

My true Love – my only true Love – take *merciful* care of yourself.

How lunatic it is to go away, and make you and myself and probably many other people too, confused and unhappy. And yet at a distance it looks as if it would be just pleasure and no harm. But Gaster's Jewish friend wrote to him today 'I start thinking that the farthest meadows are no longer the greenest, once you are near –'

But the not-far meadow is only 4 days away, not so far as to be in danger of deceiving us. My dear Love, do not, *please* do not, dread my return. *Please* do not.

Valentine

---

1 To meet Elizabeth. Chatte échaudée, tu retourneras à la chaudière. I dreaded the upshot, but needlessly. On her return she told me the pleasure was so soon swamped under the other's sullen determination to be harmful that she had called off any more such meetings.

118: VA

9 August 1950

My Love,

I have just been through a strange experience – suffering from an agony of terror and shock which at first I could not even identify, and then for a moment could not discover the cause. But the cause was the fearful peril I stood in at this time last year, and throughout all the year – of losing you, my Love, my Love –

For you might so easily, and most people would say you might so *well* – have left me and if you had no amount of trying (even if you had wanted to try) could have restored us to each other *whole*, and I do not know how either of us could have borne less than that. And indeed, if you had left me I don't think you would have wanted to come back, for *if* you had left me, you would have gone because you had already gone, or because you felt in your bones that I had, or both.

There is no way of thanking you for staying, for being you, my beloved Love: no other person alive on the earth could be true as you are, so that it isn't a fringe or fan-dangle of truth put on as a decoration, but is the substance of the whole garment you wear –

I found this sheet of paper at the end of the ms. book in which I write the details of my Wishes for disposal of small things when I die. . . . I wrote it the evening before I went to London to meet Elizabeth, I think, in March of this year. It is in one way a very sad piece of writing but in more than one other way it is all right, I think, and I shall give it to you, my Love, for all its possibly dangerous involutions. There is a wide, vast space between March and August – and if you doubt that, ask your bones!

My dearest dearest Love – my only care and Love – how I am lost without you.

Valentine

March 17th 1950
I should remember, in any event, as sharply and clearly as I know it now: that my heart's concern and anxiety are far more profound about whether S. is safe from harm, from illness, and how to keep her from anguish of heart, while I am away – than anything I feel about the very real hazards of E.'s flight over the Atlantic in these present gales.

This is, in one aspect of it anyhow, a shameful thing to know and admit, but it is true. It would always be true. Even in bed with E. it would be true –

If there is any 'salvation' for someone like me, it can only be through true-seeing: even of such strange, tangled and in some ways horrifying facts as these.

It is a total difference – *not only* in the nature of these two loves I feel, but in the potency, the vigour, the depth of the one as compared with the other.

But – I have a longing to *enjoy* myself, and I cannot feel ashamed of that, although at times I feel I ought to be ashamed of giving it so much importance.

Oh *God* I am in a bad way.

I love Sylvia so much, much more than anything or anyone – but I have lost the power to show her this.

I would pray for that power to be restored to me, beyond anything else except the one prayer I made for myself now 3 years ago 'that I may be as thou wouldst have me' – But next, oh very close to that – 'that I may be restored to Sylvia as she would have me.'

1951

Frome Vauchurch, 11 October 1951

What am I to say, my Love, in the middle of these packings and preparings, when I still don't believe that tomorrow you will be gone? Perhaps it shows how blessedly few your absences have been that when they approach I don't believe in them – though I do when you are away, with the same kind of incredulous acceptance one feels for flood over the garden.

By the time you get this my soup will have gone its way through you, my last practical hold over you will be reduced to wool. Wear the pullover, my darling, I have knitted so much love into it, and wrap yourself in the shawl; and do please try to wrap yourself in it before twelve a.m. and not be pinned in a draughty doorway, shuddering and drooping under the blast of Ruth's goodnight calamities or sudden bursts of reminiscences about cold Clays.[1]

I promise you I will observe all your commands. I will eat, and keep warm, and drink, and lock doors, and shun yard dogs.[2] I will do my part, and do you do yours. When you feel cold, or tired – and O God, if you feel ill – remember my anxious appalled stern ghost, and let it pester you into taking care of yourself. Remember that I would come at the drop of a handkerchief. I should leave Niou in the house, the key at the post-office, and ring up kind Vera[3] to come and gather him.

And remember how we love each other . . . that contains everything. If you remember that, you will do all the other things I beg and implore.

1 Connections of Ruth's, mostly dead, all grisly.
2 A German fable. The careful husband leaving a young wife warned her against every conceivable danger, and as an afterthought told her not to ride on the yard dog. Struck by this novel idea, she did so, fell off, and miscarried.
3 Vera Hickson: Niou's breeder.

O your sad pillow! But those ghosts can't come into that room now.[1]
We laid them, hand in hand we laid them.

My heart's love.

Sylvia

120: VA

Winterton, 15 October 1951

Monday morning

My dearest Love, such a FOGGY morning; cold, grey, weeping . . . I am
very well pleased with it because now I can wear my pullover and it snugs
me most comfortably, besides looking very noble and absolutely an
example of Le Sport at its finest hour.

The post this morning brought me great riches from you, my true
Love: I needed them. I always become impoverished here and although,
I hope, I am not reduced to actual shabbiness, I feel myself being
propelled to the very edge of Keeping Up Appearances, which – while I
applaud it, from superstition and fear, when I see it in others – I both
scorn and disdain when I think I am near to doing it myself.

The post also bought me a loving letter from Vera, which pleased me;
one from little Janet which touched my heart almost beyond bearing, and
one from Barbara[2] as yet unread because it is long and Ruth didn't have
so many letters as I had (!) and so I really dared not go on reading mine.
And one from Elizabeth, which refers to my careful, civil – and much
more than civil, by being easy and affectionate – explanation about the
impossibility of arranging to see her this journey, with general hopes held
out of a meeting somewhen and where unspecified but not too obviously
so – as my 'uncompromising refusal of my invitation' . . . But she had a
cold in her head, and this cd. account for almost anything that needed
accounting for. Whereas, in fact, the phrase itself – I do believe – could
have been accurately foretold, and certainly the intention behind its use.
Read directly after Janet's tragic letter it was almost embarrassingly
trivial and deplorable.

Last night, of course, there was a Conversation about all that, and I

1 The spare-room at Winterton where two years before we had been so unhappy.
2 [Barbara Whitaker.]

found myself saying cheerfully to Ruth that if ever she had to advise anyone who was suffering from any form whatever of troubled love or lust, she must remember to assure them that the *only sure cure was boredom*, and that they must wait patiently for that to supervene, and when it did they would be positively Saved. I then went on to say it was odd and remarkable but none the less gratifying, that in the 22 years or only a little less that you and I had lived together I had never once been bored in your company: I shd. perhaps have said 'by' your company, for I think I have been bored together with you, during the war, in Dorchester, but never without surprise and resentment. I then finished it off by saying majestically that you and I had never had one serious disagreement or anything approaching what is called a quarrel . . . arguments and angers, very occasionally – I said – and Ruth interrupted glibly with 'of course, but they are the Salt of Life, you know!' and I knocked her flat on her back with 'Not at all. I hate them. So does Sylvia. We have never been able to endure even an argument for more than a few minutes, and they've only happened when we've been ill or tired or – perhaps – too much bothered by tedious outsiders . . .' So that dropped.

This day is going to be awful. I have packed and packed; I started yesterday morning. I have packed continuously ever since. It is my greatest comfort. I am quite well but today I feel the strain and I wish I may get away safely! Nothing is wrong, but I feel the strain. I took a p.b. last night and the night before, to secure good dreams; and I had them, I think, though unimportant. But I have had a great headache since last evening. However, everything is going all right, so far; and I feel so violently happy when I think of seeing you, my Love, that I dare not think of it and yet I do not think of anything else . . .

Take *care*. I wonder if you will even get this before you get me? Never mind anything, so long as we are together again.

Valentine

1952

When Valentine came back from London and said, 'I can't promise I shan't fall into pits of depression. But it is at an end,' Tom the cat was still husbanding his last days – walking stiffly out into the sun, drowsing on the hearth, on a lap, borrowing warmth from familiar sources. Then he took to lying on the river-bank, at the chill water's edge. One evening in late March I heard him come downstairs after me as though he were dragging something. I picked him up. His hind legs hung like broken wings; he was paralysed. We sat up with him, and as he seemed pleased by the sound of our voices I extemporised the final stanzas of the inexhaustible Skeltonic called 'Praise of Thomas the Cat', with its refrain:

> And did purr, and purr,
> And had such soft fur.

Early in the morning Valentine carried him into the garden and shot him with her .22, shooting him through the head with a steady hand. He was the Frankfort kitten, he had known us in our happiest and unhappiest days. It was as if he had waited to see us out of our troubles.

The last ten months had stripped and battered us. We were exhausted, each of us was aware of the other's loss. During those months, we had been compelled into a no-holds-barred extremity of truthfulness. Every aspect of our turmoiled, weathercock selves had been laid bare and discussed. Good or bad, there was nothing we did not know of each other – except animosity. Apparently, it was not possible for us to quarrel.

But spring is a positive season, and we were in the power of an exceptionally positive spring. Every copse and wayside was floored with bluebells, and while we were still drowning our sight in them, and filling the house with their sleepy honey scent, the hawthorns came into bloom. They bloomed so majestically, so dazzlingly, they were like an absolution. They freed us into an unthreatened joy. We explored about to see more of them, got up early to dabble our faces in their dew, went out to smell them by moonlight.

We were coming back from one of these explorings when I remembered we needed more cider. The Acorn Inn, she said, had good cider. She left me in the parked car. When she reappeared, she had a Siamese cat under either arm. What did I think, she said. It was not their poker-work faces but the look of sensuous pleasure on hers which I instantly assented to. The inn-keeper gave us the address of their breeder: Mrs Hickson, Cauldron Barn Farm, Swanage.

As we followed Mrs Hickson's directions through Swanage, it seemed improbable that we should come to anything like a farm. The directions turned us up an avenue, halted us at its summit beside a red-brick school building. Looking down on a shaggy stone-tiled roof, a steep terraced hillside, a screen of poplars at its foot, it was as though we had come to Italy. It was also like Italy that everything was locked in a siesta. We went from door to door; we peered in at windows. 'No one lives here,' I said; 'and I don't believe it exists.' A wide-brimmed hat, a tall woman, emerged from a flower-border, and we were taken in to see the kittens. We had wanted a female, but of the current litter only two males were left. We chose, after consideration, the one who looked most intellectual. Mrs Hickson, meanwhile, sitting erect and composed, was subjecting us to a careful scrutiny. In the end, she decided we would do, and we drove away with the intellectual kitten, promising to bring him back if he were homesick. Two days later, he set up a persistent and impassioned yelling. As we already loved him, had named him, did not want to return him, this was upsetting. But he yelled for wonder and wild desire, not homesickness: we were boiling down a carcase of lobster for a bouillabaisse.

Even if we had bought the house in Co. Clare (but it was a compendium of regrettable disadvantages) I would have remembered Cauldron Barn Farm because of that first impression it didn't exist and a later encounter with what is said not to. Between impression and encounter the elder Hickson daughter had died in an accident. I had talked to her briefly while we were choosing the kitten. When we went to deposit him before going to France, I knew it was she before I knew it was her ghost who came up to the car and looked at us – very much as her mother had done on our first visit. That she should appear, neither to the grieving father who stood by wishing us a happy holiday nor to Valentine whose mind for so long had been in pursuit of immortality and the nature of the soul, but to me, made me ashamed of my irresponsible knack for the supernatural.

We wished to evade reminders, so after September in the Auvergne we rented a house on the north Norfolk coast for the winter. It was literally on the coast. The sea was within a stone's throw. Between us and the mainland stretched half a mile of ditched causeway across a marsh. The house (originally a coastguard station, then fortified for coastal defence, then made over for summer holiday use by a London family) stood on a low ridge between the marsh and the beach. It was a pebble beach, and sharply shelving. With an onshore wind and a high tide bursts of spray darkened our windows. At times, it was so cold that the waves froze as they broke on the beach. At times the wind was so strong that if I went out to empty trash into the rubbish pit, I had to go on all fours. As our tender Asiatics went on all fours by nature they were undeterred. Shan chased spindrift, Niou flirted with the breakers or walked primly to a shed where long-shore fishermen kept their gear; and licked lobster-pots.

The house was a queer mixture of splendours and hardships. There was a Bechstein but no saucepans; two bathrooms, and no drinking-water; beds quite as hard as the Horsey beds and the collected works of Edmond Rostand. We lived in wild contentment to the rubato metronome of the sea.

While we were there, I sold Little Zeal. I wanted to replace it by a house in Norfolk. We looked at several houses and fancied ourselves overcoming their various drawbacks. One and all had the insuperable drawback of being indefensible against Ruth's inroads. It had been bad enough when we lived at Winterton. Then, we were twenty years younger and more hardhearted. Now, these defences down, we would be exposed not only to Ruth's inroads, but to what might cause a festering embarrassment; for she was still bawding for Elizabeth.

An advertisement of a disused church for sale sent us to our last inspection. It was a small roofless dissenting chapel. We accepted the sign.

After the winter's hexameters, the house we reached at the end of our diagonal journey was like a poem by Anon. The swallows arrived, and the cuckoo. Everything had grown. One of the things which had grown was our friendship with the Hicksons. It was agreeable to be welcomed by people who knew no more of us than that we lived together and took pains about choosing a kitten. It was a chance-sown friendship, confident and unenquiring. When Valentine developed measles on top of pleurisy and nearly died, Vera was one of the few people I could bear to write to; when she was in the toils of recovery, the invitation to convalesce at Cauldron Barn Farm was the only invitation she could bear to contemplate. 'I believe you are doing this partly on my account,' I said. 'Entirely,' said she. I knew the depth of her love for me, but I also knew she would repudiate any other invitation with the whole force of her character; so we went, and sank into the tranquillity of the cool, gentle, untidy house; a tranquillity which seemed to flow into it from a circumference of peaceful animals – animals never hurried, never coerced, always spoken to politely. Fed and cared for and never coerced, it was as if we were on the same footing as the herd of pedigree Jerseys.

We discovered that Arthur, who looked prosaic, was a poetry reader, and that Vera, who looked poetical, was in the main practical – at any rate liked to think of herself as practical. She indulged the fancy in all directions, but especially in auction-rooms. Valentine used to meet her at auctions in Dorchester and bring her back for lunch. After lunch, Vera displayed her spoils – mixed lots, as a rule, of the kind catalogued as Sundries. Not all the sundries were immediately applicable; the uses for cricketing-pads and bears from Grindelwald are limited; but half a dozen flat-irons was just what one wanted on picnics, when the wind blows everything away, and tooth-brush trays sans lids would be perfect for the rabbits' drinking-water. Before long, Valentine was bidding, too. She did not compete with Vera's soaring practicality. Her motives were compassionate; she bought small objects which had known better days. She had a quick eye for lineage; by midsummer her finds were becoming an accumulation, and giving the prettiest to me only shifted the problem of where to put them. I can't remember which of us remarked that the long sun-parlour with its separate entrance would make a good shop. I do remember that by the end of the day I had made curtains to fig-leaf the bookshelves where Marx and Engels, Casanova and Mrs Henry Wood were wrapped in the same cobwebs, that Valentine had cleaned the range of windows and weeded the approach to the separate entrance and laid out an array of her purchases and sugared it with some things of her own; and that by the time we went to bed we had done everything – except pricing: that only occurred to us later. By then, she was sure no one would come.

Surprisingly, they did come.

Vera was an early customer. She bought so lavishly that she would have put Valentine out of business if we had not deflected her into catching fleas on Niou and Kaoru, Niou's kitten brother. Kaoru was the last of his litter. But there were still eight permanent cats at Cauldron Barn Farm as well as the old sheep-dog and Vera was at her wits' end for a deputy, since if no one could be found to keep house for them, the holiday in Provence which Arthur needed so badly would have to be given up.

Remembering how Horsey had hung on finding a locum tenens, I offered myself – and wished I hadn't, when I realised that I would have to be away for a fortnight.

*

121: VA

Frome Vauchurch, 27 September 1952

My true Love,

I do not see how to get a letter to you on Tuesday morning unless I write while you are still here and that is a dreadful thing to do . . . it makes me realise much too clearly that by this time tomorrow I shall be alone in this house which will seem to swell to a great size, to be full of draughts, to be silent as a tomb or else echoing with sounds where there should be silence: and when I have thought resentfully of all this, I realise that it will be the same but worse *for you*. And yet, I hope it will not. Because in a strange house there are at least distractions and not reminders: you will not come on one of *my* stockings, or a cup still half-full of coffee, or this or that to jerk you and make you forbode disaster, mortality, miseries of all kinds: you will only find traces of Hicksons and other people's strange ways: and you will have kind cats and grateful, deaf dogs and friendly gardeners . . . and Bea about to arrive.

I *hope* all this: I list it so that I shall remember it myself to reassure myself when I become sunk in gloom, as I shall because I am sure to think of every kind of difficulty and unhappiness besetting you, just because I am thirty miles away and I feel sure they will take the chance to run at you.

Do not let them, my dear Love: telephone me immediately the snout of a disaster shows around the door: or if possible before that. And if the telephone breaks down you *must be sure* to go straight to the school and force them to open communication immediately. And if you forget to write to me or to catch the postman or Charles,[1] please do *not* go to the post. I don't like to think of you walking anywhere out of the grounds, really: or at least not alone: because of bulls, Poles, young soldiers, polio,

---

1 Charles [Bennett]: estate carpenter and mechanic, and man of goodwill.

sleepy wasps or adders, mad dogs and all the other things that happen to people every day and that we read about every Sunday. I wish now that I had not read the N.o.W.[1] this Sunday: but even if I had not I should still have all the old ones I have read welling back into my mind like the water in the basin at the Hotel Lloret.

But above all things, and in everything else you ever think about or remember, remember that we love each other so much, my dearest heart: if you truly and clearly remember that, I think you will be prudent, wise, skilful and full of cleverness at avoiding all the frightful perils I see you exposed to when I am not with you.

Don't have any misgivings about me: first you can't, because you are a Rationalist and you know all about the whatever-it-is of averages: second, you can't because you know that this is the simplest, least dangerous of houses and that neither cat is in the least likely to go mad, and there are no bulls: third, you won't because you know that I should tell you instantly, and in the most vivid detail if anything went wrong, and above all, you don't have to think about me (as I alas do have to think about you) that there is the least tincture or trituration of Stoicism anywhere in my nature . . .

And you needn't feel sorry for me that R. and K.[2] are coming down: on the whole I look forward to it: it is a relief to my worrying kind of mind, or heart, and also it will be fun often, one way or the other: even if the usual catastrophes happen, I can enjoy them with an easy and an ironical mind, since you are safely (I hope) out of the way of their dust.

Please try to enthuse Bea about the shop, my darling: because it would be so encouraging to have someone really enjoy it: and also it would be extremely nice to have some extra pennies in hand when we go to Shropshire . . . in case we find a good shop or sale.

About the new car: if there are snags, or it all happens in a hurry, I will not invoke you, I think: it is such a weary journey and really not for much pleasure to you, because car-dealers are so horrible and you don't much like new cars and you would hate seeing the old one go. I shall hate it very sharply, too, and it might be the deciding factor, if I also distrust the new car: for the old one has been so kind to us and we have been so happy and so unhappy and so miraculously restored to happiness while we had it. But on the other hand, a car with no black association, as this poor one inevitably has, is something to be considered . . . and I think perhaps from

1 *News of the World.*
2 Katten was giving Ruth a holiday and it was to be spent in Dorchester.

a business point of view it is sensible to get a new one if we can. But all these considerations are considered already, and unless it is very easy and painless (if, for instance, it can be here on Wednesday when you are here anyhow) I don't think I will disturb you to come and see it, *unless* you would rather?

My Love, I can't think of anything else except what is so much part of me that I never think of anything, simple or complex, without it being part of my thinking: that I love you entirely, with my whole heart and soul, and have loved you so from the first moment and shall, for sure and for sure, until the last: and if there is never a last moment, how happy indeed I shall be because then I need never stop being in love with you, and I cannot for the life of me think of a greater happiness than that.

Valentine

122: STW

Cauldron Barn Farm, 2 October 1952

My Love,
  Bea's taxi has taken her off, clasping her dead leaves, and also clasping cream for Mark,[1] quinces, a melon, and three very small eggs. And her last coherent words to me were that on thinking it over she realised she had only bought things that she wanted to keep for herself, and will you please send her a list of what is in your Christmas assortment, and she will order presents from it, if you do not mind sending them to her.
  Some more incidents of Mark's aunts have come up. One of them was often to be found sitting up in bed under an umbrella. She was subject to melancholia, and revived the breed of basset hound (there could not have been a better choice, could there?). Another, spending the first night of her honeymoon at the Lord Warden hotel, rang up her parents during breakfast, and said, 'I think you had better come down. Henry has gone mad and is doing the most dreadful things to me.' Bea and I found that what really shocked about this story is that a young woman should be able to telephone and yet be so innocent of the facts of life, and that we feel the wand of electricity should have abolished all such obscurities; which is very irrational of us.

1 [Mark Lubbock: Bea's husband.]

Mark is not far behind the family record. No Lubbocks can write anything except occasionally books. A new secretary at the BBC ran after Mark, saying, Mr Lubbock, you have not signed this contract. Mark said, kindly but firmly, Don't you know I *never* sign contracts? – and the poor young woman went respectfully away, thinking that this was part of the BBC foundation, and that she should have known it.

It was a nice visit, and now it is nicely over, and I am pleased to be all myself and wholly to you. You would be impressed at the calm with which I deal with daily life on a farm. Just now the telephone rang, and it was Oldfield speaking, and did I know the bull was loose? It was dear Benno, who had pulled up his stake, and was walking about with it, so Mr Upton[1] told me. The ground is so wet you couldn't stake a mosquito, let alone a bull. This morning too, I found the egg collector dithering about whether or no he was to call next week. The hens, said I, bringing Dr Johnson to bear, will go on laying, so I suppose you had better go on collecting. Mr Upton now likes me quite well, he likes my calm. Mansfield[2] loves me, and perfectly worshipped Bea because she caught an escaped rabbit. He appeared saying, One of your rabbits has got out. Who do you think this reminded me of?

I have found out what it is that makes your story unlike any other, except its elder brother, *Lavengro*. It is because it is so completely identified with its first person singular. I don't know how it is done, but you have done it. Everything in it happened to that young man, and no one knows of them but he. They happened to him, they were not thought of by you. I don't know any one else except sometimes Borrow, who brings this off. Defoe, bless his flesh, doesn't. He knows his characters through and through, he knows exactly where he is going. But that is something quite other to what you have done. It's not imagination, it's not Yorkshire.[3] It's the private story of this young man, and no one knows it, or could guess it, if he were not telling it. The effect is extraordinary, and most of all for me, because I find myself *having to remember* that it was in fact you who wrote it.

I still do not know where to settle. The old room is too dark by day, and the fire smokes, because the chimney is still cold. The new room is light, sunny, has a good firm table, and if the telephone rings and might be you, I can hear it. But it has this damned aquarium, and only becomes

1 Mr Upton: farm manager.
2 Mr Mansfield: gardener.
3 'That's imagination,' said John Craske, showing sketches. 'That's Yorkshire.'

tolerable after dark, when the thing can be turned off, and then it boots not to be light and sunny. I have found the nicest room in the house, the real Thomas's bedroom. I realised suddenly that lurking behind the natural history bookshelf on the landing was not merely a piece of boarding, but a door with a handle. It looks over the garden, has two windows, everything handsome about it, and not a trace of handicraft. I am so glad darling Niou had it, and not that cockloft with the revolting breadbin.[1]

We will never have an Aga, my Love, not even if we had a Charles to deal with it. The hot plate is too inflexibly hot, the other one is only useful for warming cats. Tonight I may think better of it, for I mean to have baked potatoes; but except for a house with a daily demand for funeral baked meats, an Aga is no Jews harp.[2] Still, it made some lovely cream. I shall make another lot next week, and you can entertain Ruth and Katten with it, if so please you.

Bea says, may she have your secret of making ice-cream? She has always meekly complied with custard, like books say, and doesn't like the results. If she could make it as you do, she would gratefully riot in it.

I loved her as she went off today, garlanded with thanks for a nice time, and her mind already fixed on seeing Mark. Sometimes I very much enjoy seeing myself in a mirror. And though I am very sorry that you feel lost and lonely (your letter that came today, written after Mrs Lambert) I don't pretend to be surprised at it. How else could you feel? Would you expect to feel so very differently to your rib?

My Love, my Love,

Sylvia

123: VA

Frome Vauchurch, 3 October 1952

My true Love,

It is twenty-two years since you first came into my bed ... and if there is love and mercy anywhere I shall have twenty-two million aeons in which to thank you and glorify you for that, and then as much more for

1 Mrs Keates – who meant revolving.
2 A Cockney cook in my past described some labour-saving implement as a regular little Jew's harp.

each other happiness and pleasure and comfort and splendour that you have given me.

The season of this autumn must be like the autumn of 1930, I think; because I remember that so clearly, and felt appalled because I thought you would become so bored with my company unless I could dole it out in small lengths only. And you might have become so, if it had not been for that blow-up at Miss Stephensons and all that – and the pink chicken. I really do not see that you could have been anything else, except for the flurry and sudden emergency of that strange incident, and our fatigue, and so on. I am so glad the Lord moves in a mysterious way, because there is no other way at all, that I can see, which could conceivably have brought you to love me. And yet you did, and you do, and as for how I love you, my sweet and dearest, it is one of my sharp prickling and stabbing thorns that perhaps you do not know *really* how I love you: that perhaps in these years, and especially in these very troubled years, and in my dreadful affliction of inability to tell you, it has come to seem to you that I love you only domestically, or only as a comfort, or only as a dear companion. . . . And these are capacious onlies, in themselves, but they are thimbles and acorn-cups compared with the great cistern . . . larger than the cistern I wrote a poem about at Winterton so long ago . . . which anyhow overflows all the time because nothing can hold all my love for you.

If everyone has thorns to stab them, if even you have – who have no reason that I know of ever to feel a pinprick – then my beloved, my dear, know that any prick you have from any thorn which says it comes from me, or on my behalf, is a lie and a fabrication: is Maya: is completely false, forged and non-existent.

I don't believe that anyone in the world, ever, has loved more perfectly than you have loved, and I don't believe that anyone has been loved more completely, for everything and in every way, than you are loved by me, my dearest and most true heart.

But why we are such bloody fools as to be apart for half-an-hour, much less a whole interminable frightful fortnight, I can't conceive. I pray God not to hold it against us –

Valentine

124: STW

Cauldron Barn Farm, 4 October 1952

My Love,

It is twenty-two years, you say. I take your word for it, it has seemed more like twenty two minutes to me. And if you think the pink chicken had anything to do with it, for twenty two years you have been dandling an illusion. Desperate as I was to please my phoenix, and make a good impression on the creature, it would have been more likely that the pink chicken would have penned me up in mauvais honte. No, my Love, it was your sad viola voice that brought me in on what seemed then an imperative need to succour you because you were sad, and must be mistaken. The lovely, the mysterious, the enchanted creature was grieving alone; and without even considering what likelihood there was that I could comfort it, I ran in.

Do you remember the ceremony of the Brides of France – that on the frontier they were undressed, and crossed it in only a shift? And on the French side, the shift was whisked off, and the bride clothed in her husband's country – I crossed my frontier in a shift, my darling, and left everything but myself on the yonder side of that flimsy wooden door painted pink.

And not till I lay in your arms did I know that what I had gained was love, and that what I had sought, too, was love. And afterwards, O heavens: What a fidget I was in not to become a clog, a burden, an outstayer of welcome. And how I fought you with refusings of vows, and rejecting of contracts, and how I paid out such yards of free reins and long ropes that it is a marvel to me now that we didn't get strangled in them.

It was very wise of you to let me go to London, so that you could bring a longer lever to bear. Phoenixes are born wise, I believe. Their flights are wild, their flights deceive the groundlings, the wiseacres, who remark that there is no getting any sense into their heads while they are young, but perhaps in twenty years one may see a difference. You are as wise now as you were then. Often sadder, I'm afraid, and with bitter reason for it; but for all the unjust calamities and frustrations that have befallen you, you are no whit unwiser. You are as pure, as cunning, as dauntless, as cautious, as chivalrous as ever you were. And I do not say it ungratefully, either to you or to heaven, that the miracle that stopped you drinking, though it made a world of difference to you, has made no difference to me beyond a difference of demeanour, a filling or not filling of bottles. I look back on the pre-miracle Valentine, I compare her with the present Valentine: there is not a shade of alteration in my vision. She is the same, my true love and my truly loved. After the night when you told me all that, it was as if I had been – not struck by lightning, but traversed by lightning. I blinked, and drew one deep breath, and walked on, and when I looked back on the way I had come, I saw it exactly as I had always seen it. Only one difference; from admiring your good manners, I changed to venerating them.

But how can I draw the thorn from your bosom? I have seen your love for me your greatest happiness, and your greatest torment. In those appalling October days at Winterton and the winter that followed them (worse, to me, than anything that had gone before, because the interval at Yeovil with your letters and your visits had assumed a quality almost of courtship, a revenant courtship, and I had childishly thought that when we met again it would be to live happy ever after) in those appalling days, I watched you loving me with despairing drowning truth of love, and still enduring to love me, though you were half dead by it. There is some frightful story, or perhaps it is a picture, that I remember from my childhood, of a man being dragged backwards into a hole in the earth by some octopus monster – his reaching arm caught and pinioned in a fold of the beast, and another fold enveloping his mouth and silencing him, and only his eyes left, staring at the world he leaves, imploring, imploring. It must have been in some book for children; only children are granted these horrors to take to bed with them. Anyhow, it came back to me then, when I saw how you looked at me, even when we were calmly talking of Elizabeth's letters, and the date of her return.

How can I doubt what I have seen in such extremity? No more than I could doubt my own love and my trust in you, that flowed back like some gentle water as I lay on the bed while you read aloud to me those chapters from your book. There I lay, happy, safe and serene.

And now, my darling, all this is becoming almost a Winter's Tale, as we sit by our hearth. As I read those same chapters again, the words were clothed in your voice – and do you know what I thought? How happy she made me. So I am not in a way to suppose that you love me only domestically (when a chicken is pink, you know, or I forget something till the car has got out of the gate, or in the unfolding of gigantic quilts) or as a comfort (when I have a cold in my head, for instance, or stab you by looking pale) or as a dear companion. These are capacious onlies, as you say, and the last of them burrows itself into a profounder capaciousness every day and night we lie down in it; but I do not think that is how you love me. O my Valentine, I know better than that. I know a great deal more than you may suppose. Or a great deal less. But I do know that you love me, and how you love.

I don't believe for a moment that God to whom you utter these blasphemous prayers (while I just assume that if he exists at all he is somewhere about in his quad.) will hold it against us that I am here and you there. I suppose that he got confused over Vera and all the cats, and could not give her a holiday without stuffing me into her gap. He doeth all things, some of them are bound to be less well done than others, but I think you should be prepared to praise him in his comparative failures as well as in his marvellous works. Knowing what Vera and the cats are like, I can't hold this against him, and I don't expect him to hold it against us. I daresay at this moment he is in Provence, at his wits' end how to deal with her impulses to adopt several thin goats, ill-used donkeys and under-nourished cactuses, and bring them all back to Cauldron Barn.

Felix has just confirmed the truth of these suppositions by being sick at my feet.

Tib

1954

Frome Vauchurch, 26 August 1954

My Love,

The thought of your letter posted in Norwich woke me, I unpillowed my head from Kaoru's ribs and ran downstairs; even so, the postman had put everything in at the window and gone. But I was up, and there was your letter, so I took my breakfast into the shop and ate it in the sun, and now all the morning jobs are done, the letters posted up the lane, and still it is not ten o'clock. See the virtuous consequences of over-sleeping!

Last night the cats changed their dispositions.

During their last out they must have heard a sermon from an owl or the moon about visiting widows; for when I went to bed, they came in together, rushed upstairs and planted themselves dead centre in the bed in an eternity knot, nose to tail, tail to nose, and a brown plaited rush-mat of paws in the middle. I coiled myself round them. During the night, they rearranged us, Kaoru under my cheek, Niou on my neck and shoulder. And you had not as much as a mouse in the arras . . . it is horribly unfair. I brought them some delicious fillets of smoked haddock from London, as a treat, and stewed it tenderly in the Larsons' left-over milk; but they do not like it as much as their ordinary provincial food (there is plenty), so I shall make it into a fish pudding for myself.

There was also a postcard from Steven, who is in the Austrian Tyrol, rather to his surprise, and rather to his surprise is liking it. We would like it. A little biscuit-crumb village with an immensely tall thin campanile lying on the steep lap of mountain pastures, and above them some combs of fir-forest and sharp Dolomites. It looks so immensely silent; great antres of silence for one cowbell to ramble in. It is the northern slope of that landscape where my grandmother and the old woman in a porkpie hat sat side by side on the churchyard haycock telling each other about their lives. I can see their backs still, my grandmother's scotch shoulders and her toque with a sprinkling of consolable pansies, the old woman with her sunburned brown neck and a kind of skeleton girlishness, and long black ribbons hanging down from the porkpie. And afterwards she gathered all the churchyard hay into a netted mountain and went down the hill with the mountain on her back, and the rake over her shoulder.

I feel a kind of guilty concern over the end of your letter – how happy you would be in Norfolk – not so much that I am not there this time, but that you are not there at all times. I often think we should move to that side of England, in spite of the domestic difficulties. If you see a house, don't at once decide that it is out of the question. Only let it be a house and not a reed-hut or a ruined windmill, however deliciously miles from man. As I grow older, I grow avaricious about time. I do not want to waste it in machinations of how to trap a baker, in oil-lamps, and buckets at pumps, nor in interior calculations of what would happen if anything went wrong. But a house, with lofty ceilings, and a good easy stair-case, and not *all* its main rooms giving on the northeast . . . and sufficiently accessible for the shop to take a new root. This I do think should be taken into consideration. When I sat there this morning with my coffee pot I thought how entertaining it looked, and how I should enjoy a customer. And just now a young woman with a mother who loves antiques, and the usual double name, whom Nita[1] sent you, has rung up, and is coming this afternoon with the mother. So after lunch I will put on silk stockings and a respectable pair of shoes and be ready for them. As for the price of a house, we are in a perfectly sound position to buy and or in reason to renovate. But remember that it is expensive to have to make a road to one's dwelling, and it is not expenditure that one gets any particular pleasure from. The Greeks never made roads, that I know of. The sun is shining, it is almost hot, birds twitter, there is a bloom on the further trees, Mr Samways[2] is tidying the front of the house and the shop approach, and I am wearing my longest black jet earrings. You must have made very good time on your journey if you were at Norwich by noon having already got a Hen and a Luster, and a little Bit for me. How kind of dear Thetford. The first time I was at Thetford was in November 1918, the day after the armistice, going back to London in a late train full of soldiers. It stopped for a long time at Thetford, or rather just outside it, for when a soldier opened the window and leaned out to see what was happening, a

1 Nita [Edgerton].
2 Mr Samways: our jobbing gardener.

pure cold wet air came in, one of those rinsed linen airs that can only blow over wide flat landscapes. And I had just enough local geography to begin to think about Ely, which I had never seen, and to imagine an Ely which would match that cold wet air and that lamenting name. And then the train went on into the station, and stopped again there, and a soldier got out to get cups of tea, and brought me one out of loving good manners. Soldiers were much nicer then – much more English, with sad middles, like cakes. I think one must have some kind of second sighting which patterns and selects what one will remember; for why else should I remember this 1918 Thetford with such steadfastness, out of a time when Carnegie Trust were sending me on so many journeys which I now can scarcely recollect at all?

My love, how fortunate I am that it was Thetford in my stars – which I did not see again till you drove me through it on that night drive to Winterton. I love you and I thank you for your love.

Sylvia

126: VA

Winterton, 26 August 1954

My dearest Love, thank you for the little bottle of Paris which came this early morning and was only discovered by me because R. had a monologue with herself about what on earth cd. have come for her from Whiteleys . . . fortunately I heard part of it and went to examine the parcel. It is a most elegant bottle, and by far prettier than any I have seen before, and the scent *lovely*: quite as good, now, as it is when one buys it in France. And most infinitely welcome . . . it is necessary here: and besides, I like to smell of me so that I remember that I am me, which otherwise it is easy to forget after 24 hours – 25.5 hours – in this house.

And I *do* love having a parcel, too. But I also hope for a letter tomorrow – only do not feel uncomfortable about that if you haven't written, because I shall take that to mean that you are writing about the plaster Muses, which is what I hope you are doing.

Last night I went to bed at about 10.30 and lay abed reading *The True Heart* and then woke at 6 and read *The True Heart* and then woke at 8 and read *The True Heart*. I was lost in the description of the Marshes and felt a most consuming desire to be there – after my hour yesterday beside the rushes and where the water lay so close to the surface that even the main, new road shook like a quagmire every time a car flew past me . . . How *lovely* this land foundationed on water is! This afternoon I was driving Ruth on a devious way back from Holt's vicinity, and I took all the bye-roads and went to places I have never found or even heard of before and found a *lovely* little round-towered church with a painted screen half-obliterated on one side by a pulpit wickedly erected without regard to antiquity (the pulpit is dated 1624) which is at a place whose name I have totally forgotten but I did write it down and it was the *oddest* name. To that place we must go – I did not let R. go into the church and did not speak in praise of it. But took her into the next one, a joined parish, where the hole in the clock face was filled by a drooping heavy mass of green weeds (some bush or other) and where the old poppy-heads still stayed, at the pew-ends, and one of them (maybe two) carved into the likeness of a strange, venerable face . . . I took a photograph of it but it will not come out, I think. I have a torment in my feet – a hole at the tip of one toe, underneath, and a corn inside another (on the other foot, of course) between two toes. Most painful and annoying. So I did not want to walk much but those churches were worth it.

Further on, still lost, I saw a lodge and gateway and a notice saying cars might not go into the park on Sundays. So as it is Thursday I went in. Very Tibbly-roaded,[1] it was, but first a bridge and a little Broad, then a noble Italianate house and then much more road and many more holes and a branch and a magnificent 'Tower' in the finest possible romantic . . . I took the last picture of that, and that should come out. I took the house too and got a severe look from the untidy lady-owner (I suppose) who emerged in a shooting brake, taking tea to harvesters. Potatoes up to the terrace wall, and the harvesters undoubtedly included her sons and husbands. A VERY VERY old Bentley stood near-by. The oldest I have ever seen.

I don't in the least know where this place is nor what the family may be but I shall find out from a map, when I can find a map.

Then after a long wander I found the road to Trimingham and saw that house we wanted,[2] by the barns, that has the carving in its porch. It is still empty . . . damn those horrible old women.

The Sheringham shop was a disappointment, because it was all be-

---

1 It was my fate to find promising by-roads in maps, which turned out to have abominable surfaces; such roads were called Tib-roads.
2 When we were house-hunting in the winter of 1951–52.

holidayed. But I got a small Staffordshire pair for ten bob and a jelly-mould for 8/6. The former genuine and rather pretty in a dull way; the other boring to extinction.

Lunch was under-cooked pork chops and I am sure I shall get trichinopoly.

And that is all, my Love – except that time lags and drags and mumbles its way along and I think Ruth is enjoying it still but hazily and it is already running out of the heels of her boots, I suspect. She repeats all the old stories and scandals and looks not very well and is not at all happy. I think it is probably a good thing to drive her about as much as possible, and much better for me than being here, for I really do dislike this poor shabby house and everything is more and more sad and decrepit and spoiled. The rocking-horse is dying – almost dead. I hope I may rescue the little cannon, which I remember from my very earliest childhood. The pair of them stood one on either side of the Great Gong at my grandmother's house and I wheeled them with a thundering noise on the polished floor and the noise echoed in the gong. Now there is only one (I suppose the other went to Bessie – but what did M A Y [1] get?) And this single one has been out on the stoop in sun and rain and it is shrinking – the wooden carriage is almost done for. But the bronze is handsome still and maybe I can save it.

The worst thing is a dreadful tiny wired enclosure, floored with nothing but true M U D, and jammed behind the garden shed, up against the boundary of the pre-fabs. In that there are several – maybe ten – tall cockerels. Yesterday they were standing each on one leg, looking tired and parched in the way chickens do when they are very unhappy: and Ruth showed them to me and said 'There! Those are A L L for my Mothers' Union speakers' lunches! S U C H a god-send!' And I wished I had not read that Russell's [2] book and I wished I were dead and I did not know what to say to the birds, and they have eyes that can't look back at one and so there was no way to speak to them.

A well of pure fine water has been found inside the house, at The Hill: directly below the passage (typically, Ruth told me it had been found outside her bedroom!) which is an odd thing . . . If they could drain it what might not be found at the bottom?

I will send you a little Piece about Saucers [3] which will entertain you.

---

1 The eldest of three weird sisters.
2 Lord Russell of Liverpool's book on Nazi atrocities.
3 Flying saucers.

Keep it for me to send to Rachel,[1] please.

Oh my dear Love – how are you? How are the Cats? How do you get on? How do you get food for them? D O Y O U E A T ? *DO YOU DRINK WINE?* Are you warm? Is the sun shining? Here it is hot sometimes, and sometimes very bright and fair. There are 'planes all the time, and near Salthouse[2] (I did not go to Salthouse) they were firing all the time too.

Every place is full of people enjoying themselves (they really look as if they were) and the roads between here and Yarmouth are appalling: hazards worse than the ones endemic at this season, because now the Holiday camps have little 3-wheeled tricycles which hold, at a pinch, 3 people, and which have arrangements by which two people can make them work at once . . . they bear placards saying Caister Holiday Camp, or wherever – and they trudge about over all the roads . . .

My visit to Trina was a complete disaster.

Ruth is again furious with Mary.

Mr Pye[3] looks cross and ill and ill-used. He is practically stone-deaf.

Everything goes Downhill.

But I had a letter from Steven, cleverly sent to me here, and it was a happy letter, thank God.

And so no more, my Love – I am not unhappy. I loved the air and the sky and the water and the golden landscape. Some corn is all right here and was being reaped. But all the potatoes in this garden had blight: A L L – in one night – And so it goes on.

Take care of yourself, sweetheart: and do not feel worried till V E R Y late on Monday. Ruth will have to be delivered at London Colney, and it will take time. She is very tardy now and very scattered *indeed*: and quite feckless. It is saddening and rather appalling.

I love you with all my heart.

Valentine

---

1 [Rachel Braden.]

2 Village on our inland horizon in 1951–52; she avoided revisiting endeared places in Ruth's company.

3 Mr Pye: Ruth's new gardener and factotum. He had been a sergeant-major, then a bailiff, and was a consequential prater.

1955

Frome Vauchurch, 30 June 1955

My true Love,

Please do take the most careful care of yourself this evening, this night and tomorrow. Lock doors (the coal-shed back-door was unlocked this early morning) and your bedroom door as well. PLEASE DO THIS. If it thunders, take out both little plugs from behind the radio in my room. Eat a good supper and drink wine with it. And be happy.

Be tranquil too: I will drive carefully and very observantly: I will try to go to bed early: I will go to bed alone. *Thank God* there will be no anguish anywhere, this time; at most a mild discomfort, and possibly not even that. Each time these meetings[1] happen, now, I feel really ransomed, healed, restored – – – – and thanks to your matchless truth of heart, my Love, I do not feel forgiven.

I am already counting the minutes to be back with you –

Valentine

128: STW

Frome Vauchurch,[2] 5 July 1955

My Love,
    Remember the pie:
    Remember the soup:

---

1 Yearly meetings with Elizabeth.
2 A pre-departure letter. I was going to the Chatto & Windus Centenary party.

(it is in a glass bowl in the refrigerator)

If people suddenly come to tea, God forbid, there is a Lyons Swiss in the cake box.

Remember that Mr Samways takes no sugar, and three plain biscuits, and can mow the lawn and shear the grass round the lilacs.

I myself can't remember Norah's[1] telephone number, but I will telegraph it with my arrival there. Chatto and Windus in case of need is TEMPLE BAR 0127.

Proust[2] is in the black tin box with quills and roses. If you read it, I shall feel extremely proud. If you don't, it won't abate my pride. I have you to be proud of.

Remember to take care of yourself *and to rest in the afternoons*. Remember how much I love you.

Tib

129: VA

Frome Vauchurch, 6 July 1955

Evening

My Love,

I wonder whether you will get this letter: I don't see that you will, unless a new gush of intelligence bathes one or other of us. I was revived by one an hour or so ago, and went to your room & excavated your address book (and a sorry mess it is in) but although you had several past-and-done-for Ss there, you had not got Smallwood. So I concluded that this is an old a-b and that you have taken your newer one with you – to remind you of Norah Smallwood's address. It is what I should have done myself, only either I should have taken the old book by mistake, or I should have been wholly intelligent and remembered to leave my address clearly written out in the hall.

It is past nine: you are revelling, I hope, and I am just finished with walking round the garden and loving the cats & trying to comfort Candace[3] for not being able to rush down the drive, and I have also dead-headed all the roses except the drive ones. I don't think there is much use

1 [Norah Smallwood].
2 I was translating *Contre Sainte-Beuve*.
3 Candace: her poodle.

in topping the Persian Briars (if that is what they are) and anyhow, they have splendid haws – or hips – later on.

I ate an enormous slice of pie for lunch and it was *delicious*. I ate some peas for supper, and some ice-cream whipped up with strawberries and re-frozen. I have not eaten any BUTTER all day and I hope this may compensate for sugar; but I fear it won't. I would like to think I might be a sylph when you return – or a salamander. More likely that, but even that is still far off.

Nothing has happened, unless you count a gypsy at the door and – now – the thrush of all thrushes singing from a bush on the riverbank. Oh – *and a road*. . . . But I must take you there, as soon as ever it is possible after you return, my Love. It must be on a sunny, hot day, though, and near mid-day. But please remember this and remind me of it. *It is very important indeed*.

I found the tin box and read, just now, the chapters VI and VII (about the article and his mother's hair and that moment of desperate sorrow when he records her words as she lay dying). I read enough to see (a) that this – in this part at least – is infinitely more immediate – much more like a living young man in his room and in his day-to-day dress than any other Proust I have read – when he has been out calling, or sometimes staying away maybe, but in more carefully-preserved & formal clothes; that this is naturally vivid, as lightning is or as sunlight on water is, where the Work is a light flashed on and off *by him*: and (b) that it is easily and exquisitely translated, so that it unrolls like an ant-eater's tongue, and never for a moment sticks or snarls up.

I could not read more. Partly because one envelope is still sealed up and partly because it tired me – having chanced on those two chapters which are full of emotion, and on an evening that itself is full of emotion. I don't know why? Not my emotion. But it is so.

Are you being happy at this moment, my sweetheart? I like to think you are enjoying yourself *very much indeed*, and talking and drinking and eating and not smoking, maybe – and feeling beautifully centred, and not noticing that there has been any interruption to feeling like that and being in that kind of company . . . although it has been such a long and sometimes such a sad and often such a dreary, laborious interruption, after all. It is sad to me to think that – from one view anyhow – our romantic and beautifully complete love has led you into a back-alley where you pine[1] for light and air, and have so little of either. And I am

---

1 I resented having to waste so much of our life together on invading bores – I never pined for anything except her.

often aware of how I grow more steadily more heavy and dull and dumb. God knows I would not if I could by any means avoid it, but all my life I have had a strong disinclination to avoid, or delay these sad changes . . . although another of my pestering fears is that I remain in patches un-aged, and come near to being horrid, like the middle-aged are who use frayed manners and so dreadfully embarrass the new young.

Oh dear – how tedious one's dreads are, and how finicky, too.

The truth is that I love you in so much the same way as I loved you when I was 24 that, I suppose, inside all the accretion of all these years, the fat & the age & the wear-and-tear, there is still a figure intact at the core of the boring bulk, and that is unchanged and that is the Valentine I feel myself to be *truly*. Love must be something like that water at Matlock[1] or thereabouts. . . . No – much more like the chemical operation of extreme sanctity, that preserves the saints' bodies fresh and pink . . . or the manikin Valentine inside my present bulk isn't at all dead. So love must be like what ever it is that keeps fakirs alive and able to kick even when they lie buried under the sand for years . . .

Now it is ten o'clock and I don't suppose this letter will take up any of your London time at all, my Love, for it will probably go to Chatto and Windus and follow you back here. Pray GOD you will come back here. Oh how time *drags* when you are away: and how ungenerously fast it goes when we are together here. But when we are together on holiday the blessed stuff spins itself out – so let us go on holiday soon again, my sweetheart. . . .

I love you as ever and for ever.

Valentine

7 July

Now I know where you are, my Love, and now I shall post this, but add first a small postscript in case this seems to be a sad letter – which it isn't. Though last night was a sad evening in its own right. I do not know why. The moon was so large and so round and so dark and so slow, and things moved about the garden and in the reeds outside my window, and did not sound like moonlight-enjoying animals, but there were cries and plaints and hasty rustles. I am afraid that creatures are finding it hard to live,[2] now, and that they are becoming more like us, in their obsession to find

1 A petrifying spring.
2 Myxomatosis had upset the ecological balance.

food and to *make sure*.

I wander. But I shall not wander more. Because Samways is approaching and Bo has just telephoned and it is the Fête to-day and I hope someone may come to the shop. I'm in one of my moods of despair because no one comes to the shop. And I never do get new things. I am sick and tired of all the old stuff I have now.

My dearest Love — it is all because you are not here. Do come back — But do not if you could stay over the week-end, because it is G O O D for you to be there and whilst the sun shines you should stay if you can. But come back after staying. I am much less than half when you are away — and it is such a silly, half-half that is left.

Valentine

The house is crammed to bursting with Large White Moths. Thank God they sleep all day. . . .

130: STW

London, 7 July 1955

My Love,

How glad I am that I didn't telegraph the Square number (I thought for sure it would be in your little book) for to hear your voice with my morning ears was the sort of thing that happens in Heaven (Could you accept that absurd notion of eternal unwavering bliss? — never a surprise or a dayspring in it? Pooh!).

Well, here I am in that agreeable cool pigeon-coloured dress from Gorringe, thinking that in the course of the day I shall go to *Camille* . . . and see an exhibition of Pissaro and Sisley. I heard about it from Trekkie — Ian's[1] wife. When we first met at the party she was determined to like me in order to fall in with Ian's notions. By the end of it she was liking me without determination. She is an artist, a serious one. Her enormous blue eyes are blind with intensity of observing. She was dressed with the utmost chic in the 1890's — even the little velvet ribbon round her long lined neck. Chic is an extraordinary quality — she pierced that party like a knife, every time she came in sight one was aware of a completed purpose

1 [Ian Parsons.]

in apparel, and other women who were just as expensively, as intentionally dressed, either looked fumbling or fashion-plates. I liked her a great deal. I told her about the Ingres in Dublin.

When I first arrived I thought I should not know anybody, and be a drug and a disgrace. It didn't work out like that. I talked the whole evening, there was always someone I knew or someone I got to know and as I was wearing those flat black shoes I was fresh as a daisy when we sat down to hot soup at 1.30.

Cecil Day Lewis came and was polite, and for a moment I thought he was David Garnett. The same manner, the same mixture of a manner of shyness and a great deal of sexual condescension.

Jill Balcon was there: very handsome. Coal black eyes, extremely intense and not, as one says, a very nice character. I had a small conversation with David, he has written another fiction – a novella – about young girls falling in love with old men and young men with young women. He also told me about his daughters and his Jersey cows. Compton Mackenzie made the speech to the health of Chatto and Windus, standing on a table draped with fair damask, getting on and off with the greatest agility. He has three Siamese cats. While we were talking about them, we had only just started, Harold Raymond joined in to say he had never had a Siamese cat, he thought he really ought, etc. . . Out came the dirk! White with rage, shaking with chivalry, C.M. said: You shouldn't have one unless you are prepared to attend to it.

I shall come back on the train that arrives just after 4, unless something very unexpected arrests my mind. But it won't. I can't live for long, even with such kind friends as Chatto and Windus on one leg, with one lung, one eye, and only a working model of a heart.

Tib

131: STW

Frome Vauchurch, 24 July 1955

My Love,

A day before you go away is always rather like a rehearsal of the days after you have gone away; and if you want to know what I am like in your absence, you have almost seen it for yourself, for I am usually busy, and always abstracted, and always speechless, and go to and fro like a plodding ghost, planting myself with bulbs and emptying myself with wastepaper baskets. And now that I am writing to you, it is an even more exact rehearsal.

But you can have no idea what I shall be like on the day before you come back, that is something you have never seen, when I talk incessantly, to trees, to the cats, to myself, and prance instead of plodding, and look at everything with my head on one side, considering it in the light of how you will see it, and never have any notion what time it is, for sometimes, it is so much later than I think that I am horrified at the prospect that nothing will be done before you arrive, and two minutes later there is still so much time that I drown in it. And all my abstracted being rushes back into me, and I quiver like a power-house.

But you see, I shall be very dull, very discreet, very humdrum, totally unenterprising, without a flicker of impulse to ride on yard dogs. So when your fancy paints me climbing on the roof, wading in the river after a cullander, compare this to what you have seen to-day and say Fiddlesticks to your fancies. See me melancholy, but not a maniac.

I will lock all the doors at night, including the backdoor that cheats. I will eat breakfast, lunch and dinner. I will listen to at least one weather forecast during the day, and watch the heavens, and if there is any prospect of another flood, I promise you I will go to Cauldron Barn. I may be ambitious enough to wash my hair, but if I do, I will dry it. I may possibly clean the back-kitchen, but only by mild degrees, and not at all unless I feel I really want to. Still, I would like to think that when you come back the house won't smell quite so much like a marsh as it does now.

So much for me. Now, what about you? O my Love. I implore you to take care of yourself, and to preserve yourself, and to turn as deaf an ear as you can to bugaboo stories, and if Ruth has some ripe cases of cholera morbus, not to visit them with Women's papers, and not to trip on that deathly stair, and not to try to mend the kitchen hotwater pot if it is threatening to explode, just go away and leave it; and perhaps you could take a chair into the w.c. and sit there with your feet up; and if the garage door won't shut, don't destroy your back wrestling with it, but wait for someone to come and deal with it; and equally, if it won't open, wait, even if it's ever so. It is difficult to remember – and Ruth makes it even more obscure – that the reason of visits like this is that your mother enjoys your company, as well as all that incessant doing and running and fetching and lifting and picking things up and putting things down; that there is, however smothered, some element of Grace as well as works; but bear this in mind, and try to put it into practice. And try to go to bed from time to time, however Nicodemused. And remember that even if my eye is not upon you, my heart is, and attend to my heart.

Come back on Thursday if you possibly can. Norfolk is not the only place where you can find Small Antiques, and we could go on some little raids together. We have never tried Swindon, or Castle Cary, or Shepton Mallet, or Marlborough or Devizes; and there is the Salisbury auction room. If duty were very severe, we could even go to Bournemouth. But even if there were no such places, I should still say, Come back on Thursday and take me out of Limbo.

Above all, remember how much I love you, for how long, and how truly and how freshly.

Sylvia

132: VA

On the road to Acle at 1 p.m., 25 July 1955

My Love,

I am able to write to you as I sit beside a grove of willows standing in their own grove of reeds. Candace and I have lunched: we have been lunching since about 6.30 a.m., spinning out sandwiches as w e F L E W along (In the first hour I did 56 miles: I was at Thetford at 9.30).

I have just read your letter. How dreadful to think I threatened not to read it: it is an entrancing letter – I would not, not have read it for the world. I was made very happy by your Orientalising of colander; spelled Cullander it is riding on an elephant.

But now, *remember all* the good things you say, my Love; remember not to finish the iris border, and do try very hard to resist cleaning the swimming-pool.[1] I would infinitely, but I N F I N I T E L Y , rather you *sat in a chair* and read or wrote, or listened to Hi-Fi. . . . (I love the smell of river).

This won't be readable. I am hunched up as I write. I hope to write a letter on the machine, but that won't be till tomorrow, I daresay. So this is for my love and is my love. I have seen corn *cut* and in stooks. I have seen a baby black kitten and several exceptionally fine cats. I have seen

1 [The flooded store room off the kitchen.]

three dead cats and three dead hares. I have seen a purple field (what could it have been? True purple) and a vast field of roses all in flower and smelling their heads off. I have bought a table. Now it is 1.15 and I shall soon go on to Yarmouth.

I feel so revived by your letter. I feel as if I were quite new. But my Love – without you I am always vague: I feel only half-conscious and with that half, I am conscious only of not having you. I do love you so very dearly and so truly and so deeply.

Valentine

133: STW

25 July 1955

My Love,

Ever since you rang up, and I knew you had arrived safely, delightful things have been happening. The Bear[1] began to dry. When I went out to call the cats to their dinner I saw Kaoru galloping like a small Suffolk Punch all the way up the raspberry path in total unselfconsciousness. I made a delicious tomato sauce for my grey mullet. While I was eating it I listened to Campoli playing the Brahms' Concerto, he played it beautifully, and at that place in the slow movement before the theme is brought back, where the fiddle goes gently up into alt and hangs there, his tone was so pure, such fine, so poised, that I stared up into the sky as if I should see it there and saw a swallow exactly matching it. And after that, as if he had called them, the sky was full of swallows. And the moment that was finished I switched to the third and found myself about halfway through the *Magic Flute*, with the Drei Knaben singing so shamelessly out of time that I nearly turned it off, but I didn't, and I'm glad, for there was an exceptionally good Sarastro who didn't sing as if his mouth was full of his beard; most Sarastros do. It begins again in ten minutes time, and I shall go on listening, and then I shall go to bed. All the doors are shut and locked already, see how attentive I am. There is not the least trace of even an isolated, *a well-isolated*, thunderstorm, and already the house perceptibly less stinking. How thankful I am that I did the s.p. before your letter came and told me not to! A great deal of it I enjoyed, pride carried

---

1 A massive hearthrug of some nameless fur, packed away in a basket trunk.

me over the rest, and really I am not in the slightest degree overtired. I was tired till you rang up, tired in the legs. When I went downstairs after that, I discovered that my legs were as good as new.

Darling, what an unexpected day you had, arriving in Norfolk at least four hours before you expected to, and spending so much more money than you had expected to – all at one swoop, I mean. I think you must have enjoyed the first part of the drive, at any rate – though how you could go past that noble hotel in Newmarket without having breakfast there I cannot imagine. I should have insisted on it.

The line was not very good this evening, your voice did not sound like your voice; but Niou's whiskers were not mistaken. I am so glad you heard his angel strain. He was sitting on the window sill, listening to every word you said, and afterwards he tossed off a bumper of fish to your bright eyes.

By the time you get this – by the time you get this you will be thinking about coming home.

My Love, I love you.

Sylvia

1956

Frome Vauchurch, 6 April 1956

Friday Morning

My Love,

We decided this letter won't reach you, but I will take a chance on it, for all that. I woke at half-past seven and thought of you turning away from the outlines of Salisbury Plain into the hem of the Midlands, small fields and water, and dark little ponds with pale rushes round them; and then I decided that there must be an outside staircase down from your new room[1] above the re-edified garage, otherwise you will never feel safe in it; and then the postman came, and there are no striking letters for you, I think: one from Vera; and one from Burnham on Sea addressed by you, so I suppose it is about the musical boxes.

I rang up Nita. Her grandson sleeps in her room, and this morning she was awakened by a voice saying, Grandmamma, how many rings has Saturn? She said, Seven, and hoped for the best; but by breakfast he had done some research, and told her it was three. Yesterday Charlotte, who must be a nice traditional child, asked who made God. Nita replied that we can't live without some mysteries. All very well, and most dexterous, but I suspect that Charlotte will now be assembling her list of the mysteries we can't live without.

Now at this moment Dr Devereux is having a quick look round; he has brought his villain with him, who sidled in through the door like a frog in holy orders. I am sorry for the villain, he has so obviously got out of a Thackeray novel by accident, and should be put back in it.

1 A project to add an attic to the garage.

Returning to the Craskes,[1] if Janet rings up to say she will be bringing Ben. B. on Sunday, I shall hire a kingly conveyance[2] and go to fetch them. This will be ideal. The thought of another sixpence on the bill for hire will certainly cut short any conversational leanings on Mrs Henning's part. What is nine hundred dollars worth, if it can't save me from having to converse when I don't want to?

My weight has gone down again. By three pounds. And yet, as you say, I swill wine like a hog, and – as you don't say – devour cake and sweet biscuits when restoratively pressed on me like a wolf. Alas, alas, it seems to point with no uncertain paw at risotto and pasta and pommes lyonnaise.

They are gone. They did not buy anything, though they would have bought the antiquity books; but I had to say that I thought they were part of the business. The villain hung wistfully over the trout. It is a heavenly morning, and now I shall go up the road to put this in the little pillar-box. Have you put any trout in the river? said Devereux; and his voice couldn't help sounding as if the trout were for sale and might be bargains, and I could not help replying, Hundreds, rather as if I had been the weasel sentry.

I could see no signs in the kitchen that you had eaten any breakfast before starting, and this distresses me. Perhaps you ate buns, which are imperceptible. My darling love, the house is totally strange without you, and I rather doubt if I am really in it.

Tib

135: VA

Winterton, 7 April 1956

My Love,

It is only about 7.15 and I've finished Early Morning Tea. I slept badly. It was extremely cold – or perhaps I was colder than the night. I felt very tired.

Wasn't it awful about the car? But I should not have talked about money, because when I totted it up last night I had only spent half the

1 We had just learned that some paintings by John Craske, left over from an exhibition in New York City, had been deposited in Dorchester by Elizabeth. Janet Stone wanted Benjamin Britten, her guest, to see them.
2 Hired car from Mr King's garage.

money I'd brought, even with repairs and two garages and tips. So I need not have panicked.

Yarmouth was ravishing. Reeling and rocking with noise and lights because the FAIR was in its first day. Longer than ever it has been: stretching to the very door of Mr Folkes' shop.

I was delighted to see, in the R.C. church that there is now an Our Lady of Great Yarmouth who has *blue* wax votive night-lights burning in front of her at 6d each. I gave her two and she was delighted. (That may have been why the car broke down twice, each time in front of a Great Yarmouth garage?) Otherwise (but for the blue night-lights) I might have been landed at Caister or an Ormesby garage.

I don't think I've got any very good things, though I have got one or two pleasant ones. Of the 2 Toby jugs here, the best one (though I think it is N O T a Ralph Wood, though it could be) was found to be full of wishbones, all chewed by Joan and put in damp – and so they had mildewed. *And* the jug had its handle off – so that is that.

I lunched in Norwich and sat next to 2 oldish (grand) Cathedral women. Their talk was not to be believed. Two specimens. The older (Persian-Lamb-coated woman) 'He is absolutely entranced with the Army Corps'. Then when the pale, intense woman was describing (I suppose) a Good Friday service, she said 'His little addresses were M O S T wonderful – but I did feel the Seven Sorrows were just a *bit* too long'.

It was all like that, and I ate prawn curry and felt so much better for it: but Oh! to think you were not with me; and now, too, with the Strongest Thrush[1] in Norfolk singing its heart out in Ruth's garden.

My love – I love you with all my heart, whether I can sing it out or not.

Do you know that I would love and miss you even if this were Athens, and there were avenues of plane trees and legions of Peripatetics (?) walking in the sun and the shade. *I would*. And the sad poem (but not sad, truly) called 'Poem in Middle-Age'[2] which I wrote to you is still, and

---

1 'I would defy the strongest dog in Europe to eat it' – said of a wartime ration of beef.
2 Do not touch the slowly flowing water;
  If you die before me do not drink
  One drop of it, but lie on the cold bank
  Watching how sullenly the water goes
  And remembering the nameless river, in life and long ago,
  When you stood in your muslins and the air was bright,
  The water crisp and rapid; when summer was coming
  And we were together.
  Refuse to touch the water until you see me come, my Love,
  And we stoop down together.

always true.

Valentine

I will get animal's meat in Dorchester, and bread.

Narrative 14

> I stand committed now
> To the trees and the wood of the trees:
> To beauty and love and longing and loss,
> To the sweetness shown in your brow,
> Known in your hand's touch, in your glance – All these,
> And the incomprehensible fatality of Holy Cross

When her arthritis was bad, she preferred to sleep alone. One February morning I found her staring at the ceiling with an expression of extraordinary sternness and sadness. I asked what was the matter. 'A train of thought,' she said. I knew I should ask no further. Before the end of the month she told me that she intended to be a Roman Catholic again and had started the formalities of return.

Thirty-one years before, aged nineteen, she had entered the Church after a headlong conversion – to quit it, a year later. In the interval she had married a young man whom she found she did not love and could not endure to lie with. A gynaecologist she consulted told her that if she bore a child she would almost certainly die. Her priest told her that she must submit to her husband and be fruitful. Out of pride, she was preparing to stand by her vows when in confession she said she had read *Ulysses* and had a copy. The priest told her she must destroy it – enquiring as an afterthought if it was an expensive book. In this case, it cost one convert. She repudiated her Catholicism and was formally assured of her damnation.

The past cannot be revoked. When she told me of her intention to go back to the Church she was no less glorious in my eyes for her integrity in quitting it. But this news shook my whole conception of her.

She told me without any portentousness of 'breaking the news' and I tried to take it as easily. I was still struggling to my senses when she said it was not really a return, for she had never left off being a Catholic. At this I felt passionately affronted. I did not believe it; I recognised the

'Once a Catholic' appendage to the dogma of Infallibility; but that she should believe it was an affront to all the years we had lived together. Early in those years she taught me the rhyme,

> Catch a Fox and put him in a Box
> And never let him go.

Then, I applied it to her – the fox who got away. I did not like the new application.

It was a pin-prick in a wound (but still, it was a pin-prick) that my anti-clericalism had no weight with her. Perhaps she had this in mind when she told me, some days later, that she would always be a bad Catholic, felt no piety towards the Church except on the score of its universality and venerableness and would be as happy disbelieving its tenets as in believing them. It was the Mass she was going for. Instead of the holy-ghouly jargon of Mystery and Ineffability, she used the plain word, pleasure. My heart leaped up in assent. But the dishonesty of taking it easily made me self-conscious; while I was fumbling for a response, she went on to talk of the formalities involved in her re-acceptance. It had enraged me to see her complying with these pettifogging impositions. I railed at them, instead of speaking my heart. Though my heart was in the railing, too, and I only just managed to stop myself from saying, *Une messe vaut bien Paris.*

I was always stopping myself from saying things, and became increasingly glum and morose. She might have retorted on me. But her behaviour insisted that we had nothing to fear from each other, that such items as Our Lady of Yarmouth's blue night-lights would entertain us alike. This was a rope thrown out, but I could not avail myself of it. I honoured her too much to consent to thinking of her with indulgence.

Alternatively, slighting or magnifying my distress, I asked no questions because I dreaded the answers. As my father said 'Church' to forbid his following spaniel, she would say 'Church' to me. 'Church' would impend over every conversation, qualify our trust in each other; only a habit of companionship would be left to us – if that; for as a Roman Catholic she was again a married woman (her decree of nullity being void). I knew she would not go back to her husband but I did not know what else might not be extorted from her. She might have to leave me. So I thought, loving her, living beside her.

She gave me the letter and went away. She allowed time for me to read it, returned, and stood silent behind me. At the revelation of her unhappiness, her forlorn grief about her poetry, my brooded-on grievance snapped like dead twigs. It was for her own sorrow I turned to her to be comforted.

But it is difficult to recover from a trauma, and from having inflicted it. During those two months while she saw what she knew was vital to her seeming mortal to me and I stared at a door closing between us, the sense of proximity had almost drained out of our lives. We had never been so near being apart. Recovery was easier for me because I had all my eggs in one basket. She had to adjust to a dichotomy, and for a long time she was tormented by a recurrent conviction that she had antagonised and mislaid me. I am certain it never crossed her mind to consider if she could recall me by leaving the Church. For that matter, I did not give it a thought either. We never bargained.

I kept to my opinion of her Church, and she never tried to shake it. She hoped for my conversion (it saddened her there should be a pleasure we did not share) but she did not pray for it, which would be going behind my back and dishonourable. With the same scrupulosity, she attended her parish church and confessed to its priest. Catholics of intellectual pretensions were surprised she did not find a Director in one of the learned Orders – as Edwardian dandies sent their linen to be washed in Paris, she remarked. She told me all this with the unconstraint of those who talk of what makes them happy. Our differences sank into the texture of our daily lives. When understanding friends condoled with her on my impiety, with me on her credulity, they got their heads bitten off.

She was happy; she enjoyed observances, prided herself on observing them, side-stepped dogmas; all these were a framework to the liturgical magic which freed her into devotion. Devotion was inherent in her character, a constant in all her loves, where it made her dominating, solicitous, protective, watchful, potentially jealous, insistently responsible. Reversing its direction, instead of aiming it downward on its objects, she aimed it upward to an objective, a being responsible for the universe, a protecting mastering love which guided the heavens and held her in its care.

She would have been perfectly happy if she could have lived unnoticed, an anonymous addition to an unconcerned flock. But the Roman Church in England is a minority with a mission: what it lacks in mass it makes up in bustle and solidarity – like its opposite number, which in simpler days of Militant Atheism had her loyalty. She was an advantageous convert. Try as she might to efface herself, she could not avoid being remarkable, she could not help being obliging, she could not annul the sophistication which breathed from her like the spices of the Beloved in the Song of Solomon. Her very modesty was against her; it made her mysterious. Acquaintanceships of obligation accumulated: people who wanted to talk about themselves, people who wanted to talk about their neighbours, people who wanted lifts in the car, who wanted to confide, who wanted to ferret. I suppose they were no worse than any other small town bourgeoisie, but as co-religionists they were inescapably uncongenial. Bustling, gossiping, collecting trinket crucifixes, canvassing special devotions, they rattled like money-changers round the silence of her thoughts. Sunday after Sunday she came home with a racking headache, jaded by church porch button-holings. I asked her why she always went to Mass on Sundays: Mass would be Mass on any other day of the week, and quieter. 'Church' was the answer. Not to go to Mass on Sunday was a sin – mortal, if I remember rightly.

In Rome, in Provence, at St. Benoit sur Loire, she was a different creature.

From the start, she had known she must stifle her fastidiousness – endure horrors (the cause of the English Martyrs was being promoted and there was great play with disembowelling), vulgarities, bondieuseries, outrages on her native language and liturgy. She had not been prepared for schemes for putting the Church on a business footing, nor for measures for making it popular; nor for the squabbles which followed the measures. 'I shall soon be forced out,' she exclaimed.

What followed surprised me. I don't know whether it was that I hate waste – and she had spent so much – or that I value pleasure above principles, above prejudices, even. In 1962 I said that my Easter present to her would be an Easter week in a society where the Catholic faith is so familiar that there is no need to make it popular.

Faith was so real in Orta that those who didn't take part in the ceremonies were as sincere as those who did. The ceremonies were as timeless as the pullover of the stalwart man who carried pails and supported the great candle during the Blessing of Water was up-to-date. Before the Blessing of Water comes the kindling of the New Fire. The basilica at Orta is high above the lake. It was a very cold night, the wind from the mountains smelled of snow. The New Fire must be kindled with flint and steel, outside the church; the flame of the acolyte's cigarette lighter was blown out again and again before the parocco got his candle reliably burning, and entered the lightless church. There, every one held an unlighted candle; from candle to candle the original flame was passed on. By candlelight I saw the wrinkled face, the toothless mouth, of the very old man, smelling of strong garlic, who turned to me with a look of extraordinary good-will and lit my candle from his. It was as though I had seen the last of the Apostles – surviving, battered and frail, as tortoiseshell butterflies do. And at midnight, Christ rose from the dead, and all the lights went on, and the choir in the gallery burst into a shattering discordance as though they were cheering a football match.

Valentine and I had sorted ourselves together out of the congregation. We sat side by side, clutching hands when the choir hurled itself into a brief fugato. That night, at least, her wish was granted; the pleasure had been shared.

It was too late. The branch of the river she had chosen was too full of voices and jostling.

Eventually she rose out of it like a swan and returned to that other branch of the river where she had listened to Eckhart and Kabir and Epictetus and found her soul among the reeds. The reach where she alighted is called The Society of Friends. I have no idea whether she would have stayed there; but it was there she died.

*

136: VA

Frome Vauchurch, 23 April 1956

My dear Love,

This is the only way I can hope to talk to you just now, and I am so troubled in my heart that I really must, against all my acquired wisdom which says never invade anyone else's grief –

My dearest, dearest Love – do you think it is, in part, the superficial likeness to the Elizabeth summer which is frightening us both? I am concerned not to distort or to readjust facts, but is it distortion to say that the only real similarity is in your unhappiness? The rest of the situation is the opposite to the E. episode. *Being an R.C.* either makes no change at all in me, or it makes more of me to love you.

But the likeness and unlikeness, the unhappiness and misery, are only spots and aches and cramps – what is the sickness? *Being an R.C.*

My Love – for pity's sake listen this once – for I do not know that I shall ever be able to try to explain myself again.

For me, at this end of my life, *being an R.C.* means getting a Wolseley and not an M.G. It is a bit easier on the back, a bit more comfortable, and it goes as well, although it doesn't look and doesn't therefore feel, as dashing.

Since I stopped drinking – rather before that and leading to it, actually – I have been thinking and reading about God and life and death. Like, but not because of, Yeats' poem 'Now I must make my soul –'

I discovered more as I went further; and I went a long way. I think perhaps I went further than I dared believe I had gone. But there comes a time, when one is exploring these matters, when the single stream bifurcates, and one is swept either into the right or the left-hand channel. On one side, I think, one goes on into severe solitude and 'eccentricity'. These people often find what they are looking for – but often, too, they get side-tracked into other, narrow channels (as Huxley has done) or into one or the other forms of madness. But it is the way that one envies, for some reason – probably some snobbish reason, but maybe a better reason than that.

The left-hand channel takes the stream through a different country; harder going in some ways because there are so many tedious locks and hold-ups and it is much more populated.

It was not at all a conscious choice, for me; I only realised about a year ago that I had made it, and by then I was a good way along.

Now, on the illustration, my boat must travel through inhabited country, get through locks, pay tolls, and find its way among other channels and canals and so on. I am still on the same journey, and of course the river runs to the same sea; it is the route that is different, and the technique of travelling.

I found that I was getting muddled, trying to manage the shop and unable not to have still a forlorn ear open in case a poem or something might sound in the distance – like the cuckoo I could not hear. But through lack of method, mainly, I thought I might lose my power of thinking and continuing to learn.

I do not know when, or why, I began to think about going back to being an R.C. But I can tell you that it is a very great *pleasure* to me. I do enjoy it with genuine enjoyment; and it does me good – in the sense of giving me a feeling of well-being – to go to Mass. (The other observances too, but in a quite different degree, I quite enjoy – and it is like wearing a pair of comfortable old stays which ease my back without pinching my belly – to go to Confession and eat fish on Fridays!) But being an R.C. means, for me, that I can step straight into that other world which I have been finding out about and it does not trouble me to know that it is done by means of 'magic', for I have always taken magic for granted – only 'Black' magic is much easier to believe in, for our age, because it has snob-appeal and white is 'out'. For some reason I cannot explain, but which is valid and indeed inescapable for me, I need to go into this super-natural world (this may be a misnomer: never mind, so long as you know what I mean?) from time to time. I do not feel anything about 'taking Communion': going into a church where it is, or attending a Mass where it is made, are how I find my way in. And it also means (being an R.C.) support and comfort, not from its up-to-the-minute appearance so much as from the continuity, the age, the recesses of the structure that is the Church. And the dead people who belong to it.

It does N O T mean that I feel myself committed in any way as if I had joined a political party, or the Boy Scouts . . . I feel nothing of the kind: nor that sort of loyalty.

I know, of course, that I may live till the time when the political/social aspects of 'belonging' may have to be dealt with: then, if I can't evade them honourably, I will have to stand with my own feet on my own ground. But that is what I shall always do, my Love: in my own, rather abashed way, I always have: like everyone who is unsure and hates public appearances, I am apt either to whisper or to shout when I am forced to make a public declaration. I hope I shan't have to but I don't particularly dread it. (I shall never, for example, foreswear Asuncion – or nasty little James Joyce.)

Of this I am quite sure, but you aren't. I do wish I could somehow make you trust in this.

God and man, life and death, are absorbing interests for me: I have gone some distance – far enough to see a little further. Being an R.C. only alters things, for me, by making them rather easier (in the mechanics of living as if I had a soul to feed as well as a body – which may be rubbish but because I often think it is not I would rather behave as though it were true). *But the way it alters things for you* is really terrifying, my Love, and I am now at the end of my heart's tether, with worry about what to do? It is quite clear to me that you feel betrayed: as if I had changed overnight into a totally different kind of person, *and* into a kind of person you find antipathetic.

I'm afraid you also think me guilty of the Trahison des Clercs (if that is grammatical) and the implications of that.

It's no good elaborating. I can only tell you once for all that I have not changed in the slightest: I think, feel, act just as I did; my predilections are the same, so are the enemies. Simply, in the heap of nonsense, half-sense, badness and goodness and mediocrity I have found a way of finding the way. This doesn't mean that I do not see the components of the rubbishy part of the heap, my Love!

You don't realise that I have loved you *really* with all my heart, and loved you *attentively*, for 25 years. This means that I do know, quite often, what you are thinking or feeling. Bo's poor little cat for instance – I knew all too sharply that you half envied, maybe more than half, her will-to-die. I knew that Bo's disregard of the cat's bitter cry to her paired – against your will – with my 'changing' and becoming a strange person to you (*I HAVE NOT*). And I stood there in the sun and broke my heart, because that was all I could do.

It probably isn't any good to try to explain. I really feel done-for, now. I cast about in my mind this early morning to know what I *could* do, for you are so infinitely dearer to me than anything else can ever be: and beyond this I feel a disturbing sense of responsibility for your genius, my Love: as well as loving you so deeply and at times so desperately.

Would it be better if we moved to London? You have so little to feed on here. The shop might go on as a postal business, and without a car or animals we cd. probably afford it?

Think of this seriously.

I really can't endure to have you feel lonely and as it were deserted. My love, my Love! Don't you know that I would go into any despair, any damnation if it could save you a minute of fear or desolation? I cannot (I mean a literal incapacity) tell you a lie about the truth: all I can do is tell you the only certain truth I know, and that is almost untellable. Something like this:

Everything changes all the time, except something which is changeless and always there: insubstantial, like light or a clear single note on a horn: and *that* is somehow tied up with my apprehension of God and my own life and my life's love of you. A single note, a single light – quite indescribable, quite unmistakable and quite inseparable. And rather than lose my power to recognise that I would lose everything else – but in fact there is nothing else in existence, but that.

So I will move, or go away myself, or do anything that will in any way ease you or make you happier or release you if you want release. Only tell me, my Love.

But I really can't much longer endure that state of half-separation from you. I know it isn't in your power to mend it, although I do assure you that it is mainly your doing that it exists at all, for it is a work of the imagination – alas – and they have much toughness.

I'm not sure, you know, that *being an R.C.* is the root of the trouble. Did you ever recover from E.W.W.? I have so longed to believe in being able to give you happiness, in being relied on by you – have I taken myself in, and really all that went in the storm?

Oh this is so much too long. I wrote it all this early morning – it is higgledy-piggledy. I know that most of it will horrify you because it is nonsense to you, and if it is – then nothing can change it and it will make things worse. And after writing most of this I found you sitting on the bed really believing that 'They' would tell me to leave you and that I would obey . . . Once for all, my darling, get it clear in your head that I am *not* like that. Try to understand that I believe in God, and go on from there to see what a desperate blasphemy it would be to 'confess' love as a sin. Let 'Them' say what They will – They'll be dealt with in due course: I told you I was going to be a bad Catholic – and I meant it. I mean to work to rule . . . and the rule of the Church is quite clear. I made a perfectly true Confession, I think: I mean to, anyway. I am not at all afraid about that. Nor about anything except that having found a pearl of great price I may, through ineptitude or there being so many too many swine about, let it fall into the jaws of swine.

So no more. And if most of this is nonsense to you, can you see the one thing in it that matters – that I love you unchangeably, and I am myself unchanged –?

Valentine

Too long already, but one thing more: I really do not know anything sure, in all this, except that I love you with a most true, most *married* love: that I feel as I have done always, since we first lay together, a deep and absolute responsibility for you – which was my greatest joy and happiness and now is putting me very near despair. I think you must now tell me, my Love, if you have any idea of what you want me to do? I will go away, or do anything, to make you happier or more secure.

1957

Frome Vauchurch, 16 September 1957

My dearest Love,

I implore you not to grieve and fret.[1] I shall be all right. I shall be careful. I shall not come to any harm – beyond perhaps picking up some uncomfortable intonations of voice and manner, because I am like milk in the way I take taints, but I hope I do not go bad from them . . .

Don't think I have forgotten that Joan has a deep enmity towards me: I think perhaps she wants to be rid of it, but that does not make me unwary. These things do not go out for the asking, alas. Nor do I forget that she has done me much damage (and I her, I daresay). But these either have no relevance, or else they make it more proper that I should fill a gap for her, if I can.

And it is for such a short time!

I could not rest easy in my bed, my darling, if I did not do whatever I can do for her, while she is in such straits. And I think the French novelists would appreciate that what I know of her happiness now comes from the knowledge of unhappiness which I owe to her when I was first deprived of what I had thought to be a lasting love.

I know I can't DO anything; but by being there and enjoying what there is to be enjoyed I may steady her a little. So, if you can, set me free to enjoy if I possibly can – and I possibly CAN'T if I know you are seriously fretting. Try to trust me when I promise you I will take care in all ways. I love you far too much to do or leave undone anything I should not or should do.

I got into a dreadful grammatical muddle there and no time to clear it

---

1 She was going to spend a week on the river Ant with her sister. The sister had been toppled off the height of an ambition and, unaccustomed to being thwarted, was taking it hard.

up. My love – always and for ever my most true, dear Love.

Valentine

138: STW

Frome Vauchurch, 16 September 1957

My Love,

This is the little nonsense[1] I bought for you in Norwich. I lied when I said it was meant for your Christmas Stocking. It was meant for now, but I knew you would respect a Christmas Stocking. And see how well the lie answers all round, for as a result you have a solid blue wool, and I my brown slop, straight out of Craske.

The only thing I cannot as yet feel sure of is whether you will like it. Anyhow, you are not meant to like it desperately, but only sentimentally and amusedly.

My Love, I am resolved not to be foolishly craven about this trip so you are not to worry about my state of mind. Think of me gardening, or cleaning the larder, or suchlike rational lively acts; and listening to my V.H.F. and making great quantities of delicious marrow purée out of Mr Pye's monster and even perhaps selling brilliantly in the shop, though I think the weather will need to improve before anyone could think of going shopping. And if the boat goes well and there is any element of pleasure, then stay on that extra day with a clear conscience. But REMEMBER, do not force yourself to come home in one day. I would forego fifty thousand concerts (to you this would not seem a very outstanding sacrifice) I would forego even Ben Britten concerts, rather than that you should provoke a bad back or more of those headaches . . . So nerve yourself to stop and rest for a night at some comfortable hotel. Candy will protect you, she will do everything except pay the bill and tip the boots.

When I think of the sound of reeds and the smell of water and how the sky *lives* above those flats and flickers with light and shade as though it were a willow itself I feel I ought even to be glad you are going. But do

---

1 A fisherman's jersey (I relied on the sanctity of Christmas stockings to keep her from prying). We had been in Norfolk not long before, when we inspected the inn where she would stay with her sister, and her sister's motor-boat.

not let the circumstances bite into you. A grief without poetry in it, as I am afraid Joan's is, has poisonous teeth. A grief without poetry is against nature, since the two are by nature intermarrying elements. Keep yourself oiled against it, even while you are ministering to it. And do your best to keep warm. If my love could be a coat to you, you would be as warm as Kit among his shavings, his nose in his kind stomach.

Remember, my Love. Remember my Love. Forgive my qualms. I promise to be careful, cheerful and practical, and to look after myself till you come home to do it for me.

Tib

139: STW

Frome Vauchurch, 8 October 1957

My Love,

It is harder this time,[1] though we are both being so good and discreet about it – harder by the change to an autumn sky and a whole hour of earlier dusk. I thought so, a few minutes ago walking in the mute garden.

And so much harder for you by a worse drive there, an infinitely worse drive back,[2] and no homecoming at the end of it, only the bleak banality of the King's Arms; and the flattened quality of anything done as a repeat, as I'm afraid this visit is likely to have. I do think you are nobly good and magnanimous. Say it I will, say it I can on paper where you can't interrupt me, though I would much rather say it by mouth. You allow me to say that I love you, but never allow me to go on and say even a parcel of my reasons why. Yet reasons count. I have always loved you for your good character as well as for being the character I love. Your solitary courage and uprightness when you discarded Pope, book and candle was one of the first things that rivetted my love to you. It is still my pride and my glory and always will be, however you may now look back on it (but I hope you look back on it with respect, for indeed you should. Such things are ever-fixed marks). And another of those permanent admirations was when I saw that you had the kind of mercy that doesn't need to be fed on illusions, illusions about the merit or gratitude of the receiver, illusions

1 A pre-departure letter. Joan had asked her to go again.
2 Ruth was coming with her, and they were to stay the night at a Dorchester hotel.

about giver or taker necessarily being blessed or the better for it. It is for such things I love you, my Love, as it is also for ridiculous things, the inattentive piety with which you modulate from hymns to Noël Coward, all in that melancholy viola voice, or the dignified presence of mind with which, when you get yourself to Oakham five hours ahead of your announced time, you sweep on to Boston. And also, of course, because, like the girl from Bedlam, I love my love because I know he first loved me.[1] Yet today, when I saw Vera in her dream of woe, and thought, though Thomas is going back to Africa she has Arthur and Keith and Lister and Rachel, I did not feel one moment's envy. I am sure it is infinitely better to have all one's eggs in one basket, and the treasure of one's soul embarked in a single vessel – that passage of poor Otway's that haunts me whenever I see you packing to go away, and remembered today, looking at Vera.

I will not plague you with any recommendations – they would be ingorgeous lions[2] at best, repeated at such a short interval. This is merely a love-letter.

Tib

140: STW

Frome Vauchurch, 11 October 1957

My Love,

I hope you – poor Candace too – woke up this morning feeling less tired. You sounded like a shadow on the telephone last night, and my mind filled with thoughts of Asian flu, or for that matter, polio, still flowering though the more recent bloom has put its nose out of joint. I see why you stopped in Norwich to have lunch with Ruth – you were throwing yourself out of the sledge with the hope that this would abate the demand that you and Joan should go over to Winterton from Horning. A slim chance, I'm afraid; and a painful meal for the mouthful.

I am thankful for your plan for Wednesday[3] – Heavens, how far away Wednesday is! – for it will mean that I shall see you alone and

---

1 Refrain of an 18th cent. folk-song.
2 Her grandmother's mysterious term for left-overs from dinner-parties was 'gorgeous lions'.
3 An emendation, whereby she would come here alone for a couple of hours before returning to Ruth. Katten always lay down after being in Ruth's company.

unintercepted; and, I hope, have the pleasure of putting you to bed as I used to do with Katten. Katten made no two twos about accepting. Remember this, and model yourself on her dear example.

I have done all I think I can do in your workshop; what isn't done is dusting the two sets of shelves. I don't think even my Chinese editing methods could get all those little odds and bobs back exactly where they came from, and where your hands would expect to find them. But everything else has been dealt with, and the room now looks rather as though I were a missionary and had given it a thorough conversion. It is recognisably just the same, yet looks unlike itself, and wistfully furtively waiting for the moment when it can creep back into its natural being and resume the worship of large spiders. I had the company of such a nice intelligent large spider this morning. It sat on a sunny wall and watched me, and when I told it to move away, it moved. In the end it went out of the window, but without any show of fuss or malice. They are such beautiful things, the large ones – like fugue subjects. I am sorry there was one casualty: the broken-off handle of a large china ladle. It fell out of that mortuary box and broke on the floor, because I was careless in moving the box. I found several valuable jetsams on the floor: your black Japan ruler, and a beautiful mother of pearl triangle, and a dear little round whetstone, I hope this will go towards atoning.

We have grown or rather we have developed a bicoloured michaelmas daisy. Some of its blossoms are the middlesized china blue that you like, others are a bright calico pink. They seem to grow on separate fronds but from the same stems, and certainly from the same root. It is lost in a thicket near the compost box, but I have marked it, so that later on I can take away the thicket and leave it more room to express itself. I am afraid it is only a temporary freak, and because of something it has got its roots into. It is still coming out, and I sadly daresay that by the time you see it the blue will have swamped the pink. For the moment they are about even.

It is as hot as summer, and both cats are sleeping on the deck, rebrimming their clammy cells. Vera wrote me a sweet letter – Niou has just walked in at the window to send his love, personally typed – full of thanks and saying she would bring the willow slips next time. And Alyse was delighted with the coffee-pot – really delighted, I think; at any rate, delighted to write and say she was. She is not in the cottage yet. Morebath is a minute village, but it has a post master and he is writing a book.

I am perfectly well. Yesterday I had some rheumatisms, but today they are gone, and my wrist has thrived on my good cleaning works. I shall keep the yeast in a damp veil and not bake till Sunday, as I have a great deal still of your most delicious bread. Now the electricity man has come to fix the meter and *energise* the new plug. He is quite a different one. *Souvent technicien varie, fol qui s'y fie.* I hear him taking a great many things to pieces, and coughing horribly. I hope he won't say it is all wrong and heretical like the Church in Southern India. One may expect anything after a word like energise. The suspense is terrible – No! It is all right. He has a little bulb on two whiskers, and when the whiskers were put into the plug the light went on in the bulb, and now he has gone his way.

In case you don't see today's *Times*, here is a picture of the Queen going to a party given by a horse. What she thinks she is wearing heaven alone may know, but she seems pleased with it. She hasn't such good taste in dress as the old original avoid all imitations Elizabeth, who was also given to what I think is called passementerie, otherwise bugles, but wore it with a difference.

No proofs have come, either from Wells or Chatto.[1] If they don't arrive by next week, I think we shall have to pretend they have. My temper is fairly good, but I do find it rather trying after thirty years of authorship to have people being sympathetically excited about my proofs as if I had been married for as many years and were now pregnant for the first time. If I had the proofs, I would be busy, of course, and unaware of being tried, and unaware of being covered with ink, and able to show a smudged and smiling face to the world.

O my Love, I am so *dull* without you.

Tib

141: VA

Norfolk, 12 October 1957

There is something wrong with the posts, my Love. Your letter[2] which should have been here when I arrived only reached me this morning – and not *that*, because I was not on the boat and did not get a chance to fetch letters from the hotel until long after lunch. So when will you hear from me?

1 Proofs of her *28 Poems*, which I had printed by a firm in Wells, who commended themselves to us because they had a Hebrew fount; proofs of my translation of *Contre Sainte-Beuve*.
2 Letter 139.

Thank you, my Love – thank you for your letter, which gave me incredulous happiness; *on the whole* (perhaps in the much-inflated account of the qualities you think I have I am easiest with the quality of mercy: as I used to be easiest in my bird's-eye jacket over my snuff-brown trousers – *type* as well as *fit* . . .) but I was disturbed *indeed* by what you say of my feelings now, about having left the Church. For indeed, you do still misunderstand me! OF COURSE I look back on my action then with respect and with approbation. Then, as now, I could not and would not abide blackmail and bullying: *then* I knew no other way to deal with it but the direct smack in the face, and then I could not tell the garment from the man. But not for one moment do I reprobate the young creature (hard to know its sex at that stage) who stalked out of the confessional, metaphorically clutching *Ulysses*; knowing it was not an all-that-good book, but also that it was Book – *and* who told the old priest where to put it – threatened with dying and going to hell (though I wonder sometimes if he did really say All that I thought he did, for it is Uncanonical; if that is the word).

But never mind all this. What I am afraid you may forget to believe and what *is* true and is – if you are to love me – important, is that I am what I am now because I have for myself, *only one petition* I pray *always* – that I may be as God made me and would have me be. And (follies, inadvertancies, insanities, distortions apart) I was, of course, nearer to that when I was young. One gets accretions, suffers from ill-fitting theories which give one bunions and twisted bones if they are worn too long, or one wears them when one has really outgrown them – so that there *is* need to pray that one may regain one's proper shape.

If you understand this, of me (I mean, that that is my sole prayer for myself) you might not go all wrong and think I have ever turned against the things Molly-Ackland, Molly-Turpin, Valentine Ackland did; which were done by her, herself. Crude or rude, list or love – I do not regret any but the false things.

My Love, what a long-winded letter about me. I felt unhappy, for fear you let yourself think I have cast *me* off. Do not think it. I love you, you see; *all the me's love you.*

Can you read this? My hand is so tired and I cannot write by paw anyhow. I am so very LONELY here, my darling! I hope it is going all right. Joan is very happy. I feel as if I am trying to row against wind and tide, with soft rubber oars.

We went out to St. Bennets and moored there. It was unbelievably beautiful, going along the river, misty and warm, and every autumn-coloured bush and tree and reed reflected in the stream, very brilliant, as bright as it was itself. And swans reflected too; and a flying heron low along the water, its wings almost touching its reflected wings. St. Bennets' ruins so desperately lonely: empty niches and the gateway from which they hung the last abbot still bitterly grieving, as much, I think, as a living tree must grieve when a man has died on it. The marshes wide, wide – and larks singing.

But Joan cannot *stay-still*. I am very tired.

Tomorrow I go to Norwich in the morning. If I see pleasant food, cheap, I will post it to reach you on Tuesday 2nd. post or 1st. post Wednesday.

Oh *God*, I hope I shall see you early on Wednesday, my Love.

The little wireless is a deep pleasure to me. I really do love it very much, I do thank you for it.

Oh my Love, I do *thank* you. I do implore you not to wince away from ANYTHING about me. I shall never betray anything you cherish. What I am now is true for me. I love you TRULY and without ANY reservation. And totally. My love for you is all my love, and all my life.

Valentine

1958

142: VA

Frome Vauchurch, 11 June 1958

Morning

It oppresses my heart to write to you while you are still here, my Love: but I hope this small outing[1] will be as pleasant and reviving as I thought it might be, when I schemed for it in France. It seemed, then, as if I shd. be altogether gleeful about it, and now I am a little worried in case it is too tiring for you, or in some way not glorious. But do let yourself *go* into enjoyment and take whatever offers of pleasure or silliness . . . and above ALL (my darling Love!) bear in mind that *YOU* will be the Lioness of the party, and the feather in the stony-caps! Even if it is a little too much because of the topical success of your Proust, it is YOUR Proust, and could be no one else's: and in any case, that is only the red carpet, so to speak: it is SW walking on the red carpet which is the high-light.

The dear snobs will enjoy themselves heartily, and they are so innocently dedicated to this pleasure that you will love that, as well as (I hope) other and more lasting things. Perhaps you will also love the Sea: *I* do, and I envy you the sound and silken sight of it, and ask you to look at it for me and hear it for me.

Otherwise I an unenvying but only of YOU: I envy them with all my heart because you will be with them. Come back safely, sweetheart, and come back loving me, please – and for *mercy's sake* take care of yourself in practical, prudent ways. Eat, sleep, keep warm or cool, walk *carefully*, don't talk to Reynolds[2] while he is driving (he drives rather badly: I wish Janet would conduct the auto while you are in it) don't be intimidated by

1 A trip to the Aldeburgh Festival.
2 Reynolds: Stone, the engraver. [Janet, his wife; Phillida and Emma, daughters.]

Phillida's young newness and state nor put-upon by Mistress Emma. And if you are tired or feel ill, confide in Janet who is so young and so gay and so charming and such a minx – and such a sheltering Mamma into the bargain. Oh my Love, my Love – keep yourself *truly* carefully!

Valentine

1959

Frome Vauchurch, 17 February 1959

My Love,

It is not much use to ask you not to feel worried, but I do ask you not to worry: and there is a difference because feelings can be carried around and even persuaded to remain quiet but *being* worried is horribly active and tiring. So *please* don't be, but instead learn of the cats and tuck your heart's head into your mind's belly, and let it quietly stifle there, and sleep: and for the rest, enjoy the stillness[1] and the end of any necessity to cook . . . (but *eat*: eat the little tin of smoked mussels and the little pot of pheasant paste and some olives and some raisins: and drink some Good Red Wine, and if it is cold drink some Port before you go to bed, and at 11 on Tuesday and 11 on Wednesday morning. For Love's sake, eat, my darling . . .)

I don't know that I shall telephone you but I will try very hard to. There may be such ghastly complications of garaging and Candying and getting poor Ruthie upstairs (did I ever find out if there is a L I F T ?). But the hotel's number is W O R T H I N G III and the hotel is called G A R D N E R' S.

I shall probably take Candy out for her walk not later than 9 o'clock, D.V. I hope D will V that it is not dreening with rain or teeming with Teddy-Bears,[2] and that Ruth will not fall flat, as I suspect she may because she certainly does not want to go to this place, which once seemed like a paradise in view . . .

Don't worry about me because there is no reason to: I'll tell you why —

1 Ruth (whom she was about to convey to Sussex) had been staying with us.
2 Teddy boys was the current name for young gangsters. Ruth had startled a hotel lounge by remarking placidly, 'I see there's been another horrible murder by Teddy Bears.'

Sleeping even for less than an hour has twice made me feel *absolutely* restored to life and health, so there isn't anything wrong with me except boredom. And I do enjoy driving and the car is a darling little car and I am devoted to it, and it has graces already and Mr King, a moment ago, assured me that it had Plenty of Pep — P L E N T Y — which is what makes for safety as well as for pleasure. I shall not go fast, however, because I want to conserve this car carefully so that we, Y O U A N D I A L O N E, may enjoy it at its best. I want us to go away A S S O O N A S W E C A N, even if it is only for a week, and damn the weather. Even bad weather is so much less bad somewhere else . . . and once my List is done we can fly off to gather some more stuff?

My Love, I must write silly letters now: this is very silly too, but I cannot better it with Ruthie sitting behind me. One thing has *really* restored me this visit, and that is typing your lecture.[1] I adored doing it. I have now material for speculation and consideration during my drive home, and it should relieve me from that silly incessant whirligig of 'she-said-to-me-and-I-said-to-her' which besets me after being with poor Ruthie. But much more than that, it gave me back you from the cocoon-wrapping of your Works for Ruthie and your fatigue and my crossness . . . because A L W A Y S you emerge in total integrity, without a flaw or a tremor or a chip or a crack, only I cannot always manage to tear *my* sticky wrappings off and fumble through yours, because of tiredness and multiplicity. But here you were, as I typed your wild and care-free script, my Love, and *Oh Dear Me* I was glad to see.

There is no one in the World I *love* but you.

Valentine

144: STW

In the train, 10 March 1959

My Love,

If I write now and post this at Paddington, you may possibly get it by the second post tomorrow. Poor Ruth writes so many letters from trains that I think I should spare you others; but it will be a root to me to post this, so I write though all I have to say is that I love you with my heart,

---

1 I had been asked to give the Peter Le Neve Lecture at the R.S.A.

and that this picture¹ in a way expresses the depths of that love. On the surface, I know, it is vexed and turbulent with my concerns and anxieties, and rages against those who menace, prey on, annoy, misjudge, don't appreciate, bore, etc. you. But its depth is green and calm and we are there together.

The other thing I have to say is that I think you are right to fetch Ruth by car; though I wish to God you weren't doing it. Since I haven't protested or put obstacles I now advance on my Virtue's reward: that for the remainder of the visit you let me do more of the drudgery, and suffer more of the tête à têtes. Tea, for instance. You must let me develop a new passion for tea, so that I can take her on while you go off and read, or lie down. Remember, like you I find Ruth much easier to associate with if I have her to myself. There is not that mass-suicide quality about it when one is single-handed.

(The woman opposite whom I said to myself would get out at Frome has got out at Frome.)

It is warm, the sun is about to shine, the landscape looks so pretty, rather languid, but just about to feel better. I hope poor Candy will soon look the same. Ruth will probably be good for her. She *is* good for animals. They can tap some nutriment in her which those years of happiness and good works have made inaccessible to humans.

I try not to feel anxious about you. Abet me by taking all care you can of yourself.

My love always and always.

Sylvia

---

1 From a Persian silk carpet, showing two lovers standing in a wood. I despaired of our regaining such an estate. Ruth and Joan had been having a series of quarrels; Valentine was flailed with their letters, telephone calls, demands for sympathy, accusations of heartless indifference. The combatants were united in assuming that she had flawless health and would drive anywhere at a moment's notice. Their sudden decision that Ruth should come to stay with us seemed, at the moment, the last straw. There were a great many more straws. Not till April did we fight our way out and go to Brittany, where we toured about for Calvaires, lived on shellfish, were healed and happy again.

145: VA

Frome Vauchurch, 14 August 1959

My true Love,

I hope you won't get this letter,[1] but if you do, please R E A D it. I will double-space, to make it less of a labour.

Supposing I were to die (one has to think of it: It does happen: anyhow it is habitual to think of it) Shakespeare has said, of course, what is the simple truth '– save that, to die, I leave my Love alone –'. But otherwise, although I have had a *very* happy life indeed, happy and full of love and fortune, I would not have many worries on my mind: those I might have, which are tellable, I will tell you now.

First and far above the others, that you do not realise how happy you have made my life – made *me*. Because of the shredding-away process, which is partly ageing I suppose and partly after-math of drinking, and partly a conglomerate of little causes, I have become undemonstrative and dumb. This has made me very unhappy very often, because inside I have scarcely altered at all: except a *change* in fervour but no lessening of degree. I have been like the sky, ever since I fell in love with you: the sun at noon . . . standing more faithfully still than it stood for Joshua, but the *weather* changing: clouds sometimes and winds driving them; but never any diminishing of the fire of the sun, whatever passed across its bright face. And loving someone like that means matchless happiness.

My second worry would be about you: I hope I can explain what I am anxious about, because it is serious. My love – if I die before you, you will probably give away T O O   M U C H : of money, of possessions, of strength. Now – *please attend to me*. I can't argue this out at length, nor would I be able to persuade you if I did. I must do something which, in this connection, I do not think to be wrong or blackmailing: I must ask you once more in your life and mine to obey me. The few other times that I have really seriously asked this, you have done it most honourably.

Please do it again.

I want you to set aside – either in an Annuity if you would find that less

---

1 But I might well have. Her dentist found a piece of dead bone in her lower jaw. It would be a long and delicate operation, as her jaw-bone was exceptionally thin. He also knew that she was apt to bleed profusely and was alarmingly slow in coming round from an anaesthetic. As his best anaesthetist was away on holiday, he decided to put off the operation for a month, during which time she was to rest and concentrate on getting her blood pressure down. In September she went into a Weymouth nursing home. I stayed at a hotel within call.

trouble (I dislike it *because*, if the State becomes even more paternal it will be impossible to conceal from it that you have this Annuity . . . and the State may decide to spend it for you on giving you All Comforts in some place where you would not choose to be) or by investing AND EAR-MARKING IT AS FOR YOUR OWN USE *NOT* TO BE GIVEN AWAY OR LENT AWAY, the most capital you can, to ensure an income of anyhow 3800 a year, and preferably more. I don't know more than vaguely how much you can manage to put by like this, but I *do know* that when I cease to be a drain on you there will be what will seem like a good deal of money (by contrast with what there has been while I have been spending it) and I also know – with fear – that finding yourself apparently much better off than you expected, you will start to give it to Janet, Jean, and God-knows-who.

My Love, God forbid that I should let my anxiety for you to constrain your beautiful generosity . . . but you will be unhappy, you see – and you may too easily fall into a trap, and get caught, and me not there to free you. So I beg you, without arguing or questioning, to do as I ask you: keep a SOLID wall, as high as you can make it, between you and State Aid: keep your LIBERTY, my most dear Love. And live as generously and wisely as you can, in material things, *for love of me*.

By material things I do mean food and covering and light and warmth, but I also mean music and friends and cats and books, and freedom from constraint. I mean *ease*, my darling.

This anxiety I feel is a deep one: it troubles me very much. I don't want to burden you with much asking, that you should live thus-and-thus, or stay here or go somewhere else . . . simply that, in all places until you come to me, you will cherish yourself as I so passionately long to cherish you. And in little things as well as great: but remembering the great too!

Of course give away, do what you will – but always have at the back of your mind that before all else, because of our long, true love, you must keep faith and break your promise, so beautifully kept till now, *to love and to cherish*: and if I am not able to pour out the wine or close the cold windows or make you have a better stove . . . then do it for me, my true Love.

For the rest – so little. Keep anything: give anything away, of mine. I think Joan will need comfort, if I die. Try to think of her as a particularly difficult, cross-grained, sick animal: she will bite – she may snatch or scratch or go mad with fear or rage. But she IS sick, and we are creatures! She will feel bereft. You can't companion her (and should not) but from time to time you might write to her, or send her a book or a picture, and let her write to you. (Don't bother about what she says of me. She has no idea beyond her own idea of me which is both too rosy and too unreal.)

Old Bo will miss me a bit but not much. Eleanor Buller and Barbara Whitaker and perhaps Jane[1]– to a less extent – will be unhappy. No one else, that I can think of: and none of those are people you should have much to do with, but Eleanor B and Jane might possibly be linked up and manage each other quite nicely!

But all this is as *nothing*: and I don't know if I leave anything worth keeping, that I have written. For pity's sake don't get bogged-down in a mass of useless papers and bits. I don't really care, now, I think. I think one or two of my poems gave you an authentic pleasure, and one or two of them have given Barbara Whitaker pleasure, too. I have been luckier than I thought I would be, even there, you see: and it all seems rather shadow now because I've written-myself-in to being dead! This seems to prove that I R E A L L Y don't care much what happens to the papers.

If you read my diaries, *don't agonise*. Remember that I wrote almost always because I was unhappy and had to unload: and also because I've always been a graveyard bird, better able to hoot than sing! But you would find love and love and love, all through them and everywhere. I have loved you with the W H O L E of my being, Sylvia – and if my hopes come true, I shall love you changelessly for ever.

Forgive me for innumerable anxieties, pains, wounds and latterly misunderstandings which have been so largely my fault. I have *longed* with all my heart, longed to tears and great pain, that you could understand H O W I believe in God, and that by some miracle of grace I could see that we are not separated here. I have tried not to do any more and I wish with all my heart that I had never said one word, of all the thousands of words I have said to make you unhappy or show you my unease about this. Forgive me, my sweet Love – and at least believe that my unease is all because of my own shortcomings – never because I thought for one moment that Y O U were not whole worlds ahead of me, and of everyone else I know, in pure grace and goodness.

Except one thing: I speak truth to you because I must. You must look long and seriously into your own mind before you die, my darling: look with truthfulness at the truth: make yourself S E E the dead people, the imprisoned people, the people under torture, under oppression, under compulsion: of course not only in Russia and China and those countries – but *at those countries too*. At least L O O K : so that you are not *self*-deceived.

1 Jane [Long].

It may not shake your allegiance to an Idea: that is no business of mine, I know – I have tried hard not to take it on, and regretted it bitterly, as a fault, when I have slipped. But still it troubles me deeply because I think you have refused to see. It will be easier for you if I am not there, I know. I mean, if I am not there apparently self-righteous! (Believe me, wherever I shall be, I shall N O T be self-righteous!)

Oh my Love – my Love – you have been beautiful to me always, in all days, in all nights. You are my Love, my Dear, my Only One, my Burd-Alone. I don't know anything at all about being dead, nor have I the least idea of what I believe, expect, think or even feel. But one thing I know, that if 'I' am anywhere it will still be the truest of all 'Never heed' said the girl, 'I will stand by you!'

Valentine

146: STW

Frome Vauchurch, 11 September 1959

My Love,

Don't for one moment let me be a weight on your heart. It beats with mine, your courage is my courage, and as you are brave and tranquil, so will I be. I shall do everything you ask, I shall repose on Janet,[1] and take an Adelin; and I shall know that we are so close to each other that Moffat House and the Westershall Hotel don't even exist except as things on a map, above which we fly together. I grieve over you exactly as you would grieve over me, your heart beats in my breast and you won't be the only one, my Love, to be faced with woollen stockings.

But not for an instant, think that you are 'a disturber of my peace'. You *are* my peace. Even at this moment, when I feel like a stricken glass, you are my peace, and I resound you. Nothing else, my Love, my dearest Love, my dearest joy and life and comfort.

Remember Nita's advice, don't be brave. As you *are* brave, to be brave would be superfluity. Ask for things you think you'd be the better for, and quite possibly you will receive.

Only one thing – when I see you tomorrow, don't allow any toothlessness, any passing alteration, to intervene. It is you I shall see, and

1 She had arranged that my cousin Janet should be with me.

your love, and nothing else. Cast care aside!
   And try to sleep, my love.
   Goodnight.

[Sylvia]

147: STW

Lavenham, 22 October 1959

My Love,
   We must certainly come here together. The hotel is as warm as the Barn used to be: immense woodfires in large rooms; no greater luxury. I have booked to stay on for tomorrow night. On Saturday they would have to move me to another bedroom, so I think instead I shall move myself to Bury St. E.
   The things I remembered and the things I had forgotten are still here.[1] Mr Ransom is dead (I was wrong, he was a tailor not a hairdresser, it must have been his tongue that persuaded me to make a Figaro of him). But the name is over the shop, and his round fanatic blue eyes confronted me as I bought postcards (the same postcards) from a short stout middle-aged woman, who is Miss Ransom and who keeps the shop with her brother. She talks just as much and assured me it was a good thing she could keep her temper under control. She also said, 'if I may say so without offence' that too many elderly people come to Lavenham, buying up houses that Lavenham people ought to live in, which I daresay is true. And at the top of Shilling Street the monkey-puzzle has scarcely grown a foot taller in that queer little garden, though the garden itself is less bushy.
   I have bought you a dozen postcards, tomorrow I will get you some more. I have bought 4 3d exercise books in blue covers. They are of the same propitious kind that you gave me at the beginning of *Contre Sainte-Beuve*. A mad old man is soliloquising on the pavement opposite. He gesticulates, and his eloquence turns him as the wind turns a weathercock, and a large yellow Labrador dog is lying on the pavement observing the oddity of a human being. Sometimes, he thinks to himself, they bark at each other, sometimes they bark alone. I am barking alone – and I admit,

---

1 I went to Lavenham because I had heard that Mrs Parker, who looked after us when we went to The Barn, was ill. She was dying of cancer.

I feel very sad when I think of you driving towards Winterton without me. But if, today or tomorrow, Mrs Parker is able to feel pleased at seeing me again, I shall think I have done right to be here. Though I should have come before, alas!

I shall post this now and tell you how she is when I ring up this evening. My Love, never, never think that you are not real to me. You are more real to me than I am to myself. In the course of our long love I have become so grafted in you that I have no other root. When you became a Catholic you transferred me into a different climate, an air that sometimes blows chill and alien on me, and checks my natural tendency to twine and flower all over the place; but my roots are fixed. Your doings may at times be unreal, unexplicit, to me; but never you.

And I love you.

Sylvia

148: STW

London, 15 December 1959

My Love,

Judging by the extra post-office which is foaming next door in the Horticultural Hall, I shall be with you long before this letter is. But it would be an unsatisfied morning if I did not tell you that I am well, that I am good, that Norah[1] is all kindness and forethoughtedness – a fresh hotwater bottle with my breakfast tray because at home I should have the electric blanket on – and midnight pears and bunches of London violets. She is an artist in l'art de plaire. I was looking at her at dinner last night, managing a not very easy quartet, for George Painter is very shy, brooding shy, and has not learned to conceal it in conversation, as you have; and Roger[2] is a loving chatterbox, and the young waiter was full of unexpected meals, such as offering to water down my sherry (apéritif whiskeys is what he's used to, oh dear!); and there was Norah, talking with Roger, yet exchanging silences with George, and all without appearing to do so – pleasing as effortlessly as water flows. I understand why Janet Stone did not take to Norah. Le mieux est l'ennemi du bien.

1 Norah [Smallwood].
2 Roger [Senhouse].

It turned into a very comfortable quartet presently. We talked almost entirely about things, I notice, instead of persons. Ernies[1] (Roger has recently been introduced to an Ernie) hypnotism, trances, Colette's style, the British Museum, tarragon, waistcoats – not a Tiddly-Push[2] raised its head. And for me, with no talent for Tiddly-Pushes, and inexorably doomed to refer to them as Push-Tiddlys, this was very emollient.

The restaurant was one of the new S. Kensington lot; admirable food, perhaps five tables, take your own wine. We could lunch there with advantage. It is in a back street, and outside a very fine ginger cat was sitting on the nose of a Rolls Royce.

She has done up her bathroom, it is now blue – land not sea blue – with an ardent towel rail; and next she plans to recolour her ivory dining-room to match the jug with green fronds she bought from you. She was delighted with her present and has borne it off to the office, intending to write to the Royal family immediately. She commented that I filled the flat with ravishing smells – and this pleased me deeply, since it made me feel that you must be here invisibly.

Now it is raining – yesterday it wasn't – Oh dear, I hope you are not all in a flood and a morass. Not only is it raining, but Angus Wilson has just rung up Norah to say he can't manage this evening (he lives in Suffolk and was coming up) which dashes her party. She may get Mervyn Horder instead. If she does I will study him for your benefit, though I admit I disliked him when I met him before. I hate spinsterly men.

My love, my Love.

Sylvia

---

1 A government catchpenny.
2 Her generic name for local gentry. Tiddly-Push conversation largely consisted of enquiries if we knew other Tiddly-Pushes.

1960—1968

1960

149: STW

In the train, 20 April 1960

My Love,

Bruton – and you are just stretching out to have your hair washed. At the thought how they may hurt your head[1] I feel sick – idiotically, unavailingly sick. It is the flaw that runs through all loves, that one cannot suffer instead of the beloved. The inability descends on one like an iron curtain, and sets one at a remove. I remember feeling this, the night when my shingles were hurting me so much. As I went past your room I saw you sitting there with your head in your hands, as desolate as Alexander Selkirk.

This is a very nice quiet carriage, with a silent specimen of the backbone of England in each corner. The train is reeling like Billy Lucas.[2] If it began to sing a beery hymn I should not be in the least surprised.

A last thought. We have not settled anything about our letters. Shall we leave them to accumulate or shall we have them sent to a poste restante?

Another last thought. My fancy pepper plant. It is in a small pot, it will die if it goes unwatered for a week. Could you give it to Mr True? The other things will last, if I give them a good drench tomorrow evening.

How lovely to write those words, *tomorrow evening*, and to know that they portend that we shall go away for a holiday, ourselves to ourselves. London, and *Macbeth*, will be very nice, no doubt, and I will gobble up every pleasure they can give me. But really it will just seem a rather bedizened portico to my real pleasure.

---

1 An acutely sensitive place on her temple conjecturally diagnosed as temporal arteriosis – which may lead to blindness.

2 Billy Lucas of Chaldon; an amiable tippler, who used to leave the Inn singing 'I was a wandering sheep.'

If I were going to hell with you I would enjoy the journey. You would see to that, my loving Love. I look at my new ring, *and think of the giver.*

My love, my Love.

Sylvia

150: STW

Frome Vauchurch, 2 August 1960

My Love,

Today is today; and suddenly I begin to feel cold and daunted, because you are the source of my courage. All these long months you have been that, you have carried me and my care as well as your own.

There are never the words, spoken or meditated, in which one can give thanks. The fact that you have seen me mostly behaving like a rational being must be the earnest of my gratitude. How I shall feel when I come back this evening having left you in your bleak hospital (Oh, but last night we slept together in peace and happiness!) I don't yet know. What I do know is that any courage I may contrive to retain will come from you, will be yours – as I am.

Love this foolish little bottle, which still smells of distant lands, distant roses, far-away summers; and hold it in your hand, as you hold me.

Your true

Tib

151: VA

Dorchester County Hospital, 2 August 1960

My true Love,

Oh! I can't keep your letter in my pocket![1] Such a childish first-thought as I read it – but such a letter to support and stay the heart, my Love and

---

1 In the operating theatre. During the summer (when she set herself to learn Braille) the pain in her head had grown more intense, and she was now in Dorchester Hospital for an exploratory operation. The operation disclosed a piece of blocked artery, which was cut out, but no danger to her sight, as a subsidiary vein had taken over and was carrying blood to the eye.

my Dear, and I want to hold it. I have the little bottle in its little den.[1] Did you *put in* the sponge and scent, cheating me as I did over those yellow shells? If so, where did you get rose scent and how did you squeeze in the sponge? I think, otherwise, that the bottle was built around the sponge.

It is hard to write sitting up. Sister Quigley (certainly no relation to Isobel, but nicer perhaps on acquaintance) has just propped me against a bedrest: entirely uncomfortable as compared with my own way of resting my head on a bed-rail, but I could see that she believed she had done me a kindness. And she *did* by moving the dressing-table closer to the bed.

My Love, I weep to think of you this evening and this night and all tomorrow, and then the strain still on your heart. I wish to goodness I had thought to open wine for you. I did think, and then forgot again. Will this operation make me less apt to forget important things and remember all the damned stupid things like butter and buttons.

Wasn't last night happy? I slept so well and I think you did too – you looked rested, although you are so tired, my poor, poor love. It is very dreadful to me that, with all the love I have for you which is, God knows, all the love I *can* have – and a good deal – with all that, I must always be the cause of your strain, worry, sorrow, misery – it is a dreadful thing.

Try, please, to lift your head and heart: do not be afraid, or in dread *for me*, at any rate. I am all right. It may be a good thing to be a day longer, resting (as they say) and getting flattened and heart steady. I think this could make an anaesthetic easier.

Look on the bright side.

No more now. I L O N G to see you. Thank heaven you said you would come in the morning – only I must not be a bore to you, my dearest love.

My only Dear – my heart's true joy.

Valentine

152: STW

In the train, 26 November 1960

Here I am, my Love, in great peace and warmth and triumph, not having uttered a single sneeze nor barely a snuff since Maiden Newton. All your doing, looking after me so beautifully yesterday, and dosing me so

---

1 An 18th cent. smelling bottle in a leather case, still keeping a ghost of its attar of roses.

discreetly. It was very magnanimously done, and I am very grateful.

For though my heart is not set on lecturing to the Lewes Society on French literature, it would have grieved me to fail Leonard,[1] so nobly dry, so truly venerable.

But it was melancholy to leave you with a cold hearth and a prospect of plumbers this morning (I think the train is alarmed at the sight of Mr Gee's horse on the hill) when yesterday all had been so warm and so glowing. It struck me, after I'd left, that perhaps dear Mr P.[2] was too impetuous, and should not have lighted the fire so much on the heels of the pipes being set in. Thank God you brought yourself that providential pie.

It is raining a little. The sloping pattern of rain on the windows looks like newly-fledged willow boughs – when they stream on the wind. The landscape looks sad and bewintered – not at all as it did when you and I were driving through it on the outset of our holiday. Thank you for remembering to tell me that Sibyl[3] thought you were looking so much better for it. I do, myself. But I like every scrap of confirmation I can lay my ears to.

I don't suppose Mr True will be able to come on Monday. If he does, he is paid up to the hilt except 2/6 for taking down the rubbish bins; and you needn't bother about this as I can settle on Thursday. But please give him a word of Praise. And there is no need to wait at home to give him his tea. Just give him a thermos.

Look well after yourself, my Love, and eat when you can bear to, and do not let yourself be too much trampled on by those two pampered jades of Asia (kiss the P.J.s from me, nevertheless!)

I hope you know I love you. You should, by now. But to make assurance doubly sure, my darling Love, I love you.

Tib

---

1 Leonard Woolf, President of the Lewes Literary Society.
2 Mr Palmer.
3 Sibyl [Chase]: neighbour and friend, who later became our gardener and household prop.

1961

Frome Vauchurch, 7 January 1961

My Love,

What infinite relief to hear your voice. The voice of reason had become very flat and monotonous, as for the consolations of philosophy, I have never had sufficient philosophy to be able to listen to them. Now we have all dined, tomorrow's coffee is brewing on the stove, Candy is sitting on the mulberry chair, asleep with one eye, drowsing with the other, and the cats, such is their exaltation at the change in my mind's weather, are playing Devil in the Dark overhead.

Candy was very sad all the morning, and went up and down the house in a crouching attitude, giving blood-curdling howls, varied with sighs and outbursts of barking. Much to my relief she consented to eat her lunch, and during the later afternoon she brought herself in from a wet walk round the garden and felt so pleased to lie by my fire that she forgot the worst of her sorrow; and now she is merely rather pensive; and by tomorrow, I hope she will be over the worst of it; though at every car, be it van or car or lorry, she leaps up, thinking that it will bring you. She is not very flattering to your taste in cars or your management of gears, but you will forgive her that.

It has been a dank sluttish kind of cold all day. Perhaps I have thought it worse than it really was. If it had been next Tuesday, for instance, I might have found subtle beauties in it. No one has come, no one has rung up. I have written part of a small bit about things seen behind glass. I have done some more of the green table outfit for Vera. And various tidyings.

You left the first volume of *Pride and Prejudice* behind, as well as the glasses you didn't forget to take. But perhaps this was intentional. One does know it so extremely well, because of its frankness and slight barefacedness. It is a very noonday picnic, everything is there clear and

363

plain, from the sandwiches in the foreground to the distant view of the sea.

A nice example of William Maxwell's discerning eye in his letter begun on Boxing Day, 'This morning the living room is full of half played-with toys.' There he had to break off in order to read the first chapter of *Wind in the Willows* to his younger daughter. It is reviving to hear of any child being read aloud to, asking to be read aloud to, in a room full of half-played-with toys and no doubt a television.

I seem to be getting on very nicely with the Rayburn, that is, I cleaned and fuelled it like a charm this afternoon. It cooked me some delicious dried apricots in the remains of your morning tea. Better than tea'd prunes, I think. They come a beautiful sunburned colour. I have got some veal from the butcher, and with this and the hare and the pigeon and the remains of the teal, and the duck's liver, I propose to make a pâté on Monday. It will then be in perfection for your return. Owing to the wickedness of the posts, I shall have to direct this letter to Apsley.

Do not be cast down,[1] my Love. I have no doubt at all that we shall manage to make out. We have never had to live in Bootle yet. Above all, do not worry with vain calculations. There is no waste so wasteful. How much shall I put aside for buttons in 1963? Write not your balance-sheets on the clouds (T. Carlyle).

I kiss you, my love and darling.

Sylvia

154: VA

Apsley,[2] 5 June 1961

My Love. I'm writing in a snatch! waiting for supper but I should be with Ruth.[3] She's just had a third injection of heroin (4.hourly) and I hope may be resting. She is at most semi-conscious, and mostly *less*, thank God. I have been sitting beside her all the time.

I am going to bed tonight and getting up at 5.a.m.

1 She had gone to visit her sister in London, her mother in Sussex, both of whom would harp on impending ruin.
2 Apsley in Sussex, where Ruth had domiciled herself with her two nieces.
3 Who had suddenly failed, and was dying.

Don't worry about me, for pity's sake, and for love's sake, take care of yourself.

I see Joan tomorrow.

All my love. I am glad I came. I wish this were not happening.

Valentine

155: VA

Apsley, 17 July 1961

My Love,

I hope I shall be home before this can reach you, but I must write to you because I love you so much!

All is safe: your cousin[1] was extraordinarily kind, wise and speedy. I thought he was going to die and I think he is, and it was a near thing, for he had to walk up many stairs to get to the chapel, and he could scarcely speak his part – only with pauses and he had hardly any breath to keep him alive. He is a M O R D A N T man, and infinitely kind and merciful. It is a strange combination and very attractive. I *wish* you had seen him and it is perfectly possible, if he lives long enough, for you to go there whenever we can get down. It would be W E L L   W O R T H doing a day trip and I would dearly love to.

More when I see you. He gave Joan two of his books and then said I cd. borrow one which, I think, is going to be good and it might be that you wd. like to read it.

I am tired but thankful. I am going to see Dr Bousfield tomorrow about my shoulder (not because it is worse but because it will save me time, perhaps).

Love and love and love – (I have got you the 1st. bunch of those little Greek grapes. Probably sour as hell).

Valentine

---

1 A very distant one; she referred to him as my cousin in order to tease me.

156: STW

Frome Vauchurch, 22 November 1961

My Love,

I hear you in the next room, and it seems impiously unnatural to sit here beginning a letter to you. And what am I to say in it, except that we had woodcock for lunch, and drove to Gould and the Post Office?

And now, since at that point you came in, that we have painted the bathroom together and eaten snipe; and that I Love you? All of which you will know already. Yet I would hate you not to get a letter from me on Friday morning. Though I hope you will not feel much lack of me, since you will have other fish to fry,[1] miraculous draughts, and Saint Peter in butter.[2]

Oh, I hope with all my heart that this weekend will go well for you, and that you will get the relaxation and solitude and pleasure of your own society that you need so badly, that you have for so long been without. That your cold will not rise up and capture you: that you will not suffer for your wall painting; that you may not fall into the jaws and paws of baws.

When you come home, I intended you to find the bathroom a finished bower, and the remaining tulips, now looking so odd in the larder, planted in a Persian carpet in the tulip tree bed. But your black ones in a noble group near the shop door. I think I have no other projects except to wash my hair and make a cold proud pudding for Alec.[3]

Niou has come to sit beside me, and I am to tell you that he will attentively take care of me. Be happy, my Love of long loving. I never forget that.

Tib

---

1 She was going to Buckfast in Devon. She had joined the 3rd Order of St Benedict; this entailed certain devotions and a twice-yearly mass at a Benedictine centre. Buckfast Abbey was the nearest; it had a guesthouse. It was the guesthouse I fought shy of, not the Abbey.
2 From the Englished menu of a trattoria in Rome (Saint Peter is haddock).
3 Alec, her cousin, about to visit us.

1962

157: VA

Buckfast, 3 March 1962

My Love,

Your letter was on the hall-table and delighted my heart. I had to wait
through breakfast to read it, which was difficult, and now it is really very
silly of me to write an answer because – D.V. and I hope he does – I shall
have to bring it with me, and I could answer verbally. But I might forget
in the confusion of arrival and joyful greetings and, I hope, the happy
yowls of Tib and Cats (cats yowling about steak and kidney lovingly
bought for them today) and my sweet siren-voiced Poodle (Dear Ruth –
I shall never cease to remember the *gentle* warmth and grief I felt when I
found that piece of paper on her desk on which she had written, so
carefully – P O O D L E P O O D E L).

So –

Your Fortune[1] overwhelms me with astonished and (true) reverence. I
cannot conceive of M A K I N G so much money. It's quite different to get
a salary for being a Director, or someone's child, or to get £4,000 for a
picture you bought by chance, or by cunning: and I suppose some people
can save that sort of sum. But to M A K E it out of your own bowels, like a
clever, deft and beautifully-working spider – or to collect it like a Sylvia-
Warbler picking up threads and straws and little pieces of grass – and then
to disclose, all of a sudden, this well-constructed, shapely nest hanging on
the wall of the safe in the Harrow Branch of the Westminster Bank . . .
That seems to me to be something nearly unbelievable.

My Love – do you know I do not W A N T a mink coat? But I do – oh

---

1 During our first ten years together we were often pinched for money (and spoke light-heartedly
of hiring ourselves out as cook and handy-lesbian). When Mr Lobrano of *The New Yorker* gave me
a First Reading Agreement, I began to put by some part of my earnings so that my death should
not leave her penniless. I disclosed my hoard because Ruth's death had exposed her to post-obit
talk about insolvency.

I DO want to go abroad with you, and it would be glorious to go in a little room on a train,[1] and to be (you as well as me) in very nice clothes. Not rich or expensive but pleasant to wear. And to see you in sunshine again, and to look again at handsome-stepping people. And I would be glad to be in a Catholic country because I like my Faith and its doings; so long as they do not make me feel apart from me, which gives me pain so enormous that I hope you do not have any idea of it.

Let us go abroad in the Spring, if there is not too much risk of being swamped by the madmen on either side of us.

And I would feel easier to K N O W that we would be able to change our dear car for another exactly like it; which would, I suppose, take about £400 to £500, trading over against a new one?

Not urgently – but so that we *could* if it seems that Renault will decide to make some other sort of car and discard the Dauphine. A horrible thought. So – no lesser indulgence like mink. But just a holiday in sunshine (and you in fine and happy new clothes) and something left to use if it seems wise to trade in the car next year?

But it grieves me that you have had, relatively, so little of the 1800 miles the car has travelled. Let us, please, do more journeys together? Even half-days. I only love having *you* with me. *Only you.*

Joan fevered me with anxiety about money, but I have tried to keep a level head until I know how we stand. Still – if she is even half right, it looks that I shall get less than £300 a year, except that Ogle and Moodie may contrive something for me. I would like a certain income, but it seems senseless to get an Annuity and be tied to a falling Pound . . . so it is probably better to hope things will be all right, to put an egg in one basket and get millions of baskets . . . and try to keep the shop running.

And I am resolved not to stampede.

And I am equally resolved not to lie as a dead weight on you, if only I can manage not to.

But I think I am not a very profitable partner; and, God wot, I would be if I could be.

Four pages and all unreadable and my hand shaking from un-accustomed exertion.

I have been very happy here, and very well refreshed, and I am *longing* to come home.

My *Love*.

Valentine

1 We went by wagon-lit to Italy.

1963

158: VA

Frome Vauchurch, 12 April 1963

Good Friday

My true and only Love

We have heard today that I may have to have an operation:[1] it fills me with anguish because of Y O U –

I can't do anything except beseech you, for the sake of our matchless happiness in each other, to go on loving me and know that I go on loving you. We know nothing except our hope – and you do not even have a hope, I think – but if anything lives, or any part of anyone lives after dying, I am sure beyond any doubt that you and I will live in love.

My Love – my dearest Love – if I ever wrote a poem in my life, it was a poem to and about you. I wish I had written poetry. I wish I might have been worthy of being loved by you. It is my saddest sorrow that I am not: because if I were I should be all that I should have been. Do you understand?

I love you with all my heart – I always have loved you with all my heart, even when I was mad and bad.

K N O W this, and that I will have done *all I could* to stay with you and see you safe – and if I die, then if there is any power in love, I shall never leave you and I *will* see you safe.

Valentine

1 During the winter she had felt increasingly ill and her doctor had been increasingly baffled as to the cause. That morning he came to tell her he suspected tuberculosis of the pericardium, with the choice of a major operation or permanent invalidism. However, he wanted a second opinion from a London heart specialist. She saw the specialist a fortnight later. He dismissed the diagnosis of tuberculosis but found a degree of deep-seated thrombosis which needed to be treated immediately, and sent her to the Brompton Heart Hospital. There was no private room available. She was put into a cramped room with two other patients, who stared, talked at her, behaved much as caged animals do when a new animal is put into their cage.

159: STW

London, 29 April 1963

My Love

I leave you in such woe and desperation, and in such woe and desolation myself that I cannot believe we are ourselves – if it were not for our love, the only thing that substantiates us at the end of this wretched day.

There is not even the distraction of remorse. We have both tried to act rightly, and to keep faith with reason. You are ill, have been ill for months; and they say that they can cure you. Gibson's diagnosis does appear to cover your case, and is his own, no copy-catting of the T.B. and heart operation affair. And his suggested treatment[1] does need supervision and possible braking, which we could not have done at home. I see it, I recognise it; but your woes and your state of a wild animal caged in a fairground[2] makes me incapable of seeing it steadily.

I didn't dislike the medical cherub whom I saw. He was polite, and made himself plain, and wasn't overbearing. But for all that, I sat twitching to claw his blood.

I came back by underground, and dined at the Chinese restaurant, because it was cool-ish; and a sweet gentle boy waited on me. And then I walked through Victoria Square, and asked at the Goring if there were any letters. There weren't. I will ask tomorrow morning, to give Malachy Lynch another chance. If not, I will leave them your loathed address for forwarding.

And here I am, in a perfectly tolerable room, but hot and immensely sultry. I'm afraid there will be a thunderstorm.

Oh, I came away by the underground tunnel. It is perfectly straight and simple – no mystery about it and not a Cerberus anywhere. I must say that for the Brompton, it is unusually free from Cerberuses. I saw the two lounges. Both were perfectly empty with lots of windows. When you are allowed up again, we may be glad of them. I even noted a Visitor's loo. In a day I have acquired a dreadful intimacy with your jail.

I read and re-read your sweet tattered letter, and stare at that TIB as

---

1 It was a blood-thinning drug, a component of the rat-poison called Warfarin, and could be as deadly.

2 Three days later the Ward Sister took it into her own hands, commandeered a room in process of being re-decorated, sent the workmen away and put Valentine in. There I sat, reading Dryden aloud while she regained herself.

though it were a sea-mark.

Of course, you jumped out of bed and were kind to those two unfortunates. You are so infinitely better than I, more humane, more dutiful. That really at this moment is my only consolation – your magnetic-needle quality of remaining good, even when captived to Sergeant III. My whole dependence is on you, while my whole being grieves for you. I say to myself, as well as being good as an angel, she is as sly as a fox. Somehow, somehow, you will be sly with circumstances, you will lead me out of this mire. Don't try to be brave. It is unnecessary; you *are* brave. Practise Avarice; hold on to everything you have inside you, and filch and gather every crumb of repose, of relaxation, of amusement, of momentary ease, of sardony and *self-approbation*. Nota bene.

My Love, my Love.

Tib

160: STW

Frome Vauchurch, 19 July 1963

My Love,

We grieve together,[1] and our grief re-knits our love. I can't comfort you for him nor attempt to comfort myself. He was our shining kitten, and scattered sugar over the slatted table at Great Eye, and pranced with a bell round his neck at the edge of the breakers; now he is our saint.

I can't comfort you, but you comforted him. Even this morning while we were waiting for Reg Francis, when he heard your step he looked up out of his stupor. You were good to let me be with him when the time came – I wish you had heard him purring as the anaesthetic released him, though – and to wind him. It was strangely easy to do it, alone; it was as though I had been practising that very act through inherited lifetimes, and knew perfectly, but also precariously. How the thought of him comes back like the swan, and nothing is precarious any more.

But it is you who have carried me through this, and undertaken for me. And undertaken for him, too. He could not have approached death so serenely if he had not felt your strength and provision. I write this half-

1 Niou, long failing, had been given his quietus.

371

feeling you are in London[1] where you will read it. But thank God, tomorrow you will be here when I wake. And when you come back from London we will go away and very greatly prowl and poke and expand ourselves in leisure; and you will slide out of this year's fetters, my dear darling. Such is our love, we might even go to that half-promised Bootle. But it is perhaps rather too far away.

My heart's love and gratitude.

Sylvia

161: VA

Frome Vauchurch, 12 November 1963

My Love

I don't approve of Little Letters; even more I don't want to follow you like a pestering ghost, clinking your chains. But still I shall send this to Norah's, because I want to tell you that I love you and that all will be well and cats and kittens cherished and, I hope, the roof still on the house when you return.

It is good for N., too, to see that you are loved. If she puts two and two together and finds that they add up to exactly and always two.

Enjoy yourself; ignore the BBC[2] as far as you conveniently can, and for God's sake walk *slowly* up those dreadful stairs.[3] I will take care of Kaoru and Quiddity,[4] and try not to hope that when you come back you will see them walking brotherly paw-in-paw around the garden – but it would be a pleasant present to give you . . .

For your sake I wish you were staying longer, for you will be free and foot-loose and rid of the weight you carried in London during this last, poor spring. How dreadful it is to me that I burdened you at any time, and especially in the spring. . . . No one could possibly know how much I mind that.

My Love, my Love –

1 On the morrow she had to go to London to be inspected by the heart specialist. (She came home with a good report.)
2 I was recording a talk on Arthur Machen.
3 To a flat on the first floor.
4 Quiddity: a kitten.

Valentine

Remember to go to Gorringe – about that quilt but don't *order*[1] it till you tell me details.

---

1 i.e. she designed to give it to me.

1964

In the train, 5 June 1964

My Love

This is Poole, and I have just heard a ringing philanthropic voice in the corridor exclaim: 'You've left your hat!' – and from the platform a dejected fatalistic reply, 'Yes. I shall need that.'

Another dream of liberty shattered, I'm afraid. She had been nerving herself for so long to escape from that hat. Whereas I am very comfortable in mine, particularly since I turned it hind-before.

Guess what's on the page before this letter: the epitaph to Cadman who tried to fly from Shrewsbury spire across the Severn: do you remember? – it was just before you sailed down the one-way street and called the good young man a B L A S T A R D . I look on this as a direct manifestation from the Archangel Raphael that he will arrange some more paired explorings for us.

Now we are at Bournemouth. Poor Vera![1] And poor Arthur, too. He is quite as much frightened and not so deft in managements as she.

The miseries of people who love each other twang in my heart. I can never feel the same authenticated compassion for the miseries of those who don't. My compassion for them is all mixed with rage, and mitigated by the distraction of raging. But Vera and Arthur are you and me.

This now makes me feel woefully guilty at being in this train, going away from you and leaving you to grieve and be afraid. I W I S H I had never consented to the project of T.H.W.[2] There was a new vitamin in it – or there seemed to be – and I snapped at that. Instinct should not have been my guide.

1 Then in a Bournemouth nursing home.
2 My biography of T. H. White. I was flying to Alderney about it.

My love, forgive me – and as you forgive me, show it by taking all possible care of yourself. Try to go to bed early (by the way, wipe out that engagement of winding my clock. We will do it together when I am home on Sunday evening). Don't sit in wet foot and wet shoulders. Eat Buns, they will remind you – since you love them – of me. And try not to be preyed on by those who want to be just driven to the Land's End. Take care, take care, as I shall, my lovely Love.

Tib

Eat more than Buns, though.

163: STW

London, 12 December 1964

My Love

Yes, we will go to London together *before* the end of January so that we can see the little Dutch room – and stay at the Goring, and go to theatres, and the Bethnal Green Museum and perhaps find a Mozart opera somewhere; and SHUN the faces of acquaintances and be as selfish as we possibly can be.

I think that will be far better for your spirits than seeking some damp spot on the face of nature. So when I am back I will start booking bedrooms. Not that I find my spirits MUCH the worse for wear, my Love. I suppose few people so regularly wake up with a feeling of pleasure and livewittedness.

But you, my darling, do work too hard, and write yourself too many memorandums, and feel too many responsibilities. Please try to commit more sins of omission. I'm sure they're part of a healthy balance, and feed the soul with a sense of Grace abounding. You should give Grace more chance to abound. I seriously mean this. Grace is a wild animal. It won't domesticate unless doors and windows are left open for it and it is free to interrupt and rub against one when it pleases, and leave its hairs all over the floor, and mute on the counterpane and drop its feathers into the soup.

So if I come home to find the house resplendent with things undone, letters inscribed with your red pencil to PEND, and the sink full of dishes and the pigeon reposing in the frig. and the telephone ringing with unanswered reproaches I shall be DELIGHTED.

ch reminds me. Don't answer any telephone calls unless it's me. wer in a feigned voice and say you're away. It might be Don Henry.

And to your sad self be a little kind, my Love. Put your feet up. Trample on the darling animals, and rest.

My true love.

Tib

1966

164: STW

Frome Vauchurch, 22 March 1966

My Love,

Fougère[1] and Mr King have just driven off; Fou conversing, Mr King silent with emotion. They met at the gate like Maud and Tennyson. He was here before 9.15 so she did not have long to grieve; and I flattered her as much as I could and told her she was your idol and your poodle.

I am now enduring some very black looks from the cats because of the kitchen fire. The moment your back is turned, they say, everything goes to pieces, no means of warmth, no hope of dinner; and rocks on their kitchen mat. They have gone out to pace among the daffodils.

I shall collect Pericles[2] and shut him in before alarming Mr Palmer comes. So far it isn't even 10. and it seems an age since you went.

11.15. Mr Palmer is here, doing the stove. It had gone at the seams: nothing serious, for the boiler-plate at the back and the bricks at the side are all right. He has filled up the cracks. He has also remembered to bring a plinth or whatever the word is for the front-door-knob. The gate will be 'quite a job in itself' confound him, for I couldn't pin him to a date. I shall assault him about it presently, when I have thought of a way to present it as an emergency: sfz – as in hymns A & M.

I find to my rage and mortification that I can't get at the cider, not no-how. When I clinch the rope-fastener on it, the whole jar revolves like Mrs Smith the Shepherd's wife dancing – do you remember? I must wait till tomorrow, when perhaps if Sibyl clasps the jar and I work on the knob we may manage it. Meanwhile, I shall have your bread to console me.

---

1 Fougère: her miniature poodle, successor to Candy.
2 Pericles: successor to Quiddity, who died untimely.

No sooner had Mr Palmer gone and Pericles was freed than posses of aeroplanes began to go over. He fled in, bewailing. I don't see what we can do. We can't give him one of his own. There really is a great deal to be said for space-flyers and satellites. At least they don't get under one's feet.

I have an increasing conviction that I am going to turn out the larder ... an itching in my thumbs, a twitching in my toes and a general sense of uprootedness – which will go on until I have rung you up tonight. I know it.

I have written to Jean Latham.

I love you.

Sylvia

165: VA

Dawlish,¹ 22 March 1966

3.30 p.m.

My arrival was enough to daunt the bravest heart. I rang. And rang again. And opened a glass door and stood in a spacious hall, and heard low voices. And saw a door marked PRIVATE.

Eventually a lady came out: a better-bred Eliz. Brims, much made up and richly dight. She searched for a nun – saying, when I said 'Is this a bad time to arrive?' – 'Well – it is, rather. Resting and things like that. But never mind.'

I felt myself swept into a Wyndham's Theatre comedy, with Jean??² as the star. I was enthralled.

Then a tiny wizened and very old Nun came. Talking broken English. I said 'Vous êtes Française, ma Mère?' and she promptly and with infinite grace 'Mais oui, Madame – et vous?'

So we got on like a house on fire and discussed Renault cars.

Then a large kind Nun appeared – and kissed me. I thought that a little reckless but no one was there so I suppose it was all right.

I have a huge room with 2 beds in it, next to bath and lavatory. I saw 2

---

1 She had gone to sample a convent in Dawlish which took boarders and visitors.
2 Jean Cadell, an actress who excelled in fading-roles.

scowling Residents and shortly must meet them at tea. It is all very alarming, or would be if it were not totally untrue. There are huge trees: ten thousand thrushes. Only a distant sound of machines. Cocks crowing.

My darling Love – the picture of you in your sailor hat[1] has come and is beside my bed. I *wish* you were here. I really do – it would entertain you so much (so far . . .) but I fear there are no cats.

Valentine

Now it is after tea and I'm sufficiently emboldened to type. I want you to have a blow-by-blow account, though I think it may be dull by the time it is written.

I went into a huge Victorian room, with 2 sets of long windows and a lot of red plush. There was a L O N G   R O W of old ladies, side by side in different kinds of chairs, and a tea trolley in front of them. No one spoke. One was standing by the trolley. I said to her 'which is your chair?' she said 'Take any chair you like.' Silence again. I said M Y   N A M E   I S A C K L A N D . Silence. Then one said Yes. Ackroyd.

Another said Mine is Buffle. (Something like that. You see how easy it is to call someone Ackroyd.) Then, in no time at all, a plump cleanly pretty old woman, speaking broken English, began to talk to me. She is French. From near Lyons. Educated at Autun. And drives a Lanchester car which firm long since went out of production.

So we talked, oddly enough, racing cars (she had a BSA) and that driving in London used to be a sport. So I won't tell you any more about that.

Then a V E R Y old one began to steer the huge trolley out of the room: I offered to but I cd. see that it is a great pleasure to her. So I opened doors. In the passage she paused and said 'How long are you here?' I said I was leaving on Friday, and she said 'W H A T   A   P I T Y –' at which I felt *most* gratified – and relieved.

Another turned up and showed me the TV room. I said (having rehearsed it to get the phraseology right!) 'Tomorrow TV will show the H O L Y   F A T H E R 's meeting with the A of C.' 'Ah, indeed –' she said without any interest at all, adding 'The Canon will be here, you may be sure – tomorrow and the next day and the next after that! All the races will

---

1 A photograph of me as a small child. It was the only likeness of me she could accept. She had a silver case made for it, engraved with her falcon, and left directions that it should be buried with her.

be shown, ending up with the Grand National!'

Then I came upstairs, *enchanted*.

But the anonymous old ones are formidable: silent. Eating in little pecks. Knitting or sewing in little pecks. Sitting in a row. I don't think they are dumb. Some may be deaf. They can certainly all S E E . . .

One odd thing: there are no towels. I shall have to wash with Wash an' Dri tonight and race for the town tomorrow and buy a Huckaback. Whatever that is.

Nuns are so very clean. I suppose they have to keep all available towels for themselves.

I dread supper. Never mind. I take pride in being so very, very, very brave.

Now I must open my window and *smoke*. They put two ash-trays in the room . . .

Oh my dear Love. I cannot think why I should be so bloodily silly as to go away from you for even half an hour.

Valentine

166: STW

Frome Vauchurch, 22 March 1966

My dear Love,

We all feel so much better since I talked to you on the telephone. The cats are embraced in each other on the blue squab chair, blinking at me with blue eyes. I have taken your advice and left the kitchen for Sibyl; instead of doing it I am going early to bed. All doors are locked, all windows are shut. The sense of stronghold is so pervading that when the telephone rang Pericles rushed upstairs (it was an injured gentleman who wanted M.N. 286).

Our Pericles has had a trying day. In the morning it was Mr Palmer and the aeroplanes. This evening when I went to fetch him back from his park (he appeared as soon as I called, slinking out by the edge of the fence), just as we were crossing the road side by side the village siren sounded. He is a *di tanti palpiti* cat if ever there was one.

As we all dined in here I was able to observe (he sitting on the table) that he now steals exactly as Niou did: with the same air of gracious condescension. I wonder if the P. son was the same with the Swine.

I enjoyed my exeat in the larder. It is considerably improved. I combed out a quantity of heeltaps and threw them away without remorse. When you come home I shall confront you with an inordination of Carnation tinned milk. Yes, I know your sister likes it; but while we have six tins of it here it is a rather theoretical liking.

I think you should have been told about towels. If you had been going to a pensionnat I would have reminded you. But I will forgive towels and more if you have a handsome tree to look into. I long for your letter which will make me laugh and tell me all. And it is warm. Thank God for that. Bedroom too?

Did you hear the six o'clock News about the Ulster parsons wearing stencilled shirts with No Popery mottoes who travelled to Rome with the Archbishop of Canterbury? I'm afraid he is a SNOB. He let them be hounded into Tourist while he travelled First. A Christian Archbishop would have been more ecumenical. I don't think I like him any longer. I'm sure I don't. Throwing away such an opportunity, too, and getting himself teehee'd at by the Curia. Fie on him!

Your loving

Eliz: Regina

1968

167: VA

Frome Vauchurch, 6 March 1968[1]

My Love – It's writing in bed and my hand is unsteady – and so is my heart, to think of the anguish you will feel – feel now and may have to feel if I'm operated on.

Sweetheart – there isn't anything I can say to comfort you because I'm never good at reassuring you *or* myself –

But simply this – I love you as surely and truly and completely as I did at Chaldon, in London, at Winterton, at Frankfort and everywhere in the whole of my happy life – and my *happy* life is the life we have spent together.

Dear heart – *forget* my sillinesses and follies and tries at infidelity which never succeeded! Remember how deeply and passionately I love you. Go on loving me. And *fear nothing*.

I truly hope I'll live, but live or die I will never, ever, leave you alone.

Valentine

168: VA

Frome Vauchurch, 26 March 1968[2]

My true Love,

I hope with *all* my heart this won't be a 'last' letter: and if I die and my held-faith is proven, though I hope not to cause you the embarrassment

---

1 Entry for this date in her pocket diary. 'Saw Mr Hanna, surgeon, who thinks it is cancer – my *poor* Love.'
2 I did not read this letter until November 10th 1969 – the day after her death. She had entrusted it to Peg Manisty, her executor and cousin, who noted on the envelope, 'July 1969. V. said give it to S. as it stands.'

of receiving letters, I shall never leave you unless you want me to: I never have even when it looked like it and we met clandestinely because we could not *not* meet. Crossing death is far less perilous to love than poor E. was. I do believe this. You don't need to try – I do for both of us.

I ask total forgiveness, and If there is anything at all in all these years (I can't think of anything) which I might have to forgive you, of course there is total forgiveness from me. There is indeed nothing at all but pure love. Not less pure because it is trimmed with boundless gratitude, the deepest and most ardent admiration respect and delight in you, those last from the *very* beginning, before love could have been believed in as possible between us.

And, my Love, know that my life has been a truly, truly happy one. Many times unhappy but *always* happy, fortunate and most blessed.

I can't let myself speculate just now, or even recall in detail, because I know the limitations to my courage, alas. But hear this and remember it: I KNOW nothing whatever (though I have tried to) except that Love is real: that you and I love each other: that if one is needed, that is the password into the City.

Try to go on living because life is so beautiful, because of the earth and trees and music and poems and creatures – man too, sometimes and always the idea of him. And also because you do yourself give courage and wisdom and often teach tolerance, and all these are desperately needed in this desperate time.

But whatever happens, I shall *never* leave you. I have, to my capacity, stood with you, sheltered and held you, and I shall *never* not be with you to shelter and comfort and hold you, no matter what you do or what you think you don't believe.

I'm inclined to think that marriage *is* a mistake, as we have it now, and should only be declared when it exists for sure – though I am very glad indeed we didn't think of this when we were at 113 on 12th January. But there is no doubt, after 38 years, that what we have made is marriage – and while the 'death us do part' phrase is factually true, it doesn't say that death breaks the marriage – nor does it. Nothing can.

So, my most dear Love – I love you for ever, and believe with all my heart that you love me so. And I bless you.

Valentine

169: VA

Guy's Hospital, 14 April 1968

Easter

My Love,

I feel it is selfish to allow you to make these tiring journeys.[1] It worries me – not only that you make them but also that I let you.

I was thinking about why I do, and I realise that I cannot *bear* the waste of time when I do not see you. Time goes and goes and I am not with you and I gnaw my fingers for the waste.

But it is a penny-wise, pound-foolish kind of saving, my Love, that *wastes your strength*. So that, at calculation-level, you can see it is foolish? I can't write by paw . . . oh dear. And you and Peg have gone and till the jumping telephone-bell goes I shan't know if you are safe. Oh, but if you get back and have some champagne you may feel better.

The first course of my supper (fruit juice) came at 6.25. It is now exactly 7 p.m. and the second course has not come. It is like being fed in the Russian Pavilion of the World's Fair.

Your carnations are so beautiful in the evening's light, which is clear and chilly with still a radiance from the sun which has gone below the roofs, I think. The dark carnations glow and the crisp yellow ones glitter. They did not seem to hear a nurse remark that they were 'unusual' for they do not look in the least blighted.

The 2nd course came at about 7.5 and was wing of chicken sauté and then in 4.5 minutes came a little warm paper tub of Lyons ice cream saying proudly that it contained so much % of NON MILK FAT and nothing whatever about MILK fat.

I think I've finished the White–Garnett letters and I do think White was a Blessed Saint to those blind-deaf people. And how pleasant to find that Lady Docker DID give away that beautiful and desirable boat to her ex-captain of their yacht, so she *was* a good woman, you see. It is a great thing for a rich person to do.

I can't write. Oh *God*, how I wish I were home again which is to say with my Love again.

Valentine

---

1 We had moved to Peg Manisty's house, to await her summons to Guy's Hospital. Mayfield is in easy reach of London, and I went up every morning and spent the day with her.

170: VA

Frome Vauchurch, 10 December 1968

My true heart – that I should do this to you all over again[1] is more anguish than I have ever bargained for: but there is no help for it and we are bound, by very love, to be undaunted. So whatever fear we each feel, and however sharply we suffer for each other, let us somehow *always* remember to be glad that it is for each other, and that it is because of love.

I don't even attempt to persuade you not to be with me as much as you may, but for my own sake, and the desperation I feel when I think of it, I charge you *because* you love me, not to come to the hospital if you even think you are getting ill, or if your spirit momentarily fails you – one's spirit does do this, and it is not to be wondered at. I shall know whatever happens, literally *whatever*, that your love has never failed and never will, life or death, hell or high water. I know this and it is one of the few things which I have never for one moment of our joined lives not believed.

It is bitter to me that I have shaken your roots by any excursions in search of my own right way: forgive me, and from henceforth do not *ever* be shaken: one thing stands firmer than any other, and that is my total love for you, my total secure belief in your love for me (and in me for you: in our joined love become one love: 'and all is one love –' as Julian of Norwich says, and that is the most profound of all truths and one in which you and I and all the living world must believe).

So my word to you is my word to myself: we must be quiet, as best we may, and let the water flow over our heads: we *were* once fish! It will be all right. Even if I am returned to you rather chopped-about, don't mind too much: *I* don't. I'm glad it didn't happen when we were younger – the only thing that matters now is the one thing which will always stay and is for ever. I love you, my truest, my dearest, my only true love.

Valentine

---

1 Sir Hedley Atkins, surgeon at Guy's, had found another growth.

171: STW

London

My Love,

   Thirty-eight years ago I brought you a little bunch of herbs when you lay ill in a large bed with Sir Walter Raleigh and a tortoise. In all those years, my dearest, I have never doubted your love, nor my own. Much of what's to come is still unsure; but that glorious span of thirty-eight years of love and trust and happiness – care and courage too – will shine on us and protect us. I have always believed you. Even when you gave me scented shells, I believed in them. You are my faith, I will live and die in it. If I have to live on alone, I will live and die in it, and because you believe there is a life after death, I will believe in that too. Our love is the one thing I can never question.

   Now in return you must believe that I will be sensible, take care of myself, use Palfrey and the Goring amenities for all they are worth, eat an orange a day, and take care of your possession, your Tib.

   My love, my Love. And my heart's thanks for all you have given me, all your understanding, your support, your tenderness, your courage, your trust. And your Beauty, outside and in, and your delightfulness.

   Never has any woman been so well and truly loved as I.

Sylvia

Written on the back:

18.12.1968 6.45 p.m.

This letter is my greatest treasure and must be carefully preserved and given back to Sylvia if I die.

Valentine

Index

King, Mr (garage owner), 265, 325n, 347, 377
Kingley Vale, Sussex, 230
Kokoschka, Oskar, 167
Koran, The, 75, 87
Krafft-Ebing, Richard, Freiherr von, 199
Krupskaya, Nadezhda K., 142

Lambert, Mrs (charwoman), 268 & n, 303n
Lander, Dr Charles Llewellyn, 191, 198, 200-2, 244n
Lander, Mrs Charles Llewellyn, 199, 201
Latham, Jean, 378
Laurence, Brother (Nicholas Herman), 223n
Laurence, Martin: *1936*, 136
Lavenham, Suffolk, 33-6, 45, 47-8, 136-9, 353
Law, William, 232
Lawrence, D. H.: *Lady Chatterley's Lover*, 50, 98; *Women in Love*, 103
Lefanu (Nora's woman friend), 216
Left Review, The, 141n
Legg, Florrie, 59 & n
Lenin, Vladimir Ilich, 142
Lewes: Literary Society, 362 & n
Lipton, Julius, 130 & n, 144n, 145, 147-9
Lipton, Queenie, 144 & n, 145, 148
Little Gidding, 34
Little Zeal (house, Devon), 51-2, 56, 60, 65, 68, 72, 79-81, 86, 88, 96n, 98, 101-2, 106, 128, 195, 202, 212, 214, 287-8; STW sells, 297
Lobrano, Mr (of *The New Yorker*), 367n
London Library, The, 110, 122, 203, 268
Long, Jane, 351
Lubbock, Bea (*née* Howe), 150 & n, 300-3
Lubbock, Mark, 301 & n, 302-3
Lucas, Billy, 359 & n
Lucas, Mrs (Chaldon postwoman), 63 & n
Lucile (French friend of VA), 85-6
Lynch, Malachy, 370

Macaulay, (Dame) Rose, 157n, 158
MacDonald, James Ramsay, 36
Machen, Arthur, 51n, 69, 220, 372n
Machen, Dorothie Purefoy (*née* Hudlestine, STW's aunt), 51n, 69, 99 & n
Machen, Hilary (Janet's brother), 273 & n
Machen, Janet (*later* Davis; STW's cousin): VA entertains, 74 & n, 162; VA buys present for, 90; relations with STW, 131-2, 159, 352 & n; character, 160; in USA, 172-3; baby, 207-8; VA sends books to, 208; writes to VA, 212, 293; marriage, 222, 266, 269; STW's unease with, 250; VA fetches from Weymouth, 252; and STW's exile, 254; meets STW, 267, 269, 271, 273; STW orders basket for, 273
Mackenzie, Compton, 319
Madrid, 155-6
Mahomet the Prophet, 87
Maiden Newton, Dorset *see* Frome Vauchurch
Manisty, Margaret (Peg), 382n, 384 & n
Mansfield, Mr (gardener), 302 & n
Martindale, Father Cyril Charlie, 128

Mary (Catrina's sister), 202 & n, 224, 313
Maxton, James, 36 & n
Maxwell, William, 364
Mayfield, Sussex, 384n
Meep (cat), 115
Mill, Mr (of Chaldon), 251
Miller, Mr (Chaldon carpenter), 11, 133-4
Miss Green's Cottage, Chaldon: STW buys and installs VA, 9-14; furnishing, 10-11, 13-14, 19n; garden, 10, 51, 56, 59, 237; Pitmans occupy, 123; bombed in war, 189
Montagu, Lady Mary Wortley, 98
Montaigne, Michel de, 141
Moorepark, Howard, 223
Moxon, Grannie, 11-12, 36, 51; death, 116
Munich Agreement (1938), 168
Muntz, Betty, 20 & n, 63, 70
Murasaki, Lady, 159

Nation (US magazine), 102
Neruda, Pablo, 155
Nettleship, Ursula ('Nuttlesnip'), 45
New England, 169-70
Newmarket, 323
News Chronicle (newspaper), 148 & n
Newton Abbot, Devonshire, 77
New York, 163, 168-9, 175-6
New Yorker, The (magazine), 208 & n, 367n
Niou (Siamese cat), 292, 296-8, 303, 308, 323, 340, 366; death, 371 & n
Nora-and-Bailey (cook and gardener), 266 & n, 267
Nordoff, Paul, 171-2
Norfolk, 24-6, 92-5, 297; *see also* Winterton

Ogle and Moodie, 368
Oke, Anne, 72
Oke, Mary, 72
Oke, Samways (STW's great-great-grandfather), 72
Oldfield (neighbour), 302
Oleranshaw, Mr (of Maiden Newton), 265
Olney Hymns (collection), 36n
Order of Woodcraft Chivalry (O.W.C.), 40-1, 43
Orta, Italy, 330

Painter, George D., 354
Palmer, Mr (builder and plumber), 201, 362 & n, 378, 380
Panter-Downes, Molly, 198
Paris, 75-6, 81, 83-6, 91
Parisot (French friend of VA), 85-6
Park, Mungo, 268
Parker, George (of Lavenham), 136-7
Parker, Mrs George, 34, 43, 136-8, 140, 353n, 354
Parsons, Ian, 318n
Parsons, Trekkie, 318
Partisan Review, 211
Patmore, Coventry, 83
Patrick, Mrs (of Yeovil), 244, 262
Payne, Fred, 56, 59